The Years of Living Wet

For Laura — Thanks for buying my book. Can't wait for the review.

John Huetter

John Huetter

Cover: Meredith McCullough at 60, aboard S/V Quo Vadis   Photo by the Author
Photo of the author courtesy of Meredith McCullough
Formatting by Beth Kelley

© 2008 John Huetter
All Rights Reserved.

No part of this publication may be reproduced, stored in a retrieval system, or transmitted, in any form or by any means, electronic, mechanical, photocopying, recording, or otherwise, without the written permission of the author.

First published by Dog Ear Publishing
4010 W. 86th Street, Ste H
Indianapolis, IN 46268
www.dogearpublishing.net

dog ear
PUBLISHING

ISBN: 978-159858-801-9

This book is printed on acid-free paper.

Printed in the United States of America

Dedicated to All My Friends on Shore

Who Read and Responded to Messages from S/V Quo Vadis

*John and Dixie Blake
Irv and Patricia Hamilton
Jeff Hamilton and Family
Bob Hemphill and Linda Powers
*Beth Huetter
*Caroline Huetter
Betty, Bob, Mike and Pat Huetter

*Michael R. Kerley
*Meredith McCullough
Rosemary Meyer
*Jeff Morehouse and Candace Bartman
Ann and Bill Owen
*Dave Schoonmaker and Family
Steve and Geri Wallach

Staunch Supporters and Featured Subjects in the Salt-soaked Sagas

* Daniel Cartwright and Family
Jean-Paul Creignou and Christin Hardman
Peggy Huetter
Dimitri Manes

*Lynsay Matthews and Rich Helyar
*Aynsley Reycroft and Brian Schopfer
Jim and Laurie Wanko
Ben Williams

* Crew on S/V Quo Vadis

Table of Contents

1. The First 30 Days .... P. 1
2. The Next 30 Days .... P. 6
3. Two Months Later .... P. 12
4. Summer's Almost Over .... P. 20
5. Many Things Break but We Head South Anyway .... P. 26
6. Happy Holidays and Bluewater Passages .... P. 36
7. Great Gains and Tolerable Losses .... P. 44
8. Goodbye, Bahamas! Again and Again .... P. 54
9. The First Year of Living Wet .... P. 68
10. The First Year of Living Wet…and Living Well .... P. 76
11. Puerto Rico Days and Virgin Nights .... P. 88
12. Trying to Reason with Hurricane Season .... P. 100
13. Doing the Tropical Wave(s) .... P. 106
14. Singlehanding the Leewards, Windwards and Onwards .... P. 118
15. A Year on the Caribbean Sea .... P. 132
16. From Carnival to Margaritaville .... P. 144
17. The ABCs of Avoiding Pirates of the Caribbean .... P. 176
18. In Curaçao .... P. 186
19. Colombia with Gems by the Ocean .... P. 194
20. Comarca Kuna Yala .... P. 206
21. The Panama Canal Authority .... P. 222
22. Banana Republics .... P. 234
23. El Golfo de Tehuantepec .... P. 294
24. ¡Viva Mexico! .... P. 302
25. American Customs and Other Behavior .... P. 352

The Quo Vadis Conventions

In this soggy saga, I've tried to use the following conventions that reflect sailing a boat, instruments used, the way people talk, and the environment called life. Remember though, consistency is the hobgoblin of small minds, according to Dr. Johnson, and we wouldn't want to be guilty of small-mindedness.

Depths are in feet, meters or fathoms because that's the way the charts indicate depth.

Lengths, heights, widths and similar dimensions are in feet or meters, depending on the item or local usage. Inches and centimeters are used mainly for explanation (1 meter = 39 inches).

Distances on land are kilometers or miles, usually adhering to the local map. Distances at sea are in nautical miles, abbreviated nm.

Boat speed is given in knots. Miles per hour are used to describe speed on land.

Non-English conversations and most expressions are italicized. Exceptions may occur where the word is frequently used as part of English-speaking vocabulary, like gringo or panga in Mexico.

Compass directions are capitalized: North, Southwest, etc. Compass headings are magnetic, unless otherwise noted.

Names of Boats are identified with the indicated type face. Extended writing by others in the book is also identified by a distinctive type face.

A 24 hour clock is used. This fits with the reality on board, weather info and other radio times, different time zones, and also makes it easy to tell day or night. You know that 0300 is three in the morning and 1500 is three in the afternoon, so you could be doing very different things.

S/V is a sailing vessel. M/V is a motor vessel. HMS is Her Majesty's Ship, a naval vessel.

Position is usually given as degrees and minutes of Longitude and Latitude: W60.19 N12.08

Sometimes, this is spelled out for clarification or emphasis as in 60 degrees 19 minutes West Longitude, 12 degrees 8 minutes North Latitude.

Nearly all the adventures, conversations, and grisly details of each passage have been included. If a part of the book doesn't suit you, please move on to the next section. Something funny happens. If I've left out anything important, let me know. I'll correct it if there's ever another edition.

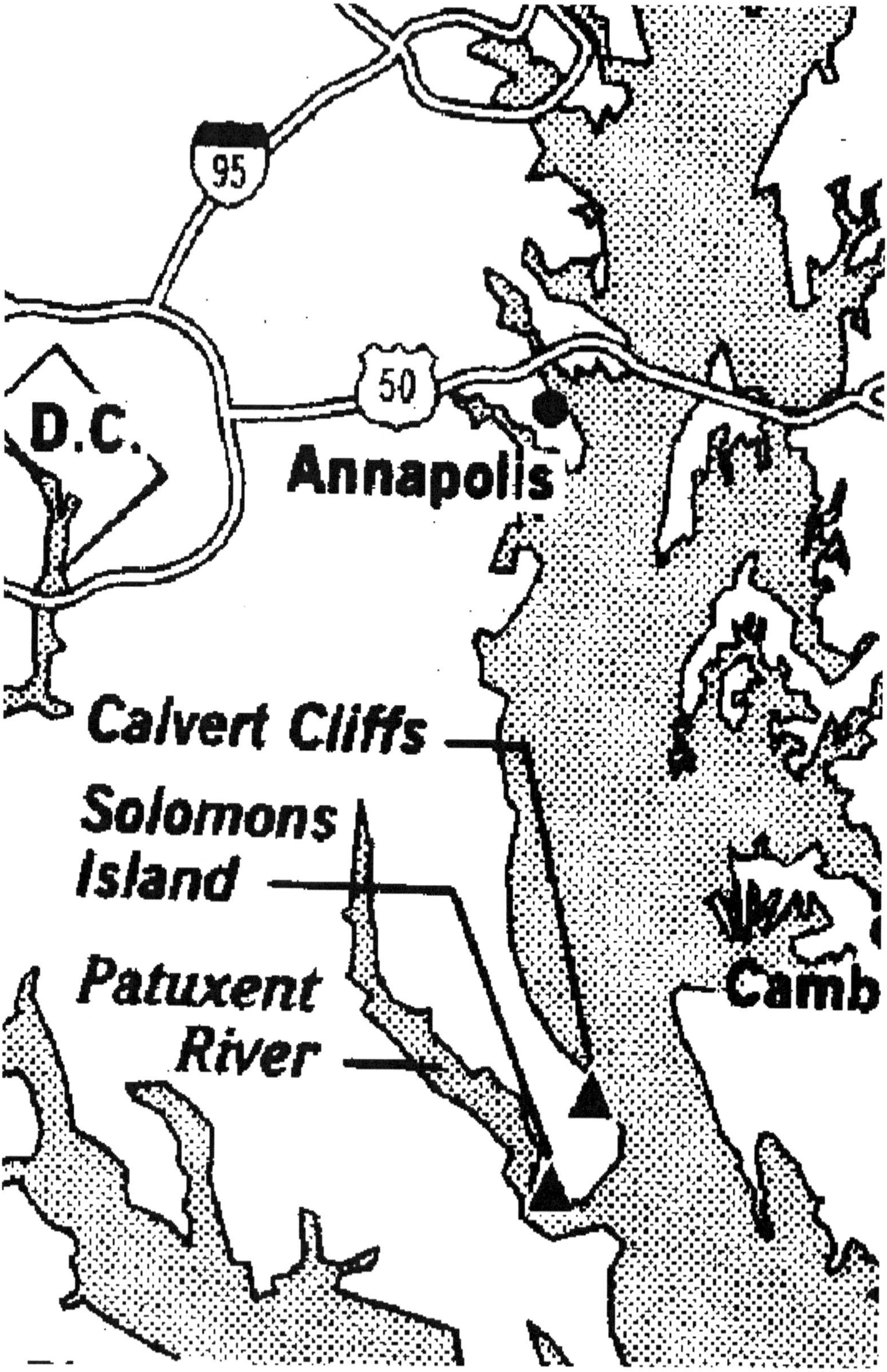
95
50
D.C.
Annapolis
Calvert Cliffs
Solomons
Island
Patuxent
River
Camb

The First 30 Days

Aboard S/V Quo Vadis, lying Annapolis, Maryland

Well, the first 30 days of owning the sailing vessel Quo Vadis have been more like "A Year in Provence" than some salty, seafaring saga except that the locals working on the boat speak in Maryland shore and other Chesapeake dialects rather than Provençal. Luckily, I can understand them and even speak a little myself since I spent three years of high school in the region. In all fairness, most of the marine sector workers are generally better about showing up than those described in Peter Mayle's book.

To update those not intimately involved in the earlier stages of this enterprise, I did finally take ownership of a 37 ft. catamaran built many years ago by the fine British boat-building firm of Prout which also chose this year to go into receivership. Ironically, the boat which met my long list of specifications (two heads, radar, solar and wind power, etc.) was in the Chesapeake; not in Florida or the Islands. I'd spent nearly six months shopping for a cat when Belinda Grimbeek, who had sailed a cat to Florida from South Africa suggested I go North and look at a boat. There was snow on the ground when we went to check out Quo Vadis in Maryland.

So the adventure begins…or continues, depending on when you came in, with a few changes. I'll be cruising the Chesapeake, rather than the Caribbean, until hurricane season begins to abate. Then, I'll head down the Intracoastal Waterway (ICW to the *cogniscenti*) toward Ft. Lauderdale and/or Key West, depending on the next island destination, for one lap around the Caribbean. If Jean-Paul can go, with his French passport, we can start from Cuba. If not, Plan B is probably a route through the Bahamas. It sounds so simple when I put it that way but it's all new territory to me. If you were educated in the classics, or by Jesuits, you already know the name of the boat is appropriate to the situation. Transliterated from the Latin, it's "Where are you going?"

So far, everybody has been right! Dimitri's advice to slam the shithoses, rebuild the heads and that the rigging survey was bogus was spot on. Except that I installed all new impermeable sanitary lines and a new holding tank. That's just one example of the mostly invisible stuff I've been doing for the last four weeks.

So you'd better admire my USCG Standard A1 fuel lines and shutoff valves when you come aboard, if you can find them. Irv's observations on the nature of boat preparation and cruising hold true so far. A lifetime of accumulating technical knowledge, planning ability, and decision-making under pressures of time, money and physical discomfort have proven more important than sailing skills. No doubt I will get into trouble due to a lack of such skills in the next five months. I hope I've acquired some by then. I could use a little help here, guys. And I haven't even gotten into using all the navigation and electronics stuff. When is the last time any of us read a radar screen? Years? Decades? It's all green smudges, man, and that's when it's working. I'm also trying to figure out my new internet-capable cell phone.

One of the major challenges my fellow sufferers in boat ownership can relate to is finding a slip for the summer that will accommodate a 16 ft. beam. Plus these crazy locals have driven pilings in every possible location you might reasonably want to dock a boat. What's with this pilings stuff? Is it to compensate for dock area the size of a commemorative postage stamp? Finally, I found a place way down the bay at Solomon's Island, a funky former crabbing/fishing hamlet which has recently become seriously gentrified. Ironically, it is just across the river from the Patuxent Naval Air Test Center: the Navy's equivalent of Edwards AFB, the Air Force Flight Test Center, which is way out in the Mojave Desert. The Navy always gets the good spots.

One of the major lessons I've learned in my short time on the boat is that everything has to be done right every time and you can't leave anything to be done. Stuff left unattended on deck will fall or blow overboard. You can't forget to turn out the lights or you may not get the engine started when you return. I have already left the stereo circuit on and bilge pump circuit off. Wrong! In this sense, it's a lot like flying: many hours of meticulous and expensive preparation for a relatively short time airborne, or underway.

I hope this transition period is over soon with all the stuff stowed where it makes sense and I can find it in the dark. Half the time now I can't find whatever it is I'm looking for but often come across something whose purpose I can only guess. It's too much like work just getting the items from the marine survey corrected and I'm feeling way outside my comfort zone, which of course is part of the reason I'm doing this: to enlarge that zone.

Having said all that, the few times we've actually sailed, Quo Vadis is great on the water and I feel good about the boat. This design is not as fast as other cats, which still makes it faster than nearly all cruising monohulls, but it is built "Prout Stout" so I'm told. We did the sea trials in March with 35 knot winds gusting to 50 and it felt very confident; even comfortable. It's dry, has no perceptible heel and responds very satisfactorily for a multi-hull. All right, I've only sailed two others but it feels OK to me.

Meredith was at the helm for nearly the whole trip when we took possession of the boat and appears to be a natural at that position. This is good, because I have everything else to learn…and do. We were also initiated to navigation on the Chesapeake during this maiden voyage. The float line of a crab trap snagged around the engine drive leg. I had not seen the float in our wake after it went between the *amas* but didn't make the connection until our speed dropped off. Bill Mattox suggested the problem came from unplanned drag, also noting it was massively illegal to do anything to a crab trap. He told me of watermen watching their traps with high-power binoculars and a high-power rifle. I can't help but glance furtively at the shoreline before I hang upside down under the aft deck to cut the line wrapped around the prop.

Bill was on board because he is a local sailor who knew what the docks in Eastport looked like from the Bay and we didn't. He also took the dimensions to weld up a new stainless steel tank to double our fuel capacity and still fit in the existing space. This was just the first on my list of both new and necessary survey items. About US$15,000 later, most of them had been attended to. Carol Haase, proprietor of Port Townsend Sails, was in town for the week and agreed to meet us at the dock. While she is inspecting our sail inventory and rig prior to preparing a quote for a new suit designed for cruising, Meredith starts confiding to her intimate details of our personal life and lack of sailing knowledge: stuff that guys would never divulge. Carol is taken aback. I sense it is mainly because we have never been cruising. "Well," she states in her matter of fact way. "Experience starts now." The meticulously prepared quote is almost another US$15,000.

To supplement the experience, Mer also insisted we take the USSA "Safety at Sea" 2-day seminar at the Naval Academy, the USCG Boating Safety four week course, and a 2 day hands-on sailing experience with Womanship. (I didn't get to do the last one. Aside from being gender-challenged, I spent that weekend replacing and plumbing a pump.) So now she is totally convinced that all sailing is focused around maritime disasters. And that I am totally crazy.

John Blake was good enough to connect me with some of his pals who live and sail around Annapolis. Jim Wanko and Dave Campbell agree to help me move the boat some 50 miles down the Bay to Solomon's next Friday, weather permitting. What's even better is that one of them has actually sailed this route a couple of times. I'll let you know the results of this effort, especially if we manage to miss all the pilings leaving the docks in downtown Annapolis. More accurately, we will be embarking from the Maritime Republic of Eastport which doesn't want to be confused or associated with all them snooty city folk 150 meters across the water in Annapolis, many of whom are bureaucrats…or worse.

I look forward to having John and Dixie on board in June, when we plan to sail up to his ancestral estate at the far north of Chesapeake Bay. My excellent children, Beth and Caroline, will be joining me between schools and summer jobs. I'm thinking we could cruise up the Potomac to Washington. I hope Michael the K and my high school roommate, Maddog Morehouse, will come aboard to help me sail this bloody thing. Not that I expect a lot more nautical expertise but I'm sure there will be strongly held opinions. Stay healthy, guys. Better yet, bring your mates. The reward for such effort by any and all intrepid crew (OK, maybe even the not-so-intrepid) is another invitation to cruise and dive in the Caribbean this winter.

Another right thing that Irv and Patricia told me was that most sailing people are pretty good folks. This has really been true to date. Since my boat and I are both mature, some of the nicer folks flatter me by assuming I'm the old Prout catamaran expert until they observe some monumental goof or hear me respond, "Gee, I don't really know about that. I just bought it."

I also remembered we need to get diesel, the first aid kit isn't complete, and I haven't finished provisioning or paid the last day's dock fees. I am faithful about keeping the daily Captain's log, however, just like Capt. Kirk on Star Trek. ("Seadate 2002.5, in the Severn quadrant.") I have lost 10 pounds: another event I didn't see coming.

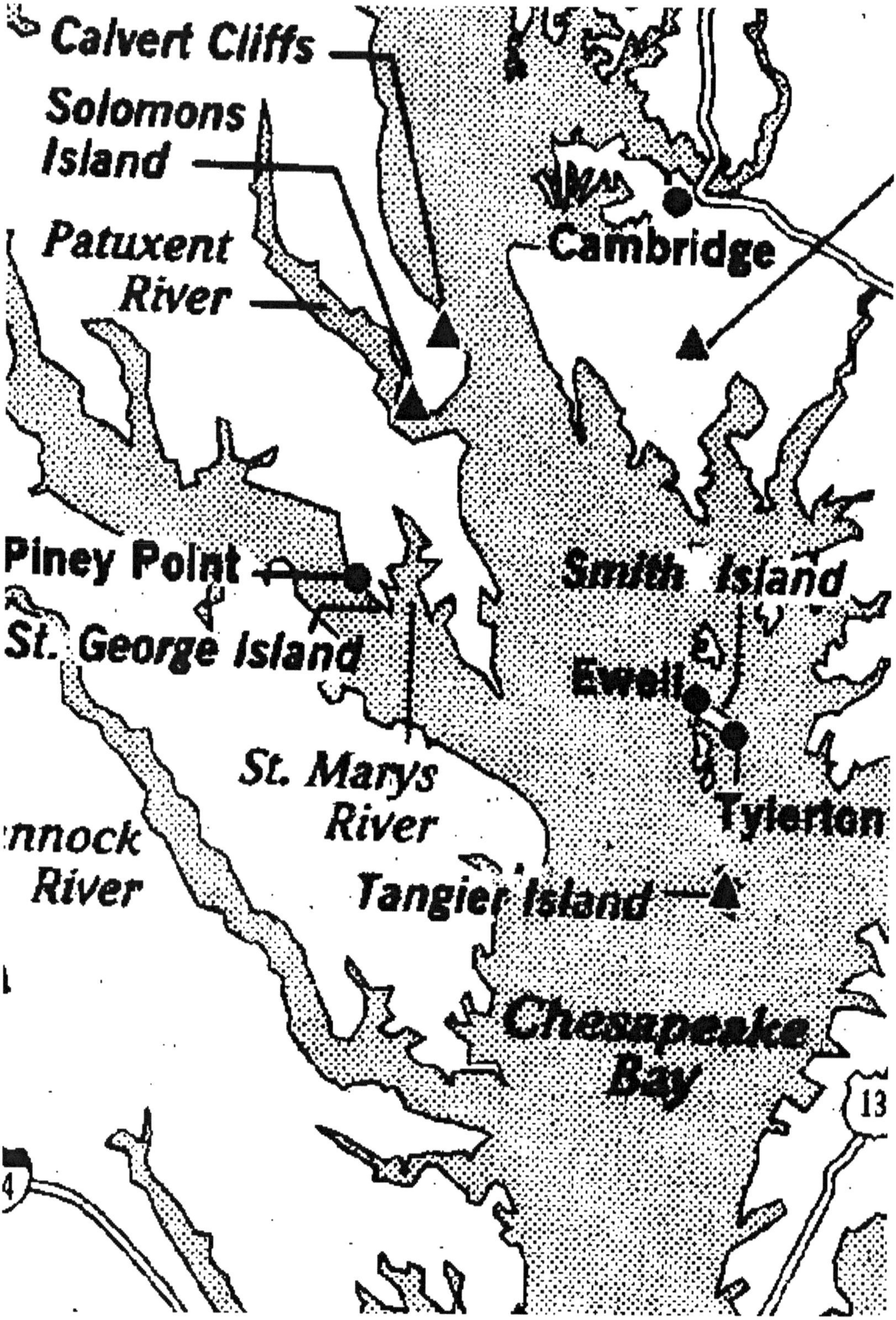
Calvert Cliffs
Solomons Island
Patuxent River
Cambridge
Piney Point
St. George Island
Smith Island
Ewell
Tylerton
St. Marys River
nnock River
Tangier Island
Chesapeake Bay
13

The Next 30 Days

Aboard S/V Quo Vadis, lying Solomon's Island, Maryland

Just before leaving the Catamaran Center at Eastport, I made the monumental decision to buy some real davits for my new dinghy and have them professionally installed. These accessories turn out to be pricey, but we all know by now that "marine", when used as an adjective, means triple the normal price for almost any item.

The ship's carpenters are finishing in the davit mounting blocks on the aft deck when I overhear a conversation between Ron and Felix. Now, these guys look the part: two days' stubble, Felix with belly coming out from under his faded purple T-shirt, work boots, etc. But Felix is telling Ron how he is taking violin lessons from Rhonda. He is trading her some baby-sitting time in return for being taught to play violin. He confides that the violin is something he always wanted to do. Ron replies, "Yeah, the violin is nice but I always wanted to be a tap dancer." He turns, seeing me now, and gives us the requisite grin. "Tap dancing. I really have wanted to." They finish the installation work neither playing nor dancing. The davits haven't fallen off.

Jim and Dave show up before 0800 to sail down to Solomon's. Meredith is already on board. The wind is fresh from the North-Northwest and we are underway within 20 minutes. Dave applies his experience to get *Quo Vadis* out of the Maritime Republic while missing most of the pilings. The few owners on board their boats move quickly to their sterns to fend us off. We have about two feet of leeway but manage not to scrape anything.

"Where's your catamaran grease this morning?" asks one jolly wag. Something else I didn't know I needed.

As soon as we cleared the mouth of the Severn, we set all three sails and were soon running down the Bay at over 8 knots. The maximum observed was 9.4 knots with a following wind. Dave commented that this may be the best day we would see on the Chesapeake. Meredith and I are, like, "What! This is as good as it gets? Now we've done it all?" Mer is soon engrossed in Dave's precise, workmanlike explanations of the parts and functions of a sailboat, which she seems to like better than her Womanship course or anything I've said. Jim is wonderfully witty but I am in my serious "Let's not screw anything up." mode since this is our first real trip.

The sailing is going very well with Dave predicting a quick 6 hour arrival until about 1230 when the wind starts to die. I propose one of my favorite solutions: Let's eat lunch. That activity completed, we start the diesel. (Yaay! It kicks right in. I'm so happy when that happens.) We motor the rest of the way, eventually dropping all sail as the wind goes to nothing. Jim and I alternate at the helm. Dave is still busy conducting his sailing seminar while Meredith diligently takes copious notes. During his final trick at the wheel, Jim manages to spot and miss the fish traps, crab pots and shoal flats leading into Back Creek at Solomon's Island. I decide to take advantage of the full crew to refuel but the first fuel dock turns us away. It's just 1645 and we note that it's not yet five, the listed closing time. "We close at quarter of," informs the dock attendant. "That's the difference between an employee and an owner," observes Dave.

We turn to port and cross the harbor entrance to the Town Center Marina fuel dock. Jim can't get the engine into reverse to ease QV up to the dock. So the clever crew jumps off and snubs spring lines to arrest our headway while I toss out fenders to lessen the crunch. The nice girl sells us all the diesel we can hold at a very reasonable price. Later, I learn her name is Linda.

We discover the reason Jim couldn't get into reverse is that the tackle rigged under the aft deck to raise and lower the drive leg has come untensioned and tangled in the prop. Oh, goody. This whole arrangement is a default in British engineering and execution. Here's a handy, retractable stern drive for your boat. You go figure out how to get it to work. What!? I go upside down with my deck tool and cut the tangled line so I can push the drive leg into its full down and locked position. This is not very elegant but works. Also, I don't know what else to do.

Having the advantage of both forward and reverse, Jim took QV into slip C-10 where Laurie Wanko and Chris Campbell were waiting to give the male crewmembers a ride home. They first joined us on board for drinks and on shore for dinner. Mer changed into a white turtleneck and jeans which, incidentally, set off the color she's gotten during Dave's Day on the Bay Sailing Seminar. As night falls on Back Creek, the Annapolis crew departs and this happy skipper escorts his sweetie back to QV's port cabin. Which of us has learned more on board today?

I thought that first voyage went pretty well but spend the next two weeks trying to come up with solutions that: a) Do not involve putting more holes in the hull, b) Can be done with the boat in the water since there are no local lifts identified that can handle the beam. Meanwhile, the drive leg stays locked in the down operating position, secured with a remnant of cut line. I'm told some Prout owners accept this as a permanent solution. I'm thinking of a new approach.

In the following weeks, we are cordially yet warily welcomed by other folks on C dock, I try to deal with a non-functioning water heater, and the port head breaks. Now, a major reason I wanted a boat with two heads is that I figured one of them would malfunction at the wrong time and place. I just didn't think it would be quite so soon. The 8HP outboard that is delivered to propel the new dinghy refuses to run for more than about 30 seconds, so it goes back to Annapolis. The first two repair kits I order for the head don't include replacements for the broken parts. I do have some informative conversations with Patrick, the tech rep at Groco, who still remembers how the old style toilets were built and what parts they require. Fortunately, he is just a couple of hours up the road near Baltimore and can arrange to ship parts overnight. Six years of college and I'm struggling to rebuild a very used boat toilet. I remind myself this was my idea; no whining allowed.

I end up buying a new 9.8HP motor locally for about the same price as the smaller one. This makes the dink wicked quick with just me in it. The Maryland DNR patrol also noticed this fair turn of speed. The officer further advised me I had to have state registration to operate anything. I explained how I'm new to this turf, sympathize with his expanded responsibilities in the face of departmental budget cuts and don't get a ticket. I do manage to lose one of the oars which I had naively left clipped to the gunwale. Gee, the picture showed it like that. (Further research reveals it's legal to row the dinghy but not motor it.) I just hope the dink-motor combo works when fully loaded and in surf. After way too many hours of patchwork plumbing, I abandon the water heater for another option, still to be determined. OK, are we having fun yet?

Meredith admits me to her colonial style home in the trees near Mt. Vernon. I immediately achieve a new perspective. Later, we drive to the horse country of South Carolina to celebrate the nuptials of Katy and Jerry. Katy is the daughter of my pal, Jeff. I experience an unsettling rite of passage: my friends' children getting married. My own children are much too young for any such thing as, so far, we all agree. But am I?

Katy's long-time canine companion, Dixie, is the maid of honor. She behaves at least as well as the two-legged guests. The reception is held under moss-draped oaks on groomed lawns at the horse museum, with genteel Low Country hospitality. Later, we visit the newlyweds' new business: 88 acres with stables, where they raise and train polo mounts. I am moved by their enthusiasm, the generational difference, and the contrast with my new life on board.

For me, much of learning about such living and the workings of a medium-size vessel is just being on it. I am now more comfortable moving around the boat, doing tasks, establishing housekeeping routines, cleaning up things, checking rigging, but still stub my toes on some deck cleats. My personal effects arrived from California and got stowed. The new interior has been completed despite protests that I was using the wrong material in the wrong color. It gets installed with M's help and will, no doubt, be spilled on and perhaps fade in the harsh tropical light. Family photos have gone up in the main cabin. All the bunks have been made up, unmade and re-made. Putting the new bed sheets on the queen berth with Mer's help is a turn-on. I let her know this effect she has on me. She admonishes me, "We're not going to be doing it doggy style in the salon with guests on board. You're just going to have to figure out some other way to get me." I am speechless in awe and anticipation.

I do a full provisioning from the Solomon's Island markets after bringing my East Coast car back to the marina. Food and drink are stocked and stored. The main reefer works well, keeping its contents at cold temperatures. This has become an important thing to me. With the stereo playing some early jazz pieces, the house batteries charging from the wind generator, and the oil lamp swaying to the lapping waves, Quo Vadis is beginning to feel like a new home.

Things were going along so well that I had time to notice green stuff growing on the hulls, mostly around the waterline. I figured I'd just jump in and brush it off since the bottom paint had seemed to be in such good condition when we did the marine survey. It would also look really shipshape when John and Dixie Blake arrived, or so I figured. Nobody had warned me about barnacles. Beneath a relatively benign covering of green slime lay an equally dense coating of sharp, nasty barnacles! So this is what the Navy swabs do. Scraping at them is really not so much fun and surprisingly tiring. It disturbs me, overall, that I can expend only 6-7 hours/day of effort before tiring. I don't know what that means for the longer passages ahead.

There was apparently no anti-fouling treatment on the drive leg. That will be remedied before setting sail next week for the Eastern shore, Virginia, and other exotic locales. I'll even try to get both heads working at the same time, if the parts show up. Now, that's luxury yachting!

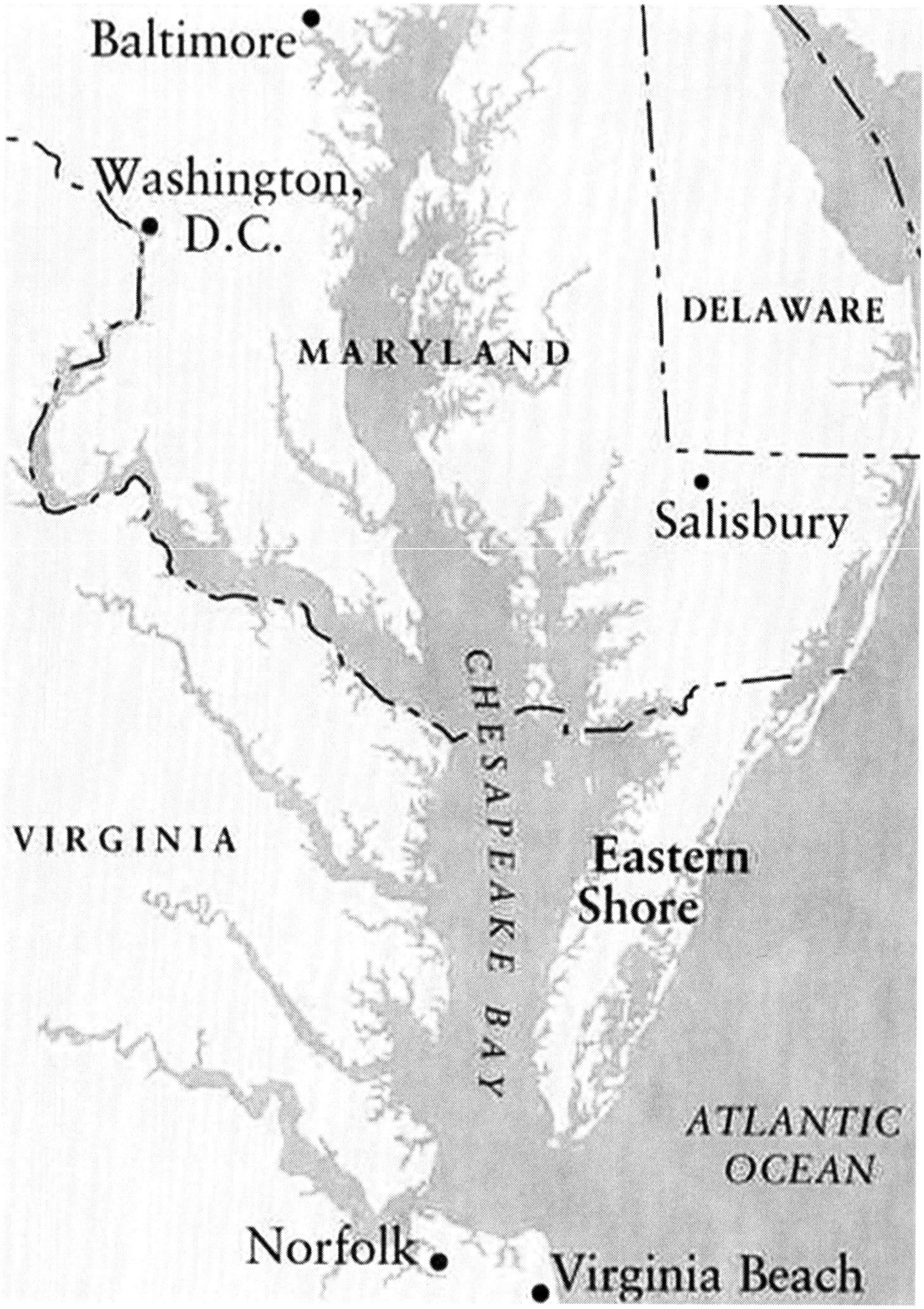
Baltimore
Washington, D.C.
MARYLAND
DELAWARE
Salisbury
VIRGINIA
CHESAPEAKE BAY
Eastern Shore
ATLANTIC OCEAN
Norfolk
Virginia Beach

Two Months Later

Aboard S/V Quo Vadis, cruising the Chesapeake

Cruising is cool. Yes, we finally get to the object of the exercise. Chesapeake Bay is muddy and the water is not gin-clear but it is full of tasty crabs, which is some consolation. For those of you who have been anxiously waiting to find out, the parts to rebuild the second head did not arrive before John and Dixie Blake did. They were good sports and agreed to ship out anyway. My clever plan to sail to the other end of the Bay where John's family manse sits at Hance Point was vetoed by everybody else. As John pointed out, he'd just come from the house so he'd seen it. Meredith also observed that they might actually like to see some other parts of the Bay instead of making a five day forced sail that would leave me alone on board somewhere near Philadelphia.

Wiser heads prevailed and their plan to make one loop around the central Chesapeake was implemented. I had asked John what we needed on board for an extended cruise. He unhesitatingly replied, "Beer". No argument there but I provisioned a few other items, as well. Call me crazy…

There is much good news to tell. For all of you who were concerned about such things, a week's provisions (and beer) for four adults with hearty appetites fit very handily in Quo Vadis' pantries and reefers and wherever else I stowed stuff. Extrapolating by bulk, it looks like we could handle a month's worth. Well, maybe not a month's worth of beer. We'll need those two 90 gallon water tanks. John and Dix are experienced, capable and great fun. John is one of a select group of Pacific Coast sailors qualified to handle a square-rigged ocean-going ship as well as his own 35 ft. sloop berthed at San Diego. Dixie is one of a select group who puts up with all this, as well as being a calm, competent sailing companion. I had doubled everything from PFDs to toilet articles in preparing for this daunting voyage so, of course, John shows up with everything including his own handheld GPS. And he didn't even know that Meredith would commandeer my handheld GPS for the entire trip. You can't have enough redundant systems, or clean towels.

For those losing interest, or who want to skip right to the chart (Go ahead, Irv. We'll wait for you to dig it out.), our cruise plan was Solomon's Island-Annapolis-Rock Hall-St. Michael's through the Kent Narrows-Oxford through the Poplar Island Narrows and Knapp's Narrows with a stop in the Choptank River. This watercourse featured large in James Michener's book "Chesapeake". (That book has a lot more relevance if you're living and sailing here, believe me.) Oh, yeah. Then back to

Solomon's Island. All the crew seemed determined not to leave me to get the boat back on my own. Probably a wise move.

To summarize: it was great. In more detail, the cruise featured only one squall, moderate to light to no winds, most evenings anchored out in postcard settings, a few hours of pucker factor due to our first time in these waters with very shallow, often narrow channels, great camaraderie, and lots of seafood. In personal accomplishments, Dix did get Quo Vadis bouncing off the sides of the channel going into St. Mike's which, I later learned, is not uncommon as it's only 5-6 ft. deep, and JB forgot his shoes going ashore. My new dink with the 9.8HP outboard gets up on the plane quickly so that oversight was corrected. In Mer's first experience dealing with navigation markers out in vast expanses of flat water, she assumed the platforms were built as nesting areas for the ospreys which have made a healthy comeback. She charmingly called out the channel markers and checkpoints as "Go to the next osprey nest." Mariners, take note: the town of Oxford, Maryland is closed on Wednesday. John B. was desolated that the shopping opportunity was lost after Dixie had made such plans. As skipper, I felt it my duty to console the crew so allowed JB to buy us a large dinner ashore. One of the highlights of this cruise was being met by Jim Wanko in his 16 ft. runabout as we approached Annapolis after a 50 mile slog back up the Bay; then being escorted through the channel to his private anchorage in Lake Ogleton.

Lake Ogleton is not really a lake in the same way many of the creeks in these parts aren't really creeks. Attached to other bodies of water they would be called coves or inlets but not on Chesapeake Bay. The experience of sailing Quo Vadis down to Solomon's Island the month before apparently did not deter Jim or he has selective memory. He ferried us ashore for a yummy dinner Laurie had prepared. He also served a better grade of beer than I had stocked on board. Bob Hemphill and Linda Powers drove over to join us in Annapolis but declined an invitation to visit aboard my new home. I sensed they may not have been captured by the seafaring spirit that so infused the rest of the assembled. OK, OK. Maybe Meredith was just being really nice about all this. But she was sharing the experience, on board.

Highlight #2: Anchoring in a small cove off the Wye River, lowering the dink and the swim ladder and jumping in. We knew there were jellyfish in the water (Here called "sea nettles"). We all got stung; poured vinegar on the welts and jumped back in. No whining from this crew. Stout fellows and gals all! Filtered gold sunlight lit the great blue herons flying around the anchorage like a flock of updated pterodactyls. Ospreys wheeled overhead and occasionally dived to grab a fish. And, sit down for this one: No bugs! Meredith had sewn screens for 12 of the 15 hatches and we did encounter some visiting insects at other anchorages but not so bad as I'd been told to expect.

After a warm shower and cranking up some of JB's traveling music, how could drinks and dinner on board be bad? After Knapp's Narrows, we encounter a skipjack, one of the last wooden sail-driven working boats on the Chesapeake. We watch living history pass us on a broad reach.

There are some photos, taken during this cruise, featuring two really suave guys wearing cool hats and swimsuits. One of them is rowing a 9 ft. inflatable while the other sits in the bow of said tender wielding his high-tech camera. These photos are available by special request only. Overall, sea and other sickness was non-existent or controlled (Cats really don't roll.) We lost a piece of rubrail on a piling at St. Michaels and everything ran pretty well until the engine over-temperature alarm went off about 10 miles out from Solomon's Island on our approach.

It was time for a command decision, so I had to make one. This time it was not "Let's eat lunch." This proved logical, as I recalled we had already eaten lunch and it wasn't yet time for dinner. Complications arose as neither the engine nor the alarm would stop with the kill switch. After a couple of moves not covered in the operating manual, I got the engine to stop dieseling (Ha, ha.) and we started sailing. About two hours later, we were at the entrance channel for Solomon's Island. To end the suspense, the engine did re-start, we made it to the dock and bid John and Dixie a poignant farewell along with many rolls of exposed film and dozens of digital images. We still had clean towels but, after Meredith returned to her estate near Mt. Vernon, I pumped over three gallons of ugly water/fuel slop out of the engine compartment. I suspected a leak.

After some marine diesel repair (Remember? Marine as a descriptor means triple the normal price.), my third re-build with the arrived parts for the second head (This was Dimitri's prophesy. You're gonna get yours, Greek!), and an intense deck-swabbing I was then off to Baltimore Washington International (which many of us remember as Friendship Airport) to collect my excellent children: Beth and Caroline. At least I think it was them. The one called "Caroline" was way too tall and mature while the "Beth" person had short, blonde hair. But, they both called me "Dad" so I went along with it. Each of these familiar strangers, supposedly my own kids, chose their cabin and moved their gear on to the boat. They travel light and efficiently, as usual, carrying only the minimum cruising necessities and several hundred essential CDs. Meredith joined us again at Solomon's so I find myself the happy skipper of a really fine, good-looking female crew. Maybe they are not long on experience but I realize they are all on board Quo Vadis because they care about the skipper who cares even more deeply for all of them.

We plan a four-day cruise to Smith Island and Tangier Island which are geographically out in the middle of the Chesapeake and politically in Virginia. It also seems vaguely exotic to sail off to islands where they really do speak a different language: this one is a variant of 17th century Cornish. These islands are reputedly the blue crab centers of the Eastern seaboard as well as the subject of documentary films about disappearing lifestyles in America.

Beth shows a handiness with rigging, sails and lines. Caroline is an effortless natural at the helm. She also uses those sharp teenage eyes to read markers from half a mile out and spot the crab pot floats which are scattered thoughout the Bay like multi-colored minefields for sailboats. Sailing with these young women fills my heart with pride and wonder. I am later informed by Mer that I talked in my stern Daddy voice when they were not able to execute boat tasks like seasoned salts. Sorry, gals. We'll all get better at this.

We are one of the few vessels and the only non-commercial boat at the pier when we dock at Smith Island. Meredith and Caroline put on their swimsuits and go swimming in the channel with the local kids. This activity consists mostly of whooping and jumping off the pier. It is such a nostalgic vignette of American life, now starring these two ladies of 16 and 59, that I get all misty. Unfortunately, all 110 lbs. of Meredith gets hypothermic. Yes, it can happen in 85-degree weather and warm water. We press on to Tangier with M. not much better and Caroline getting queasy. The docks here work better as they offer power, water and shoreside heads. Tangier is fairly quaint as an island in time. In fact, tour boats from the mainland show up on weekends packed with gawkers. The locals consist of descendants of the seven families who settled here back in the 1600s. They bury their dead in shallow graves in their front yards, speak another version of English, and one descendant chastised Beth for wearing her swim suit to the beach. Go figure. There is also a small, seldom-used airstrip and lots of working watermen's boats motoring in and out from the faded-to-gray wooden docks and crabhouses. We Californians really cannot understand their speech which seems to be made up of Cornish-inflected nautical terms most of the time. The watermen enliven their discourse with ample profanity. We know this because that part we understand. Maybe those old English words haven't changed much in 300 years.

The remote island charm is not totally engaging and Meredith is now running a fever. Another command decision: we can't diagnose what's wrong with her so let's head back to the mainland. There were lots of crabs though, curiously, not always available for eating by visiting cruisers.

The bad news is Mer is really sick, bedridden and still undiagnosed. The good news is Beth, Caroline and I spend time together doing touristy stuff in D.C. and environs. I learn quite a bit from them. I'm having such a good time I ask them to stay longer. Beth feels obligated to get back to her summer job and Caroline, after finishing high school at 16, wants to get on to college. This is hard for a father to argue with. Job? College? I decide I should not discourage anybody; certainly not my children, from these goals. We plan to sail again in the Caribbean where the water is clear and we can snorkel together.

I "walk on" and get a crew slot on a C&C 35 to race the Screwpile Challenge. This is a three day, six race regatta commemorating the screwpile lighthouses once common in the Chesapeake; only two remain. Depending on who answers the question, this is either the biggest or second biggest racing event on the Bay. This is my first time racing on this coast and it's a long time since my last race anywhere. Skipper Fred Dreyer is a great guy, I like all the other crew, and I learn a lot. I am also a little sore after three days of hauling and grinding but, overall, feel pretty good. Is this to be my new life? Cruising and racing and going to the after-event parties? Oh, well…so it goes.

I am really pleased when my old pal, Dave Schoonmaker, agrees to come on board for a three day jaunt. I have not seen Dave since the days of the "Mother Earth News" Eco-village. We spent many years before that testing and racing motorcycles including some memorable dusty runs into Mexico. Neither of us makes a point of how long it's been, as that would imply too much: time passing, babies growing up, us getting older. Way too much to consider. Neither had realized we'd also been doing some sailing as these things happened. The question arises: do all old motorcycle racers move on to this sailing thing? There are other examples we can think of, some reading this.

This is as short-handed a cruise as I've attempted. Dave is a competent and technically correct sailor so this seems like a good time to go for it. We plan to head out once more to Smith Island, overnight there and return, allowing a buffer day. The forecast looked good two days out so Dave flies up from North Carolina but the forecast was wrong. There is only light wind, from the East (on our nose) and it is raining heavily. We shove off into the teeth of the weather. After about an hour and a half in falling visibility, more rain, colder temperatures and no useful wind, I decide I'm not having fun and, more to the point, we won't get to Smith Island today. I propose we turn around and sail up the Patuxent River which, despite two months of sailing past its mouth, I have never done. This is also very colonial.

We jibe up the Pax River in fairly good form and continuing rain to Broome's Island. We anchor in about 9 ft. of water off the dock at Stoney's, world-famous for crab cakes. A quick dinghy drop and a short row brings us to the dock. We are wet, hungry, cold and in pretty damn good spirits. Dave allows as how this is the best workout his new foul weather gear has ever had. The crab cakes are world class; the seafood chowder is thick and hot. How can I keep losing weight while we eat like this? I like it. Quo Vadis looks pretty good resting at anchor. Even better is that we remembered to close the companionway. We decide to find a snug anchorage for the night and attempt the Bay crossing again in the morning. The rain stops. And starts again. "There's our 80% chance of rain," observes Dave. "It rains 48-50 minutes out of each hour."

St. Leonard's Creek is written up in the cruising guide as the scene of a U.S. naval victory in the War of 1812. We head up into said creek through a Z-channel entrance and anchor in a quiet cove in front of a very expensive-looking house. It appears only the servants are in residence for the weekend. We later discover, from historical sources, that the U.S. victory probably consisted of a motley American flotilla temporarily escaping from the British fleet that ruled the Chesapeake during that conflict. Nobody can remember what the 1812 war was fought about. One result of the war was that an American prisoner, Francis Scott Key, wrote some new lyrics set to the tune of an old British drinking song, "To Anachreon in Heaven". Key's lyrics started out, "Oh, say can you see by the dawn's early light?" The victorious flotilla later scuttled itself to avoid capture.

The anchorage in St. Leonard's Creek is good. A blue heron cruises low to check us out and there is lots of fish action. Thankfully, no bugs; especially since there is no wind. In the morning, there is still no wind. Dave is a real sport about cleaning the primeval ooze off the anchor chain, which explains why the anchor set so well. He takes the helm as we head toward the Bay—one more time. I act like a skipper and inform the helmsman we'll take a decision by the Hog Island Buoy. If we can't make Smith Island today, we'll put the wind on our starboard beam and head up toward Calvert Cliffs and the postcard-picturesque Cove Point Lighthouse to take in the scenery. The wind is 4-6 kts; still East to South when we get out on the Bay so we turn North. After about three hours, we have a no-kidding 0 kts wind speed (Not apparent wind, smart guys.) so it is not what you might call a great sailing day. Dave quotes the bumper sticker, "A bad day sailing is better than the best day working." Dave later shares his coastal guide and Caribbean charts. We agree to sail together in those places within months; not years.

There is little drama in a smooth docking back at the marina on Solomon's Island. Meredith cannot join us for dinner but confirms she is recovered from her undiagnosed affliction. Dave wears his new Quo Vadis Crew shirt to a dinner of tasty soft shell crabs. I feel a very lucky man.

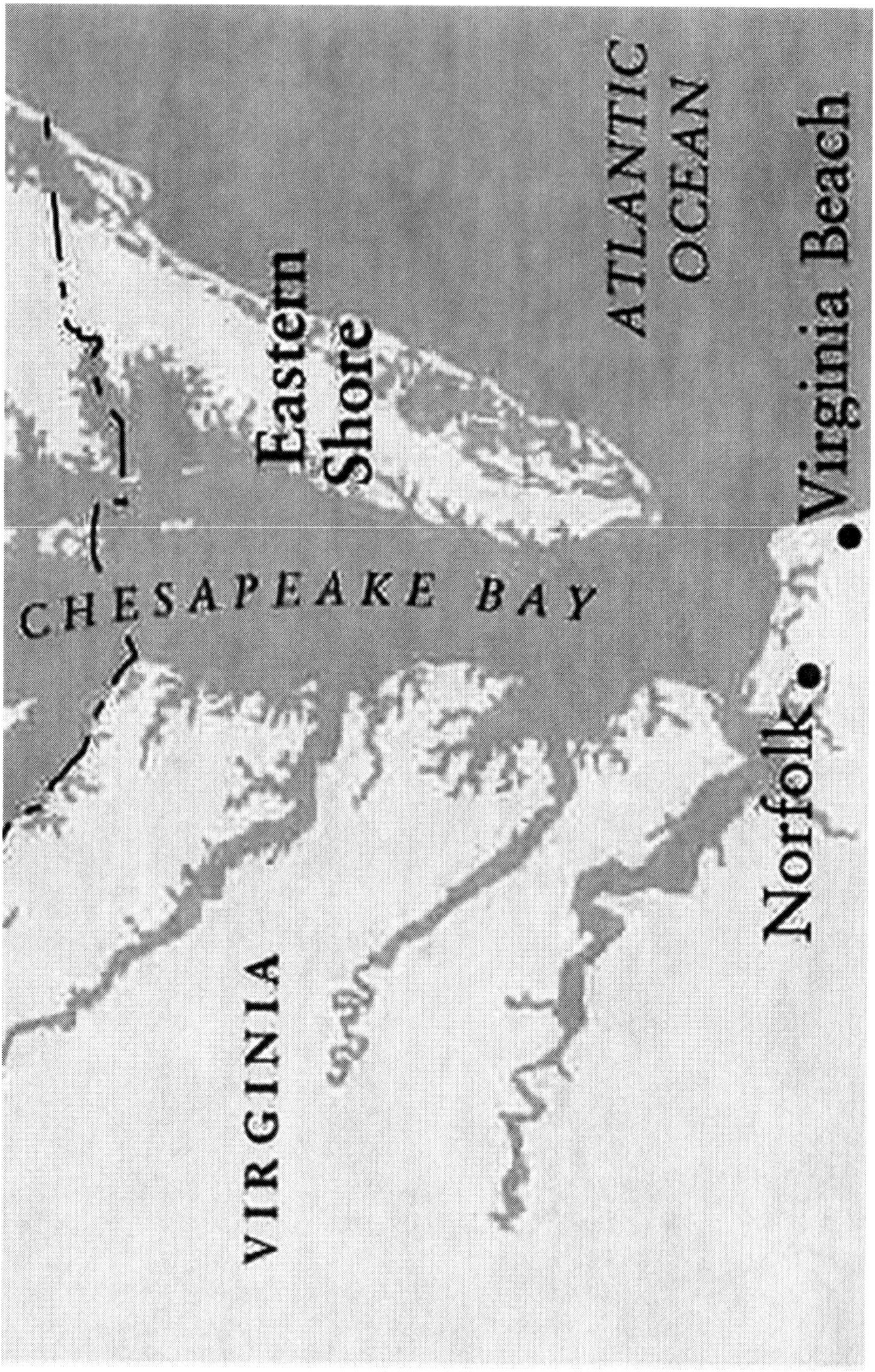
ATLANTIC
OCEAN
Eastern
Shore
CHESAPEAKE BAY
VIRGINIA
Norfolk
Virginia Beach

Summer's Almost Over

Aboard S/V Quo Vadis, docked back at Solomon's Island

It came as a (minor) shock to count the calendar pages up to nearly four months of living aboard Quo Vadis. This is further reinforcement to enjoy each day of this voyage, because they seem to pass so quickly, sometimes in bunches. This is especially true for those of us with more yesterdays than we have tomorrows. This passage on twin hulls is getting to be too much like a metaphor for "real life". More later on that subject.

Some of the best days were spent with my kids. I want to recapture some of their comments not recorded earlier, mostly so that I'll remember. (I keep forgetting to take that gingko biloba stuff.)

We had gone from sailing to motoring due to a severe lack of wind out there on the Chesapeake. After a while of diesel-thrumming, Beth looked up at me in the helm chair and said, "It's too bad Grandpa John's not here. He really would have liked this." I am touched and silently wonder: Did she remember that he had commanded an Army amphibious boat battalion which operated on the lower reaches of the Chesapeake? Grandpa John, my father, died last year. His ashes were scattered on the Pacific Ocean at sunset from a family-conned sloop. I think he would have liked this. He definitely would approve of his grandchildren sailing on this Bay.

I received what I considered a most important Stamp of Approval when Caroline turned to me the second day of that same cruise and told me, "Dad, you really do have a nice boat." I was speechless, which is rare, as many of you know. Of course, this is the same daughter who told Meredith, "You must put your face in Tupperware in the refrigerator at night." We're pretty sure she intended this as a compliment.

Meanwhile, the never-ending process of boat work continues. I finally got the ship's bell, brought from Alameda, installed near the companionway but can't remember how many bells means what time…or however that works. Something else to research. My old pal and former LCU bos'n's mate, Mike Kerley, joins us on Quo Vadis after being led astray for hours by MapQuest or some other literal and misleading computer program. The poor guy also had to endure several local 100+ heat index days. I must be getting acclimatized as I planned a two-day sail into the Nanticoke River, referred to in the cruising guide as the last wild and scenic river of Delaware. Given its location, it's fair to wonder if this riverine description may speak to the level of industrial development rather than periodic salmon migrations as a "wildness' index.

There is enough wind but it is not favorable, so we tack for about four hours until Mike's shoulders give out and Meredith is officially seasick. I sympathize with his specific accumulation of physical traumas accrued by our mature bodies. If I had to tack with my knees, I wouldn't be out here. So we return to civilization with its discontents of air conditioning, chilled drinks, and professionally-prepared food, forfeiting the wild and scenic experience. Mike and Mer have lost the opportunity to savor my inimitable on-board meals, generically known as "Skipper Specials". (John and Dixie pretended to like them. Or maybe they didn't want to cook.)

The run back takes less than two hours on a single tack as I hit and hold the reverse course to the degree. This cat really can be trimmed up and sailed hands off, like the propaganda claims. I am thrilled with this new experience. The rest of the crew is less enthusiastic about the event. Mike abandons the teak-paneled Old World charm of the Quo Vadis for an air conditioned room at the Holiday Inn. Mer is seriously concerned he has suffered heat stroke. Since he did a tour in Viet Nam; some of it in the engine room of an LCU, I am not so convinced, but agree he is suffering. This was my crazy idea to start with.

Unfortunately, another chance to improve my sailing skills is canceled when Corain, the boat I crewed in the Screwpile Regatta, cannot muster enough other crewmembers for the two-day race from Annapolis to Oxford. Hey, I was ready! Whatever happened to the commitment to competition? Or anything else people say they're going to do? I am disappointed.

My roommate from high school, Dr. Jeffrey Morehouse (aka Mad Dog), and his wife, Dr. Candace Bartman, join us for a cruise despite our warnings and their personal knowledge of what it's like on the Chesapeake in August. The second day finds us motoring toward Smith Island when a note in the cruising guide about entering the channel on a rising tide prompts me to check the tide tables. After a quick adjustment for the distance from Ft. McHenry (the tidal reference), I conclude that we will arrive within 2-3 minutes of dead low tide. Since we plowed the channel a little wider the last time QV visited Smith, we re-think our destination. On to Tangier! We have another two hours of motoring with this option but possibly avoid exposing Meredith to whatever at Smith Island made her deathly sick for three weeks: in itself, a superior plan, I think.

When we enter the Tangier channel, the tide is running high and we have 8 ft. under the hull. A corollary of the tide rushing in, however, is the current doing the same. Nobody on board noticed the speed of the current until Jeff jumps off onto the dock with the bow line and the stern immediately whips out into the channel. There are at least 3 knots flowing as I now see the turbulence around the pilings. I blow several more approaches (but avoid hitting the pilings) accompanied by much hand gesturing and shouted advice (mostly in 17th century Cornish) from the locals now gathering on the dock for this entertainment. Is Jeff, now standing on the dock, actually laughing? I also don't seem to have much control in reverse with the drive leg. This is a problem for me with a 37 ft. vessel of 16 ft. beam, and a channel about 50 ft. wide. Another boat comes close enough for the helmsman to sneer at me, "You want a tow?" He then keeps going. I don't find this helpful but suppress the correct reaction which is to tell him to fuck off.

The boat swings 180 degrees with a notable benefit: it is now heading into the current. I finally bring it alongside the landing I wanted in the first place and "Gander" Park, patriarch of the Tangier community, is content to let us tie at this dock to keep me from cluttering up the channel. After a yummy dinner ashore of crabs served about four different ways, Jeff, Candy and Meredith are persuaded to take a motorized jitney tour of Tangier narrated by one of the locals. With the length of negotiable roadway on the island, this takes about 15 minutes at 5 MPH. I hate feeling like a tourist when I cruise to someplace, perhaps because I'm aware that, to the locals, I am one. Jeff, Candy and Mer all liked the tour. We sail 'til the wind dies; then motor up the Potomac River and overnight in Smith's Creek, north of Smith Point and west of Smith Island. Besides getting a real break from Pocahontas, John Smith sure got around a lot for a scrawny little Englishman. He was not shy about attaching his name to any thing or any notable accomplishment, whether actually his own or not. I like the local legend that he got spiked by a sting ray while he was wading ashore. So, naturally, there is a Sting Ray Point.

The wind shifts to the North, which is predictable since that is the direction we want to go. The wind has been on our nose every hour of every day, no matter our course. Jeff wants to go sailing, so we head East. We sail to the other side of Chesapeake Bay and our planned tacking point where even the North wind dies. Since I have already started preparation of today's "Skipper Special" down in the galley, my traditional response to contrary events afloat is easy to implement: We eat lunch.

Later, motoring over a glassy surface, discussions turn to sailing short-handed as it appears that's what I'll be doing. (Responses from the good, experienced sailors invited to join the cruise have been negative to non-existent. What are you people doing with your lives?) The sea conditions support a decision to actually do some Man Overboard drills. No one on board has yet done such a drill from *Quo Vadis*. I fall in first to test if Meredith can actually get the boat turned around, get a Lifesling out to me, position the boat and haul my dripping, chunky body up 3-4 ft. of freeboard and on to the deck, all by herself.

It is a very interesting feeling, bobbing around in the middle of the Bay with nothing else in sight from water level, watching your boat sail away from you. The psychological relief when the boat turns around shouldn't be, but is, surprising. With some procedural suggestions from Jeff and Candy, Meredith gets flotation and recovery gear overboard, brings the boat alongside without running me down, and manages to winch me aboard in the Lifesling. Well done, and good that it was done at all. So we try again, with the changed condition that she can't winch me up but needs to launch the tethered dinghy and pull me in. This also works but takes a little longer. One lesson we learn is that once the crew overboard is secured and calmed down, the other crewmember has some time to work through the rescue and get them back on board.

Jeff and I suggest that there be some signal from the boat to show the victim they've been spotted: like waving and yelling "I see you." As we start the second drill, Meredith stops the boat and looks back at my bobbing head. She smiles, waves and shouts: "I'll see you!" before putting the engine back in gear. Note: Must review life insurance beneficiaries.

I manage to pull her from the murky depths under similar circumstances and discover that the stainless steel D-rings on the Lifesling are nearly corroded through. This leads to replacement with new stainless triangles, re-rigging the sling and a review of other safety gear. As my old business partner, Les Haug, used to say of engineering solutions, "You can't check enough."

Despite a year-long effort to walk away (or sail away) from it, business continues to intrude into my cruising plans. My client Alameda Power & Telecom still owes me an interesting dollar amount and isn't returning phone calls. This is potentially the bad news. I develop some more prospects for electric Powerbike rentals in resort areas which was a major part of the last business plan I wrote. The development effort wasn't too arduous since the Harleys were docked one slip over at Solomon's on their power cruiser High Heels. They bought a sample bike after riding the one I had on board, so this could be construed as the good news; especially if they buy a bunch more for the resorts in the Bahamas. The basic question I'm still grappling with: Is this something I want to do?

It was neat to spend a little time with Jim Wanko getting his new boat ready to take home from Solomon's Island since he was in the first crew bringing Quo Vadis to Solomon's from Annapolis. Unfortunately, he didn't need my help to sail his pretty Cape Dory 30 back up the Bay.

A 3-day cruise planned over Labor Day weekend was canceled by me based on the NOAA long range weather forecast. The immediate personal feedback I got was: You're a wimpy skipper and not flexible. This opinion was supported by initial conditions featuring light morning sprinkles and 10 knots of wind. The next day was a full-on Nor'easter: the scourge of the Chesapeake. This particular version featured sustained 35-knot winds (from the North, of course, where the fun ports are), 4 ft. whitecaps, sheeting rain all day, and falling temperatures. The next day continued wet and cold with winds from the wrong direction. This experience reinforced the concept that once the skipper makes a "go/ no go" decision, it's probably a good idea to stick with it. If the result is that you're not out in that stuff, it's an even better idea.

An increasing amount of time is spent planning the cruise South. I'm plotting each day of travel down the Chesapeake; then courses for either going offshore or on the Intracoastal Waterway, how and when to make the Gulf Stream crossing to the Bahamas. I've calculated the miles to be covered both motoring or sailing based on some prevailing and storm wind assumptions, planned anchorages, and necessary dockings: all with the innate understanding that it will probably be different. In this sense, it is like a more focused version of life itself. (I've lost 10 more pounds; so should be that much easier to winch up if I go overboard.)

26   John Huetter

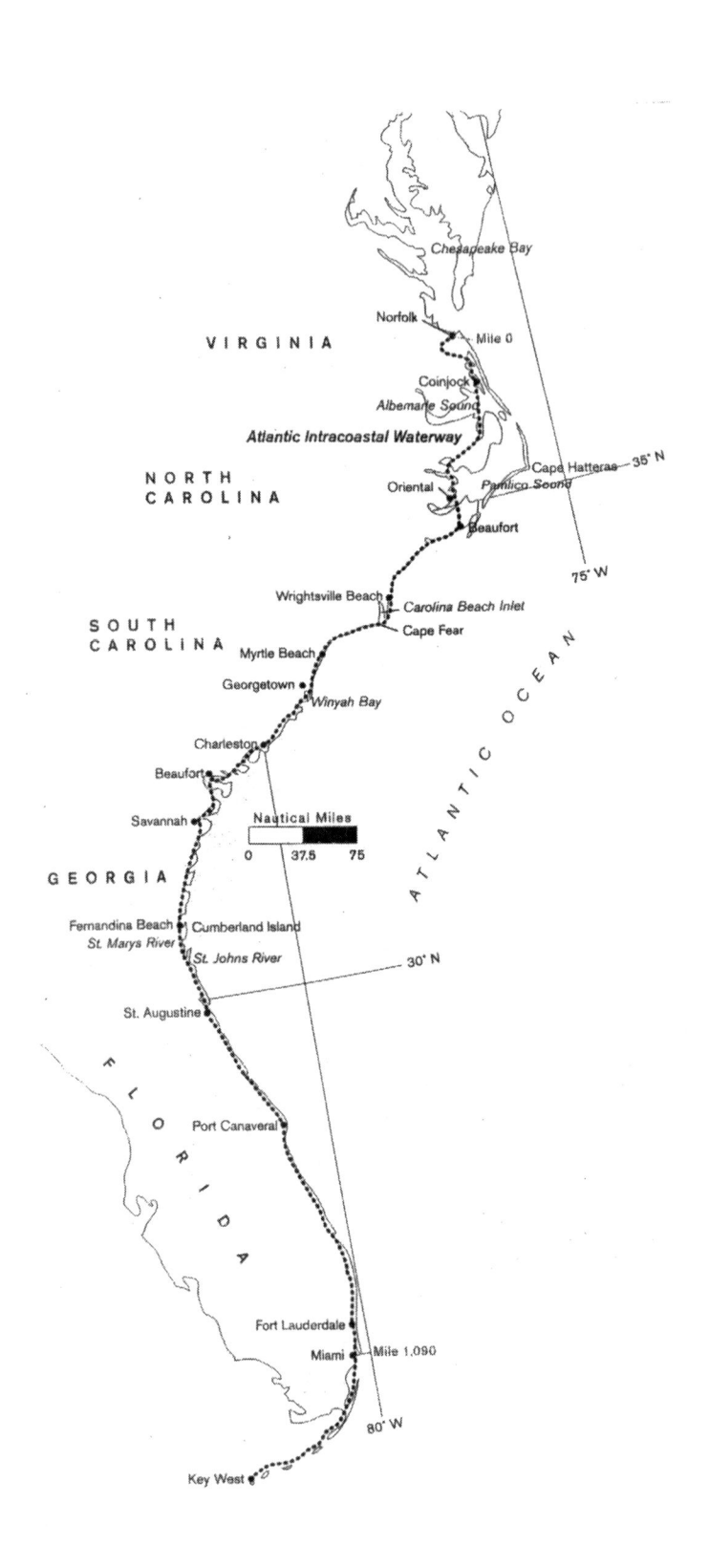

Many Things Break but We Head South Anyway

Aboard S/V Quo Vadis, docked Pompano Beach, Florida

The last two months of this crazy trip called my life can be summarized as one month of everything breaking and trying to fix it and one month making a 1200 mile cruise from the Chesapeake Bay to South Florida. (Or, for Dr. Seuss fans: Month One and Month Two.) Which month could possibly be more interesting? Here: you decide.

Month One began on a very upbeat note with a weekend of shore leave at Meredith's house in the autumnal leafiness near Mt. Vernon. Her residence also features a king size bed and air conditioning. Upon returning to my nautical abode, now a rested and happy sailorman, I noticed that the reefer and the freezer weren't working. I discovered a short from a burnt connector behind the first panel I removed. (You boat guys and gals will appreciate this minor miracle as you usually have to remove all the panels to find the fault.)

Buoyed by my ability to fix the reefer, I jumped in the water to clean the algae off the drive leg and scrape some barnacles. To my sodden surprise, the steering yoke holding the drive leg was snapped in two. One piece was dangling from the pivot pin. I was also forced to admit that the bottom paint was flaking far worse that I had hoped, or noticed even a few days earlier. Things did not improve. After a fairly perplexing exercise in calling overseas with my baffling new cell phone, I finally got hold of Sonic Sillette in Surrey, U.K. who made this outdrive for catamarans.

Alan answered and was very cavalier about the whole thing. "You're going to tell me you didn't hit anything. They all do." (We hadn't hit the leg or somebody on board—we're talking ocean experienced sailors, some with Ph.D.'s — would have noticed.) "Yes, we have about 1500 of these units in service and we ship about two of these yolks a month as replacements. It's really supposed to break to protect the pricier bits." Since this chunk of cast aluminum is costing me over 350 pounds sterling (about $500 at current exchange rate), I shudder to think of the pricier bits. Is this sacrificial part which breaks to render the unit unsteerable another British design coup? I've had British sports cars but this is my first British-built boat. Alan then started giving me verbal instructions for repairing it in the water—working from the dinghy under the aft deck.

"You've got your mate to put a line on it and now you've got your bowl floating on the water to catch the oil." I stopped him right there, agreed to pay full price and shipping charges for the part, then started calling boatyards to see if any could haul twin hulls with a 16 ft. beam. Sue (Bless her.) scheduled me in to the only yard in this part of the Chesapeake that could handle it. The good news is that the yard was close enough that I risked the move with the broken steering yoke by lashing the drive leg in position and steering with rudders only. With some help, I made it to the Travelift slings. The bad news is…well, everything got expensive and messy. Even me.

The colorful royal blue anti-fouling paint cost $178/gallon. People that haven't done boats really don't believe this. By the second day of scraping and sanding the bottom, the yard workers were calling me "Papa Smurf". Yes, I was blue; very blue. While the boat was hauled, more stuff happened until a couple of B.O.A.T. units later (Break Out Another Thousand), it had a working knotmeter, new drive leg parts installed, electrical system readout and calibration, drained and repaired rudders, and a bright blue bottom. One very positive aspect of this episode is that I came to appreciate the hydrodynamic design and hull shape of this catamaran. Prouts can look somewhat dowdy and dated; not as pretty as the new French cats in the water, but the hulls' design with the integral skeg and the rudder arrangements give some confidence in both the sailing manners and seaworthiness of *Quo Vadis*. For future reference, I never want to do another bottom job. Nor should you.

During this out of water experience, Dave Schoonmaker confirmed that he could sail for a week during the passage south. The incredibly good news was that Mer decided she would go with me. I was overjoyed and still am. Dave is quite an optimist in this enterprise as his previous experience aboard *Quo Vadis*, on the Chesapeake, had been wet and windless. Meredith had to overcome the admonishments of several professional mariners that the Intracoastal Waterway was both boring and dangerous as well as her continued skepticism about my sailing abilities.

Bob Hemphill continued to avoid actually boarding my boat but gave us a nice Bon Voyage dinner and some presents, including some inspirational reading entitled "A Voyage for Madmen" or something like that. I continued working on understanding and upgrading the boat's electrical systems. I acquired more ICW guides and charts; in fact, every one that I knew existed and began the provisioning for an expected 20 days/2 crew and 7 days/3 crew underway.

We set October 9th as the departure date from Solomon's Island with a targeted November 5th arrival in Ft. Lauderdale. On October 8th, I finished preparing the boat about 1830, got Meredith on board about 2230, and everybody to sleep about 0130. The net effect was about six hours sleep before a planned 0800 cast off to catch the ebbing tide and make our first anchorage by 1630: an hour before sunset which is one of the few *Quo Vadis* rules when underway. So much for Month One. It was a character-building, cash-depleting experience. It was also not much fun.

The next stage of the adventure now begins. It won't spoil your fun if I tell you right now it was one of the finest experiences of my life. Twenty-five days underway, five of them under sail, and three days in port: two of them unplanned. During the months QV was based at Solomon's Island, there was much talk and planning of next passages on other boats, changes of plan, boat preparation, and trial sails. As the winds across the Chesapeake turned chill, we were still the only vessel that actually cast off from the docks to make that "next passage" during the whole season.

Quo Vadis was under way by 0855 with a hand from Alan Reese, Canadian owner of Gringo, a Vagabond 47 docked next door at Solomon's. Destination: Ft. Lauderdale, with our first anchorage in the Great Wicomico River on the western shore of the Chesapeake. We set the sails as we passed the green Patuxent River 1 buoy for the last time and headed almost due South.

Mer did a great job at the helm during anchoring, following hand signals only, as she would continue to do for the rest the voyage. For dinner at our first night's anchorage double-handing together, we had seared tenderloin on arugula salad, clam chowder with fresh lemons, and a Chilean chardonnay. I added a half quart of oil to the diesel. The next morning, I raised the mainsail before pulling up the hook and we fell off in 10-15 knots wind with intermittent rain all day. Mer plotted an aggressive route on her GPS which took us over some shallows but it worked out OK since QV draws just 1 meter (39 inches) in its current cruising trim.

We docked in Fishing Bay to take on fuel, beginning a pattern of docking for fuel and holding tank pump-out every second or third day; then anchoring out when we could. Another pattern that seemed immutable was my ability to be docked at the slip furthest from essential shoreside facilities (like toilets and showers) and still be in the same marina. This makes for some long, dark, and rapid walks. We left Fishing Bay under power but I determined we could go faster under sail, so we set them all. The wind kept building. Boat speed went from 5 knots to 7 knots and waves to 3 ft. with flying foam. The max observed speed was 7.8 kts but conditions were deteriorating with heavy rain and limited visibility.

Quo Vadis passed another legend of the Bay, the skipjack Claud W. Somers. We hit all of M's waypoints which was very useful in reduced visibility and intermittent rain in our face. I didn't like the weather after about six hours sailing and reduced sail while Mer took the helm. My USS Hopper ship's cap blew overboard while I was scurrying around the deck furling the genoa. I had gotten the cap at the commissioning ceremony in San Francisco for the first Navy combat vessel named for a female: Rear Admiral Ruth Hopper, the co-inventor of COBOL computer language.

I was very glad to see the channel markers for the Salt Ponds north of Hampton, Virginia and less glad to surf between them on a five foot breaking wave. We avoided both the markers and the rock jetty. Mer did a great job of docking us in drenching rain but I was tired from anxiety and fighting the helm for nearly seven hours. She insisted that the only remaining dock hand ("I was on my way home when you called in 'cuz I didn't think anybody'd be out in this weather.") take our photograph because, as she gleefully insisted, we looked like a couple of drowned rats.

This weather was the Northern edge of Hurricane Kyle which was later announced to be arriving in Hampton Roads at noon the next day, just as were scheduled to. We opted instead to stay in port after enjoying a dinner of turkey and sun-dried tomato sausages, black beans and rice, and fresh red peppers and onions in vinaigrette. I drank shiraz; Mer drank skim milk. I also discovered the wonder and benefits of a rest day after three days underway.

Kyle took another one of his record number of directional jogs the next day. This one was away from our planned course. I felt very good heading across Hampton Roads with the goal of going through the Great Bridge Lock into the Intracoastal Waterway and meeting Dave somewhere around North Carolina. About halfway across the Roads, I was regaling Mer with still more fascinating tales of my childhood in this Tidewater region when I looked over my shoulder to see DD982, the Nicholson, bearing down on QV at 20 knots. We're on the same course; headed for the Navy piers. I drop off to port with 982 looming large over us. The destroyer steams past. I'm sure they do this with small craft all the time but it definitely got my adrenaline flowing. I punched Mile "0" of the ICW into my brand new knotmeter/log where one of the guides said it was. This reference point never matched any other distance readings for the rest of the voyage.

We locked in to the ICW behind a young family headed for the Islands. Their Rutland wind generator had blown off during their time in the Kyle-related weather we'd also experienced. Did I know where to get parts? I think this was the older skipper-older boat syndrome, again. Maybe we are both starting to look broken-in; maybe just well-used. At least the locks were easy to traverse, contrary to most of the talk back at the marina docks. There were only a few feet of elevation change and the lock-keepers were experienced in handling the many novices to the ICW.

We docked at Pungo Ferry Marina about 1645. Dave arrived at 1710 after a long land route diversion. He was equipped with the new, spare alternator and a basketful of goodies (fresh-baked bread, fruit and wine). Daughter Elizabeth had bravely pressed on an extra two hours from the waterless locks we couldn't use to deliver her Dad. She said "Hi", got in her Saab and drove home. The crew of Quo Vadis, now reinforced to three, decided to sail off to Albemarle Sound.

High winds closed the swing bridge at the entrance to the Alligator River before noon the next day so we diverted to an anchorage in Broad Creek where we were on the hook by 1430. This was the scene of another episode of Meredith's continuing love affair with boat dogs. Buck, a black standard poodle, was invited on board with his crew, Sandy and Ann, from Windwalker. Though Windwalker's hailing port was in central Texas, they had made an overnight run the length of the Chesapeake to get this far: standing watch and watch. I begin to understand there are other ways to do this thing. Buck nearly got Shanghaied by Mer but the "First Mutt" jumped gracefully back in to his tender and took his crew back to their boat. We did not have the appropriate food.

The next morning we headed South with the goal of making 65 miles across the Sound. We set sail in the channel, right out of Broad Creek, making 5.7-6.8 knots and entered Albemarle Sound at 0830. One reef in the main and a fully deployed genoa provided 8 knots along our intended course, moistened with intermittent rain. The max recorded boat speed for the crossing was 9.8 knots, as quick as the boat had gone since our first day sailing that Norther down to Solomon's Island. We anchored out, after a long but satisfying day, in the Upper Pungo as dusk fell along with heavy rain. After Italian greens in lemon and olive oil, my version of the hot sausage with onion/oregano red sauce was well-received. It's likely there was some red wine along in here.

The week cruising with Dave on board was outstanding, marred only by one little incident. One morning, I elected to start the engine using only the start battery. This is recommended to ensure that it still works independently of the house bank. It started with no problem. About two hours out, I observed smoke from the engine compartment; then smelled electrical overload or meltdown. The start battery was a problem: it was cooked. We lost instruments. I stopped the engine and set the sails in 1-2 kts. Wind. About this time, another cruiser motored past the silent and ghosting Quo Vadis. He observed, "You guys are hard-core purists." Well, not intentionally.

After a considered joint analysis of what went wrong and why, we decided to try the other battery bank after isolating the "bad" battery. It worked and we proceeded into the Neuse River to complete 60 miles under sail with Dave at the helm. We docked at Oriental where Dave soon disembarked for a 10-mile run before dinner. He is training for another triathlon. The search for a replacement gel cell battery also begins. It took another two days and a layover in Beaufort, the North Carolina one. We are encountering dolphins almost daily near the ocean inlets to the ICW. They feed, frolic and, on this leg, several jump clear of the water. I like their presence as a good omen and a prediction of good things.

I had called ahead to the marina and was told they had the gel cell we had described. They didn't and the dockhand tried to sell us something else. This was not OK and I let him know even my meager intelligence was insulted. Steve, the owner/manager of Town Creek Marina, is informed of the situation. He located the correct replacement at the Morehead City West Marine store, ordered it on his account, and arranged for pick-up and delivery. Again, the difference between an employee and an owner is underscored. The next afternoon, technician Mike Collins comes wheeling a roll-on cart down the dock.

"Somebody here need a battery?" he smiled. Mike used to be an aviation electronics tech with American Airlines. He declined to move to Oklahoma City when American relocated their maintenance base. "Me going to Oral Roberts country? No way." He's now fixing boats for which this skipper is very thankful. He installed the battery and it immediately ran up to 16 volts: too much for a traditional 12V boat battery. He quickly determined the APC-built regulator was shot which explained the start battery overcharging and toasting. Using my cell phone, he ordered a new "Smart" regulator for UPS overnight delivery. I hope it is smarter than the last one...or me. This is all starting to get pricey.

The agony is eased considerably by the excellent company who retain their sense of humor even after all the days on board with Capt. Mean-o. This same crew shares a very good dinner ashore prepared by young chef John Wade. He made some first class fajitas with local seafood among other culinary feats. Mer selects Beethoven's cello concertos for the evening's music on board. We are soothed for hours without concern for the batteries; we're on shore power.

Mike gets everything wired in after much cell phone talk with the power controller factory rep. We're ready to go as soon as I can find Mer and settle our tab: now approaching a B.O.A.T. unit. She often goes wandering off on her own as if she were an independent grown woman, for God's sake. Finally, we see her walking down the dock. I start in on one of my "Where were you?" things. She gives me an "Oh, get real!" look with her turquoise eyes and informs me, "Everything's settled. I was going to get you an EPIRB for your birthday but it seems you needed this first." I stumble and mumble thanks with feelings far stronger than my feeble words.

The new voltage regulator kept regulating, the new battery stayed charged at 12-13 volts, and the engine started when we punched the correct button. Still, we finally had to let Dave ashore at the South Carolina border. Son Devin arrived to transport him back to his day job editing <u>American Scientist</u> magazine and his family. Brave Meredith would have to endure two more weeks aboard QV, alone with me. All had been warned the floggings would continue until morale improved.

Well, some of the time wasn't so bad. We reunited with former crew, Jeff and Candy, for a long dinner in Charlestown, South Carolina. Jeff drove two hours with his broken arm still in a sling. He fell out of the hayloft at his daughter's horse farm. I wondered out loud if his arm still hurt, after the drive and all. His reply reflected the acquired wisdom of our years, which I sadly lack.

"Of course it hurts. You live with it. We're all used to being in pain by now. Aren't you?" He's right. We have grown used to chronic pain. My knee and left shoulder joints ache in empathy.

We are favored with many quiet anchorages all to ourselves at sunset. One of these is in a cove in front of Ft. Frederica. It was, we discover, a British fort which controlled this water route during the Revolutionary War. Florida, which included parts of what is now south Georgia, remained under British control. The fort is now isolated from maritime traffic: just a few ruins, low walls with some cannons and a Union Jack flying. The sunset is spectacular and Mer likes to make love under the open sky. In minutes, we're sprawled naked over the front of the coach roof. The cries of the not-so-young lovers ring in waves over the surrounding sawgrass while our legs wrap around each other in surprise and delight. The pink and orange light of the sunset colors everything, including our skin and the air itself. The weeds and water are very still. No bugs arrive to spoil the moment, even as it gets dark. Later, I prepare chicken piccata, chilled asparagus with mayo, slice a baguette, and open some sauvignon blanc, served inside the salon.

Quo Vadis cruises into Florida at Fernandina Beach and makes it to St. Augustine by Hallowe'en. We get a Mexican food fix, then check out the old fort and the Spanish Quarter which are both surprisingly deserted. Mer buys this outrageous black and silver witch's hat from a milliner. It's made in the traditional style with a wide brim and pointy crown. When we get back on board, she goes below to change into her Hallowe'en costume for our small party. Mer emerges on deck wearing her new witch's hat with an orange coral necklace as her only accessory. Well, she adds an enchanting smile. I am charmed. It is a very Happy Hallowe'en with both tricks and treats.

The dolphin sightings are more frequent as go further South on the ICW, even as the good sailing opportunities diminish to zero. Mer wants to feed the dolphins, so buys some bait fish from one of the docks where we've stopped to re-fuel. The bait seller says that if you pound on the hull with your hand, the dolphins will come over to the boat to be hand fed. Equipped with a couple of bags of small, dead fish we venture out to lure the dolphins to our side. We see a pod over by the edge of the main channel. I'm willing to stop QV but not keen to go outside the channel. Mer gets the bait fish out and pounds on the outside of the *ama*. The dolphins ignore the supposed signal and soon disappear. She later tries banging on the hull with no dolphins visible, thinking to attract those who are cavorting below the surface. This variation doesn't seem to work, either. We try this for a couple of days whenever we spot more dolphins, until the bait fish start to smell way too fishy. Finally, the slimy little carcasses get tossed over the side, never having attracted any of our fun mammalian pals. I wonder if the bait store guys tell this same story to all ICW novices.

The weather very suddenly gets warmer. We have gone from sweaters and foul weather gear to swimsuits. Mer is sunning herself on the foredeck in her black bikini bottom when we see our first Florida alligator sunning itself on a gravel bank. She does a half push-up off the deck to look at the 'gator, thrilling the guy in the nearby fishing skiff as well as the skipper of the Quo Vadis.

The route opens up into a wide expanse with the channel marked by the ICW mileposts. After another half hour of feeling the engine vibrations through the foredeck, Mer comes back to the cockpit. She announces, "You've got a horny woman here." As she pulls the white stool over to the helm. She slips out of her bikini, pulls my shorts down and steps up on the stool in front of me. I'm still thinking we shouldn't be doing this while underway when suddenly I'm in her. Her very firm white bottom is framed by her tan back and legs. With my right eye, I can see the fathometer. It is set in "feet" to match the local charts. We start to move together along with the digital readout: 10-9-7-8-6 (Damn!) 8-7-9-11-10-10 (OK, back in the channel). I relax and go tense in the same moment. We're not a hazard to navigation much longer. Some minutes later, I catch my breath.

In Florida, the powerboat wakes got bigger and their operators ruder. There were a lot more bridges to contend with as well as 3-5 knot crosscurrents. Every day, I thanked whatever God or goddesses were looking after us that most of the currents worked for us (as planned) and nearly all the bridge tenders were friendly to courteous; opening their spans when they said they would.

We dragged anchor only once, on an exposed flat when the wind shifted North. We recovered in the dark with no damage, grounding or injury. Good for both of us. I may even have scored some extra points for getting us back on the hook with little drama. Having been intimidated by the advisories from those intrepid boaters back on the Chesapeake, Mer did not want to sail out into "The Ocean". It was so calm during most of our passage after Albemarle Sound that I had to tell her after we had made our excursions from the ICW into the Atlantic that she had been sailing in "The Ocean". Perception is not all, but it is sure a big part of how most folks see life.

I had planned for our last night together before making Ft. Lauderdale to be at a secluded, quiet anchorage about 50 miles to the North. Well, neither the guidebooks nor the charts had been updated for a while. The supposedly hidden anchorage was experiencing a major construction boom. A shiny, new condo building overlooking the mangrove swamp was nearing completion. The workers enjoyed the view directly down onto the decks of a Quo Vadis anchored in the narrow channel between island and mainland. Well, it was Florida waterfront property…sort of.

We survived the last day which featured 17 bridges, countless big wakes, and a tricky sideways docking at the Sands Marina which cost the starboard *ama* some bottom paint. It turned out the dockhand handling the lines was from New York. I'd chosen the Sands because it provided access for my friend Paul Sturman, a former Marine now in a wheelchair, to come on board. I found out he'd moved without informing me. My friends Steve and Geri Wallach had not moved, though they didn't pick up when we phoned while passing by their condo. A hot shower, fresh clothes and great dinner ashore with them made for a very civilized ending of this passage. They are, however, not candidates for crew in the Caribbean. Steve and Geri are leaving next week for a cruise in the Gulf of Mexico on something that has air conditioning and a walk-up bar, is considerably longer than 37 ft., and carries hundreds of other people.

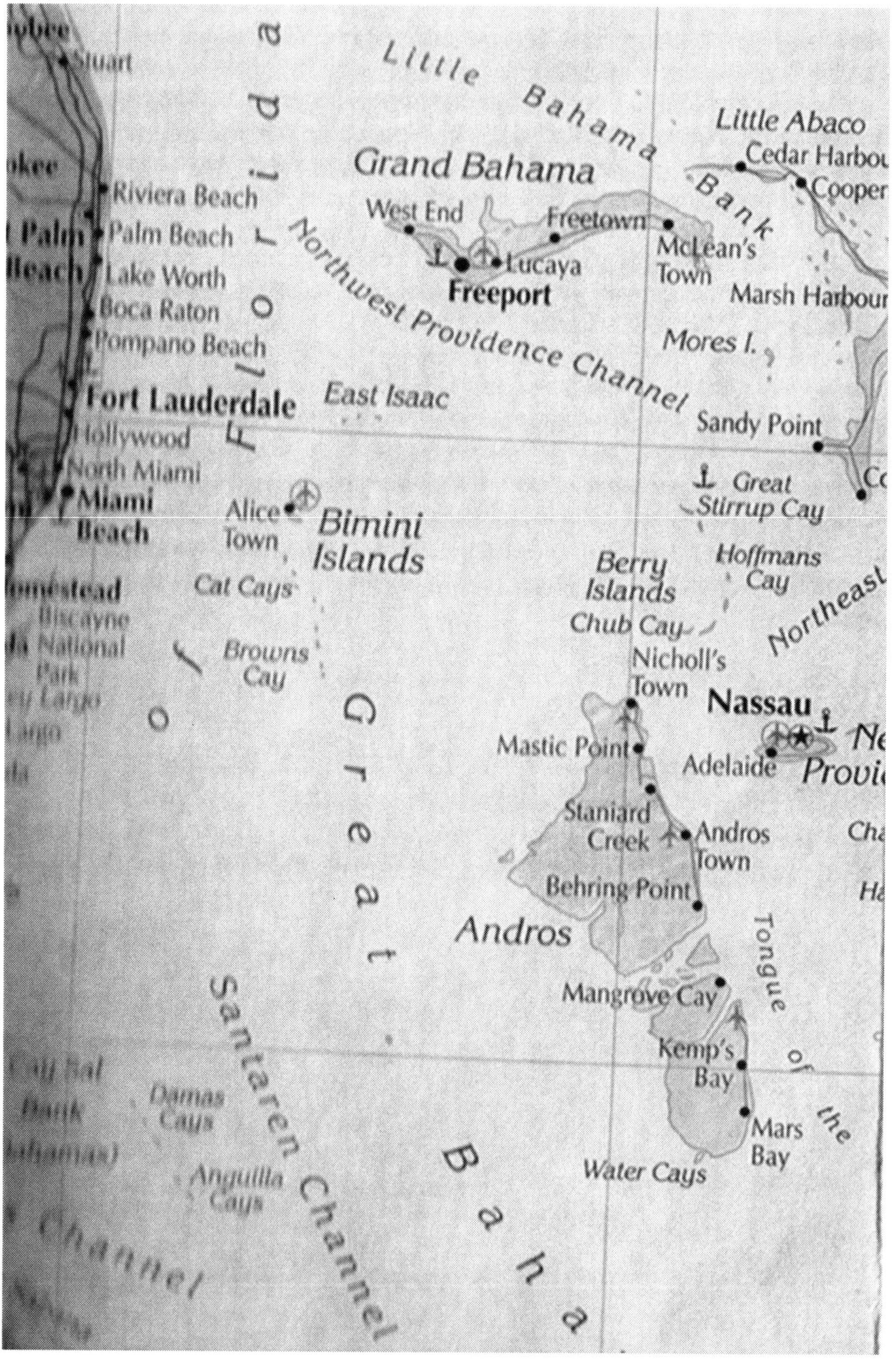
Stuart
Riviera Beach
Palm Beach
Lake Worth
Boca Raton
Pompano Beach
Fort Lauderdale
Hollywood
North Miami
Miami
Beach
Florida
Little Bahama Bank
Little Abaco
Cedar Harbou
Cooper
Grand Bahama
West End
Freetown
Lucaya
Freeport
McLean's Town
Marsh Harbour
Northwest Providence Channel
Mores I.
East Isaac
Sandy Point
Great Stirrup Cay
Alice Town
Bimini Islands
Berry Islands
Hoffmans Cay
Cat Cays
Chub Cay
Browns Cay
Nicholl's Town
Northeast
Nassau
Mastic Point
Adelaide
Staniard Creek
Andros Town
Behring Point
Andros
Tongue of the
Great Baha
Mangrove Cay
Kemp's Bay
Mars Bay
Water Cays
Santaren Channel
Damas Cays
Anguilla Cays
Channel

Happy Holidays and Bluewater Passages

Aboard S/V Quo Vadis, lying Nassau, The Bahamas

When you last heard from the Quo Vadis, we were mucking about in Southern Florida after a voyage of 1200 miles down from the Chesapeake. The Sands Marina had too many winter slip reservations and kicked me out—to a dock behind the dockmaster's parents' house on a canal at about one-third the cost. There is no shoreside head or shower, however. This reinforced my plan to go visit friends, relatives, lovers and others for a few weeks, so I did, leaving Quo Vadis securely tethered to the Johnsons' dock. I also did not have any crew clamoring and eager to make the Gulfstream/Bahamas Banks/Northwest Channel/Deep Water with Scary Sharks In It Crossing. Then, John Blake called to inform me that he and Dixie would join me for just this activity the second week in December. Cool.

Burning the last of my Frequently Flying Someplace Miles, I set out for a brief sojourn with the lovely Meredith, languishing at home since early November, and a visit to California family. It was very good to check in on the home turf with Auntie Ro, Irv and Patricia, Jeff H. and Dimitri (who still refuse to come sailing—argh) and my excellent children. Birthday celebrations were caught up, accelerated and accomplished by at least three of us. It is my continuing pleasure to make Thanksiving dinner for all who will show up to eat it, including those traditional favorites: mushroom *risotto* and *pommes frites*. There was a fowl course in there, too, someplace. Ahh, life is good. So is shore leave. I verified that my mother and brothers were alive and well. Except Mike has the gout. And he was supposedly the clean-living one.

Gathering all the weapons I can remember how to use, I ship them and myself back to the boat to prepare and provision for John and Dixie's arrival for our passage to a foreign land. I accomplish all of the assigned tasks except getting the holding tank pumpout I had been calling for all week. There is a personal downside to all this environmental correctness.

John and Dixie arrived on the red-eye from San Diego along with "The Weather". Days of high North winds were accented by hours of lashing rainstorms. "This is very unusual," said the locals. And how did that help us? The real problem with 25-35 knot North winds is they blow from that direction which is against the northward flow of the Gulfstream resulting in the waves called "Elephants" because of their size, shape and frequency: one closely following another.

John also arrived with a custom-made deepwater fishing rig, gaff hook and filet knife with plans to use all three during the passage. I can use a filet knife and that's about it. Their rental car also meant they got to ride through the rainstorms to Bluewater Charts, West Marine and other essential marine voyaging venues beyond bicycle range or my carrying capacity. However, NOAA predictions for the next week were getting no better and the otherwise capacious salon of Quo Vadis was getting no larger, so they returned to the other coast after a stalwart stay. Florida weather responded to the departure of my would-be Bahamas crew and cleared the next day. The "Elephants" did not necessarily disperse with similar speed.

This wait for the weather window is not trivial, a joke or anything else to be taken lightly for a 37 ft. sailing cat. You hear over the VHF:"Seas 9-13 ft. in the Gulfstream" which I'm assured have square edges to them. The prudent sailor waits. And I did, too. Meanwhile, there were not a lot of takers for an All Expenses Paid Trip to the Bahamas. Maybe I'm not marketing this opportunity correctly.

Then came Captain Larry. Along with his pal, Al. Brian Becker, of acrobatic flying fame, had told them I was in need of crew to Nassau. They both came on board, told me how many times they had done it, how to do it, where to anchor, and several other sea stories. Larry said he'd contact me tomorrow and Al said he'd see about looking after his parrot. (He wasn't going to try getting that through customs, again! Heh, heh.) Larry's "real job" is flight instructor.

A couple of days go by with me calling Larry's number and not much else happening. I have begun consuming the provisions for the passage. Another crossing window has opened with the wind East; forecast to go South. I bought more engine oil, another VHF radio (waterproof for the dinghy), 35mm film, and lots of other stuff which I'm storing when Larry shows up on the dock and commits to going to Nassau at 0600 the next day. We negotiated for something less than his captain's rate plus a plane ride back to Ft. Lauderdale from Nassau. Al is too busy.

Oh six hundred arrived right on time but Larry did not. Apparently, he really wanted to go at 0700 and that's about when we got started, still trying to make it past three bridges on the ICW to the Hillsboro Inlet. We were using this gap as an outlet to the Atlantic, but going either direction the cruising guide characterized it as too dangerous and requiring local knowledge. Well, I had a local on board so we motored out of the inlet with its reputation for fierce currents, albeit I had planned this activity for slack tide, at 0800. We avoided the reef, dredge and spoils—bound for the Islands across the 'Stream. Cat Cay, to be specific, in the Biminis. This meant, among other things, that we were looking at a night arrival amongst the reefs of the Bahamas. The cruising guides are clear on this matter: "Don't do it!" Larry told me not to worry. He'd been to Cat Cay "hundreds of times".

I'd calculated a heading of 150 to point us South enough across this river that runs North in the Atlantic Ocean at speeds of 2.5-5.5 knots. You don't want to stall out in this crossing. If you're heading South at 5.5 kts in the middle of the 'Stream, you're going nowhere across the surface of the planet. We came up to 120 to better cut across the flow. I was at the helm in the afternoon when the furled staysail head cable snapped and the whole thing fell into the portside signal halyard. It didn't hit me and, I thought, rode pretty comfortably cocked out like an outrigger. Larry had felt sick in the afternoon, which I thought strange for a veteran captain, and gone below to his bunk where he stayed until after sunset.

I hear what sounds like empty cans rolling around the deck, so go below to check and get Larry up for his watch. He is lying across his bunk in his jockey shorts with about half a dozen empties scattered around the cabin. It looks like he didn't take me seriously about one of QV's few rules: no drinking or smoking underway. He assured me he was trying to feel better and popped another beer.

We end our night crossing of the Gulfstream north of Bimini. Larry came on deck when I yelled down that I'd spotted lights. He asked if I wanted to go to Bimini to clear in. I didn't. He said he'd take the helm but then somehow managed to get Quo Vadis pointed back toward Florida. I am new to cruising the Bahamas but couldn't see the benefit of this move.

"Larry, I don't think this course is going to get us to Cat Cay," the scattered, few lights of Bimini now astern. "Oh, yeah, this is what happens when you're 60." This is to become his frequent excuse but I get him to relinquish the helm. He goes back below. He's not really 60, yet.

On the run South from Bimini, I had a full moon for illumination. Since any navigational aids were really unknown, I actually did steer by "Orion, Lucky Star" just like the Jolly Mon song that Beth and Caroline learned as kids. Gals, it works pretty well. It's the brightest in the South off his belt. I'm still paying attention to wind direction with occasional compass checks and watching the cays start to appear out of the dark to port. I stay in 5-10 meters depth. I call Larry back on deck when I get close to the waypoint. Between his prior experience, my chart study and some working beacon lights, rare in the Bahamas, we made it to the fuel dock at Cat Cay at 2330. This midnight arrival was through a 1-2 meter channel at low tide, cutting closer to the edges of the rocks than I ever had. Definitely not the guidebook way. The 52nm rhumbline turned into 72nm traveled. I had calculated 65nm along the plotted courses but had 20-25 knot winds all across the 'Stream. Except for losing the furled stays'l, the crossing wasn't that bad. The seas were consistently 3-5 feet but then I'd planned for that. Ri-i-ight.

It is an incredibly (Or typical? I don't know.) beautiful morning in the Bahamas. The water really does have a special clarity and quality in all its colors. Larry's beer can count was up but so was he; acting fairly chipper. We waited until the Customs office opened at 0900 and met with Ms. L.T. Collie. It was all very nice and proper with Bahamas$20 in the tip jar from Larry and the required US$100 accompanied by multiple forms from me. No waiting in line.

It was after 1000 by the time we'd gotten the cruising permit, valid for 100 days, and immigration visa, valid for 30 days, so I got a brief tour of Cat Cay. (Am I the only one noting this inconsistency? It's very Bahamas.) The island is actually a private club and the former hangout of Richard Nixon's pal, Bebe Rebozo, and Nixon himself. There is Rebozo's house, just up the beach. I can remember seeing newspaper photos of Nixon out here on Bebe's fishing boat. Nixon was wearing a suit and tie. Larry is especially proud of the 1000 ft. airstrip on which he'd operated his STOL-kitted Cessna 206 as a contract pilot for one of the owners of Cat Cay. It looked really short. This particular owner isn't in residence but Larry gets a hug from the maid.

After paying the highest dock fees and diesel fuel prices ever: US$2.50 per foot and gallon, we finally got underway about 1130. The Bahamas do not seem to be the place for budget cruising. As it's 80nm east to Chub Cay in the Berry Islands (waypoint to waypoint), most sailboats can't make it in daylight. The plan is to anchor out on the Bahamas Bank, which is basically a 50-mile stretch of flat, sandy bottom 2-15 ft. deep. We set sail until the wind came around right on our nose, again. Wind direction 105 with a course of 110 to Chub, so we motored into fairly significant chop over the Bank for six hours.

No matter how much you think, plan, or hear about it, dropping anchor with nothing but sea around a 360-degree horizon feels strange. That's what we did at 1730 (sunset) in still fairly brisk winds of 20 kts. We must have found one of the deepest spots on the bank at 4 meters (about 14 ft.) The tired but elated skipper switched hats to prep a steak, salad and cabernet sauvignon dinner on board. Well, we didn't have anyplace else to dine with nothing in sight but Atlantic Ocean. It was the first solid food I'd seen Larry eat.

I greeted a beautiful, stark sunrise over the Banks with some stretches and improvised Sun Salutation yoga moves taught me by Mer and took down the new anchor light which seemed to work well, turning off and on with a photovoltaic cell signal. We were still anchored at N25.35 W78.51 with absolutely nothing in sight around the watery horizon but everything under the boat visible in the totally transparent water.

We started motoring with the wind still on the nose. After figuring out that Quo Vadis was doing only 4-5 kts actual speed over the surface, I decided to set our two still-functional sails and continued on motor-sailing at over 7 kts. What a tremendous difference! Basically 50% better actual speed. There may be something to this, as I'm discovering. Larry turned up quite sick today, unable to rotate turns at the helm and spent most of the time in his bunk.

About 1500 I felt a new, disquieting secondary vibration. (Meredith thinks I'm paranoid and that I find something new like this every day.) I finally isolate the source back to the stern drive. Larry came on deck, roused by my de-clutching the stern drive, trying different engine RPM, etc. His recommendation was keep going until the drive quits or maybe the vibration will go away which I interpreted as the "Delivery Captain with Deep Pockets Owner" approach. I decided to shut down the engine/drive leg to save its final minutes for anchoring, docking, the last hour into Nassau, or similar events which may be the "Cautious Skipper with 2% Deductible Insurance" approach. I also decided to sail until about 1600 and see where we were by then.

Well, the sailing speed was also 7-8 kts as QV came off the Bank into 3-5 ft. confused seas in the Northwest Channel. Larry was vomiting over the side and shaking by 1600 but Chub Cay was in sight, about 12 nm off, and the boat was really moving. After a brief consideration of possible anchorages, I decided to go into the marina for calm water and a MedEvac for sick crew, if needed. Chub Cay responded on CH16 and assigned a slip for a 16 ft. beam which turned out to be moot since there were no finger piers. This marina has an interesting range-guided entrance between limestone cuts and coral into a narrow, shallow (2 meters) channel. Larry seemed a little apprehensive of the width and especially depth. His prior experience was on keel boats. I struck sail, restarted the engine, engaged the drive leg and felt no vibration in this low RPM range. Quo Vadis was docked with dockhand help by 1730. Larry was still shaking sick and not eating. I made cold sandwiches on board for dinner which, actually, were not too bad.

I was awakened by a squeaking, scraping noise in the dark and finally got up at 0400 to investigate. The bow sections of the *amas* were stuck under the dock with the tide coming in. I managed to push the starboard side out with the result that the port side jammed still tighter. I couldn't push it out with my legs and back braced against the dock but did manage to cut my back on the metal cap of the piling and strain my left trapezius muscle. So I woke up Larry to get his weight on the port *ama* before the tide rose another inch. This worked well enough to push it out. We re-rigged the spring lines to hold QV away from the dock which put her too far away for stepping ashore and went back to bed at 0445.

Up again at first light which, this being the shortest day of the year even in the Bahamas, was around 0700 to check out the stern drive. I re-tied the docklines, got out tools and lubricant; then woke Larry up again before I went in the water to investigate. The bad news and good news were the same: the lube level in the drive leg was good and quality of the lubricant looked excellent. The rest of the unit was visually intact. The drain plug was in. Nothing looked broken. I removed a moderate amount of Sargasso seaweed twisted around the prop. George Carver of Chub Cay showed up at 0830 with a bottle of gear lube, which didn't appear needed, and his 8 year-old son, who was always with him. A couple of dollars "For your trouble" were accepted by George Carver. Larry said he was doing better. He still had shakes and chills but had stopped vomiting. Larry asked the dockhand if the Chub Cay liquor store was open today. It was.

After looking at the sea state on the horizon and listening to Nassau weather (7-8 ft. seas and winds 25-30 kts.), we decided not to go there this morning. I made a ham 'n' eggs brunch (which was the first solid food for Larry in 36 hrs), hooked up shore power (which is a major expense in these islands), got wet clothes out of the locker and trash ashore (which incurred no additional cost). Later, I went for my first swim in the Bahamas where I was fascinated by large red brittle stars and good-sized stingrays winging away. Larry stayed on board; not offering me any Bloody Marys on the beach this morning. I had it all to myself. Very nice. The restaurants on Chub Cay seemed closed so I made chicken piccata for dinner and ate most of it myself with a Pinot Grigio. Aside from my back stinging from the cuts, I feel pretty damn good.

Larry was doing better next morning; winds were way down, so we cleared the Chub Cay channel by 0715 followed by another Nassau-bound cruising boat. We stayed on the back range out through the reefs to a 6 meter depth, then set course of 127 magnetic to Nassau. The diminished wind was, you guessed it, right on our nose. The crossing to Nassau was uneventful and the vibration was gone. I hope the Sargasso weed entanglement was the only problem.

S/V Quo Vadis called and cleared Nassau Harbor Control at 1330. I expected to dock at East Bay Marina, noted in the guide as being least expensive yet adequate, but could not raise them. We barely cleared under the 50 ft. bridge span to the alleged marina location but nobody was there. Instead of new docks, as promised in the cruising guide, the few remaining were falling into the water. There was no apparent docking for a vessel with our beam, anyhow, so we turned around to Nassau Yacht Haven which was almost twice the price but had the distinct advantage of being there. Dockmaster Sidney Wilson filled the fuel tank and then directed us to a slip "other side across from trawler". Well, I thought I followed his instructions but Sidney soon advised me I was in the wrong slip. Later, moving the boat to a slip

I thought QV could fit into, I put the starboard hull aground on a sand bar trying to make the wide U-turn into the dock. I had waited until slack tide which is the key for maneuvering with limited power in Nassau Harbor. Unfortunately, it was the low slack. I finally prop-walked QV sideways off the bar and backed into the slip with dockside help from the owner of Sea Spirit out of Montreal. Larry was quite agitated during and after the grounding, yelling at me; calling me "Buddy" which I hate. I didn't figure out til later he was embarrassed because the veteran captain (him) thought he had lost face in front of the Nassau locals. Enough excitement.

The next day I checked out other marinas. It being Christmas week, there was no space for a newly arrived catamaran featuring 16 ft. beam. A visit to the dilapidated docks confirmed that the East Bay Marina was really not functioning as such. Larry speculated the owner was waiting for the next hurricane to blow it away to collect the insurance. This was an early lesson in the fallibility of cruising guides. I put the almost-back-to-normal Captain Larry on Chalk's seaplane service to Ft. Lauderdale after I bought brunch of Kalik beer and scorched conch: my first taste in the islands. I liked it. After Larry boarded the twin Grumman, I walked across the bridge to the open air market stalls to buy fruits and fresh vegetables to eat over Christmas. I found some likely tomatoes, bananas and limes but was running out of cash. The limes were 5/$1. I had 30 cents left. The stall owner looked away; said, "Take two." Then, "Take three." As I gave him the coins, he clasped my hand in his calloused black hand twice the size of mine, shook it once and said "I wish you Godspeed."

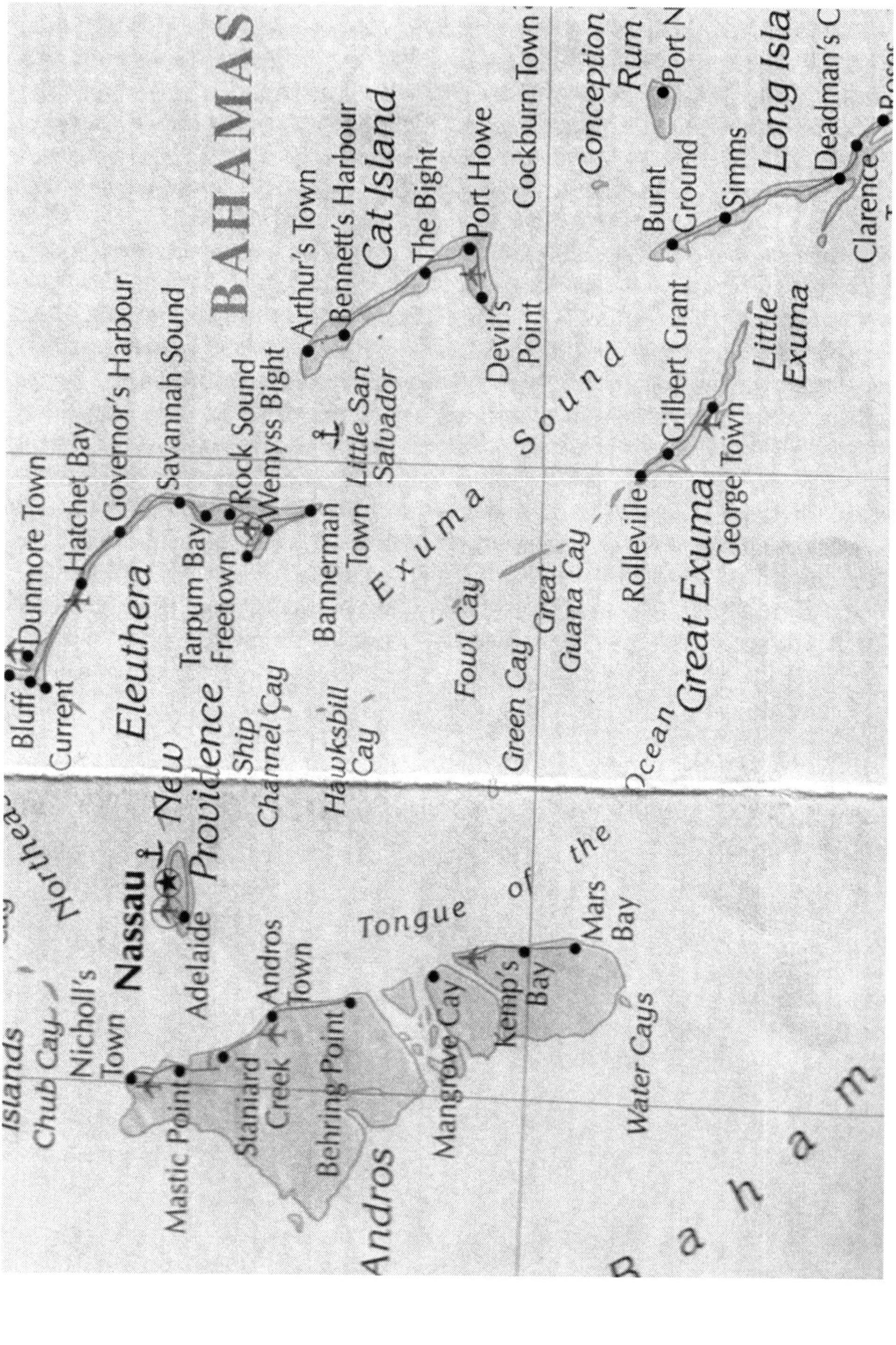
BAHAMAS
Andros
Chub Cay
Nicholl's Town
Mastic Point
Staniard Creek
Andros Town
Behring Point
Mangrove Cay
Kemp's Bay
Mars Bay
Water Cays
Nassau
Adelaide
New Providence
Tongue of the Ocean
Ship Channel Cay
Hawksbill Cay
Bluff
Current
Dunmore Town
Hatchet Bay
Eleuthera
Governor's Harbour
Tarpum Bay
Freetown
Savannah Sound
Rock Sound
Wemyss Bight
Bannerman Town
Little San Salvador
Exuma Sound
Fowl Cay
Green Cay
Great Guana Cay
Great Exuma
Rolleville
George Town
Gilbert Grant
Little Exuma
Arthur's Town
Bennett's Harbour
Cat Island
The Bight
Port Howe
Devil's Point
Cockburn Town
Conception
Rum
Burnt Ground
Simms
Clarence
Deadman's

Great Gains and Tolerable Losses

Aboard S/V Quo Vadis, anchored Red Shank Cay, Great Exuma, Bahamas

As Steve and John B. will no doubt recall with appropriate eye-rolling behind my back, in Florida I was obsessing about anchor chain. This has been a major focus in preparation for cruising the Bahamas, slightly ahead of stowing enough beer for several months in the Islands. This obsession is not quite as weird as it seems. Really. The conventional wisdom (and cruising guide) dictates an all-chain anchor rode so the nasty reefs, marl and rocks don't chafe the anchor line to shreds. And, if not an all-chain rode, then have at least 50 ft. Quo Vadis is equipped with only 22 ft. of chain rode. I was seriously suffering from chain inadequacy as well as shame from being so woefully unprepared for the Bahamas.

You'd think buying 30 ft. of chain is a no-brainer. You'd be wrong. In weeks of searching, sampling and mis-matching we could find no chain to match the British (we assume) original that was also compatible with the windlass. You not-so-nautical sorts now will know the windlass is the rotating wheel with ratchets that pulls the anchor up. In wooden ship days, you'd see poor swabs pushing it around by hand while groaning sea chanties at each other. The one on QV is electric-powered. It got to the point where at least one West Marine sales guy in Florida (there were many) was trying sell me a new windlass since he couldn't match the chain. I have not previously confessed to this but we set out for the rode-eating reefs of the Bahamas with what I believed to be a serious anchor chain deficiency.

On Christmas Day in Nassau, I am returning to my boat (now properly tied in the assigned slip) when I overhear some rather charming British accents whose owners are engaged in (Surprise!) boat talk. "Perhaps," my mind races wildly, "they will know all about British anchor chain!" I breached the topic to them, noting that the chain on Quo Vadis didn't seem to be any of the 3 standard types of 2 regular sizes.

"If it's an older Prout, it could be Leonard-Barbour chain," observed the charming lady, introducing herself as Barbara Adams. Her husband, John, thought it was worth a try. So off we go to their 43 ft. ketch *My Bonnie* to check things out. (Yes, as in "lies over the ocean". I've previously noted there should be a commissar for screening boat names.) Their chain was not a match but we're still not sure whether it's 3/8" or a metric size that I will need.

John Adams asks, "How much chain rode do you have?" This has become a highly personal question but, bravely revealing this inadequacy, I confess to "Only 22 ft."

"Well, that's enough then," John allows. "We know folks who cruise the Bahamas with only 10 ft. Some swear by an all-line anchor rode" This advantage, if any, escapes me but their invitation to Christmas dinner does not. What a gift! I am so relieved to hear from an experienced Bahamas cruiser that I have adequate anchor chain.

Barbara prepares a fairly elaborate traditional English dinner from the galley of My Bonnie. Only instead of overcooked roast or joint, there is medium rare Chateaubriand accompanied by oven-roasted potatoes; steamed veggies (Hey, I said it was English.) washed down with "Marques de Caceres", a Rioja which happens to be one of my favorite wines with meats. The evening passed in focused discussion on motor racing and vintage aircraft, in which they trade. We agreed Formula One had gone all wrong and both the Formula and format should be changed. We were mutually impressed that they had found an original Hispano-Suiza engine and that I recalled it was the type most used in the SE5-A, the principal British fighter of WWI. They had recently re-built one of these aircraft with all original parts for an air museum in the UK. I'm liking this couple.

John had hurt his back getting off an AJS many years ago. I had hurt lots of body parts getting off lots of different motorcycles over too many years. We agreed we weren't going to do that anymore. Barbara downloaded images of their recently acquired farm near Pau in the Pyrenees. After I remembered out loud that the French Parachute Training School was near "Pow", they corrected my Fox Pass with dry British wit. She also downloaded two weather reports to share with me: another thoughtful present. Happy Christmas to all and to all a good night.

They left directly for Staniel Cay the next morning. That sounded pretty exotic and distant to me at the time. Meanwhile, the broken stays'l had not jumped up to the mast and re-attached itself. Fairly diligent research led to the discovery that the only sail loft in Nassau was closed for the holidays. Part of this research included attendance at the weekly Nassau cruisers' lunch, hosted by Nick and Carolyn Swardle: locally famous for their morning weather reports.

Carolyn graciously invited me to the Sunday games at the Nassau Lawn Tennis Club which, naturally, had clay courts. I dug out my whites, bought as cheap a racket as I could get away with at the local sports store, and dutifully showed up at the appointed hour: not Island time. It was the first time with a racket in my hand in quite a while and the second time in 30 years on a clay court. This resulted in pretty rusty play but a great workout for wobbly sea legs. I managed not to disgrace my hostess, or so I thought, going down 4-6, 6-7 in a tie break. I also provided local entertainment as my tennis shorts, which I'm pretty sure fit the last time I wore them, kept falling down. Luckily, not to my ankles.

Junkanoo and Endangered Species

The end of 2002 arrived in Nassau and so did the lovely Meredith. When I spotted her at the airport, I couldn't understand why she was following the porter pushing a cart piled with luggage for a family of four. Or why he was pushing it away from the taxi driver who had agreed to wait. Well, I got the porter turned around and it turned out the bags were actually hers—for a two week cruise. Some guys never learn. Both of her swimsuits, which is what she mostly wore, fit in the back pocket of my sailing shorts. Maybe it's all those necessary accessories.

She managed to get most of her gear stowed before midnight, but I couldn't stand watching her leaning over in to the lockers any longer and attacked her. We ended up in the forward queen berth in the missionary position which she prefers after we've been apart for so long.

We had a light supper about 0130 and went out into the dark streets of Nassau for—Junkanoo! This is a uniquely Bahamian New Years celebration that combines elements of Carnival and the Pasadena Rose Parade or, maybe, more like the "Doo-Dah" parade now that I think about it. One explanation of the name is that the masked revelers become, in French, Gens Inconnu: people unknown to each other during the celebration so they can get away with almost anything. Claims about what really goes on vary widely. The parade was scheduled to begin at 0200. About 0300, we hear Island tunes and see one painted guy blocked by the constabulary from joining his crew.

Associations with names like "Mighty Saxons", "Valley Boys" and "One Family" spend the year making elaborate floats, costumes, music and dance routines all for a few glorious hours early on January First. I have never seen such innovative use of crepe paper, baling wire and feathers even at my kids' school pageants. I'll bet you haven't either. Some of the floats are nearly the width of downtown Nassau's streets but none of them are motorized. There are "pushers" inside on their hands and knees moving the floats forward with their shoulders. They can't see where they are going from inside so there are float guides who keep instructing them. "Turn left! Left! No, go straight!" until inevitably a float runs into the crowd to much amusement or dismay, depending on where you are in this unfolding tableau. In many cases, the distinction between costume and float is completely blurred as some guy or gal comes dancing along with 60-70 pounds of serious spangles, oversize wings, tails, etc. attached to them. I think I got a bigger kick out of Junkanoo than Mer, or most of the more sophisticated, cosmopolitan Nassau residents I chatted with, but we enjoyed a very sober and safe walk back to the boat about 0500. The party in Nassau was sort of winding down; at least the public parts. Mer was, of course, dressed impeccably.

On to the Exumas

We had just two weeks to cruise to, and down the Exumas: the chain of smaller cays that stretch from the central to the southern Bahamas. Some of you will think that schedule was rushing it. Others may wonder, "How could you spend two weeks on a 37 ft. catamaran and only go 160 miles?" My viewpoint? I'm happy life can be this good and I get to be part of it.

Sailing (or motoring) all new territory with the Bahamas' typically shallow depths can get fairly intense. Especially since screwing up has really undesirable consequences. Mer's concern about cruising in "The Ocean" seemed to abate considerably, maybe because you could count the starfish on the bottom out to, say, 20 meters depth. If you planned the sun angle (and got it right) you could see every coral head in water so clear you wonder what's holding the boat up. And that's how we crossed the Yellow Banks down to Allan's Cay. We were on the hook by 1400 in 1.4 meters of water. I introduced Mer to her new mask and fins; then dove on the anchor at 1.2 meters low tide. This left less than a foot under the rudders. I'm adjusting, JB, OK?

The rising wind woke me about 0445. I checked the anchor and we seemed to be stuck pretty well where we'd dropped but, over 20 minutes' observation, Quo Vadis and Northern Star were getting closer than I thought prudent. I got M. to the helm at 0515, pulled up the hook and drove around in fairly heavy wind to get separation; then dropped again in 1.5 meters. I monitored position 'til after dawn and we seemed to be well-stuck, again, 'though maybe it was on the sandbar which we knew was in the middle of the anchorage. The Canadian skipper of Northern Star later confirmed he had dragged down on us and apologized.

We decided to sit out a forecast cold front and did, in 30-35 knot winds and tropical gushes of rain. Quo Vadis was holding well through the squalls; avoiding another Canadian boat that had anchored too close and had a really noisy wind generator. I also made the unpleasant discovery that my super-wunderbar photovoltaic cell-controlled low amperage anchor light wasn't working after only 5 uses. Neither was the original masthead light. I flipped on the steaming light and made cheeseburgers. That venerable cruising maxim was, again, confirmed. Something breaks on your boat every day. Sometimes you see it; sometimes, you don't. Mer washed her hair with ample, freshly caught rainwater. Observing her ablutions on deck made my day. She got clean, too.

Allan's Cay supports a sub-species of iguana all its own. We got the dinghy rigged, outfitted and motored ashore to check them out. Bunches of iguanas came running out of the bush as soon as we hit the beach. Despite prohibitions on feeding them, it appears somebody has been. The big Alpha Iguana staked out prime territory (near Mer who knelt down to their eye level) and intimidated the others into waves of descending size. Some other cruisers later came ashore and spoiled the scene for me, including poking the reptiles with dinghy oars. Yes, I told them "Stop!" We're talking rare iguanas here; not Komodo dragons. Buncha idiots. So we now have photos of ourselves with yet another endangered species on a remote island.

The weather forecast sounded good for a passage South…and it was. We had a nice, easy sail in winds N-NE 15 kts. down to Norman's Cay. We went into the lagoon to check out the former lair of druglord Carlos Lehder. The lagoon is known for the awash remains of a dope-laden DC-3 which missed the runway—but only by about 200 meters. The dope has long since gone. I've forgotten if Lehder is doing umpteen life sentences or was offed by competitors, but his former residential compound was for sale. "Fixer upper, ocean view, private dock and airstrip"

I am surprised how many of the cays, especially in desirable areas, are private. Did the government hold a big auction after independence to fill the treasury? Or the governor's offshore account? (Lame joke intended) Later that day, we elected a solo anchorage over an expanse of white sand off Shroud Cay. It was very peaceful after a good day's sail, island hopping. I made dinner of fresh greens spiked with chunk tuna (Yes, Linda, QV is well stocked with canned tuna.), chicken piccata and a Pinot Grigio. I'm somewhat tired, so sliding into that big forward bunk with my favorite companion felt so-o-o good. We survived another anchorage with a big swell, which I don't seem to be predicting very well, and took the dinghy into a "creek" through the mangrove swamps in a deep, clear channel. We emerged on a small beach on the outside of Shroud Cay. We were all alone. Not even another footprint. There was more snorkeling orientation in the afternoon. Mer doesn't seem all that confident of herself or my instructions.

We sailed on to Warderick Wells, former pirate lair and water provisioning site. It is now the center of the Exuma Land and Sea Park which, no surprise, is mostly sea. It was too rough for my taste out on the Sound so we took a mooring inside. There are just about a dozen which helps protect the surrounding reefs and prevent overcrowding. We had a little more adventurous snorkel around Emerald Rock in open water. Mer wanted some flotation which, frankly, had not occurred to me. My old yellow buoyancy vest from the L.A. County Advanced Diver Program seemed to work for her.

I joined the Exuma Park support fleet for US$20 and decided to spend that night at the South Anchorage. This was the real pirates' lair, carved out of the bush near the freshwater well, and marked with non-native vegetation they tracked ashore centuries ago. I returned to the wells to fill the water jugs. Mer was concerned about parasites in the water. I thought it was too tannic for parasites, but maybe they've adapted .

On an absolutely beautiful day, we sailed on to Compass Cay, reputed to have the best beach in the Bahamas. We later discovered it has among the most hospitable hosts in the islands: Turner Rolle (owner) and brother, Patrick. We got to the markers which lead into a very narrow cut by 1500. With Mer at the helm, I caught the line on a mooring buoy only to discover my snap shackle was about one-quarter diameter shy of opening enough to clip it. I caught the second mooring buoy line but lost the boat hook so looped a bowline, quickly. The friendly fellow who had greeted us on CH16 jumped in a runabout and retrieved the boathook: now floating away in the gentle current. It was not our most skilled performance and I'm still leery about having a mooring ball slip between the hulls. Later, we had the "Best Beach in the Bahamas" totally to ourselves and captured the moment with slow, soft sex in and out of the warm, buoying water.

Swimming with Sharks and Other Diversions

Mer initially thought it would be neat to have her picture taken swimming with the sharks that gathered near the Compass Cay dock, expecting a regular feeding. Then, she thought I should swim with the sharks and take their pictures while she watched from the dock. As I recall, what finally happened was Mer was on the dock taking pictures while I was in the water with the sharks. Now, lest you think I am crazy adventurous, or just plain stupid, these sharks are so tame they have names. (Actually, so do some man-eaters like Great Whites. Hmm.) But these denizens of the not-so-deep had names like "Bill" and "Pug". Not too imaginative even for these mostly docile sand and nurse sharks. Maybe somebody should also vett pet shark names.

I later snorkeled the outside reef of the Bahamas' Best Beach looking for lobster; instead saw my first good-sized barracuda of this voyage, guarding his section of the reef. Some things never change. But I saw no antennae; no bugs. Later, I overheard comments by the locals about how they weren't finding lobster this year and weren't sure why.

"Captain Larry", of Nassau passage notoriety, had told me that we just had to cruise down Pipe Creek, which is actually a shallow draft passage down the inside of the cays. It was too tense to be fun and did not offer much variety in landscape. The route involved minimal depths, a narrow unmarked channel and motoring. Finally, we heard and felt the bump. An immediate look at the fathometer showed 0.9 meter. QV draws 1.0 in current cruising configuration. It was the first time I'd heard Mer use <u>that</u> word. Well, maybe the second time. It was suited to the occasion but we didn't stick to the bottom, weren't taking on water, and my later inspection of the starboard *ama* indicated we had hit sand; not coral. We found deeper water, like 1.1 meters, (Ya-a-ay!) and made it over the final sandbar to the Sampson Cay channel, headed on to Staniel Cay. I raised Staniel Cay on the VHF to request fuel and dockage but heard we needed to be there in an hour to get either one. Unsure of the route or the speed attainable in this channel, I turned back to Sampson Cay. We topped off at the E-Z Access fuel dock and were on the hook by 1630, all alone in a neat little protected cove just off the resort. For US$60 more, we could have been 300 yards to the South; tied to the dock. Just for drill, I did a solo anchor up and departure the next morning. It was not a problem with the minimal wind and current early in the day.

Cuts and Caves

Staniel Cay was not very crowded, including by *My Bonnie* which had moved on. It was an easy sail and approach to the sand anchorage off the "yacht club". We went into town to get water, lunch and advice on the tidal effects for diving the grotto made famous in the James Bond film, "Thunderball". The locals call it The Cave. It is accessible only by diving through a submerged passage leading into a large chamber inside the rock. Holes in the roof admit shafts of light during the day. The play of light on the fish schools and corals give the dark inner pool a surreal look and made it a good movie set. The underwater swim is shorter at low tide.

Low tide is at 1030. Mer wanted to go to church at 1100. She bought me lunch (Grouper sandwich. Yum.) and a Staniel Cay Yacht Club shirt. The "yacht club" part is pretty amusing if you've been there. It never occurred to me this might be a subtle way of softening me up. The next morning, I got M. and snorkel gear in the dink by 0830 and off to Thunderball. As I ease the dinghy up to the mouth of the grotto, a 30 ft. motor cruiser rudely anchors right in front of us.

Sitting on the stern swim platform is a strikingly handsome black woman in a swimsuit. She has short cropped hair and appears to be in her 20s. Mer, not looking too shabby herself in her python print string bikini, tells her, "You're so beautiful. You look like a James Bond girl." I didn't know this was a female category and the irony of our location was wasted on me. The black girl smiles, accepting the compliment gracefully. This is something neither Mer nor I have ever learned to do because our parents instructed us not to think too highly of ourselves.

Mer put on my old ADP vest, told everybody in the other boat she had never done this before and was truly afraid to go into an underwater cave entrance. But in we went, hand in hand. Once inside, I gave Mer some bread to feed the reef fish and she did. Sergeant majors, purple wrasses, little pink and green parrotfish all swarmed around her as she held out bread chunks. Then, she wanted to take my picture and took off the vest. Next, she was free diving for the camera in front of the light shafts that made this cave a film icon. This is the same gal that, 10 days ago, didn't know why to spit in her mask.

We made it to church, tying the dink to a stake on the shore below, with no time to spare. Mer was dressed in a long skirt and Victorian-style blouse. I'd managed to find some long pants and a clean dress shirt. We carried our shoes. The Mt. Olivet Baptist Church on Staniel Cay sends up some joyous noise to praise the Lord. We were both surprised to see the preacher was the same man who told us about the tides when we'd encountered him on the road to town. My favorites were the little girls in the pew ahead of us banging on their tambourines. Mer and the choir leader sang together at the church door after the services were over and left each other still singing. God must work in some mysterious ways. After we got changed out of our Sunday-go-to-meetin' clothes, Mer wanted to take a nap and I thought we should head down to Little Farmer's Cay. So that's what we did, in that order. I dove on the hook by 1645 in a solo anchorage off the west beach. We reviewed our options and M. said let's go to George Town if the weather's good.

Of interest mainly to sailing types, there is a surprising amount of discussion and controversy over which cut to take from the shallower Banks on the West of the Exumas to the deeper Sound on the East side. We had been told that Doug, the dockmaster at Compass Cay, was the Grand Guru of cut selection and passage. I engaged him one evening before green flash time with just this question and a chilled can of Miller's. "With your draft, you can take almost any cut you want. Just don't get caught in a 'rage'." So much for controversy and discussion. Did I mention that a "rage" is a wind-tide opposition in a cut that can set up a standing wave or series of white water haystacks. You either can't move or, worse, broach to the reef. There was some bumpy action coming out through the Farmer's Cay Cut but we were OK to start a beautiful sail. Mer said she felt like she was "really doing it".

The wind came to the Southeast at 10-15 knots after about 3 hours under sail, so we motored to the Conch Cay Cut. So far, all these guidebook-described "difficult approaches" have not been that intimidating. Good timing? Good light? Good luck? We came through the cut, lining up on the "landscape" range for Elizabeth Harbor, which is actually a road off Great Exuma. We had a lovely anchorage all to ourselves off the beach in Jolly Hall Bay, open only to the North with the winds steady at 10-15 Southeast. The next morning, it's blowing from the North at 20 kts. I feel like I have a bad line from a bad movie, "We're fine so long as it's not from the North." Groan. I wanted to anchor at Red Shank, anyhow, ever since I saw a photo of the Red Shank Yacht & Tennis Club members standing at the bar in ankle deep water. The bar of the RSY&TC is a long limestone shelf fronted by two benches and a small table assembled from driftwood.

We scouted Red Shank Cay and its inlet by dink; moved Quo Vadis and anchored in 2 meters before heading back to town for the night to ensure Mer could make the 0630 check-in for her flight. It is a longish, wet ride from Red Shank to the dinghy dock behind the George Town market. After getting Mer's bags to our room at the Green Turtle Inn, we had a lobster dinner, checked out the "Rake 'n' Scrape" Bahamian music named for the instruments used to make it, and enjoyed a little dancing. We checked the dinghy at 2130 and it was still chained to the dock. Then, we strolled back to the Inn in the soft, starry night.

The canted mirror beside the bed reflected the tangle of tanned limbs and white buttocks that happens when passionate lovers come together without inhibitions. The single, shaded bulb does not provide flattering lighting but the recumbent, naked Meredith looks sexy, beautiful and very toned after two weeks sailing and snorkeling through the Exumas. Clifford (His friends call him "Greasy".) showed up with his taxi at 0600, as previously requested, for the ride to the airport.

So, on 16 January: 1) Mer left me, 2) I returned to the dinghy dock to find my new outboard motor and gas tank stolen, and 3) the propane tank ran empty while I was making lunch, later that same day. However, the weeks with Mer were bliss, the cruiser net at George Town had a loaner 9.9 HP Nissan clamped on the trashed transom of my dink within 90 minutes, and the other propane bottle was full, thanks to John and Dixie's patience with their rental car back in Florida. I made my comfort food for lunch: tacos.

Derek Lewis, upon contributing his outboard and fuel tank to remedy my misfortune, explained to me: "You can't always pay it back. So I pay it forward." This feels very real.

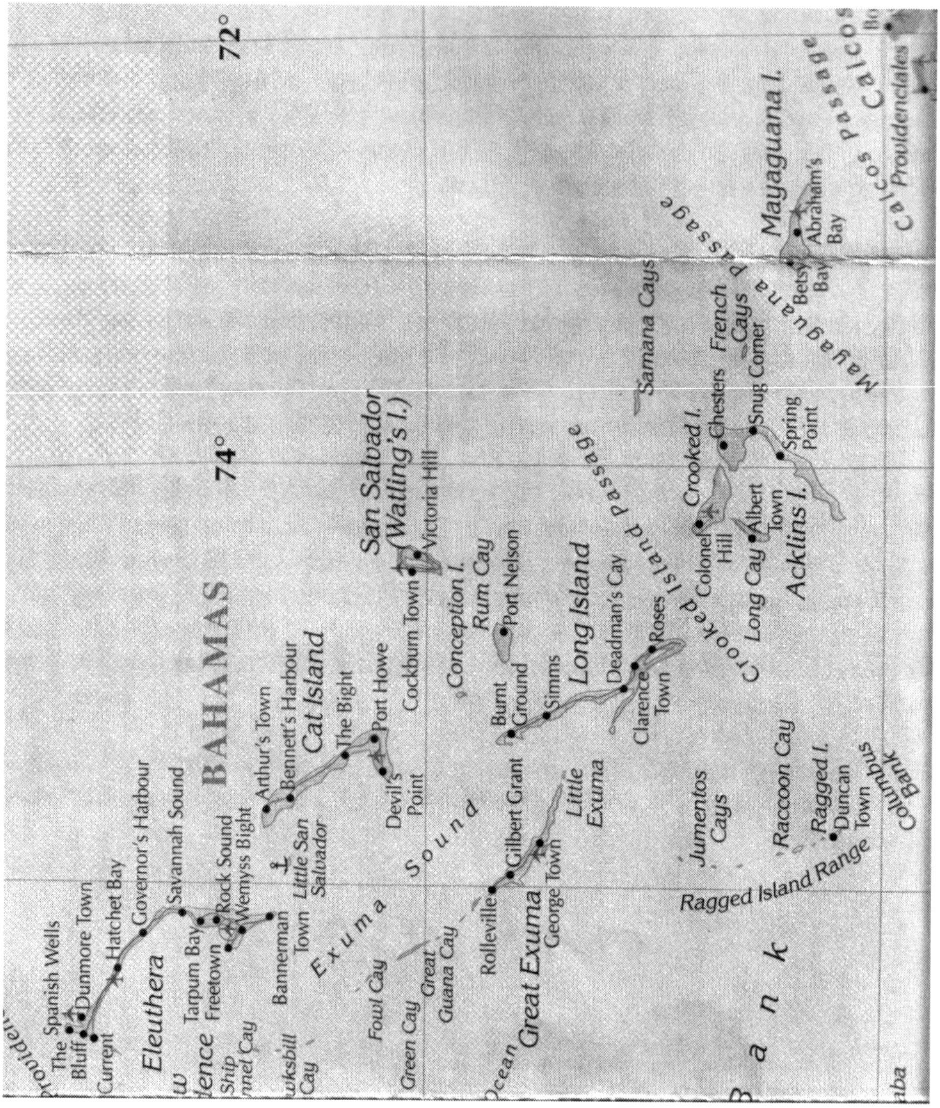
BAHAMAS
74°
72°
Spanish Wells
The Bluff
Dunmore Town
Current
Hatchet Bay
Eleuthera
Governor's Harbour
Savannah Sound
Tarpum Bay
Freetown
Rock Sound
Wemyss Bight
Bannerman Town
Little San Salvador
Arthur's Town
Bennett's Harbour
Cat Island
The Bight
Port Howe
Devil's Point
Exuma Sound
Fowl Cay
Green Cay
Great Guana Cay
Rolleville
Great Exuma
George Town
Gilbert Grant
Little Exuma
Cockburn Town
San Salvador (Watling's I.)
Victoria Hill
Conception I.
Rum Cay
Port Nelson
Burnt Ground
Simms
Long Island
Deadman's Cay
Clarence Town
Roses
Crooked Island Passage
Jumentos Cays
Raccoon Cay
Ragged I.
Duncan Town
Ragged Island Range
Columbus Bank
Samana Cays
Crooked I.
Colonel Hill
Long Cay
Albert Town
Acklins I.
Chesters
Snug Corner
Spring Point
French Cays
Mayaguana Passage
Mayaguana I.
Betsy Bay
Abraham's Bay
Caicos Passage

Goodbye, Bahamas! Again and Again.

Aboard S/V Quo Vadis, docked Providenciales, Turks & Caicos Islands

I've been hearing the voices. They are both male and female: pleasant, soft-spoken but with excellent diction. They speak in a way that makes the content of their sustained; probably very interesting conversations barely indiscernible. It was a while before I realized the conversations were between the wavelets lapping against the insides of the twin hulls of Quo Vadis: talking each to each. It was, somehow, slightly disappointing to figure this out. What benefit did the reality offer compared to listening in on what were probably very interesting conversations?

I've also taken up residential membership at the Red Shank Yacht & Tennis Club, located in the exclusive Red Shank Cay District of the southern Exumas. The promise: Free Beer Tomorrow. The advisory: If Irene starts looking good, it's time to go. Irene being a driftwood-based mannequin, adorned much like a tastefully, or tackily (It's hard to decide.) dressed scarecrow. She semi-reclines on the ledge above the club bar. As previously noted, the club is mostly a 50 ft. beach awash at high tide but never too deep for Happy Hour. This lasts, generally, 'til the conch shell is blown to mark the sunset. It's BYOB except for heavy hors d'ouvres which many of the members compete in providing. Dues are payable, in arrears, beginning in 2050. Originally, the dues were to begin in 2025 but that was looming up too near. Planning for the tennis courts continues, intermittently. Some of the preferred areas are subject to flooding. The club is short on tunes and, with Mer gone, short of feminine company; otherwise, it's my kind of place.

Just a few hundred yards from Quo Vadis' well-protected and blessedly bug-free anchorage, the skipper and mate of the motor yacht Bali Motu hosted a Superbowl party. I had no particular interest in watching two John Gruden-coached teams making still more money but the whole concept of seeing onboard satellite TV, anchored in this Bahamas cay most people won't find on a map while many of those on board made football pools, made drinks and dinner, and yelled at the 36" screen, etc. was mind-blowing. That was the real show. One of the Gruden teams lost.

The international crime spree, in which I had suffered the greatest losses, continued for another few days until the alleged perp was arrested, tried, convicted and sentenced to six months hard labor. This did nothing toward the return of my outboard and fuel tank, however. The local constabulary could have acted sooner, I'm sure, since it did not take them long once the formalistic cruiser community of George Town was officially incensed. The cops know what's happening in these small islands, often before it does. I did not get much sympathy for my loss since I was the totally new guy in this very structured, hierarchical assemblage of folks on boats.

The new motor I'd ordered from Lightbourne Marine in Nassau, over the Exuma Markets' always popular pay phone, arrived in 24 hours on the inter-island cargo boat Sealink. The US$10 delivery charge for the outboard was the best deal of this cruise, so I gave the burly cargomaster another five. He was very surprised and cooperative. During this time, the staysail was re-rigged under the lead of Norm Gwindon who came over on his Manta 40 Walkabout. Despite the boat name, Norm is Canadian. The re-rig is simpler and appears more rugged than the original. It was a good experience in re-rigging a furling sail with scrounged parts; working strictly from the foredeck. The new bos'un's chair, given to me by Meredith as a going away present, got lots of compliments. I also went back to vintage style oil lamps for the anchor light and the salon night light. Call me old-fashioned, or paranoid about draining the batteries. The boat has been operating on DC input from renewables only for nearly three weeks. Sun and wind happen.

Sun, wind, and renewable energy are a completely normal experience for most of the high school-age cruising kids I volunteered to teach. I gave a few lectures on "Energy and the Environment" under the casuarina pines on a white sand beach on nearby Stocking Island. About two dozen very precocious, polite and privileged 13-17 year-olds dinghied over for the lesson. It was also the first time I can remember ever taking a boat to class. Most nights there are too many stars here. I feel like scooping some up and sending them to you.

Overhead Activity

On another clear, blue day in the Exumas, I hear the unmistakable clatter of rotor blades and look up to see two Blackhawk helicopters sweeping directly overhead at approx. 200 ft. altitude. They are painted flat black; have no markings but I notice they are very up to date models with an IR pod, what looks like a refueling probe: all the goodies. "Wow", I think. "I had no idea the Bahamas Defense Force had anything so modern—or expensive." I mention my observations at that evening's gathering of the RSY&TC and a couple of the returning guys chuckle.

"Those aren't Bahamian choppers. They're U.S. They stay over on the other side of the road at the Army base. There's also a company of Rangers and the support crews for the choppers and a big communications center. It's part of drug interdiction." So, I find we have a Blackhawk detachment and a Ranger company working for the DEA to keep the Exumas safe from drug smugglers. This is supposedly a Secret base but they have organized a softball team and a regular schedule of games with the cruiser community's softball team. The soldiers get out of P.E. if they play on the softball team. That night I see a regular pattern of high intensity lights across the channel where we know there is an access road. I had naively thought they were street lights. Well, some of them were—for the Secret Army base on Great Exuma. They were also building a Four Seasons hotel when I was anchored at Red Shank. There goes the neighborhood.

I'm below deck when I hear very excited voices coming from the VHF announcing a hot air balloon is passing over the cay. The message passes from boat to boat. I go to the aft deck to see this hot air balloon. I observe, instead, a blimp motoring southward at 500 ft. It is emblazoned with "RON DROGAL" in yellow and blue. The radio chatter continues which confirms my belief that these people don't have enough to do in their day. Finally, a world-weary voice comes on to inform us that Ron Drogal is the national rum of the Dominican Republic and very good rum, at that. Further speculation is that said blimp is headed down to Trinidad for Carnival. It seems just as likely that the blimp's destination is, in fact, the Dom Rep. I'm guessing that any company sponsoring its own blimp must have some deep pockets, especially in the Caribbean. Much later, I discover that Ron Drogal damn near sponsors the entire country. I also discover, as have many sailors before and after me, that their dark rum is very tasty. The reaction to the blimp from my nearby neighbors, the Holloways on Eagle Light ? What a fantastic way to see the Bahamas!

Off to see the...?

Dave Schoonmaker and son, Devin, are scheduled to arrive near George Town the second week in February so I pay even closer attention to the single sideband weather forecasts for all areas to the South. Winds permitting, the plan is to sail to the Turks & Caicos Islands with a couple of days for diving at each end of the passage. The planned route was Great Exuma-Rum Cay- Mayaguana-Providenciales (in the Turks & Caicos). The key, so I read, is to wait for—and ride—a Northern front down the islands so the Southeast wind is not on your nose all the time. This is also the key to making the windward trek "thornless", so says the cruising guide. I moved from Red Shank to the George Town dock, fueled up, provisioned for a week, got gasoline for the new outboard, and got Dave and Devin on board, right on time. They are equipped and ready to go.

We staged out and anchored off the small beach at Fowl Cay for an easier Northerly exit through the cut in early morning light which even you landlubbers know is mostly in the East. You have a better chance of missing the edges of the reef and the odd coral head scattered about. This part, so far, was working pretty much to plan as we passed out of the cut about 0730, headed for Cape Santa Maria at the north end of Long Island. Sails were set with the wind shifting between 45 apparent and on the beam. It was really a pretty nice sail to Rum Cay although, after rounding

Cape Santa Maria, it proved more expeditious to use some engine. We raised Rum Cay with plenty of light (well, about an hour before sunset) and figured out the zig-zag entrance channel even though the surfers who run this marina were a shade too casual about coming through the reefs for this old gringo's taste. The ambience and dining at Rum Cay were great. This was my introduction to single island resort fixed price meals and almost everything else. Dave had done it before on family charters and earlier dive trips. He did not think US$35 was a rip-off for the three courses served. I'd hoped for fish but Krista from the Kitchen had thawed the leg of lamb.

Dave, Devin and I managed to drop the dink for a snorkel on the notorious reef and were not disappointed. Items observed: a boldly marked four ft. leopard ray, a barracuda about the same size looking after his piece of reef, lots and lots of nurse sharks: some sleeping in caves; some nosing around, and extensive fields of living staghorn coral. You may remember Dave's day job is editing <u>American Scientist</u> magazine so he was intensely interested in the health of the coral which, I take it, is not so good other places. But, enough fun!

We're off on a planned 24 hour run to Mayaguana, identified in the chartbook as one of the "Far Bahamas". After a near miss with a coral patch at 0815 (My bad), we set course of 126 True for Mayaguana and run down that way in increasing wind and swell until we hear the 1130 weather forecast. I wasn't interested in another 20 hours of 25 knot headwinds, so made the painful decision to come about toward Clarence Town, over on Long Island. The wind died from 25 to 5 as we approached the Booby Rock waypoint (which I'm beginning to feel like) so we motored to the nice, shiny new Flying Fish Marina, docking by 1700. The five o'clock weather tells us to expect N-NE winds 12-20 knots over the next 24 hours. This is good, as we want to go South.

Once again slipping the docklines, we cleared Clarence Town harbor for the overnight run to Mayaguana as the sun rose to reveal the reef(s). The above-noted wind forecast arrived—and went. It was blowing 25, gusts to 35, and clocked right back to Southeast where we were headed. We hate it when that happens. Despite our feelings, the winds stayed steady and the seas started building from 3-5 ft. to 6-8 ft. Once again, Captain "Wimpy" decided 18 hours of pounding wasn't much improvement over 20 and diverted to Crooked Island. This was an easier downwind ride, accompanied for over an hour by a large pod of small whales. As they were mostly 15-20 ft. long with small dorsals, I proclaimed them to be pilot whales and the rest of the crew went along with it because they couldn't come up with anything more likely. These are like mega-dolphins with pointy noses and white chests. Around, behind and under the boat: surfing the swells with their noses out of the wave. Also on this leg, we took evasive action to miss the Panama-registered freighter Firmeza on a collision course. Hello, anybody on the bridge? Z-z-z.

After sailing past a lone catamaran tucked in closer to the point, we anchored in slight swell off the sandy beach and ate cheeseburgers: the unofficial comfort food of frustrated sailors without fish. The next morning, we're still in the same spot, which is good, and wind is E-SE 20-30 knots, which is not good. The weather net is now giving small craft warnings for the Central and Southeast Bahamas, the latter of which we are in. It is now 86nm to Mayaguana into weather and 38nm back to Clarence Town. The tough decision was to go back. I knew this would doom any chance of making it to the Turks & Caicos with Dave and Devin: they are running out of time. With a second reef in the main and the genoa furled under-100%, we ran back at 7-8 knots in seas with the same vertical dimension in feet. By now Devin is wondering, with some cause, why we are going back and forth without really getting anywhere. Dave offers some fatherly philosophy: How it's not the destination, it's the journey that matters. I nod and grin in a manner intended to be helpful and supportive. Devin looks at us both skeptically.

Flying Fish Marina was becoming like a second home…with mortgage payments. So, now we'd all been to Crooked Island for the first time with winds on the nose at 30-35 knots; gusts to 40. I am beginning to find my tolerance level: under 8 ft. and 40 kts. It's also beginning to sound like we won't see Mayaguana today, or tomorrow, or the next day. Dave and Devin felt obliged to get home regardless of where we weren't going any time soon. As they laboriously tried to find flights from Long Island in the southern Bahamas to North Carolina in the southern U.S., they discovered that you can't call BahamasAir from here because there's nobody at the terminal until an hour before flight time and the operator can't connect you because it's in the same area code. Be advised. Remember this Captain's answer to seemingly insoluble problems on board: "Let's have lunch." We actually had lunch on shore at Max's Conch Bar & Grill which was by the roadside, covered by a palm roof on posts with tall stools on more posts. From here, we could see the airport and any airplane's arrival. Dave and Devin seemed to make it aboard the ATR turboprop with their gear so I maneuvered the US$65 rental car back to Mr. Cartwright at the marina. It was the first time I'd driven a car in two months. Now, it's on the left side of the road and it's an automatic which I'm not used to. It felt weird but so has lots of stuff lately.

Did I have a Plan B? or C?

Back at Flying Fish Marina, the "River Rat" thought his friends Paul and Judy over on Cat Island might be interested in crewing down to the TCI (as we now are calling these islands) Hey, they were even looking to buy an older Prout 37 so they'd get to try one. It crossed my mind ever so briefly, but I refrained from offering mine. I called Paul and Judy. They were initially very enthusiastic but 12 hours later declined the offer. I recall similar situations back on the Chesapeake and believe there is some male-female interaction that goes something like this:

"Honey! Let's go sail with this guy we don't know very well on this boat I'm interested in down to the next country South of here." "No, honey, of course I didn't forget it's (Pick one or more.) your birthday/our anniversary/Christmas eve/you just went into labor. It's just for a few days, anyhow." I sort of understand how this happens but it doesn't help me now, or then.

Ever helpful, "River Rat" introduces me to Ambrose and Edith Cartwright. The Cartwright family makes up about one-third of the population of Long Island, mostly descended from two old colonial families: one white and one black. Ambrose and Edith have several adult children, including Daniel, currently in residence. He's spent 13 years fishing the Bahamas but has never been to the Turks & Caicos. "New horizons for you," says Ambrose. Daniel agrees. Ye-e-ess!

Dan is one of those fairly frequent phenomena on Long Island: a white Bahamian. We're talking red beard, blue eyes, blonde forearm hair and skin several shades fairer than mine. The white side of the families came to the Bahamas as refugee Tories during the American Revolution or, later, as Confederate states slaveholders after the American Civil War. Now, they are white, black, brown and everything in between. Edith, for example, is half Native American. They all speak the same language. It da Ting. We be beyond "Jah" here, mon.

We're ready and agreed to go to the Turks & Caicos in convoy with "River Rat" and Annie. They will be on his Irwin 32 Mr. Sippi. The wind is still SE 15-20; seas 4-6ft. so we also agree to postpone a Mayaguana attempt and spend the morning provisioning with Dan's help, harvesting the fresh fruit and veggies from his family plots. Cousin "Scalpie" cut a stalk of bananas for us and, yes, the galley of Quo Vadis soon does look like the interior of "Das Boot" as it left the port in Spain. We're armed with Hawaiian slings and fishing poles instead of torpedoes.

The next day provided a window. The weather was clear. Winds were from the Southeast but down to 10-15 knots. The plan is to go for Acklins Island; accepting the fact of a night arrival. "River Rat" is not as enthusiastic as before but we both decide to go and, with Dan on the lines, Quo Vadis is out of the slip smoothly and seamanlike. Until we had to turn to port after clearing the reef and there was no rudder response. This was a problem. I used the engine drive leg, kicked hard over, and Dan grabbed one rudder by hand to turn it. (Dave said before that it was a real advantage we could see our rudders, though I'm pretty sure this is not what he had in mind.)

We brought the boat back to a leeward docking. I pulled the inspection panels to the aft spaces of the amas and saw the bolts gone on the starboard side and connecting plate weld snapped on the port side. Uh-oh. Only later do I wonder: How had we made it back to the dock the last time? When did this happen? I didn't know enough to check this. "River Rat" and Annie continued on; not knowing what repairs QV would need or how long it would take. Neither did I.

Dan called his Mom, Edith, for a ride in search of a welding machine and some stainless steel welding rod. Cousin Ronnie Cartwright had both, sitting dust-covered under a coconut palm in his front yard. Dan used the last piece of SS welding rod in Clarence Town to draw the bead on the connecting plate and we went back to Quo Vadis to re-assemble the steering linkage. I added stainless steel welding rod to my list of essential stores. Dan knew what he was doing and was willing to crawl into those very tight spaces. When he finished bolting the rudder arms, I made gaskets and re-installed the inspection and cover plates. It was now 1300, too late to make it anywhere before dark, so I bought lunch at Harbor Rest, where Annie Minnis opened the kitchen at Dan's request. We had mutton stew, which was actually made from goat and pretty tasty.

The next morning, all crew are on board, prepared and ready to go by 0630. As I'm doing the engine check, the wooden hatch cover hinge tore out. This was supposed to have been re-built back in Florida but I didn't yet take it as an evil omen. The oil level was good and everything else looked right. Observed wind at the dock was E15-20. Once we were out of the channel, with the rudders working very well, the wind came up to 30 and on the nose for the rhumbline to the NE point of Acklins Island. After an hour, I decided not to sail 63nm to Acklins in these conditions and fell off on a more southerly course to Crooked Island. I'd tried this once before. The wind came around to within 10 degrees of our course and seas were still building. A position check at 0900 indicated we had made 5.15nm progress in approx. 2-1/2 hours.

Boat speed was dropping from 5 to 4 to 3 knots. My tolerance level seems established: 8 ft. seas and 40 knots on the nose and we scurry back to the harbor, if we can reach one. Of course, sanity would dictate you don't leave the harbor under those conditions. Dan did a great job at the helm and securing the docklines in 30 knot winds while white water was breaking around and over the dock. He's gained skills in all those years crewing on his family's fishing boat that I'll never have. Dan was very chagrined about turning back and wanted to sleep on board. Turning back is not what Bahamas fishermen do, at least this one. He did tell me it was the first time he'd ever been on a sailboat. Oh. I guess I hadn't asked that question. Good to know…I guess.

Pipin' and Conchin'

The winds continued: right around 30 kts SE. Dan said, "The coconut trees bendin' over to touch their toes." Dr. Hugh Dundee, singlehanding the Cape Dory 30 Patience, made it into the slip next to us fighting the channel current and winds down to a headway of one knot. After a circumnavigation four years ago and three seasons in the Caribbean, he said he was headed back North because the big winds were spoiling all the fun. I silently agreed but, then, I didn't know any different. He'd been down at Samana Cay for 3 weeks. He didn't say why. Continuing weather checks and solicited opinions of locals indicated no change in conditions for 3-4 days so I left Quo Vadis to help with construction of Ambrose and Edith Cartwright's new house further north on Long Island. Edith said, bringing lunch out to the construction site, "It's pipin'." And it stayed pipin' for 3 days but we did get the roof and eaves on the house.

Meanwhile, this 40 ft. open deck runabout with three 200 HP outboards on the stern had pulled in to the marina. It had no name, no numbers and three 55 gallon fuel drums lashed on the deck. Dan asked them, "What was doin'?" and they said they were conchin'. Well, harvesting conch is a major island occupation and they could certainly get out to the conch beds and back in record time with that kind of horsepower so we started calling this type of vessel a "conch boat". As the sea state did not improve, the next morning we discovered another "conch boat" had tucked in during the night. This one had four 250 HP Yamahas screwed to the transom. Dan knew two of the crew: Lennox and Naugy. Lennox told us, "Mon, you couldn't get me back out there for a million dollars." So we assumed he wasn't getting that amount after the split four ways. Dan was of the opinion they couldn't make it to Jamaica with their fuel consumption against the current sea state. I wondered if the arrival of the only high speed Bahamas police boat I was ever to see had kept them in port. Dan said the police boat was diesel-powered so it had a cruising range in pursuit that the "conch boats" couldn't match. He knew a lot about this sort of stuff.

Once more, with feeling

The "conch boats" left in a couple of days during which I'd been to church and picked up a hitchhiker. Father Jerome was apparently one of those self-assured colonial Anglican prelates of the late 19th century who arrived in the Bahamas with Episcopalian Edifice Complex. E.C. is actually common in many organized religions. As the wooden frame churches most common at the time were blown away in most hurricanes, he set about building stone churches. He did this on several islands including Long Island. A few years later, he converted to Catholicism (still as a priest) and built a stone Catholic church one hill over from the stone Anglican church he'd first built. The last-built church of SS. Peter and Paul is, frankly, more impressive though the sermon had more about sins and the singing was not nearly so good as at Mt. Olivet back on Staniel Cay.

Did I mention the wind? The mast top anemometer was reading 40 with frequent gusts to 50. Dr. Hugh and I put two thick cables across to the opposite dock: the lines I'd hoped I'd never need to use, ending up with 8 lines securing QV. His boat had about the same number, though smaller diameter. We then helped the French Canadian 50 ft. ketch **Tiger Sea** as they were even more screwed up, trying to jam fenders between their very expensive hull and the dock pilings while Mr. Cartwright (No direct relation, according to Dan.) shouted instructions not to damage his dock. With my masterful command of Quebecois French, we finally convinced them to hand us some lines which we then pulled across to windward. All the tomato plants on their deck were knocked down from the pounding. The tomatoes were still green.

During my extended sojourn on Long Island, I was pleased to get a FAX from Meredith, a phone call from my Aunt, and sing Happy 80th Birthday to my mother, using up the final minutes on my Batelco phone card. I checked over the drive leg lower end, filled the diesel tank, took on 6 gals. of drinking water, and monitored the 1700 US Coast Guard weather. Reports were inconsistent but supported a decision to go. Except for slipping docklines and shipping fenders, the boat appeared ready so I checked charts and courses, again.

My crew of Dan, Bahamian fisherman and emerging entrepreneur, and Gailene ("Don't call me Gail."), nautical hitchhiker and probable Canadian lesbian (We think.), appeared on board in a timely manner and we cast off for the Turks & Caicos Islands, again. This time, we made it.

Dan rigged two rod holders on the stern rail, prepared his lures, and set the lines for game fish. He figured our sailing speed of 5-6 kts was just about right for trolling. He's planning on reeling in dorado, wahoo, tuna; serious stuff. "Anything under 30 inches we're throwing back," he announces. Poor Dan was skunked during all of his days deep sea fishing from **Quo Vadis**. Not a single pelagic fish, not even a strike. He caught enough reef fish and I gathered enough conch at anchor that we ate wonderfully for the entire passage. Dan's conch salad was the best. Plus his grouper strips, a fish stew in a brown sauce reduction, pasta, and an artichoke salad. We managed to finish the last of the wine loaded on board at Pompano Beach, Fla. three months ago.

Still sailing to windward, we made anchorage again at Crooked Island. Next day, we made a 40nm motor sail East to the NE point of Acklins Island. We passed Mr.Sippi, who left during our first attempt a week ago, now going the other way. They were returning to Clarence Town with a broken mast. We discovered their condition after raising them on VHF. "River Rat" asked us to give thanks and reassurance of their condition to the folks who had helped them jury rig the mast. We wished them best of luck and to see them in the TCI. Before sunset, we saw the mushroom rock marking the entrance to Atwood Harbor. The wind favored this anchorage tonight. It was delightful. I swam to the wide, white beach and took a walk. It had been a few days since touching land. That night, we three sat in the cockpit under a blanket of stars. One of the crew commented out loud, "What are those poor people doing who aren't here?"

Landfalls

We cleared the reef by 0715 next morning, with the intent to end up at the Plana Cays or Mayaguana, and sailed the wind very comfortably until it went away. The sea got fairly smooth with a long swell. Dan was of the opinion this might be our chance to motor to Mayaguana, so we cranked up the diesel and headed for the NW point of this last of the Bahamas. We left the Plana Cays to starboard, passing by another of the many landfalls supposedly made by Columbus. He must have covered a lot of territory during his voyages to make all the landfalls, landings and settlements now claimed. By midday, I saw the clouds building up in the direction of Mayaguana, as well as convection over both the Plana Cays and, astern, over Acklins. Dan was just wondering out loud how long it was to Mayaguana. I informed him that we were seeing the marker cloud dead ahead. This surprised him, even as I pointed out the white puffs over the other cays and explained how they got there. "I never knew that," he admitted. "I would have thought we were just seeing five clouds over the sea." This gap in his sea-going knowledge surprised me. He is Bahamian with 13 years fishing and small boat handling, reads the water very well, senses currents, but did not know or ever figured out islands were often under clouds.

We made that landfall about 1530, still 9nm out from the waypoint. We passed through another pod of whales who were not going anywhere. This gang was feeding and spouting. They allowed us to pass through and continued eating. We dropped anchor in front of a small, empty beach by 1730 into what looked like a sand pocket amidst the coral. When I dived on it 10 minutes later, I discovered it was white marl. This is not so good. I relocated the anchor in a crevice which would be OK for every direction but South wind. Dan fished the rocks again with good success but twice sharks came in and bit through his wire leader taking bait, lure, hook, etc.

The clever captain had planned this anchorage just 1 nm from the new government dock so we could easily refuel after the long day's motoring. We started calling the fuel dock but got no response, so started calling Mayaguana—anybody—and still got no response. It looked more promising when we went into the dock next morning as there was at least 50,000 gallons of new tankage right there. And nobody to pump from it. We walked two miles up the road where Miguel, driving his pick-up over to check the island's electric powerplant, informed us that the "new dock" would not be open 'til next year. The nearest fuel might be in Abraham's Bay Settlement: 18 miles across the island. I calculated we had just enough fuel on board to make it to the Turks & Caicos if we had to motor—with no margin.

Miguel had to go to work (It was nearly 1000. Work time is casual here.) but volunteered his truck and his wife, Nathalie, to drive us in search of fuel. After some introductions around the new church construction site near Abraham's Bay, with an invitation from the foreman to come back to Mayaguana soon, it was agreed that Miss Mable had fuel. Which she did: in a drum in a shed in her backyard. Dan found a blue plastic drum, rinsed it out, and offered to try first on the hose, so he got the mouthful of diesel fuel. We siphoned as much as I thought we could lift onto the deck while still taking enough fuel to motor to the TCI, if we had to.

As we walked back from the shed into the house, Miss Mable gave us a loaf of fresh-baked bread: warm from her oven. She handed it to us with this explanation, "I hope that bread would be given to me or my children if we were traveling." Including the little something we gave Nathalie for the use of her truck, our "insurance" fuel ended up costing $5.50/gallon and was worth every bit of it.

The concrete dock had cut through a new 50 ft. springline and was chafing at the bow and stern lines by the time we got back to Quo Vadis. Dan apologized for how he had fastened the lines but I realized that I was the one who was way down on the learning curve. It is always the skipper's responsibility to make sure the vessel is secured properly. He trimmed the frayed ends and re-tied the line in a Fisherman's knot. I was skeptical about trusting it or how long it might last.

Later, we snorkeled and spear-fished off the stern, both of which were surprisingly good in only 6-10 ft. of water between the rocks and reef. Mayaguana appears to be seldom-visited and sparsely settled even though it has an 11,000 ft. airstrip left over from the years when the island was a U.S. missile-tracking station. The waters remain Bahamas-clear and seem to have lots of critters still living in them. I am told the airstrip gets shorter every year as the end cracks and crumbles. It is not maintained. Our good time was interrupted when the "No see'ums" arrived about 1730. We quickly moved the boat and anchored further out in the last of the day's light. All were in their bunks by 2000 for a scheduled 0200 departure for "Provo" in the TCI.

Quo Vadis cleared the anchorage before 0200 with a responsive crew on deck and no problems. Dan took the first trick at the helm and spotted the lights of a tanker coming across our bow on a Northwest course. I confirmed distance and track on the radar. The radar apparently uses lots of power. I kept it lit up for 20 minute interval checks on the tanker and another vessel 'til dawn but later recorded significant amp-hour drawdown on the house battery bank. It was a beautiful night as we steered down the moon and planet Venus into sunrise.

I made the Providenciales landfall during my second trick at the helm, about 1130. Then the wind died. This was not necessarily a bad thing as we had to maneuver a fairly intricate path through the reef to Turtle Cove. After a couple of calls, the guide boat came out to meet QV and this big motor yacht that had barged in front of us; then led through about two miles of doglegs around the reefs to the very narrow marina entrance. We shut down the engine by 1545 and waited 'til Customs officially closed so they could collect the overtime charges. At US$23, I didn't think they were too excessive. Officer Carl Gardiner gave us no hassle (despite three different nationalities and passports), a 3-month cruising permit for the islands, a welcome to the Turks & Caicos, but only a 7-day visa. With no complaints, we hauled down the Q-flag given by Ian and Anna before I left California and hoisted the British Red up the signals halyard for the first time.

An osprey: a large male, we thought, from its coloration, stood on the piling at the end of the slip as the sun went down. We were sipping something cold and wet, watching the white and black fish hawk outlined against a red sky. It had been a long passage in the making but, once again, I appreciated how good life is.

68   John Huetter

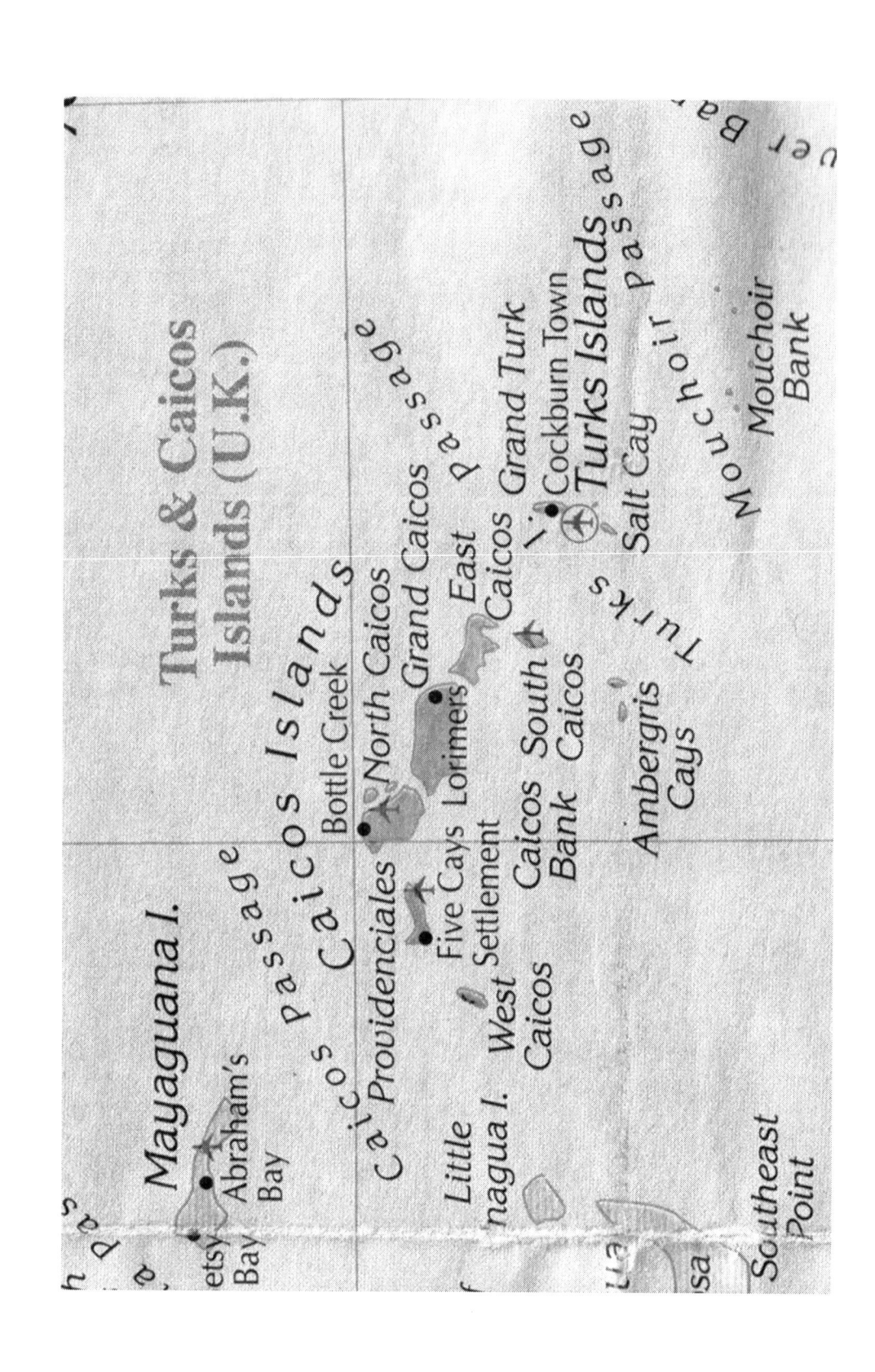

The First Year of Living Wet

In transit, anchored and docked, Turks & Caicos Islands, British West Indies

When Beth and Caroline came to cruise with me this month, they told me Mr. Rogers had died. At the time, I just felt a little older. Later, when I read his "Appreciation" in the journals they brought me, I wept slowly for a while. Not like when Jim Henson died: I went into a funk for days. If there is a God, she wants us to rely on ourselves a lot more than most folks think.

I heard there was another war started by a non-elected, non-combat politician who somehow ended up as President. Anybody know how that's going? My kids and I found out about it when we took the dink into the fuel dock from our anchorage off Little Water Cay. As we got the dink tied up, the dock boy came down and tore the posted fuel prices off the pumps. "Boss said price going up." I started to make some sort of protesting noise but he just looked away, over the water, and said, "Blame George Bush." Fuel price increases are the only visibility of that conflict here in this part of the world. Regardless of price, the fuel is priced and paid for in U.S. dollars. This still baffles me since the TCI are among the last of the true British colonies. I was figuring out the pound sterling exchange rate since the Bahamas but needn't have bothered. Itsa greenback dollah, mon.

Surprisingly, overall fuel costs for this voyage of personal discovery have been a fraction of the amount budgeted. Dock fees, more than double. But this is a personal, not a global perspective. And from that narrow perspective, a year has passed since I bought this vintage Prout catamaran and made it my home, which leads me to ask: How are all of you doing? Happy and well, I hope.

As a cautionary example, I was just advised of Dave and Devin's misadventures since strolling innocently on to the BahamasAir flight departing from Deadman's Cay. I knew that was a poor choice of names for any kind of port: air, sea or I/O. It took them days to get home, being stranded; then frustrated by several air travel Nazis due to an ice storm that swept the U.S. East Coast. As we used to say in the Air Force, with particular reference to Military Airlift Command: "Time to spare? Go by air." If you come back on board, we'll make it up to you, guys. How about the Spanish or British Virgins? Mona Passage bookings are also still available, though I can't promise anything about ice storms.

Lots of advice and other cautionary notes

At the end of this first year, I look at all the charts and cruising guides already retired: the Chesapeake, the Intracoastal Waterway, South Florida, Near Bahamas, Exumas, Far Bahamas, Turks & Caicos. I'm going through the national courtesy flags, too. OK, only two so far. Next will be the Dominican Republic. I also remember and reflect on the (mostly) unsolicited comments of other sailors. Many non-sailors, too, were full of advice as well as their opinions.

When I was cruising and racing on Chesapeake Bay, it was "Wait until you get out on the ocean. It's a whole different world." Did that. Also, most of my sailing experience before this has been on "the ocean". It's called the Pacific. Before embarking from Solomon's Island, Meredith and I were warned the Intracoastal Waterway was long and perilous and boring, to the point where Meredith was again questioning both my judgment and abilities. We did that. It was only long: about 1200 miles. From the Chesapeake through South Florida, it was "Wait 'til you get to the Bahamas." as if this were a really scary place. Did that. At Nassau (capital of the Bahamas), Captain Larry admonished me, "You're going to have to really get better and ready for down in the Exumas." Did that…again with Meredith, who had never sailed offshore before. At the end of the Exuma chain, I was told repeatedly, "90% of the boats don't go any farther than George Town." What? Even if their motors aren't stolen? This, however, turns out to have some validity as this heavily-populated anchorage has earned the nautical sobriquet "Chickentown." Most cruising vessels from the U.S. and Canada do not continue any further South from there.

But my faithful crews of Dave, Devin, Dan and Gailene helped me through the "Far Bahamas" to Mayaguana and on to the Turks & Caicos. While the air and water temperatures are in the 70s (Fahrenheit), we are still in the Winter North Atlantic conditions which inspired Lloyds to create the Plimsoll line for insuring commercial vessels by sea and season. There is big swell, waves, and winds 30-40 knots all the way down to the Dom Rep. I have the advantage of not knowing it should be any different and so I deal with it—or not. What have all these other, mostly cautionary, types been doing? I'm expecting Southeast trade winds all Spring and Summer.

Sometime in the last month, I finished reading all of the "Voyages of Joshua Slocum", a Bon Voyage present from Irv and Patricia. Most of you will remember Capt. Slocum was the first person to circumnavigate the planet alone. He did it in the late 1890s. His vessel Spray had, surprisingly, about the same overall dimensions as Quo Vadis even though Spray was a hand-built monohull in varying rigs and Quo Vadis is a factory-built cutter-rigged catamaran. Capt. Slocum treated himself to a hot meal daily, as I do, being mostly alone or underway with few crew. It took him three tries to get through the Straights of Magellan as it did me to get from the Bahamas to the TCI, though the passages themselves have little comparison. He whined and complained when treated unfairly in a foreign port where the officials did not speak English and did have guns; then wrote a protest letter to the President of the U.S., Grover Cleveland. Oops. I didn't do that last part. I'm pretty sure Grover Cleveland isn't the Prez anyhow, though I have been off shore for a while. Plus, I can deal with no English and guns. As it turned out, his complaining and letter of protest netted him nothing. Gee whiz, why am I not surprised?

The writing of this report on the first year living on board has been languishing for many reasons, not all of them worthy, so we'll proceed directly to what you probably have not been waiting for.

(Some of) The Best of My First Year of Living Wet

Best New Beer: Presidente, Dominican Republic. US$1.25/24 oz. bottle.

Best New Food: Bahamas Conch Salad, especially as prepared by Bahamian entrepreneur, fisherman and QV crewmember, Dan Cartwright. Chesapeake Bay oysters and blue crabs were not really a "new" food, so do not qualify in this category.

Best Anchorage: Red Shank Cay. Despite the hype, or because so many spurn it, the Home of the Red Shank Yacht & Tennis Club looms large as the best for all the right reasons you anchor out. There are too many Honorable Mentions to mention— with white sand bottoms and starry skies above. You had to be there. Why weren't you?

Best Personal Experience: Cruising South through the Exuma Cays with Meredith.

Best Personal Experience Publishable in a Family Magazine: Beth and Caroline Huetter on board Quo Vadis in the Caicos Islands during Spring Break 2003. We partied like it was 1999!

Best Shore Leave: Late November/early December in California. Family birthdays all 'round and Thanksgiving dinner prepared by your very own Chef Giovanni *in cucina*.

Best Personal Progress: At the helm of my home; especially under power. Everybody except Meredith tells me I'm getting more skilled at driving and navigation. Under sail? Hey, that's what us skippers do best! "EE-HAW! Look at us: 10 knots at 45 degrees apparent wind." No, I'm not crazy. Just lovin' it.

Best Bread: Miss Mable's in Abraham's Bay Settlement, Mayaguana. Given with love and 10 gallons of diesel siphoned from a drum in her backyard shed. I still don't know the ingredients.

Best Meals On Board: Dan's and my cooking from Long Island, Bahamas to the TCI.

Best Dive Spot: No "One Best", because at some you could take sea critters to eat and others, you couldn't. So: Northwest Point, Mayaguana; Smith Reef, Providenciales; Big Sand Cay, Turks Islands. We must go back to the Dominican Republic as we did no diving on those shores; sailing quickly both times through.

Most Exotic: Tangier Island, Virginia. 17th century Cornish in the middle of the Chesapeake.

Most Expensive: Turks & Caicos Islands. A dollar-based tourist economy, EU subsidies through Imperial Britain, off-shore banking, and opportunities for drug money laundering.

Least Expensive: Dominican Republic. We need to check this out in more detail.

Most Frustrating Sailing Experience: Trying to head South from the Bahamas; having 35-40 knot winds on the nose. Several times.

Most Frustrating Personal Experience: Those long times when Mer is not on board.

Best Thing that Did Not Happen: Did not sink or even wreck my boat on a reef.

Next Best Thing that Did Not Happen: No shark stories. Everybody else who has put a hull in these waters has a shark story. I don't and am glad of it. Unless you consider being photographed with the sharks in the water off the pier at Compass Cay.

Best Time Going Nowhere: Pompano Beach, Florida with John and Dixie Blake. Waiting for the Gulf Stream to get tolerable enough for a crossing to Cat Cay. It never did but we were cool about it. Too bad John didn't get to try out his custom fishing gear.

Best Religious Experience: Skipping right over the "Oh, God. Oh, God." type expressions: Singing and hearing praises of the Lord at Mt. Olivet on Staniel Cay (just after diving the Thunderball grotto with Mer) to the locals' accompaniment on organ, drum and tambourines.

Best Thing I Didn't Expect or Even Think About: Losing 20 lbs. and being very healthy the whole time, though increasingly brown and skinny.

Most Profoundly Unexpected and Sobering Sight: Shipwrecks. Lots of them: some very new with sails still flapping; some not so new and rusting. All the way along the route of this voyage.

Best Bet: Being on board. This should only get better as Quo Vadis heads East and South.

Meanwhile, back at the Marina…

There have been other noteworthy events this month. I helped the "River Rat" and Annie bring their now-repaired Irwin 32 from Turtle Cove to Luperon, on the North coast of the Dominican Republic. After getting the mast re-stepped back at Clarence Town, they made good time to the TCI and were ready to press on. We took the northern route around the Caicos Islands, past the Turks down to Sand Cay. This involved two longish night passages. The first one was unplanned but was always a contingency given there is only one anchorage on this route and it is, at best, problematic. The planned overnight passage was from the chunk of rock and sand that is the last of the Turks down to Luperon, including the crossing of the Windward Passage to Hispaniola.

The latter was made in significant wind and sea state which made me appreciate having a 37 ft. cat. Small monohulls heel and are bouncy. The only comfortable position I could find was lying down. Still, I stayed focused during my night watch by pretending we were in an ocean race and trying to maximize our boat speed, even by tenths of a knot. Rat's navigation must have been pretty good and the sailing was not too sloppy as we beat 38 and 40 ft. Island Packets that had left two hours earlier down to Luperon. After the fact, I'm not sure how much help I really was but it was a good learning experience. Things learned included: 1) Making longish overnight passages, 2) Having a crew of three makes the watch schedule a lot more comfortable, and a lot safer if one body gets sick or injured; 3) Nice to have a preview of a passage I planned to make in a few weeks and a better understanding of the entry to Luperon.

At a critical point in this journey, I discovered my Spanish was not as wonderful as I'd previously thought while executing key tasks like ordering lunch and beers. The ride to the airport in Hector's mini-truck cost twice what I'd understood in our negotiations. He muttered noises about the soaring cost of gasoline. The DR is within one degree longitude of the Turks, but in a different time zone. What a surprise for these Yankee sailors when we arrived at Puerto Plata International Airport. I was only then informed by the counter agent with the box full of cash that Sky King (the airline; not the old radio hero) accepted only local pesos should you want to actually purchase one of their airplane tickets. Just making reservations didn't count. I asked the pilots (in what I hoped was better Spanish) not to leave without me, scurried around shoving plastic at various ATMs and bank branches, dodged the incoming phalanxes of German tourists, and still made it to the aircraft in time to fly back to the TCI and meet my excellent children.

Beth and Caroline flew into Providenciales during Spring Break. We hung out around Turtle Cove for a couple of days. We snorkeled Smith's reef (where they saw their first shark sleeping under a coral ledge), ate on shore, and went shopping. Beth had forgotten her board shorts. We sailed up to Little Water Cay to see the iguanas running around the Cay and large rays with 3-4 foot wingspans gliding over sand bottom in 6-12 feet of water. We heard about the invasion of Iraq with the instant jump in pump price when we dinghied to Leeward Marina for fuel.

We later motor-sailed over to Western Caicos and dropped anchor not far from a deserted village of palm-frond houses with large communal spaces and sprawling verandas. This is not the native architecture of the island. It was a set, built for a French TV game show. It was intended to look like the audience's dream version of a tropical island. The game required the contestants to dive down and collect treasure coins from underwater sites. These tokens had different values that were redeemed for swell prizes. The treasure sites were attended by resident mermaids who offered refreshing hits from their air tank, allowing the contestants to stay down longer and collect more treasure coins. Part of the droll Frenchness in this show was the inclusion of random "bad" mermaids who swam away with the air tank rather than offering the mouthpiece. Heh, heh. Fooled you.

The local story is that one of the coin-laden contestants drowned after being denied air by a bad mermaid and the show was canceled. The village, complete with dance floor and restaurant on the beach, was abandoned. Given the prevailing state of TV programming, I'm surprised their ratings didn't go up. My kids thought this story was pretty interesting background as they explored the village and its long, white sand beach wearing only their underwear. Since we had the place to ourselves, part of my parental psyche was glad they were comfortable enough to do this. The Dad part of my brain was sending a different message, but I kept my mouth shut.

We sailed back to Provo with Caroline at the helm; through Sellars Cut without a guide boat this time, and made it to the Turtle Cove docks in time for Beth's 21st birthday. I had over-tipped the hostess to arrange a dinner at one of those fancy indoor-outdoor places featuring candles on the tables and lots of polished wood. About an hour before sunset, my daughters stepped off the boat and on to the dock wearing long black evening dresses. They led me, in the fading light, up the steps carved into the limestone bluff to our table overlooking the northern reef break off Providenciales. With the candles flickering in a gentle wind, we celebrated a birthday and being together. They each had two desserts, of course: the ice cream and the cake.

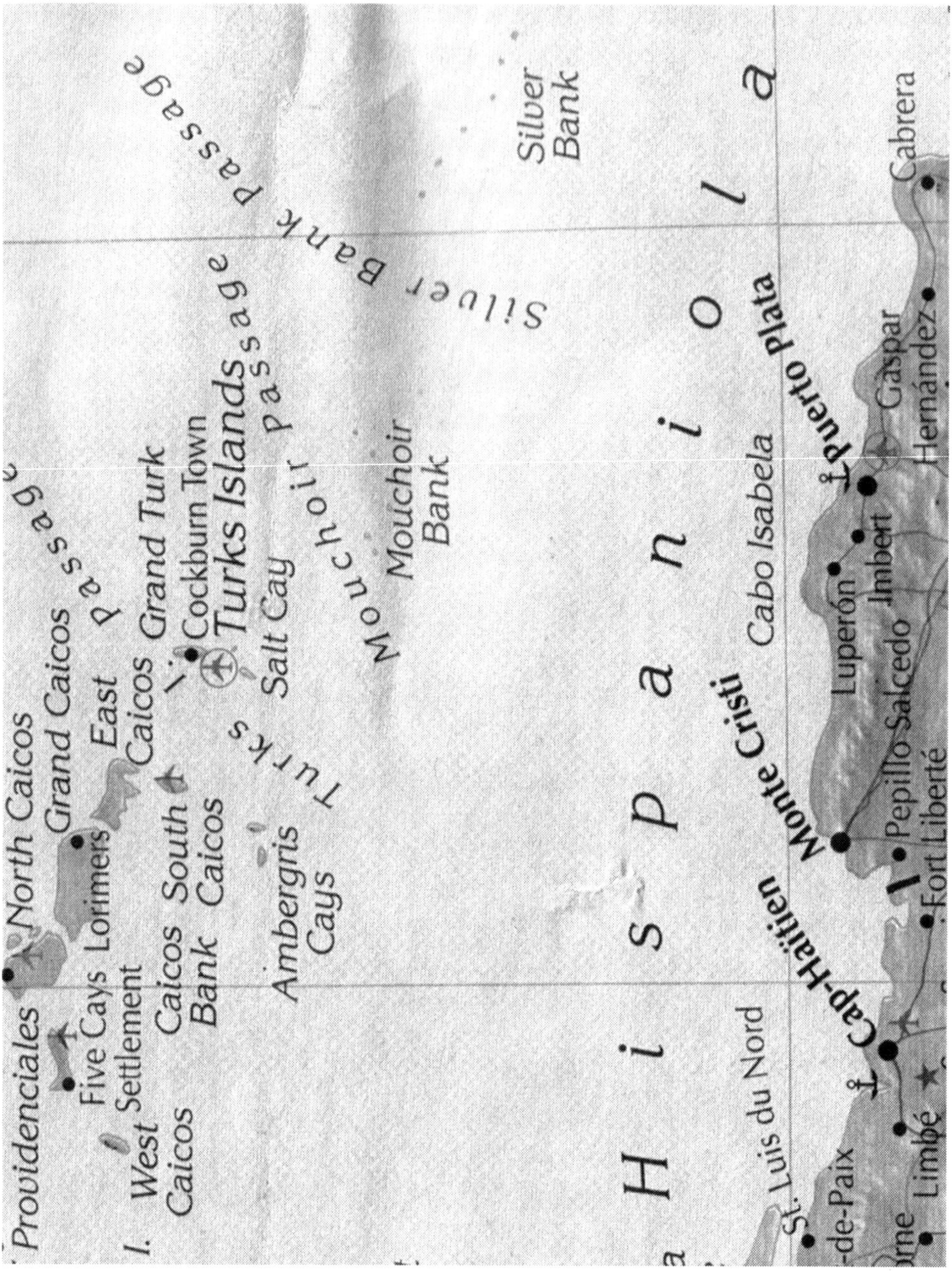
Providenciales
Five Cays
Settlement
West Caicos
North Caicos
Lorimers
Grand Caicos
East Caicos
South Caicos
Caicos Bank
Grand Turk
Cockburn Town
Turks Islands
Salt Cay
Turks Passage
Ambergris Cays
Mouchoir Passage
Mouchoir Bank
Silver Bank Passage
Silver Bank
Hispaniola
St. Luis du Nord
Cap-Haïtien
Monte Cristi
Cabo Isabela
Puerto Plata
Limbé
Fort Liberté
Pepillo Salcedo
Luperón
Imbert
Gaspar Hernández
Cabrera

The Real First Year of Living Wet...
and Living Well

Aboard S/V Quo Vadis, lying Ponce, Puerto Rico

I'm smoking a 12-cent cigar from the handful purchased in the Dominican Republic and listening to the sounds of the Romantico quartet coming across the water from the Malecon—whether you want to hear them or not. The Malecon is the boardwalk of La Guancha, the harbor district of Ponce. Meredith, a dancer, is not here to dance the Gaviota with me, which is the dance you do to the Romantico-style tunes. Other than the Malecon and the Ponce Yacht and Fishing Club, this is a serious commercial-industrial port. That might be the coal dock for the AES Guayama power plant across the channel. I'd expect there to be a pier at the powerplant. The AES guys wouldn't be so inefficient as to double-handle solid fuels, would they? However, this is Puerto Rico...

Quo Vadis is staying put in 25 kts with 190 ft. of scope out after dragging this afternoon in 35 kts with 120 feet out. This is only the second time ever that QV has dragged! But it's the first time with me alone onboard. You'll just have to believe the clever seamanship I displayed re-anchoring under these conditions. Seamanship I probably would not have been compelled to display if I'd let out more scope in the first place.

I've just enjoyed an on-board dinner of fresh, local tomatoes: a New World food considered poisonous by British-American colonials well into the 19th century, Caldo Gallego (a sort of Galician stew), corn tortillas: Aztec creations originally but Hispanicized in the past 500 years, and a bottle of Castillero del Diablo: the last white wine in the reefer. And, inevitably, I'm still hearing the Battle of the Puerto Rico Bands which would actually be OK if they competed serially rather than in parallel. The Romantico quartet went home some time ago.

Since we chased the remnants of the cruel Spanish out of here in 1898 and took over the place, it surprises me that Puerto Ricans still wax nostalgic about the days "under the Spanish crown", as they put it. I know, most U.S. mainlanders' response is either "Huh?" or "So what?" I won't pass that sentiment on at the Ponce Y. & F. Club until after I get fuel and the wind generator tower welded back on and rewired. Maybe, not even then.

During the first week of April, I crossed the palms of Kyle and Katis, sublords of Turtle Cove Marina, as incentive to remember Quo Vadis while I was carried to the shores of the Potomac by the great silver bird to participate in Meredith's 60th birthday celebration. If you've checked the photo of her, you know that 60 never looked so good. Or 50, or 40 for most women. She is very toned, and all natural. Other shoreside events included a swell day hosted by my Goddaughter, Elika. Too bad that she and husband Rich are decidedly not interested in cruising on QV. I also discovered that the "River Rat" will not be available to help me get on down to the Dominican Republic but he did return my charts and personal PFD left aboard. You sailing types will recognize that as a classy move on his part as he was sailing on to Vieques. But, still no crew.

Ten days later, I'm lugging US$850 in boat parts back to Providenciales in my carry-on duffle, including a complete replacement set of Yanmar diesel fuel injectors. They are my talisman. If they are on board, they won't be needed. I'm still not sure how to get down to Luperon from the Turks & Caicos, since I am quite confident I can't stay awake for two overnight passages and don't really want to go alone, anyhow.

Then came Brian and Aynsley. They looked like a couple in a Tommy Hilfiger ad, except Brian was letting his beard grow. (Aynsley, on the other hand, shaved regularly. Mostly her legs, though.) Should I really trust my home to them? They had just docked next to me on the Halberg-Rassy ketch *Alcyone* during a six month voyage making a direct-to-video documentary on cruisers and cruising, with Jon (skipper of said vessel) and 'Becca. After reciprocal dinners on board (I grilled triggerfish for the QV dinner. It's tasty but the meat sticks to the bones.) and serious consideration among the *Alcyone* crew, all agreed that Brian and Aynsley would crew on *Quo Vadis* to Luperon. This D.R. port was also as far as *Alcyone* planned to go but not for a couple of weeks as Jon was going to hang around the TCI to meet family. After further discussion and a few sundowners, B&A allowed as how they would stay on board 'til St. Thomas in the U.S. Virgins.

Once more into the Leeward Cut

Easter Sunday was "Prep for the Passage" day including jerry-jugging diesel fuel, engine oil and filter change, filling and treating the water tanks; you know, the usual household chores. I had sailed the Northern, deep water route with River Rat and Annie but we figured going South, across the Caicos Banks, would save a day. Some sources of information flatly stated the "Leeward Going Through" was a serious misnomer because the route was impassable. The local boat guide and a local guy were both saying the "LGT" was not a problem with over 4 ft. of water after the conch farm. Local computer guy John Lawson showed us a route on the chart and allowed as how we'd be " laughing all the way". I see a lot of "1.0" places on the chart: one meter. This is exactly the 39-inch cruising draft of *Quo Vadis* but I decide to try it anyway—on the high tide.

So we're off to the South Caicos as the first stop on the Thornless Path to Luperon. We clear the Northern Providenciales reef through Sellars Cut with breakers on both sides due to the swell, cleverly planning to catch high tide an hour and a half later coming back in through the Leeward Cut. We did, again with big reef break on both sides. The cautious captain surfed QV into the Cut with Brian's young, sharp eyes on the foredeck checking for sandbars and coral heads. So far, Caroline and Beth can totally relate to this, having done it a few weeks earlier. Well, by now I was so skilled at surfing this particular island's North shore that we ran aground on the inside bar of Leeward Cut in 2.5 ft. We had all mistaken it for the outside bar which has a channel through it, as Caroline had also pointed out. No excuses, but—the channel had shifted. It still wasn't high tide. Which was a good thing, as I worked QV off the bar using power when she lifted on the very small waves of the rising tide. Six inches really does matter. Brian and Aynsley commented on the lack of salty language from this skipper after we went aground. If such language would float the boat, I'd swear like the crusty old guy I am becoming but there is little evidence that really works.

Now, with this little drama resolved, another interesting situation presented itself. Do we continue or go back out the Cut and try to make the only anchorage on the Northern route before dark? We press on, partly because the already-noted North swell is still building. As noted, some of the cruising guides say this is not do-able. They are almost right. After feeling our way through the spontaneously re-named "Leeward Maybe Going", we ran the more strangely named "Ship Channel" in indicated depths down to 2.3 ft. Do I need to point out we never saw another ship? It was a tense 10 hours on a tight, shallow route across more than 50 miles of banks. I was on the foredeck, hoping to correctly foresee how the channel went, with Brian at the helm most of the time. This turned out to be good because if I'd seen the indicated depths he later reported I would have been freaked out. I'd already run aground that morning in 2.5 ft. Perhaps burnished by the glowing patina of success, the passage was strangely beautiful as sky, sea and sandbar merged, hopefully not under the *amas* of Quo Vadis. All the sea critters were close enough to touch; even those on the bottom. But I don't recall laughing even part of the way—or at all.

I can't figure out why this route is even on the charts. There is no escape if you have a problem. The only way I can explain QV not being hard aground is the depth transponder location at the top of the skeg, which extends about 18 inches from the main hull. When the depth meter was reading 2.3 ft. I guess we had 9 inches under the hulls. We made it to the dock at Sea View Marina on South Caicos before dark. The marina owner couldn't find us when we informed him on CH16 that we were approaching. He was looking East toward the harbor entrance and we were skimming over the impassable sand flats to the West. Docking was free, possibly because the dock consisted of a concrete slab with trash piled on it. But with a sense of relief, we were in 7 ft. depth; not wanting to make that passage again or anything remotely like it. After the Captain re-composed, our dinner reward was Aynsley's excellent salad, sourdough, chef-sautéed grouper filets, and a 2000 Greenvale Chardonnay that Brian had liberated during his recent gig working at that winery near Newport. It was the first time I'd ever tasted Rhode Island Chardonnay. It was just great.

Wherein we leave Britannia's rule for the next country South

At 0900 the next morning, all the crew strolled into Cockburn Town. Brian and Aynsley headed to the bakery and the captain to call Customs again, so we could legally clear out of this British colony. Capt. Norris (the owner of all things "Sea View") called Tina, who I assumed to be the Customs agent, and informed me she'd be down. Applying my hard-won cruising experience, I think to ask, "This morning?" "Yes" is the reply.

The bakery was sold out by nine, but I figured if I started scraping stuff off the bottom, Customs would show up. After about 1.5 hours in the water, I had the knot meter impeller cleared, most of the barnacles off the central nacelle and had seriously mutilated the strange black growths on the *amas*. Despite these efforts, no Customs agent appeared. I hoped Brian and Aynsley had enjoyed some private time while I was submerged. I was pretty well worn out from scraping.

Aynsley had the clever idea, after we'd been waiting three hours, that since Customs had not come to the Quo Vadis perhaps the Captain should go to the Customs office. After following directions that took me on a trek around the periphery of Cockburn Town, which fortunately is not very big, I arrived at the small but air-conditioned Customs office at 1210. Tina was there; her crisply pressed uniform un-mussed by movement; with no apparent intention of leaving her temperature-controlled domain until it closed for the day at 1230. She did give me a bureaucratic break by not making me walk back with crew passports so long as I agreed to leave all the information at "Sea View". Otherwise, everything would have had to wait until 0830 the next day.

The GPS told us it was 23nm to the Sand Cay waypoint after we cleared the trash dock at 1315 in 1-5 kts wind. So we motored over a near-glassy four foot swell at speeds up to 7 knots. I'd never seen Quo Vadis make that speed under power. I complimented B&A for their good influence on vessel performance. I also put the anchor down in 12 ft. over white sand by 1730. We had the anchorage, and Big Sand Cay, all to ourselves. I had some concern due to our proximity to shore break with the North swell but figured we would be OK in the probable worst case: low tide. Brian made great cheeseburgers, served with sliced avocado and Greenvale Gypsy

Red. A peaceful sunset was followed by some serious star-spotting as the swell dampened and the wind came to the Northeast. After a well-executed surf landing and launch of the dink next morning, we were back on board with a haul of beach glass and small shells from our solitary exploration of Sand Cay. We had not seen another human being or vessel since leaving Cockburn Town. It is wonderfully strange to have a good-sized cay in the middle of the ocean all to yourself. I made salad and pasta for lunch; then checked the fuel—twice. We had the anchor up by 1500 and were headed for the Windward Passage.

We spotted a small pod of pilot whales and, again, got some nice shots of where they had just been, both above and under water. About an hour and a half later, dolphins started appearing ahead. I always like this omen and the 1800 offshore weather report doesn't contradict the good vibe claiming winds NE 10 kts and seas 3-5 ft. However, as Dave will always remember, this offshore report has not always been accurate. I got the autohelm set for our 176 Magnetic course after quite a bit of tinkering. Still, we had reasonably good performance from the ST1000 which I guess must have been one of the first commercially available autohelms for sailors. I understand they're up to ST7000 by now. We stood three hour watches through the night, passed two cruisers on a reverse course and avoided a westbound freighter in the shipping lanes North of Hispaniola. I remembered the freighter traffic from my prior cruise to the Dom Rep on Mr. Sippi.

The Transition to Capitan Juan Begins

By 0600, the mountainous coast of the Dominican Republic was looming large but looking friendly. We had set the sails on my midnight watch to good effect: running at 6.5-7 kts 'til dawn. As the wind came up with the sun, it also came back on the nose with seas building. B&A furled the headsails and I was back on the helm from 0615. I recognized the cliff face to port, the beach hotel populated mostly by Germans, and other landmarks from the March passage. Quo Vadis crossed the waypoint at 0725. The GPS had predicted 0730.

We negotiated the fish trap floats and lots of small fishing boats in the channel between the rock cliff and the sandbar. They all waved. Well, the floats didn't. We could not pass over the mud flat I had charted in March with the tide this low, so anchored in five feet of the opaque Bahia Blanco by 0800. Customs, immigration and public health guys, as well as the local version of Spanish, were easier to work with when they came aboard. There was a new Port Captain who was formerly the C.O. of a Navy combat vessel (*"Un Canoñero"* he proudly told us.) and seemed a lot less sleazy than the previous guy. It's always a relief when the outboard starts; especially after a long passage. This event and the Port Captain let me complete documentation on shore; then treat the crew to lunch at the corner café with the big arched windows. We were back on board by 1400: siesta time. Aynsley was doing watercolors, Brian was reading and napping, and I'm working on the ship's log; enjoying a D.R. see-gar which really did cost ten cents.

There is a fellow named Bruce Van Sant who wrote "The Thornless Passage" in which he insists sailing to windward in this part of the world, which we're doing, can be accomplished easily by going in the night lees of the islands when the wind drops and changes direction. So we decide to leave at sundown, as prescribed. Brian and Aynsley are off to Cabo Isabela, site of the first European city in the New World and Columbus' American house. I'm still trying to get fuel, water, propane, and laundry on board. Everything just listed was a no-show so I went ashore to check on stuff. I also got a shave and a haircut for US$2 at a barber shop with one chair and a red, white and blue-painted wooden pole out front. The young barber snipped away for a while; then asked me if I wanted to *"limpiar"*. Literally, in Spanish, "to clean up". I didn't know what he meant. He showed me a razor blade: just the blade. He then proceded to dry shave my beard, using just the blade, into a *conquistador* configuration. The result is very precise and somewhat angular. He does the same thing for the hairlines of the black guys who really don't have much beard. He uses one blade per customer with no lather, aftershave or talc. So the transition begins.

Finally, everything happened at once; almost by surprise. Rafael showed up with fuel and water. I found rum and beer (next on the list of critical fluids) and B&A returned with lots of provisions and some good stories about their trip to Columbus' house. We are ready to take advantage of the recommended "Night Lee" and weigh anchor just before sunset. Well, Van Sant can take his "night lees" and put them where the sun really doesn't shine.

We're out of the Puerto Blanco channel before dark (barely) and clear the supposedly fearsome Punta Patilla after 2100. However the wind is building, not dropping, and soon the seas are over six feet and sneaking up behind us in the night. The surprise drenchings in the dark are not fun so I decide to divert to the anchorage at Sosua. We have the anchor down in 20 ft. off the beach by 0115. The wind is still against us. Like a fade-in from a movie, we awake to a calm, sunny morning. Bird calls, children laughing on the beach, the whole thing. QV is the largest of a handful of boats anchored off what is evidently a local resort area. We all go swimming.

Cruising the Capes and Making some Crossings

The next two legs bring us to the Rio San Juan and on to Bahia Escondido. We make the tough decision to work around the next big cape, though it is too late in the day to make it according to Van Sant's guide. We manage to get around the cape and head across Bahia Escosesa (Scotswoman's Bay). This is a long but not especially difficult passage. The Rio San Juan disgorges cold, fresh water through the mangrove swamp at its mouth into the anchorage. When you dive down from the warm surface water, you are swept into a cold stream surging along the bottom. Bahia Escondido is described in the guidebooks as "fjord-like". Well, fjord-like doesn't really capture the whole scene. The approach to Bahia Escondido is toward rocky escarpments 500 ft. high and, says the guide, "Go around the island visible from miles out." Since it will add more miles to go around the island, we head inside. The depth decreases rapidly but the readout is never less than 18 ft. After the Caicos Banks, this feels like surplus water under the hulls. I further stretch the protocol of chart and GPS. Since we can see the anchorage as we round the point and it is now 1730, I make the command decision to bypass the waypoint and go directly in to Hidden Bay. "Whoa, Ca-pi-tan Juan..." intones Brian. This must be the wildest move they've ever seen me make and is another, unplanned step in the transition.

Bahia Escondido is surrounded by 300 ft. rock walls, faced by two sand beaches and fringed with coconut palms. Dugout canoes are pulled up on the beach, where fires are set at night to guide fishermen home. This is as Columbus described it in 1493 and as we saw it in 2003. Except in 2003 there is a sign on the small, postcard-worthy beach where we anchor. Translated, it reads: "This property for sale. Approx. 200,000 sq. mtrs." followed by a phone number. For us, this only adds to the intrigue. Dozens and dozens of snowy egrets fly across our bows to their night roost in the trees East of the beach. We see some of the fishermen shove off and the beach fires are lit. At dawn, we see the egrets leave while we have coffee on deck. Shortly after they leave, so do we.

That day we round the three capes which define the Northeast side of Hispaniola, passing solitary fishermen bobbing in brightly-painted dories. That night we dine at the French restaurant in Samaná. I order a carpaccio of sliced grouper and green peppercorn steak in cream sauce. We all share the different orders. The next morning we also decide to lift the hook and go in to the fuel dock since we can use some of that petroleum product. We should probably also clear in to Samaná since nobody came out to see us.

As Brian and Aynsley secure our lines to the dock, everybody suddenly appears and all start to come tromping on board. I hear many demands, most of them conflicting for attention and timing. I don't like how the fuel is delivered or the crowd hustling us gringos and I start telling them so, in Spanish, using (as it turns out) my Capitan Juan voice. Strangely, this sort of works. Things get sorted out with the officials and we only have to pay a port use fee of US$15...plus tip. All of our boat papers and passports are in order, of course. I decline to deal with the self-appointed dock agent and go directly to the guy silently watching us from beside the fuel pump.

We like Samaná and take a day off to go to the waterfalls riding in Wally's *motoconcho*. This vehicle consists of a 125 Yamaha pulling a carriage. It appears to be the major mode of municipal transportation. I like the D.R. It is inexpensive with friendly people who seem to enjoy a dignified quality of life in an essentially poor country. The locals are proud of their town or region and seldom talk about wanting to be someplace else. Rafael described his town of Luperon as "Paradiso". His paradise is a muddy bay with a crumbling quay in a buggy jungle. The people in Samaná brag about its natural beauty and rich abundance. Non-believers might see a steamy, tropical port. Brian, Aynsley and I talk about returning to tour the D.R. on dirt bikes. I'll want a 250 or a 350, though, instead of one of the prevailing 125s.

The rudder problems continue. I am sure I tightened the nuts at South Caicos but notice the right rudder flopping around uselessly as we ready Quo Vadis to try the "night lee" theory again. We pull off the inspection panel and see nuts and bolts scattered about in the rudder post compartment. Brian bravely wriggles into the space while I perch on the end of the *ama*, holding tools from the top. Sweating on each other while barking our own knuckles, we manage to re-attach all loose pieces. Hopefully, the correct way and for the long term.

Surprise bleeding, the Mona Passage, and then some

Our next effort to cruise thornlessly in the night lees is another bad joke. After three hours of bashing into strong night winds and seas we've covered about 6 nm, so we head back to Samaná. It takes about one hour to return to the anchorage. I had back-ranged the entrance and the few lights when we left for just such a reverse course in the dark. It worked. From now on, it's only going to be friendly daylight passages on Quo Vadis. Well, most of them.

We continue down the East coast of the Dominican Republic. Punta Macao is a fine anchorage but appears to be a weekend getaway for locals and a destination resort for Germans. You know they're German even before they speak because both genders are wearing rubber swim caps and doing the breast stroke while snorkeling. Also, they only seem to exist in different shades of pink. We manage to look at some fish and swim in solitude after the tourist gangs leave the beach on dune buggies.

You other sailors will understand and agree: bleeding on board is always a bad surprise. Half the time when you see blood on the deck, you don't know how it happened and all the time it is hard to clean up. I seem to leak the red stuff all over so I go through lots of hydrogen peroxide. Some of it ends up on me and the rest on the decks in an attempt to get the bloodstains out. You'll also remember it's impossible to keep bandages on these unplanned holes in yourself when you're underway. They inevitably get wet and fall off. Eeyeww. Gross. Call me Scarleg.

Punta Cana is the sticking-out chunk of land on the East coast of the D.R. and a jumping off place for crossing the Mona Passage to Puerto Rico (the P.R.). It has also become a luxury destination-type resort. Punta Cana did not, however, have many folks luxuriating the weekend we arrived. It had the eerie feel of near-vacant big places with lots of staff wandering around not doing much. The channel into the marina may be the best-marked I've seen since Florida which is a good thing because the marina basin is small, shallow and has rocks on three sides. We fuel up at low cost; have a luxury resort lunch at high cost and rest up for the crossing of the Mona Passage.

The literature describing the Mona Passage is mostly intimidating. It is replete with tales of terrible thunderstorms, strong currents, and long passage times of 32-40 hours. In planning, I figured on 20-25 hours to the bay at Boqueron on the Southwest corner of Puerto Rico. The intrepid crew of the Quo Vadis did it in less than 16 hours with an average speed over 6 kts; putting 95 nm under the *amas*. I know that doesn't calculate precisely but then neither do all the instruments on board nor those who read them. Here's how we did it, despite buying in to Van Sant's "Thornless Guide" one last time.

We set sail across the passage about 1900 with winds 20-30 kts Southeast. Despite that, it was decided to take one long Northern tack across the top of Mona Island and its dreaded outlying rock: Monita. We experienced good sailing speeds on a beat: 7-8 kts consistently; 9-10 often at 35-45 degrees to the apparent wind. Brian grins and shouts, "We are sailing the Mona Passage!" So it seems cats, at least this Prout design, can point up if the wind speed is greater than what most folks would sail in. Again, there is no frigging night lee. I manage to sleep for 5-6 hours of the crossing. Brian and Aynsley woke me up about 2230 as a squall hit us with 40-45 knot winds; gusts to 50. Despite my heightened powers as "Capitan Juan", I couldn't get the wind or rain to abate but did give the order to shorten sail. Well, maybe not order. It was more like, "Hmm. We could take in some sails." This clever move did bring the boat speed back down to single digits.

Well, we got to someplace

I took the helm as the stars emerged and we continued pounding, rapidly, towards Puerto Rico. It was wet and bouncy but the crew were great. We had the anchor set in Boqueron and the yellow quarantine flag up by 1200.

We Q-flagged Boqueron while I made ham and cheese omelets with tomato and guacamole on the side. Officially, we weren't there. We didn't want to give cause for any other impressions, so cleared the anchorage by 0530 the next morning. There had been some very unsatisfactory exchanges with somebody at the port office up in Mayaguez, which is about 50 miles North. Something about how it was the only Puerto Rico West Coast port of entry, and we had to bring ship's papers and passports and Luis, the taxi driver, was the only guy to conduct and advise us on this journey. Some more talk about fees. I was not going to Mayaguez!

What I was trying to do was get around Cabo Rojo, the southwest corner of Puerto Rico, before it got nasty. We almost made it with me at the helm until 0830 when I handed off to Brian. Then the wind turned on and it got all choppy out. I was plotting to tack across the rhumbline as our sailing speed was about 50% faster than plowing into the waves with only 25-30% increased distance. It was working pretty well with short out tacks and longer inbound tacks at speeds of 7-10 kts. The pounding must have been more than I understood because about 1015 the wind generator tower snapped off and went overboard behind the starboard *ama*. Seas were up to 7 ft. and gusts to 40 kts. Brian controlled the boat while Aynsley and I pulled the wind generator back on the aft deck and lashed it down. I'm still not sure how we did that, even with adrenaline saturating every cell.

I took the helm with (or because of?) seas breaking over the bows and coach roof. The gas tank for the outboard surged up and out of the latched forward locker and lodged in the lifelines. Brian went forward, recovered and re-stowed it. A starboard dorade cover popped off. Brian grabbed it before it washed overboard and re-installed it. He was of the opinion it would need glue to stay on. The headsail was starting to look a little frayed, too. I tried to explain to the intrepid couple that I wasn't a complete maniac but, rather, they should think of me instead as a mature guy with a keen sense of adventure. Brian looked at me quizzically between soaking waves and, still smiling, asked the non-rhetorical question, "But you're loving this, right?" Not exactly how I'd have put it but Aynsley laughed. Only later did I wonder if it was from hysteria or her keen sense of humor.

Brian navigated the approach into Bahia de Ponce very effectively while I hung on to the wheel and pinched the wind very hard so we didn't blow past the entrance to the harbor. We finally cut inside the lighthouse island and motored to windward on up to the Ponce Yacht & Fishing Club fuel dock. No visible pilings were sticking up high enough to catch the wind generator tower which was lashed down sideways; extending several feet over the starboard side. It was 1645 but too late to buy fuel. I quickly became a Guest Member of the club and we all found hot showers.

We didn't make it to St.Thomas on *Quo Vadis*. Our last night's dinner aboard included antipasto, Aynsley's famous salad, pasta with my infamous red sauce and the last bottle of Brian's Gypsy Red. The next morning I arranged plane reservations and a cab to take them to the San Juan airport. I had some help from the ladies in the front office of the Ponce Y&FC. Brian and Aynsley had bravely earned their Quo Vadis Crew shirts. I eagerly admit I prefer hanging out with intelligent, competent people; preferably ones with a good sense of humor. (This is another reason I enjoy my own kids so much.) We had shared a great adventure. I'd do it again tomorrow. In fact, I'd prefer to do it compared to what is likely to be on tomorrow's agenda! Wouldn't you?

Meanwhile, in other news…

Despite no informative responses from my friends on shore, I did catch up on how the thing in Iraq is playing out—at least, for now. I see Cameron Diaz playing Pvt. Kelly Lynch. I hope Cameron doesn't have a schedule conflict and I hope Pvt. Lynch recovers completely and makes E-3. It seems it's OK to invade any country we want now; especially if it has oil. Now, oil is something the guy running these United States knows about. Hell, Dick Cheney was CEO of Halliburton for years and it that's not the premier oilfield services company, then Schlumberger is—and they sound French. But I want somebody running the country who knows about teak. Teak is really expensive in world markets and sometimes hard to find at any price. Nearly all sailboats need teak. Right now, I need a starboard rub rail and a cockpit hatch cover fabricated in teak. So why don't we invade Burma? (Now, self-styled "Myanmar") There's an oppressive dictatorship that threatens a Nobel Peace Prize winner with death under continuing house arrest. They use slave labor, too, but they have lots of teak. Seize that teak and put it on the market at competitive prices and you're talking big time yachtie trickle-down economics. Probably trickling down to rum in the yacht world. Rum is an important product of all the U.S. territories in the Caribbean so we'd also be strengthening the domestic economy. Getting that teak is definitely a win-win situation. So, on to Burma! The Brits need teak on their boats, too, so they'd probably help out. Maybe we could even re-use some of those bases we left in Thailand from that other war.

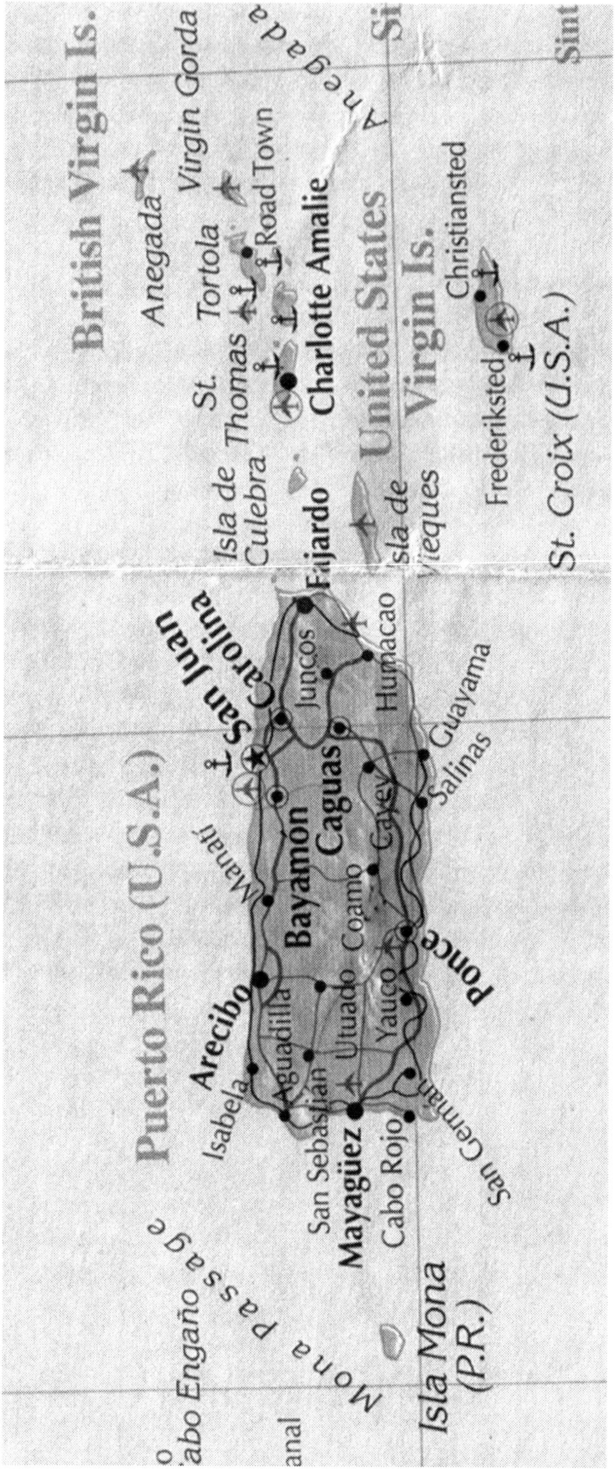
British Virgin Is.
Anegada
Virgin Gorda
Tortola
Road Town
St. Thomas
Charlotte Amalie
Isla de Culebra
United States Virgin Is.
Christiansted
Frederiksted
St. Croix (U.S.A.)
Isla de Vieques
Fajardo
Puerto Rico (U.S.A.)
San Juan
Carolina
Juncos
Humacao
Caguas
Bayamón
Manatí
Cayey
Guayama
Salinas
Coamo
Ponce
Arecibo
Utuado
Yauco
Isabela
Aguadilla
San Sebastián
Mayagüez
Cabo Rojo
San Germán
Mona Passage
Cabo Engaño
Isla Mona (P.R.)
Anegada Passage

Puerto Rico Days and Virgin Nights

Aboard S/V Quo Vadis, sailing Puerto Rico and the Virgin Islands

Puerto Rican gals have absolutely cartoonish asses. Even R. Crumb doesn't have the imagination to draw some of these posterior realities, many of them adorned with tattoos. Some of you probably knew this already. If I did notice on my last trip to Puerto Rico, some 20 years ago, I forgot. These gals also have pudgy tummies but this doesn't stop them from wearing Brazilian-style jeans and bare midriff tops which results in most females over 18 looking 4-5 months pregnant even though some of them really aren't. This may indicate a dreadful ordering of my priorities but these Latina lovelies were not the reason I was docked at Ponce for nearly a month.

The cumulative effects of a year cruising and a couple of recent, fairly bouncy passages dictated the need for services of a sail maker, electrician, welder, electronics tech, and some fiberglass and teak repair. I observed to Brian and Aynsley as they were leaving Quo Vadis that the repair work would take 2-3 weeks. They couldn't believe it would take that long. I reminded them I had worked in Puerto Rico before.

In my search for some of the above-listed skills, I asked Alicia and Jeanette in the *Oficina* of the Ponce Yacht & Fishing Club for suggestions. Puerto Ricans are very fond of nicknames. So I was not surprised when the guys in the boatyard who did fiberglass and woodwork were identified as Pipo, Pichi, Ponchi and…Wenceslaus. As I diligently wrote down these names, one of the ladies commented, "I think Wenceslaus just works in the office." Poor Wenceslaus. Did the stigma of having a desk job prevent him from acquiring a cool boatyard guy nickname?

It was nearly four weeks 'til the work was done. I elected to have two deteriorating wooden hatch covers rebuilt in fiberglass. I had the time since Russ and Lynsay weren't able to schedule their time for a boat trip halfway around Puerto Rico. I also called the former managers of Prout (builder of my Hull #223), looking for a solution to the rudder posts constantly coming undone. (Well, OK, it's been three times but the timing and location have always been damn poor.) I again got this cavalier British attitude about the rudders coming unbolted from the control arms. "We see some of that; especially in boats that have been doing offshore work," explained the former Prout manager. He had survived their bankruptcy. "Oh, really?" I thought. "Where exactly do you expect us to be sailing your frigging boats?" but said nothing aloud.

The fix (He knew it needed one.), as I understand it, involves removing the rudders and re-machining vital, expensive-sounding parts that can only be accessed when the boat is hauled out. Deep breaths, now, Capitan Juan. I calmly verify the UK phone number. Maybe I will get back to him when I can do something about the problem besides Loc-tite all the accessible nuts, which I finally busted my knuckles and did with the boat in the water. Wish I'd thought to have Brian do it in Samaná when he was busting his knuckles.

The wind generator tower gets re-welded, reinforced and re-installed by Raul. The genoa gets patched, taped and sewn by Fraito. Pipo does wood, fiberglass, and things until two B.O.A.T. units later, our work is finished here or as much of it as we can figure out how to do. During this effort, I learn that Raul is actually a graduate chemical engineer who chose welding for both the money and independence. His academic emphasis was metallurgy. Fraito is representing Puerto Rico in the upcoming Pan American Games. He is skipper of their #1 boat. Eddie the electrician just retired after 20 years with the PR Electric Power Authority which means he fears no voltage and money is no object. This is pretty classy dockside help. Ponce Y& FC wants it like that.

One of the aspects of these repairs is that the identification, negotiation and installation of the work were all conducted in Spanish. The tradesmen of Ponce, and most of the moneyed professionals I meet at the Y&F Club, do not gladly speak English. This is not a tourist town and they don't need to. I realized after the fact that I had gone nearly three weeks without speaking English except for a few phone calls. Though I seemed to be generally well-understood, perhaps because I was paying in cash, I was accused of having a "Spanish" accent, like from Spain. I could not pass for Puerto Rican, possibly because I continued to pronounce most of the consonants in most words. It's an old habit; hard to break. While speaking English for the first time my cell phone has been in coverage this year, I discover many folks are not doing too well. I am truly sorry. A Caribbean cruise would be good for you: sun, sand, warm water, good rum, and Capitan Juan singing at the helm. Well, OK, the last item could be "by request" only.

Hot Time in the Old Town

All work and no play do indeed make Cap'n Jack a dull old boy. Not expecting to sharpen my edge, I still take off a couple of Sundays to visit downtown Ponce and the indigenous peoples' settlement at Tibes. The former was founded in the 18th century; the latter in the 4th. Old Ponce is Victorian; not Spanish colonial. To this day, the town is highly commercial in outlook and performance. It is a capitalist, independent-minded place that achieved maximum prosperity after the U.S. took the place from Spain. Tibes is a pre-Columbian series of settlements which include the largest ceremonial center in the Caribbean and several ball courts. There are no pyramids at Tibes, just big rocks rolled up from the nearby river. The same river flooding first exposed the ruins only 40 years ago. Our self-described New YoRican guide tells us the ball game played here required the teams to keep the ball in the air without using their hands. Unlike the similar Mayan game, however, the losing team captain was not sacrificed. However, the winning captain was awarded a solid stone belt he had to wear until the next game. Makes you wonder.

I was intrigued to learn that in the Tainu* and pre-Tainu pantheon, the evil god or presence was called "Juracan". (I forget the good guy's name.) When the devastating winds would seasonally roar across the island, the locals attributed this bad stuff to the presence of Juracan. Those unimaginative Spaniards leapt to the conclusion that this was the name of the terrible winds. Juracan became hurricane. One of which I hope we never encounter, despite it being the season.

Meredith flew in to Puerto Rico still suffering the lingering effects of cold, wet D.C. area ailments. Demonstrating the already-noted benefits of remedial sea cruises, she left a short 17 days later a healthy woman. No more coughing or sneezing, biscuit brown, looking like a Victoria's Secret model; with her immune systems built back up from healthy food, many days in warm water, and frequent sex. She swam greater distances and saw more coral reef and reef critters than she ever had before.

We eased into this experience by decompressing for a couple of days in Old San Juan. We stayed in a converted Carmelite convent: El Convento, ate tapas, and explored the Spanish fortress and walls. I hadn't been in San Juan since a business trip in 1980 and it was the first time for Mer. She appreciated the room with a view of the harbor and the governor's mansion. I appreciated her.

After this onshore interval, we set out for the docks of Ponce which, when I left two days earlier, were still on fire. I woke up the morning scheduled to collect Mer at San Juan airport to see the commercial docks opposite my vessel engulfed in black smoke and red flames. Quo Vadis was still tied to the Y& F Club fuel dock but I didn't see a threat to the boat unless the adjacent gas and oil tanks blew. In that case, Ponce harbor would immediately get deeper and lots of hot, nasty stuff would probably start falling from the sky. Despite their long, proud history the Ponce *Bomberos* did not respond quickly from their famous red and black-striped fire station. (As a former LA County firefighter and transplanted San Franciscan, I think of fire response times in single digit minutes; not hours.) They did not have it under control within the first day.

*Tainu: Early indigenous inhabitants of Borinquen, the island now called Puerto Rico.

So we cast off QV, left this smoking industrial ruin, and sailed out into the Dreaded South Wind. We were the only boat that did. This pattern continued for quite a few days. We beat to windward into Salinas, a funky little beach town noted for gringo derelicts and having the only marine supply store on Puerto Rico's South coast. Feeling the tropical sun, Mer scissors a QV boat shirt into a crop top. The high collar and long sleeves protect her shoulders and back from sunburn while the modification still lets air circulate and a little color on to her firm midriff. Paired with a black bikini bottom and a black fishing cap, it is definitely a fashion statement. Quo Vadis was one of two boats that left Salinas. There was a gringo on a resident boat about 30 yards away who ranted at us for operating the diesel engine. He yelled, over his barking onboard dogs, that the fumes would infect his recent and expensive throat surgery. The commercial fishing boats that chug in and out through this channel wouldn't? There are some strange characters afloat there.

When we made the next leg to windward into Puerto Patillas, a really funky little fishing town, there were no other cruising boats in the bay. There was one voyeur panga driver who kept racing out from the beach towards the anchored Quo Vadis while Mer showered and washed her hair in the welcome soft rains of the afternoon. The next morning we negotiated the bay-girdling reefs and made it around Punta Tuna (the southeast cape of Puerto Rico) without the wind generator tower blowing overboard or any other structural failures. Later that day, QV surfed a rolling wave through the gate in the breakwater at Palmas del Mar. This is a very un-funky upscale "Own your slip and condo" development built for really rich Puerto Ricans. We tried to eat at the fishermen's co-op on the beach but they had closed an hour early that day. Palmas del Mar is trying to look Mediterranean and prices things accordingly. The garish primary colors of newly built condos and shops give it away as Puerto Rican.

We left the crowded anchorage next morning in 30 knot winds and 6 ft. seas: the only boat weighing anchor. Shortly after we had passed beyond the rollers outside the breakwater, we heard a radio call from a larger cat still anchored inside. They wanted to know the conditions outside. I somewhat surprised myself by answering, "Tolerable." (Some may recall my personal "Stay Home!" numbers are 35 and 7.) Brave Mer saw no reason for concern.

"I expected it to be like this", she informed me. Maybe neither of us knows any better. I do know and recall vividly that for the first time since January, the wind came around to the Northeast the day we rounded Punta Tuna and wanted to head, yes, you guessed it: Northeast. The wind abated to about 20 knots while clocking around from the South and then piped right back up to the 30 we were getting used to. The computer-generated voice on the radio weather reports informed us it was *"Muy ventoso."* for over a week. That translates as "Very windy". We had already noticed.

We saw absolutely no other cruisers underway but had a dolphin escort for quite a while beyond the Palmas del Mar breakwater: my favorite good omen as we kept beating to the North.

Fajardo is a region of a half-dozen marinas and boatyards along Puerto Rico's Northeast coast. In discussions with the sporting types at the Ponce Y&F Club, Puerto del Rey was recommended as the best marina for easy entry and exit, considering the prevailing winds and tides. Despite its size (biggest in the Caribbean) and glitz, this was also the last chance for fuel, water, shoreside showers and provisioning until we didn't know when. The cruising guides were getting more than a little vague on these key items. Puerto del Rey also proved to be reasonably priced, surprisingly efficient and a long walk to an Amigo Supermarket (Their motto: "Here, you have an Amigo.") I shouldered the packs, trekked to the Amigo, and shopped while Mer did laundry at the marina. I don't <u>think</u> that's a sexist division of labor. The 100% cotton custom crop top that Mer had fashioned shrank in the wash. The shirt still protected her shoulders, back, and arms from sunburn, but now also provided teasing views of her firm, rounded breasts—from the bottom. This look was new to me and unexpectedly erotic. Always practical, she continued to wear that top when she had the helm.

Filled with fuel, water and as much food, wine and Coke as I could carry from the market, *Quo Vadis* sallied forth from the Puerto del Rey breakwater toward the Spanish Virgin Islands. I don't really know why they are called Spanish. Not owned by Spain since 1898 nor do they speak that language; only their personal version of Reefbreak. Happily, that is one of my favorite idioms.

Isla Palominos is the first of these Virgins but, observing the beach chairs and umbrellas implanted thereon, she didn't appear unviolated. We moved on and anchored about 30 yards off the beach at nearby Palominitos, going inside that island's reef. Mer did not want to leave. Ever. OK, we've got the glass-clear waters, white sand beach, the island to ourselves, a cluster of palm trees for shade, and reef break for background sound. She figured this was it. We were not going to find anything better. The boat was freshly provisioned. Why go anyplace else? She also persuaded me to anchor in 5 ft. depth so she could virtually walk ashore, 'though bouncing on tiptoes since she stands 5'2". There is minimal tide in this part of the Caribbean but it still looks strange to see substantial 37 ft.long hulls hanging just a foot and a half above a sandy bottom. With the water so clear, you wonder what's holding the boat up.

After a couple of days lying on our own island, snorkeling the reef and sharing some quiet moments, I manage to drag Mer off to Culebra, which is looming mistily on the horizon. After more heavy duty tacking to windward, we anchor in Bahia

Tamarindo by mid-afternoon, get wet on purpose, and kick back with sundowners. The only boat that had stopped briefly by our Palominitos beach recommended the adjacent islet of Culebrita for having the "Best Beach in the Caribbean". Happily, I have heard several beaches described this way by the local residents.

Next morning, as we turned through the opening in the reef north of Culebrita, we looked out on a sweeping arc of white sand backed by palms and tamarind without another boat or body in sight. For about 10 minutes. By the end of the afternoon, a dozen or so powerboats had arrived and their inhabitants started to par-tay in the P-R style. Boom boxes, rum drinks, coolers full of the local beer, shameless bodies that shouldn't ever be seen in swimsuits. We guessed the word had gotten out about this particular "Best Beach in the Caribbean". No complaints, though. The beautiful Mer and I coupled buoyantly in the warm, clear waters off Culebrita. I slipped our swim suits around my right ankle so not to lose them in the surf. She lay back floating; pulled the twin triangles of her bikini top aside to let her hard nipples point up toward the hot sun…and me.

Quo Vadis was on the hook in 7 feet about 50 yards off the beach. I seized the opportunity to get some of the more obvious growth off some of the more accessible parts of both hulls. The weeks in Ponce harbor had not been kind to QV's bottom. The result was still not wonderful but at least served to impress Mer with my industry during her cooling dips off the aft deck. Most of the red and green beards that had grown so quickly, ignoring the anti-foul paint, were gone when I quit.

The cruising guide was incomplete or inaccurate, or both, about clearing U.S. Customs for the British colonies. I worried about this like a responsible skipper until Mer suggested I phone the Customs office on Culebra and ask them. Brilliant! I punched in the number on my cell phone. "Hallo!" answered a voice with a noticeable PR accent. I inquired about the regulations for clearing out of this U.S. Commonwealth for the British colonies. "U.S. boat?" the voice asked. I confirmed it was; captained and crewed by passport-equipped U.S. citizens. "You keep going to the British Virgins and have a good time over there," he instructed. So we did.

Denizens of the Deep Surface Nearby

I hear whistling and chirping as we hit the open sea. QV is just emerging from the smaller islands clustered on the east side of Culebrita. The sounds are from dolphins so close that I first thought they were the bow waves; jumping as high as the 4-5 ft. seas. A few hours later, while crossing the Virgin Passage, a Boomer surfaces barely half a mile to starboard. That long aft deck with the 16 missile silos gives the sub away as to type. I figure it's headed for Roosevelt Roads, our main Naval facility in this part of the world, probably for shore leave. Mer doesn't really take much notice of this happening while I'm all goo-gaw and jumping around. "Trident sub off the starboard beam!" kind of stuff. It is completely surreal to see a big missile sub surface out at sea, especially from the deck of a 37 ft. sailboat. I check the fathometer and realize that 160 ft. is pretty shallow running for a Boomer… which may explain why it surfaced. It continues to plow away through breaking seas. It also gets me to wondering what the Navy uses Boomers for, now that we supposedly don't target the USSR. China? France? Watch out, Dub-ya! They've both got nukes!

We complete the Virgin Passage and tuck in to Santa Maria Bay on the north side of St. Thomas. This inlet is not identified in the charts or cruising guide as an anchorage so we are, yet again, doomed to be the only boat facing an idyllic white beach backed by high, jungled cliffs and very few houses. This being the U.S. however, I see paved roads connecting the scattered houses and street lights. Mer takes a break from the boat, swims to shore and chats with the one family spreading their picnic on the beach. We had no reason to go into any other USVI harbors or towns, most of which are on the south coast of St. Thomas and St. John. I have been told these places include many big cruise ships and the many people who ride on them.

We do follow the recommendation to clear British Customs on Jost Van Dyke, largely to avoid the hordes of charter boats at every other Port of Entry (POE). Learning another lesson in small degrees of error in navigation, I do not quite sail into White Bay but, having already dropped the sails, have to motor around the point to Great Harbour: the actual POE on Jost Van Dyke.

Another cat that seems to have made the same error beats me to the anchorage I had in mind, so I ask Mer to drive around to another spot while I get the anchor ready to drop. She complains all the while that this spot is too far from the beach (maybe 100 yards) and too near the dock and all that "loud honky-tonk music we'll have to listen to all night." After further explaining that the moorings she next wanted to take were private, I noted aloud that the music (actually fairly tasty to my ear) was streaming from Foxy's. This is one of the major ultra-cool destinations for both cruisers and charters in the Northern Caribbean. Founded and run by Foxy Callwood: composer, singer, restaurateur, boat builder and legendary host of the hand-built Wooden Boat Regatta. Sometimes, she just doesn't get it. Other times, I don't. She _is_ more into classical music.

Other Countries' Customs

We launched the dink and beached it in front of the Administration Building of Jost Van Dyke. We were, once again, the only visitors there. I like this condition. The British colonial logic (reminiscent of the Bahamas) allows a one year cruising permit for the boat (a bargain at US$15) but only 30 days on a personal visa. Jost Van

Dyke is small scale but, perhaps as a sign of the economic times, Mer and I were the only patrons at Wendell's World for a dinner on the beach. We shared a Greek salad. I have local red snapper in a creole sauce. Mer orders a chicken sandwich to save money. Her intentions are good but I philosophize that life doesn't last longer if you're abstemious. It just feels that way. The cost of a dinner ashore, even at resort prices, which Wendell definitely does not charge, gets lost in the rounding of the repairs at Ponce or any other boat work that I've experienced. A handful of locals in all skin colors stop by later in the evening to dance and drink Guinness. Foxy's is very quiet. He must be off the island.

I am surprised how much it freaks me out to see this strange type of human: Vacationing Tourist. It has been quite a while since I've seen any humans who weren't locals on islands or cruisers on boats. These new type of creatures mouth strange words and are slow, pudgy and pink. They are dressed inappropriately for anything. Or not dressed enough. They are creeping me out.

Dave mentioned something about charter boats when he was on board but did not warn me explicitly. They are anchorage accidents waiting to happen. Mer goes for a swim but I stay on board to fend off as charter boats beginning their 1-2 week odyssey motor in from the many Tortola bases. One such vessel is on its second lap around the bay looking for a mooring or some place to drop the hook. A guy is standing at the wheel yelling and getting red-faced while his wife looks both frantic and harried. She is holding a boat hook but she is standing on the aft deck. Three kids are running all over the boat, loudly ignoring the parents. I don't see anybody on the bow where the primary anchor is stowed on most boats, including this one. Bizarrely, an adult male in a Speedo is on the swim step putting on mask and fins to go snorkeling, as if all this had nothing to do with him. I doubt he was preparing to dive on the anchor since they hadn't yet found a spot to drop it. From recent observations, most people don't check the anchor set anyway unless it's their own boat, mainly because most bareboat charterers have limited experience anchoring. I cannot believe we were this inept when chartering with Jean-Paul in Guadeloupe.

We make a quick day sail across the channel to Cane Garden Bay. So far, this is the only time I've succumbed to a Jimmy Buffet song. "Things'll get better, at least that's what they say, as soon as we sail into Cane Garden Bay." Mer is handling the helm. She gets better, and better-looking, each day she's on board but she still has little regard for my planning, navigating or sailing. I've been cruising for 14 months now and avoided sinking or holing the boat, with no casualties. This does not impress her. Like most guys, regardless of age, I want to impress the girl without being too obvious about it. I'm not asking her to feel my biceps or silly stuff like that.

I had planned a two day sail down the Sir Francis Drake Channel from Cane Garden Bay to Virgin Gorda. Mer says we should do it in one day. We sail back to the Thatch Island Cut in about an hour; then turn into Sir Francis' Channel. It is immediately obvious why we had such a quick run to Little Thatch Island. The wind is pushing 30 knots at just 10 degrees south of our rhumbline course to Virgin Gorda. Norman, Peter, Salt, Cooper and Ginger Islands loom up as we tack toward them, consistently making 9 and 10 knots with apparent wind at 40 degrees. The same ilands fade into the haze as we tack back to the Northeast.

On one of these tacks, Mer asks, "Why are we meandering all over? Let's turn on the engine and go where we're supposed to go." The last time I was in these waters, I had promised myself I would come back and sail my own boat down the Sir Francis Drake Channel. That was more than 20 years ago. It has taken me that long to make this happen. I respond, "Mer, I've been planning on sailing here for a long time. Don't take the joy out of it." She turns and looks at me quizzically as her sky-blue eyes start to fill with tears. I didn't mean to make her cry. I move away from the wheel to hug her and hold her wet cheeks against my chest. We both gulp out words like "OK" and "Sorry" and keep sailing.

It is a long day from Cane Garden Bay to The Baths on Virgin Gorda. With windward beats and close-hauled pinching, it is too long by my current standards. My first injuries in a long time happen. A finger gets caught in the cleat as I shorten sail for easier tacks as the wind builds. A muscle gets pulled around the left rib cage from jerking on a sheet while being tense. They are painful but not crippling injuries. As I step up to bring down the mainsail, my red cap from the George Town Regatta blows overboard. We can see it floating not far astern but by the time we get the boat turned around, it is lost. I am impressed how quickly anything, even when you're focused on it, disappears at sea. It is a sobering lesson provided by one of my favorite caps.

After tacking past the anchorage, we fall back down to The Baths where I spot a public mooring still available. I'm told these are rarities late in the afternoon. Snagging a mooring is still not one of our best maneuvers whereas we have anchoring down pretty well, even in adverse conditions. Part of the challenge for me is you can't let the mooring ball go between the hulls and under the bridge deck or it will hit the drive leg. I finally jump overboard to rig a bridle around the buoy since there is no mooring line loop attached to it. Maybe that's why it was still available.

The Baths is a jumble of really big granite boulders tossed on to the beaches and in to the waters at the south end of Virgin Gorda. If you've seen a travel calendar of the Caribbean, you've probably seen the place. The snorkeling is surprisingly good, especially considering the level of tourist traffic this scenic site endures. The conditions build Mer's confidence so that she is soon free diving again. We take underwater snapshots of each other amidst the fishies and the staghorn coral. The afternoon we arrive, it is not crowded but there is a smallish black guy striking Greek statue poses high on a rock. He is completely naked. What, exactly, is his purpose? Mer gets out the binoculars for further inspection but alleges she can't see anything. Finally, around sunset, he put on some pants and went away. Still without a modeling contract, I'd wager.

Virgin Gorda Yacht Harbor is surprisingly fancy, modern and clean. When I use a credit card, I discover it is owned by Little Dix Bay Corp., a RockResort. I spread some US$ among the dock and yard hands, thinking I might be here for a while. It's not long before it adds up to more than a chicken sandwich. Speaking of which, the neatly manicured look of Virgin Gorda Y.H. is slightly compromised by the flocks of black and brown chickens free-ranging all over the place. Most of these roaming fowl are followed by small broods of 1-3 noisy chicks. Dozens of these chickens are nesting under the oleander bushes and pecking at the garbage while the nattily uniformed staff sweep, trim and water around them. Is there chicken on the menu at Little Dix Bay?

From Being Wet to Being on the Hard

The time with Meredith has been too short: just enough to get re-acquainted and not quite enough to get re-adjusted to life on my home. She takes me to dinner at the fancy café down the road from the yacht harbor. We eat outdoors amidst the rocks, waterfall, and tropical plants. We wear our Quo Vadis boat shirts as a private joke. This part of the BVI is one place you can get away with it. She has lobster and I have a whole baked fish. I still cannot get enough seafood. (Note to Bob and Linda. The "Island Cuisine" you were seeking on your vacation is, at best, today's fish which better be just caught, pigeon peas 'n' rice, peppers and fresh tomatoes, if available. On the Brit islands, they might try to feed you steamed formerly frozen vegetables and macaroni loaf. That's "Island Cuisine". Believe me. I've been eating in the Islands for months.)

I am torn as we hug and I wave farewell to Mer from the end of the Customs pier. The 0830 boat takes her away, toward Trellis Bay and the first of several flights back to D.C. Virgin Gorda is best sailed to or from. Otherwise, it involves the ferry, small plane, medium plane, big plane and all those opportunities for lost bags and missed connections. Plus a five minute walk to Quo Vadis at the dock. That's the least taxing leg of the journey

After a little persuasion, by 0930 that morning QV is in the slings of one of few lifts in the V.I. that can haul a cat. After the bottoms of the *amas* are sprayed down, it is pretty obvious my quart can of Pettit Ultima RS anti-fouling paint isn't going to make it for the needed touch-up. My Solomon's Island paint job lasted less than a year. Pamela, Queen of Yard Services, is now in sales mode (after previously telling me the boat couldn't be hauled for 3 days) and gives me an estimate for painting the bottom. I am beyond gasping at the price; so add the taping of new red boot stripes to the job.

Meanwhile, I serviced the engine drive leg completely; adhering strictly to the instructions of the owner's manual. I hope I did a good job of it. No matter how I prepare for it, there are still gallons of messy used lubricant. I prepare my home for a month-long lay-up and myself for a trip to California during this early part of hurricane season.

The next time we see Quo Vadis, it should have a spanking new blue bottom with fresh red stripes. You'll have to take my word, dirty fingernails, and the log records for the drive leg work. It looks just the same. When back in the water, QV will be prepared to sail for Anguilla, St.Martin, St. Barts and points South, goddess and Juracan permitting.

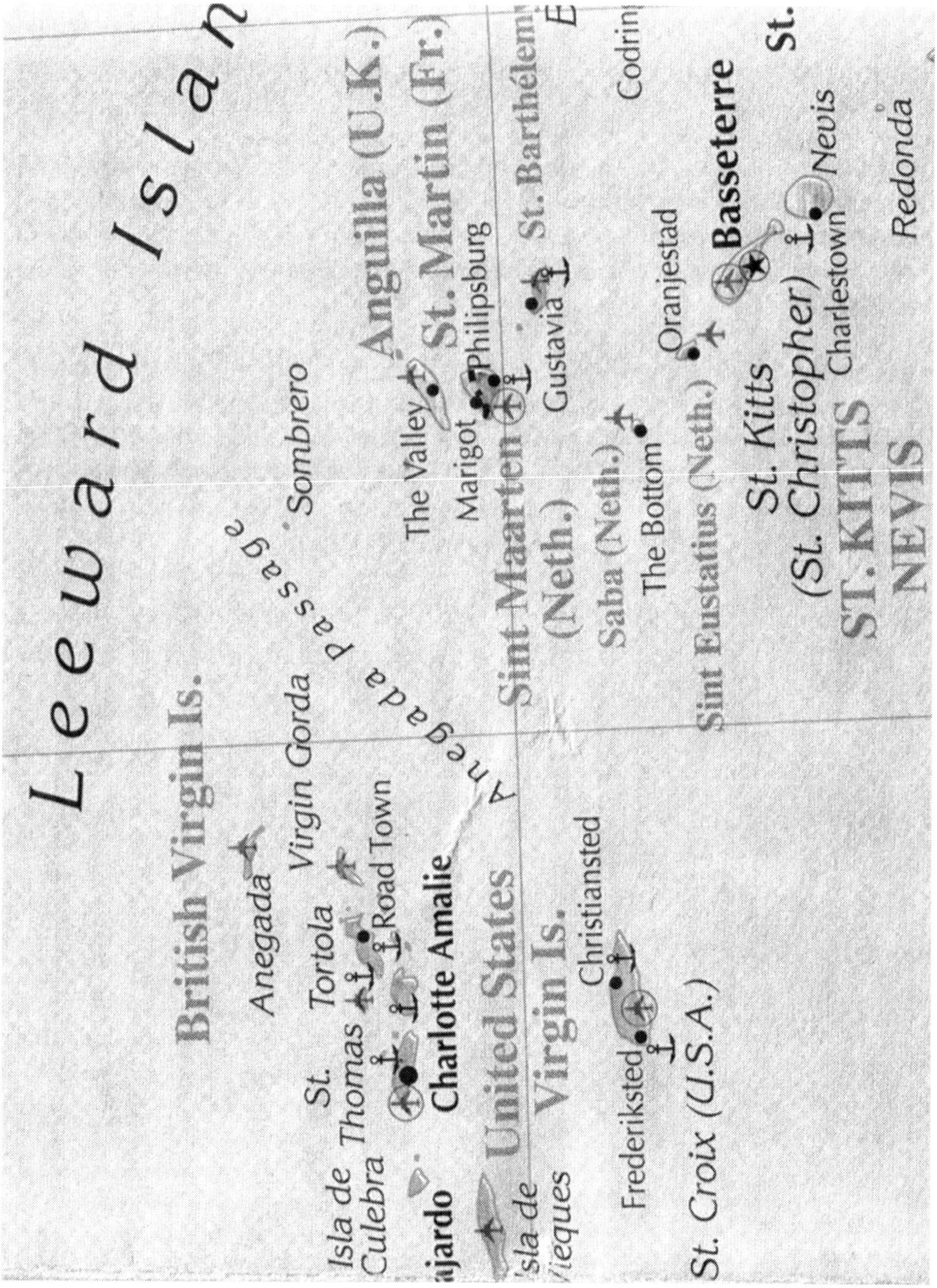
Leeward Islands
British Virgin Is.
Anegada
Virgin Gorda
Tortola
Road Town
St. Thomas
Charlotte Amalie
Isla de Culebra
United States Virgin Is.
Isla de Vieques
Christiansted
Frederiksted
St. Croix (U.S.A.)
Anegada Passage
Sombrero
Anguilla (U.K.)
The Valley
St. Martin (Fr.)
Marigot
Philipsburg
Sint Maarten (Neth.)
St. Barthélemy
Gustavia
Saba (Neth.)
The Bottom
Sint Eustatius (Neth.)
Oranjestad
St. Kitts (St. Christopher)
Basseterre
Nevis
Charlestown
ST. KITTS NEVIS
Redonda

Trying to Reason with Hurricane Season

Aboard S/V Quo Vadis, anchored Tamarind Bay, Nevis, West Indies

Hurricane Fabian missed us! Avoiding disaster is such a high. Russ and Lynsay flew out two days earlier to avoid being stuck, or hit, by this tropical storm. It turned out to be a bummer for all of us since, as it developed, the local weather was pretty decent. I indulged in a solo dinner celebration the day after Fabian went further North and hammered Bermuda. The brown egg omelette with Bayonne ham and Camembert was washed down with a bottle of the "Mis en boteille au chateau" good stuff, all acquired on St. Barth's.

We discovered the hurricane had formed during our passage from St.Martin>St. Barth's>St. Kitts. It was honking over 110 MPH and headed toward the Leeward Islands by the time we got there. The Port Authority guy said, "Leave. Get out of here. Go to Antigua." That island reportedly has better hurricane holes but was 50 miles further into Fabian's path. This same helpful fellow took only 21 of the 22 U.S. dollars he'd assessed Quo Vadis, even though the advertised fee for port entry is US$10. Alas, where does one find virtue? Or consistency? Are they both hobgoblins of small minds?

Forty-eight hours of sweat; then Caribbean weather gives Fabian's position: north of St. Kitts. Woo-hoo. Latitude 18 North and it's outta here! But, that still leaves me docked at this barely emerging marina at Basseterre, capital city of St. Christopher & Nevis, which together call themselves a country. The passage from St. Barth's was classic Caribbean cruising over cobalt blue 3-5 ft. seas with a Northeast wind. We were doing 8-9 knots; seeing over 10 knots surfing down the larger waves. QV never heeled more than 5 degrees.

After the misadventures of St. Barth's, we were initially headed for St. Eustatius (Statia); then decided to go directly to St. Kitts since we could already see it, as well. We thought this would buy more time to dive, explore, and all that fun stuff before Fabian made everybody's plans "contingent". No, actually, very screwed up. I was sorry to lose the company and skills of my fine crew but figured I could try to singlehand QV out of the prevailing storm tracks down to Montserrat and Guadeloupe in easy passages. More on that line of thought in a future episode.

Visiting France

No need to fly to Paris for fancy shopping. Most, if not all, of the big name shops are here and much more accessible than in Paris. At least, once you're ashore. The nice chef at Chez Domi stayed open by request to make us a late lunch. He was completely charming about the whole thing. I have this strange condition about having nice places in other countries to ourselves: I like it. It's sort of like having a private chef, because they'll whomp up pretty much anything to order, if it's available within walking distance. Russ observed, "Most sailors have a girl in every port. John has a favorite restaurant in every port." In my defense, not all ports result in a favorite restaurant and I'm a one-woman guy.

Brace yourselves! I also encountered nice and helpful French port officials. They were willing to speak English when my vocabulary failed me and were also the ones to inform us that the fuel dock was probably closed because the girl was on vacation. But maybe the auto-pump took a Visa card. At the dock, there are regular hours posted on the door of the pumphouse but no sign or explanation as to why it is closed. Nor is there any possibility of some one filling in for the girl since it's during the last two weeks of August when all French are vacationing. Even the locals apparently didn't have this information since the French guy, smoking while leaning on the fuel pump, called on his cell phone for somebody to bring him a Visa card.

The tiny harbor at St. Barth's is a water-filled square in the middle of town. The watery part is filled with double end-on-end moorings. I'd never encountered them before and, in fact, had only been on moorings 2-3 times, preferring to anchor out. Thanks to Russ' many days on dive boats, he is pretty good at snagging and securing mooring balls. Entering, leaving, or moored, your vessel is no more than a beam's width from the next string. I am pleasantly surprised we make it in and out without hitting anything. I'll bet there is a lot of multi-lingual yelling and cussing in there during the winter high season.

My sense is that St. Martin is a place you could stay and explore for a long time: under, in and off the water. Not at Simpson Bay which all boat folks hear about and most go to. But there is good snorkeling, good eating and several pretty cool anchorages. Some are fancy; some aren't. It was a very welcome landfall (and several hours later—anchorage) after a night crossing of the Anegada Passage from the Virgins. The women in the marketplace at Marigot were confiding that the season was slow and they were cutting their prices since there were no cruise ships visiting. There were apparent bargains in Caribbean art, including some interesting primitives I will probably regret not collecting. The eateries and galleries along the single road through Grande Case are mostly high quality with very little tacky tourist feel. I learn later it's where the locals go for dinner. The days spent in St. Martin are not regretted. It is a place to come back to. Maybe we'll even check out the Dutch side next time. This is, after all, the smallest property on Earth governed by two sovereign nations so the charter flights come in from both Paris and Amsterdam.

To France from the UK, not via the usual Channel

To get to this happy piece of France, Russ, Lynsay and Capitan Juan headed Quo Vadis out of the North Sound of Virgin Gorda, one of the dwindling number of British colonies, across the Anegada Passage. (It's called Sombrero Passage on some charts. The UK owns both islands, so what's the deal?) The boat's knotmeter log said 89nm under the amas. I'd estimated 90nm and a 15 hour passage time. Russ noted later he could have done without the last 3 (or was it 4?) hours which were a hard beat to windward. Russ and Lynsay had arrived only the day before from St. Thomas on the fast ferry so their first passage was a fairly harsh introduction to the Caribbean. We three had rendezvoused at Jeremy's cybercafé on the beach of Trellis Bay, Beef Island, BVI within minutes of the appointed time. All the crew had a large English breakfast. As it turned out, none of us eaten and it was mid-afternoon. Thank God, no bangers and mash. Just a big hug from Dorothy the cook after we'd polished off her yummy victuals. Then, a thankfully short dinghy ride out to Quo Vadis where I plugged in the new anchor light they'd brought me.

I had solo'd around the BVI a bit since Mer left, mainly to get the boat over to the airport. I'd always assumed everybody took the flight to Beef Island. I find I'm not that crazy about singlehanding, despite its virtues as extolled by some old salts. I prefer crew; even inexperienced crew if their attitude is good. Hey, if there's nobody to inflict my corny jokes on, point out the whales and dolphins to, or share a toast with, what's the point?

Anyway, I'd been back on Virgin Gorda for a few days getting Quo Vadis back in the water after its haulout, tanked up, provisioned and (hopefully) ready for a 10 day cruise with Russ and Lynsay. A couple more B.O.A.T. units had disappeared but the bottom paint job looked good and thick. I promised last year I'd never do it myself, again. Maybe this stuff will even stay on the bottoms of the *amas* longer than last time.

So, whilst I'm preparing for this passage in the Virgin Gorda Yacht Harbor, this 80 ft. Merritt sportfisher (Merritts are only custom-built in Pompano Beach, Fla.) guns up to the face dock, spins 180 degrees on its axis using all the thrusters; then rumbles sideways over to the dock. A crew of six ,wearing matching T-shirts stenciled with the boat name, scramble out carrying these wrist-thick black docklines and lash them down nice and secure. Then out wanders a guy who acts like a hired captain. He's wearing a faded baseball cap, smoking a cigarette, not doing much of anything. He's soon followed by a grizzled-looking gray-haired guy wearing a collared knit shirt with the boat name embroidered on it. (When I think about it later, he was probably my age.) Then come three young ladies, appearing to be Latinas between 18 and 26 years of age but, being Latina, they could be 12 to 20. One has on 4-inch spike heels that coordinate nicely with her barely butt-covering spaghetti strap minidress. Another one has on this yellow 2-piece sarong outfit with fluttering cloth tabs on the bra part. I'm not sure of the role of these flutter tabs, either for mating ritual or dressing for success, but they appear to be all the rage in the Caribbean this season.

Then emerges from the opaque, black-glassed, air conditioned interior of this vessel a man with brushed back white hair, smooth pink skin, and very thick prescription sunglasses. He is attired in a more expensive-looking, blinding white polo shirt with the boat name and something else stitched on it. His name, maybe? He is assisted on to the dock by the grizzled guy. He then places a hand on the bare, brown shoulder of the yellow-bra'd Latina as most of this entourage starts moving in a very measured fashion up the dock. I figure this is not a guy worried about cuts in Medicare—or the minimum wage. A couple of the T-shirted hands stay with the boat.

But he does care about property taxes. I cleverly deduce this because the hailing port gold-leafed on the stern of the 80-footer is just "George Town". I have become very peeved at snooty, mostly corporate-owned boats whose users choose a tax-preferred or tax-exempt hailing port and just expect everyone to know which country, province, state, or planet it's hailing from. Quo Vadis is proud to have "Alameda California" spelled out across the back of the engine compartment in stick-on letters expertly applied by Meredith back on the Chesapeake. Given, Quo Vadis has never been within 3000 miles of California but many people in the Caribbean are still not real sure where either place is. Please stay tuned. It gets worse.

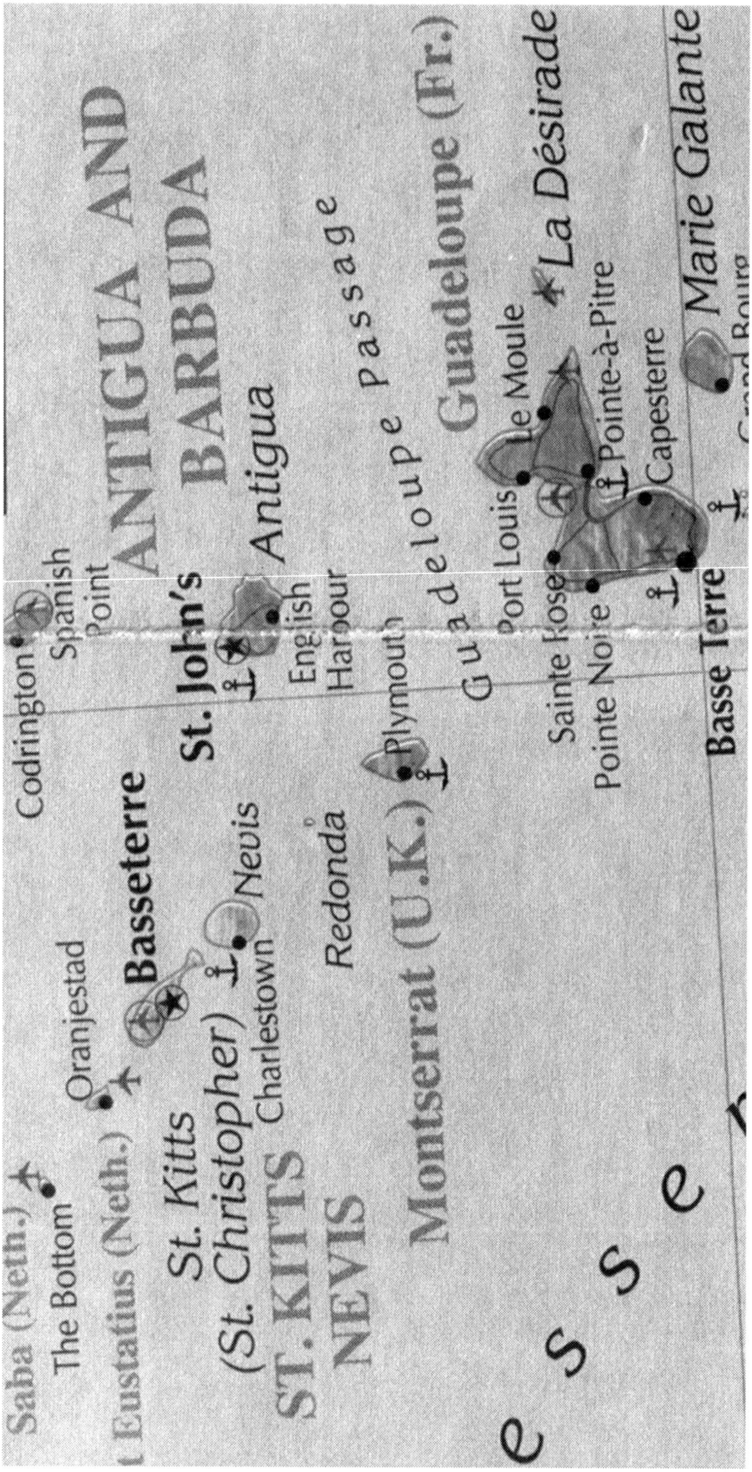

Saba (Neth.)
The Bottom
Eustatius (Neth.)
Oranjestad
Basseterre
St. Kitts
(St. Christopher)
ST. KITTS
NEVIS
Charlestown
Nevis
Redonda
Montserrat (U.K.)
Plymouth
Codrington
Spanish Point
ANTIGUA AND
BARBUDA
St. John's
Antigua
English Harbour
Guadeloupe Passage
Guadeloupe (Fr.)
Port Louis
Le Moule
La Désirade
Pointe-à-Pitre
Sainte Rose
Pointe Noire
Capesterre
Basse Terre
Marie Galante

Doing the Tropical Wave(s)

Aboard S/V Quo Vadis, docked Jolly Harbour, Antigua

A very large white egret lands just 20 ft. away, trying to escape the tropical downpour that is pouring down on shore, which is also where I am sitting. Just then, whirring across my field of vision comes a black hummingbird, about 3 inches long, sticking its beak in the colorful flora of Antigua. I note the contrast: 3 ft. white bird, 3 inch black bird; backgrounded by lush tropical vegetation. I further note that I've left the companionway hatch open on Quo Vadis.

It has been that kind of a month and it's not even done yet. We will try to keep this part of the story from degenerating into a tale of woe and see what nuggets of humor or knowledge can be extracted…but no promises!

For the minority of you not familiar with the terms, a tropical wave is the least threatening level of atmospheric disturbance in these parts. As it gets better organized (I hate that meteorologist's expression.), it may become a tropical depression, a tropical storm (winds 35-64) or a hurricane (winds 65-150). The Caribbean population on or near the water lives by the waves. As you have probably figured out by now, that includes most of it. So when the morning report includes the notice that a wave has become a depression, I figure it is time to head South of Latitude 16 N where these tropical waves don't usually organize into hurricanes. I also plan to boldly go where this man has never gone before: Nevis, Montserrat and Guadeloupe, solo.

With predicted favorable winds, I stage an easy 12nm down to the north end of Nevis on Saturday, planning to continue the 32nm to Montserrat on Sunday, Q-flag that volcano, and complete the last 37nm in time to clear French Customs before they close on Monday. Clever, no? As a final check before lifting anchor, I go under the boat to make sure everything's OK. I see the bloody, God-awful steering yoke on the engine drive leg is half-gone. This item had already been replaced last September. I ruefully conclude it <u>had</u> cracked entering the harbor at St. Kitts. This was not revealed by visual and tactile inspection and just fell off on the trip over to Nevis. So it begins.

Days of St. Kitts and Nevis

There is a boat-building company on St. Kitts which builds big 60-70 ft. custom catamarans. I figure they can fix this problem including ordering in the part from the UK. I put the dinghy back down, get the outboard on (which is a real pain single-handed) and buzz back into Charlestown: the only town on Nevis. I call the now-renamed Indigo Yachts and catch David in on a Saturday afternoon. He says bring Quo Vadis back to St. Kitts and he'll look at it Monday. The next morning, I head back to St. Kitts. During this return trip, the alternator belt shreds. So, I'm now reliant solely on wind and solar power. The batteries were, however, nearly full, as I had planned for the passage to Guadeloupe. There are no staff at the Port Zante docks of St. Kitts on Sunday.

I manage to raise a security guard on CH16 and alert her that I'm coming in to the docks. I ease up to the fairly high seawall and throw her a dockline. She drops it in the water. I retrieve the line and toss it again, only now she won't catch it because it's all wet and drippy. Ee-yew. Another guy who is just walking by dressed in his Sunday best catches the other line I toss, looking very surprised. I'm finally snubbed on a cleat but the boat is drifting gently toward a 90-degree angle to the dock face while the fat security guard watches placidly and the snappy dresser remains confused. I knot two lines together (Yes, I used a sheepshank, Meredith.), run the eye through a stern cleat and jump off the starboard bow clutching what I hope is sufficient length of line in my gloved hand. It is long enough and I pull Quo Vadis in to the dock. Pant, pant. All this is just getting back to where I left a couple of days ago. This is not exactly what I had in mind when I was shopping for a cruising catamaran—how many months ago?

Note for your files: In current and former British colonies, everything is closed on Sunday. I don't think you could get arrested. The constabulary would not be in 'til Monday. Which was the day David Risdale-Shaw came to inspect the damaged drive leg. Subsequent to phone conversations with the infamous Alan at Sonic (who seems to be the only person in the company or, at least, answering the phones), David declines to do the work with the boat in the water due to the risk of oil spill in the small harbor. The way Alan has explained the procedure, a spill seems possible.

"All right," I continue, "Damn the expense! Let's take it out at your boatyard."

He then informs me that he can't haul out a catamaran as small as Quo Vadis. I have a real problem grasping this as the problem of size usually goes the other way. Never-helpful Alan also won't ship the part unless he talks to me on the phone personally which I didn't find out til the next day because of the time zone difference. David recommends I go back to St. Martin and have the work done there. He knows some people. I'm reluctant to make a longish sail back North; then have to come back South again. The distance is about the same to Guadeloupe and I know the wily French can figure out how to haul a small catamaran with only a 16 ft. beam. After a lengthy, contentious, aggravating conversation, the result is that Alan of

Sonic officially advises against setting out for anywhere and David of the Boatyard won't do the repairs on St. Kitts. I decide to head South even as Hurricane Isabel moves North. I also arrange for payment and shipping of the fragile yet vital part to Guadeloupe where it should be waiting for me in 2-3 days. That was a mistake. Perhaps, you are thinking, another mistake.

Despite being the same country, St. Kitts and Nevis officials require separate clearances. I had already cleared out of Nevis for Montserrat, planned as the first overnight anchorage. Being back at St. Kitts for non-repair, I'm required to clear out again. So I do. As Russ and Lynsay will recall, this involves fairly expensive taxi rides down to the commercial docks. However, this time I am not charged entrance or clearance fees and get still another official-looking paper with rubber stamps on it. I had nearly made it out of the building when the young Customs guy came to the door and called me back. Uh -oh. What now? He said he could notify the St. Kitts Coast Guard of my situation. Maybe they could escort me as far as Redonda: a big rock jutting out of the sea about halfway to Montserrat. I am touched by what sounds like a good idea. Checking the track of Hurricane Isabel, it has gone beyond the Leeward Islands so it looked good to go in the morning.

I had spare alternator belts but the way the diesel is installed in the engine compartment, it takes a third hand to install the belt. As most boat owners know, this is not uncommon. A scary-looking Rasta Man came down from the boatyard: this was my third hand. He turned out to be a soft-spoken guy who did not overcharge; shook my hand as he left, and wished me good luck. I doubt I could have done that job by myself. I picked up a couple of moves watching him, though.

With the alternator now alternating and, presumably, the inverter inverting AC to DC, the battery voltages still were not coming back up. Something seemed amiss with the electrics but the batteries were full so I lashed the drive leg on with a section of 2" X 4" and some dockline. It was not really a great job but might keep the whole thing from plunging to the bottom if the rest of the yoke snapped. It was late in the day to make Montserrat, so I set a waypoint and course for an anchorage off Pinney's Beach, Nevis which is really just a "road" protected from easterly winds.

Days become Weeks

I clear Port Zante at very low engine RPM and turn into the wind for a mainsail raise. I have a double wrap of the mains'l halyard around the mast steps. As many of my crew will remember, that cannot be cleared from the helm or the base of the mast because of the lazy jacks. I'm also not totally clear of the area described on the chart as "Unmarked Obstacles". These cracked the drive leg coming in to this port the first time. I decided to set the staysail which worked OK except the luff had come unstitched. Considering its condition, it set pretty well. The alternator started charging normally; then the amperage ran away so I shut off the generating field. Hmm.

By 1630, the hook is set in a rippled white sand bottom about 200 meters off the palm-fringed beach with cloud-wrapped Mt. Nevis as background. I put a bridle on the anchor rode, like a good cat Cap'n, and untangled the main halyard from the mast steps. Current status report: 1) Steering yoke on the drive leg is half-gone, so that could fall off any time. 2) Probably will not get a battery start on the engine based on voltage readings. 3) Alternator charging does not appear to be an option. 4) Torn stays'l. 5) I cannot seem to get a clean raise of the mainsail singlehanded, ever.

Ironically, I'm anchored off the beach shared with the Four Seasons-Nevis. It is generally ranked as the #2 high end resort in the Caribbean. For $$$/night, folks staying there have avoided all the above-noted hassles but have the identical natural environment. Actually, the views from Quo Vadis were better. I replaced the batteries in the Garmin GPS12, thanks to Dave S. It tells me it is now only 31.7nm straight line to Montserrat. I am pretty tired after a frustrating 10 hour day.

The engine would not start the next morning; not even turn over. All battery voltages read around 10 volts which, even you non-electrical engineers can figure out, is not good for 12 volt batteries.

"But," I brightly remembered in the clear light of dawn, "I can hand crank the diesel to start it."

I opened the engine compartment and dug out the hand crank. It was right where I stowed it many months ago, thinking I'd never have to use the thing. The crank did not fit into the flywheel socket. If it had fit, its rotation would not clear the alternator belt pulley. There may be several mistakes compounding here. From 0700-1000 there was not enough wind to sail to I spent the hours going through all the compartments on the boat in search of a possible tool to turn the flywheel. It is, as Jeff H. will appreciate, strictly a dealer part. I tried different battery selections and start modes until about noon. By then, it was too late to reach Montserrat before dark.

The Days with Willett: Episode I

I dinghied ashore to make some calls. The cruising guide did not identify any support services on Nevis. Because it was right in front of me, I walked in to the Nevis Tourism Office. The guide said they were encouraging yachties. It didn't say to do what. The gal behind the counter contacted Reuel who arrived 5 minutes later to call Willett who was working on "The Government Ferry" but would be back about 1400. About 1600, I called Reuel. Everybody on Nevis uses VHF CH16 like it was a party line, which I guess it is. No Willett. About 1630, I jump overboard and swim around the boat, just like last week. Gee whiz! Nothing had changed. It was still broken or out of trim. The sunset is stunning.

Reuel came on CH16 about 0730 the next morning to let me know everything was set up with Willett. "Look for a red pickup on the beach around 0815 and come pick him up in the dinghy." Sure enough, a guy gets out of a red pickup truck not too far up the beach. I eagerly launch the dink and head in to make the first of what turn out to be many sloppy surf landings. A middle-aged white guy stares at me uncuriously. He is not Willett. I raise Reuel on CH16. He shows up on the beach. Then Willett shows up with his helper Bill, who doesn't seem to speak much English which doesn't matter because I can barely understand Willett. The latter stuffs some tools in his pockets and we go back out to Quo Vadis. They looked at the digital display like it was an alien TV; then read 10 volts directly off the engine start battery with a hand-held meter. He takes out the start battery to charge it and we make another crash landing in the beach surf but manage to save the battery. Willett's plan is to get the engine started with this battery, then let the alternator charge the house bank of batteries. I hope I have successfully fixed the alternator regulator and agree to pick up the freshly charged battery at 1030. By 1130, I have neither the weather update nor Willett with the battery, so I won't be going anywhere today. About 1215, I spot Willett waving to me from the beach. I retrieve him, we install the battery and the engine starts. Willett cheers out loud. Everything looks good initially, then all the voltages start dropping. Willett said a slow charge would take care of it and charged me US$150 for removing, charging, and installing one battery. He also recommended cleaning the battery terminals with bicarbonate of soda. The antacid I had in the medical kit didn't seem to cut it.

This time we land the dinghy on the beach in front of Sunshine's. This is another one of the Caribbean's cruiser destination beach bars known almost entirely for the owner's personality and attitude. Sunshine's also served the best island food I have eaten. Many of his clientele are folks who wander through the hedge from the Four Seasons resort next door because his food is a whole lot better and the drinks are a whole lot cheaper. I go back to Quo Vadis to re-start the engine for the slow charge and get water jugs to fill. The engine would not start.

Back at Sunshine's a few minutes later, surviving another of my surf landings, I called Willett. No answer. It turns out on Nevis you can only call cell phones with other cell phones; not land lines. One of Sunshine's many nephews calls on his cell phone. Everybody on Nevis seems to have a cell phone. Sometimes they hold them and stare at them wordlessly— is that true in all cultures?

Willett came back to the beach and we're back on board QV around 1630. He thinks now it's the alternator. No, that's not it. Maybe one of the house batteries is dead. "The battery store is closed today," he informs me. We agree to meet at 0800 the next day, get a new battery and see if it works. After delivering Willett and Bill the helper back to Sunshine's stretch of beach, I'm back on board before sunset. I feel like I've made more beach landings than a SEAL team; not all of them graceful. My shins also feel like it: they are bashed and bloody.

The Days with Willett: Episode II

The next morning, I again launch the dinghy and head in to meet Willett on the beach. (If this is getting tiresome reading about it, I promise you it was a lot more tiresome doing it.) I caught my left foot on the gunwale jumping out of the dink and ingloriously fell in the sandy surf. I then spent the next two hours riding around in Willett's amazing (that it's running) pickup while he does some errands. By the way, his pickup is red only in the sense that rust is often called red. I am soaking wet and have sand in my crotch but no working battery.

During our tour of Nevis, we go by Willett's workplace. This is demarcated by the hulks of partial engines and vehicles in the front yard of the two shacks he lives in: one is for sleeping; one is the kitchen. To one side is a sort of cage made of a wrought iron gate or two; some pipes and wires. Inside the cage are piles of things that may be tools or parts. He mutters some instructions to his mate who is as plump and large as he is skinny and small. She appears, briefly, from Shack #1 with documents which he hands to me. "This is who I am," he boasts. "Everybody know Willett." The first document is a laminated license of a marine chief engineer issued by St. Vincent & The Grenadines. The second is a safety and first aid course certification jointly issued by the U.S. and British Virgin Islands. The last document in the stack is a certificate for 5 shares in the Nevis Credit Union. She has obviously interpreted his request as showing me all of his official stuff. Now, it's official.

We do eventually find a marine gel cell battery at Nevis Tyre & Hardware. Willett had announced that he wanted a battery for a boat. It is much smaller than the 4D types purchased from West Marine, has no listed amp-hour rating and the clerk is clueless. She observes that it says 950 CCA on the label. Willett has a new helper today named Anastasio. He really doesn't speak any English; only Spanish. I can actually understand him better.

With the new battery installed, the engine starts in all possible battery combination settings and all the voltages level out above 12. It was noon by the time I took Willett and Anastasio back to Sunshine's beach, one more time. Willett wanted US$60 more plus something for Reuel. I had left exactly one US $50 bill, so that's what he got. I also bought us both a beer, using EC$, which seemed to cheer him up considerably, not least because we were drinking them together.

"See, a white man like you can have a beer with a little black man like Willett," he proclaims.

I hadn't really thought about it that way but it was a reminder how up front almost everybody is about race in the Islands. A lot of the frankness is racist, by both blacks and whites, but I find it refreshing that it's very up front. There is none of the hypocrisy or discomfort that are often part of race relations in the U.S. The relationships get especially interesting to an outsider, like me, when there are former slave and owner families on these small islands living literally side-by-side; even inter-marrying. The social structure is sharp and obvious and nobody tries to hide it.

It was, once again, too late to make Montserrat by daylight; so I indulged in a longish lobster lunch at Sunshine's. I'm not feeling particularly leisurely, though, after spending over US$400 just to get a substandard battery replacement. Grousing about this situation as I'm eating lobster on Pinney's Beach, listening to some blues while drinking Carib beer does, however, strike me as a small-minded reaction to my circumstances, both at the time and in retrospect.

Wind and Waves or…No Wind

Hurricane Isabel is now a Category 5 storm. This is the maximum rating: winds 150 MPH and higher. Although it has gone north of Nevis, her effects are wide ranging: out to 350nm from the eye of the storm. It is suggested to me that I wait as the seas in island crossings are predicted to be 12 ft. while retaining the frequency of Caribbean chop. Isabel's counter-clockwise sweep brings the winds around to the West by morning and the sea state starts to build.

I decide to move to the only local bay with westerly protection, back at St. Kitts. To save time, I leave the dink in the water, adding a safety line. I have the anchor up just before 1000 and estimate about an hour for the 6 nm across The Narrows back to the protected South end of St. Kitts. Quo Vadis went over a nice clear sand patch in a sheltered corner of Majors Bay. I got the hook on to it, put out lots of anchor line and had the bridle on by 1110. Submerged in the middle of this nice sandy bottom was a very large concrete polygon. It looked like something left over from an old James Bond film. As I've anchored way down wind of this strange structure, we should keep well clear.

The first squall came raging over from the West at 1120 featuring 40 knot gusts and bouncy chop. I re-opened the hatches after the rain and peered into the temporarily calm waters to see Quo Vadis floating directly over the mystery polygon; the skegs clear it by inches and the anchor line is casually draped around one corner. Just as I decided to move, I looked up and saw the next squall bearing down.

I got the anchor up and gingerly moved Quo Vadis to another sand patch. Some small increment of tide and calm water kept us from being stuck on top of this concrete platform or alien landing pad or whatever it was. I dropped the hook again in the between-storms calm. Since there was no wind to set the anchor, I backed down gently at low engine RPM. The dinghy painter with the floats installed on it just so it wouldn't get caught in the prop wrapped up in the prop. With a quick shift into neutral, I was back on the foredeck; set the hook by hand and finished rigging the bridle just as the next squall hit. After it passed, I put on a mask and snorkel to go under and clear the tangled prop. While it had scoured some of the black protective coating off the prop, the painter itself was remarkably undamaged. I looked up to check the drive leg. It had popped out of the locked position, though still hanging by the pin. I grabbed the bottom of the leg and pushed it forward until the lock caught. I saw no further cracking but then I missed the crack the first time, didn't I? While I was salty wet, I paddled out and shoved the anchor a few more inches into the sand.

The squalls continued with 40 knot winds on their leading edges. The Carib weather report was not just the small craft warning, as usual. It was: Small craft and sailors stay in port! The anchor held as the wind clocked West; then Southwest until there were breaking seas in the Bay—for the next two days. A small sloop came in and anchored directly in front, upwind. The boat bucked wildly in the chop and looked supremely uncomfortable for the young couple aboard. I guess wherever they had been was worse but that small boat sure bounced around a bunch. That may be more tolerable when you are a couple in your 20s.

On day three of the refuge from Isabel's effects, the winds return to sort of normal direction and speed. I have the boat prepped and ready for Montserrat by 0630. But forgot to bring the dink up and get the outboard stowed. Uh-oh. So I cleared the point by 0700, motoring along at 2000 RPM. I managed to set the mainsail in a satisfactory manner, so maybe I am learning something, but was hearing some strange mechanical sounds. I looked through the inspection port in the aft deck to see, two inches above the coursing waters of the blue Caribbean, the remaining half of the steering yoke vibrating half off its pin. One possible interpretation: just as clockwise prop rotation (forward) pulls the boat to starboard, the same effect pushes the yoke that same direction if there's no balancing force, or restraining arm, on the other side. I could not see from the deck if the rest of the piece had broken through.

Somewhere in here, I got the genoa unfurled and started sailing to miss the westward bulge of Nevis. The wind was back to southeast with the rhumbline to Montserrat 145 degrees as I cleared the southern coast of Nevis. Hey, this is supposed to be a sailboat. So let's tack. The winds were light (9-15 knots) which was OK for solo sailing but didn't allow for any pinching back to course. I did this for another two hours during which the big rock Redonda and the small island of Montserrat became defined above the morning haze. Then the wind dropped to 4-5 knots which leaves Quo Vadis fairly dead in the water. I also did not have confidence the drive leg would stay attached. I tried vise grips but the jaw aperture was too small. I thought of C-clamps but did not have any on board big enough to go around the yoke: about six inches. At 1130 I was 31.5 nm from Montserrat but only making 4 kts with the chart telling me I had half a knot of current coming at me. I calculated that I would still be 5-7 nm short of the one and only northern Montserrat anchorage before nightfall so turned back to Charlestown to get bigger C-clamps…or baling wire. I already knew chewing gum was out of the question for this particular fix.

Approaching Nevis from the South (This, at least, was something different.), I decided it was better to go into the harbor, turning up into the southeast wind to drop anchor without using the engine. I turned downwind and furled the genoa; brought QV back up with mainsail only at much reduced speed. I couldn't hold it so let out some staysail. This gave better balance but barely kept headway at 1.5-2 knots. I worked Quo Vadis through the harbor moorings into a 10 ft. depth. The staysail furler chose this moment to jam. I dropped the main and went to the windlass, letting the hook go as forward motion stopped. It felt like a good hold so I rigged the bridle. And it was only 1230! What an exciting morning. Between the exertion and the anxiety, I had drunk all four of my water bottles by noon and still hadn't peed.

The Days with Willett: Episode III

By the time I'd put the dink and motor down, found a working ATM in Charlestown, and walked back up to Willett's, it was 1430. I had been warned to have him do any work before he started in drinking. He was fairly loaded and belligerent this afternoon though, admittedly, I did rouse him from his siesta. In a pile that consisted mostly of welding gear, there was a big C-clamp. I wasn't sure if the foot of the clamp was bigger than the pin holding the steering yoke, so asked them to find a larger diameter washer to weld on to it. Willett decides Bill should weld the washer to the C-clamp. Willett then wanders off mumbling about all the work he has to do. Bill (We're conversing in Spanish now.) holds a shard of green glass in front of one eye, squints the other eye shut and tack welds the washer. I hadn't been sure' til now there was a welding machine in that pile. I also grab some insurance baling wire to twist around the clamp so maybe it won't back off from the engine vibration and wave action.

Willett is mellowing a bit now. He says to pay him whatever I want for the C-clamp. I have EC$40 (about US$16) figuring that's what a new C-clamp would cost if the hardware store had one. Willet then takes the two 20s and hands one to Bill who looks very surprised. On the road back to the harbor, I stop for ice, limes and beer. The checkout girl at Friendly Market will not let me slide for 6 cents EC (two cents US) so I put a lime back. I have the dink back up, outboard secured and deck fairly squared away by 1700.

I hope I'm not seeing smoke and ash from the Montserrat volcano creating this red sunset but that's just what it looks like. On a personal note, this is the first place since Florida where I've been panhandled, hustled and felt ripped off. The residual Brits have been unhelpful to the point of physical endangerment. I'm confident there are solutions I haven't been offered or figured out. There were a very few good guys.

The newly modified and installed C-clamp did not fall off overnight. I clear Charlestown harbor on a fairly clear morning over a long swell on a heading of 135 to Montserrat. After setting sail, I could only hold 190 on a southerly tack and 90 on the easterly tack. I continued this until ending up in a field of fishtrap floats in 100 ft. at 1230. I had progressed only 12nm toward Little Bay, Montserrat on this beat to windward. I confirmed the C-clamp was still in place, turned the engine on and pointed QV toward Little Bay. At 2000 RPM, there was no movement of the drive leg yoke. I edged up to 2500 RPM, hoping it wouldn't fall off. It didn't and I'm so grateful because I can't think of any more clever things to do. The boat starts taking a pounding even though I'm steering across the swell.

After spending hours getting past Redonda, I spot a naval ship apparently anchored directly over my waypoint at Montserrat. Even weirder, it then disappeared. It's been a strange couple of weeks but now I'm a little freaked. For the next 10 minutes, this ship is gone. I'm beginning to think it's an illusion until a sun shaft hits the area. When not frontally illuminated, that vessel is painted to disappear. I cross the waypoint with enough offset to miss HMS Manchester, which is a heavily antennaed British frigate or something similar, at 1655. The hook drops into 18 ft. and moderate swell in Little Bay, Montserrat. The volcano is not erupting tonight.

All the cruising guides describe Montserrat as desolate, destroyed, forsaken; even mournful. Well, this evening it's a pretty busy place. One of Her Majesty's warships lies at anchor at the entrance; there's the current version of a Caribbean tramp steamer at the dock. This boat is later hooted out of that position by the ultra-modern high speed ferry from Guadeloupe which comes in to unload people and provisions. A tanker came up and anchored out just before dark; then put on its red Hazardous Materials lights. And Quo Vadis rests at anchor with the Q-flag up and anchor light on by 1800. After dark, HMS Manchester lights up like a fancy passenger cruise ship for the rest of the night. I consider diverting to Antigua instead of beating down to Guadeloupe.

Just after first light, I'm awakened by the sound of voices just outside the starboard portholes. They sound just a few yards away. The dock, beach and other ships were about two hundred yards off when I went to sleep last night. I poke my head out to see what appears to be the Montserrat Morning Swimming Society bobbing in the bay outside the shore break; just a few yards away from Quo Vadis. Their number varies from 6 to10 over a half hour of immersion, about equal in male and female members. In normal tones of voice, they discuss their plans for the day, exchange greetings and make the usual sort of neighborly conversation floating and paddling into the morning swell in the shadow of the cliffs. I wave "Hello" but only one guy waves back. The others are engrossed in news of the day. The bemused white sailor is probably not as interesting.

The wind has come East to 110-120, making the run to Antigua less attractive. The heading to Guadeloupe was not much better at 156 magnetic and 48 nm to windward. Contrary to conventional practice, I head out around the North end of Montserrat to test the conditions on the windward side. I wave to the only two guys visible on the deck of the Manchester. One is shirtless; the other has added a knit watch cap to his kit. Neither seem to be standing watch. They wave back. I imagine the rest are below having morning tea as the now-you-see-it, now-you-don't warship swings on one anchor off Montserrat, just like QV had.

After clearing the Northwest bluff, Antigua looked attractively closer as I could, for sure, make the passage in daylight. Also, just getting to Deshaies, the northernmost port on Guadeloupe, would not get the drive leg fixed. Antigua has haulout facilities. I could not hold a course of 80 degrees to English Harbour, as planned, so fell off to make Jolly Harbour on the west side of Antigua. It turned out to be a fairly rapid crossing as QV got close enough to the waypoint for me to pick up the outer marker by 1130. I rigged docklines and fenders on both sides while the boat sort of steered itself around. The cruising guide said to use Channel 16. This produced no response after several calls. A helpful soul came up on 16 to say Antigua monitors Channel 68. Still no response from Jolly Harbour on 68. Quo Vadis was moving along at over 8 knots toward a waypoint just north of Irish Reef, so I thought I better slow things down. I furled the genoa nearly dead downwind. I was so inspired by this success, I tried it with the main but the battens got caught. I heaved to and stalled the boat, now in much shallower water; got the engine started, the main under control and put new batteries in the handheld VHF radio. It was pretty busy onboard for a while; definitely for this new single-hander. I did raise Jolly Harbour with fresh batts in the handheld VHF. The response was very helpful. Leslie met me in the channel in a guide boat. With no directional control from the engine drive leg, I managed a smooth starboard docking as William and Leslie took the docklines I tossed them. What nice guys, huh? I heard "Welcome to Antigua." It was just after noon.

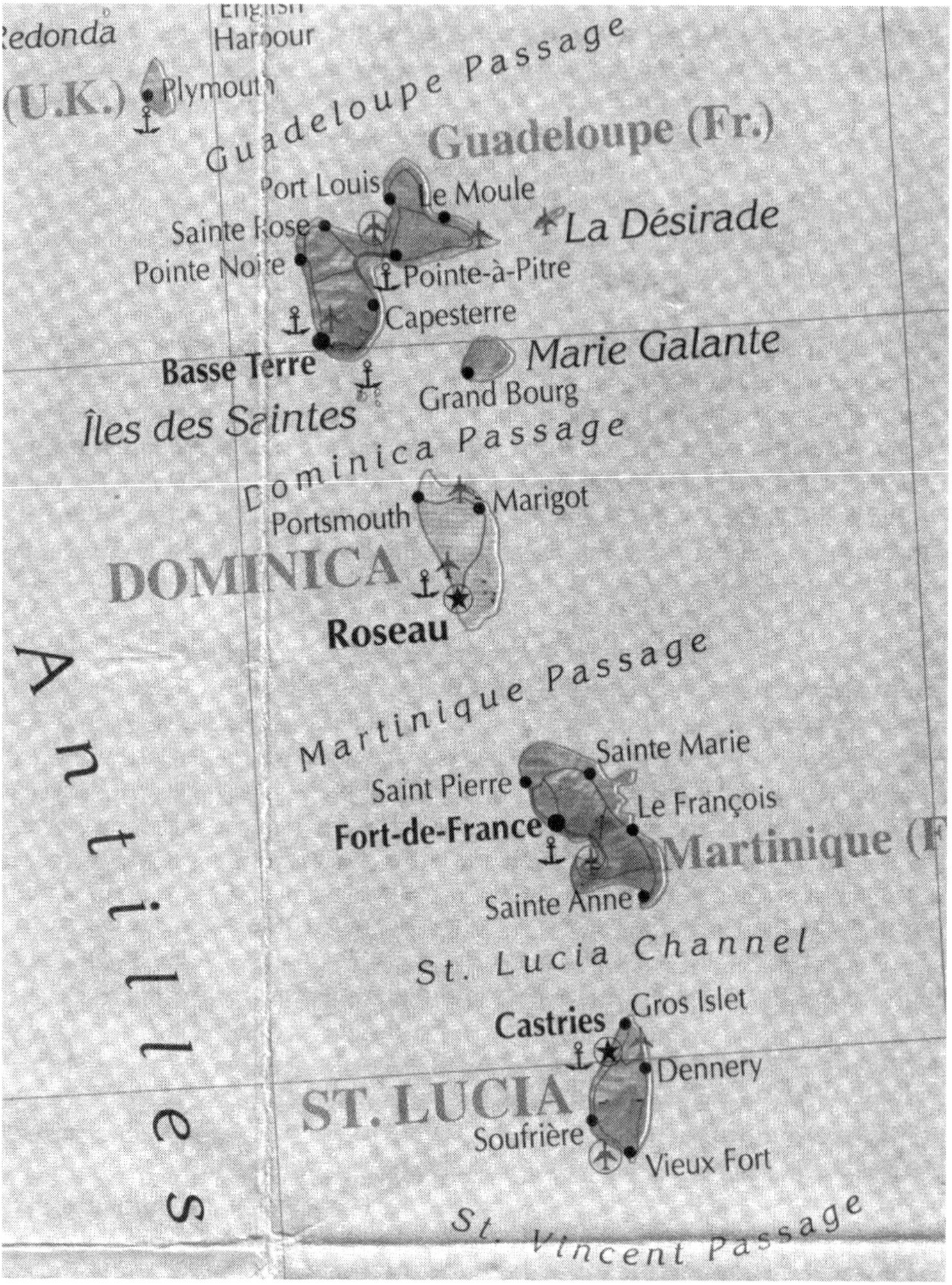
Redonda
English Harbour
(U.K.)
Plymouth
Guadeloupe Passage
Guadeloupe (Fr.)
Port Louis
Le Moule
Sainte Rose
La Désirade
Pointe Noire
Pointe-à-Pitre
Capesterre
Basse Terre
Marie Galante
Grand Bourg
Îles des Saintes
Dominica Passage
Portsmouth
Marigot
DOMINICA
Roseau
Martinique Passage
Sainte Marie
Saint Pierre
Le François
Fort-de-France
Martinique (F
Sainte Anne
St. Lucia Channel
Gros Islet
Castries
Dennery
ST. LUCIA
Soufrière
Vieux Fort
Antilles
St. Vincent Passage

Single-handing the Leewards, the Windwards and Onwards

Aboard S/V Quo Vadis, docked Rodney Bay, St. Lucia; anchored Salt Whistle Bay, Mayreau

Most of my friends on shore know I don't even like eating alone. I prefer candlelight dinners for two, Chinese banquets for many, and grilling feasts for friends and family. Imagine then how much I like single-handing this catamaran with fractured out-drive through the reefs and across the choppy channels of the Caribbean.

I do not embrace the motto of the Air Force recon pilot: "Alone, unarmed and unafraid." I never wanted to be a recon pilot; especially the alone and unarmed parts. I'm not so much afraid as in a sustained state of anxiety. What if something breaks that I can't fix? What if I fall down and can't get up? Not a healthy state of mind.

I am well outside my comfort zone and into the realm of stuff I didn't think I could do, like sewing. I sewed up a torn batten pocket on the mainsail. I sewed up the ragged and fraying U.S. ensign, feeling like Betsy Ross without the patriotic encouragement. There I sat in the tropical sun emptying my sail repair kit with the big curved needle, clad in naught but faded cut-offs. (Hey, I'm in France. I could be naked.) I also have on Ben Franklin-style glasses so I can see to thread the damn thing; then poking thread through fabric. I cover the stitches in cloth tape so nobody can see how bad it looks. How long will this last? I realize just because I whine and complain (without benefit of audience) that doesn't mean things are going to stop breaking. Right now, they are breaking at just the rate that I have the capacity to fix, which means I'm not making much progress.

Before I forget (most likely) or drown (less likely), let the logs show that I've singlehanded Quo Vadis from St.Kitts to Nevis (and back and forth a couple of times) to Montserrat to Antigua to Guadeloupe to the Iles des Saintes to Dominica to Martinique to St. Lucia to St. Vincent to Becquia to Mayreau—way down in the Grenadines. These are mostly fun places and the French ones have great food and wine. People pay real money to come here on vacation. I'm paying for fuel and boat expenses and still can't attract crew. Oh, yeah. Almost everything on board is working now. Really.

A lesson I have learned on these Caribbean passages but, sadly, have not fully internalized and implemented is: Start half an hour earlier. Making an ocean passage? Start half an hour earlier. Have to work on the engine? Start half an hour earlier. Launching the dinghy to motor ashore? Start half an hour… Well, you get it.

Although docked in this shallow, dirty water, former mosquito bog marina in Jolly Harbour, I've seen sea turtles, a school of fluorescent-striped needle-nosed fish swimming under the hulls, and wonderfully marked pelicans diving within a few feet of the boat for fish they're willing to eat. When these big birds hit the water, it sounds like somebody fell overboard which always startles me to attention. Kuh-sploosh!

After a week or so of saying "Hello" or "Good morning." I introduce myself to Bob and Linda Sikorski. Their Beneteau 50 50 Ways is at the next dock. After he invited me aboard to test some of his Antiguan rum, Bob said he'd been wondering if I were anti-social or preferred to be reclusive; he'd seen that before in single-handing cruisers. I informed him I had no such intentions and didn't realize I'd given that impression. Back on Long Island, in the Bahamas, Edith Cartwright characterized me as "The Quiet One" among the cruising skippers. At Red Shank Cay in the Exumas, I was referred to by the long time residents of that floating colony as One of the Two Skinny Guys. I doubt any of my friends on shore would describe me in either of these ways. Am I undergoing some type of transformation? I can't tell objectively if there's been a personal sea change, but I have figured out some things I don't want to be.

Life lessons and local observations

I don't want to be a 61 year-old ex-Captain with injuries; working on somebody else's boat. I don't want to sit in the cockpit of a used-looking boat and get drunk most afternoons. I don't want to be one of those ex-patriates who blatantly don't fit into a post-colonial island society but probably couldn't make it back in the home country. I don't know how to be one of those rascals who scam their way around the islands one clearance ahead of the customs man, though they do seem to get the hard body babes on board. And, surprisingly, I don't want to be one of those guys attended by a full-time staff who drive him around to various places on a boat so big it requires that staff to operate it. Such boats are usually listed as the assets of a Delaware corporation and registered someplace like the Cayman Islands where there's no property tax. All these are observed examples and all, it seems to me, pitiful in their own ways.

Bob Sikorski, skipper of 50 Ways, had made other accommodations in his life. Bob is an interesting guy. He did two tours as a Marine in Vietnam. He was up in I Corps, Khe Sanh; all that bad stuff. He turned down Captain's bars and a third tour ("Told 'em to go rotate on it.") He came back to California, saw the ad in the back of the magazine and used his G.I. bill to become a commercial diver. He worked that trade for 17 years which, as I understand it, is about two lifetimes in that line of work. He now lives and sails in Antigua with his wife Linda. Our conversations eventually get to my reason for being in Antigua: repairs to Quo Vadis.

He advised me not to let any local labor even start work on the boat until I figured out what the problem is and how to fix it, so I can explain in detail. "This is a Third World country," he observes correctly. This resonates when I see $50/hr Antiguan "helpers" trying to tighten steering nuts on Quo Vadis with my pliers. I advise them to use a socket wrench. They ignore this advice, so I tell them to stop work. Similarly, most of the work done in Puerto Rico has proven worthless with the notable exception of Fraito's re-sewing of the Genoa and Raul's welding up the wind generator tower. The other Latino labor clichés proved all too true in my case. Sorry, guys, but you got my B.O.A.T. units and I don't have working stuff on board.

I also realized after two weeks at Jolly Harbour that I am in sorry shape physically and mentally. I have cuts in the tips of my fingers from boat work. This means all acids (citric, acetic, hydrochloric) that I deal with burn them. My knees are scraped and seem to always be bloody. I think this is from the fiberglass ridges on the rigid bottom of the dinghy. I put pads on my knees, as working from the dinghy under the aft deck must continue. The pads fall off from sweat and saltwater so I find bloody kneeprints all over the deck. This is not exactly the Shroud of Turin but it hurts. It's nearly two months since I've had crew or companionship. Mer informs me she won't be joining me in Guadeloupe, even if I do get there. Each article I read about transiting the Panama Canal is more discouraging. And…the CD player broke! My morale is not good.

Contributing to my poor morale is the continuing frustration of trying to get another steering yoke to replace the one that has snapped in two. Carl thinks there is one like it on a boat that has been sitting on the hard for about a year. I drive up the hill to check it out with one of his yard guys, Joel, who I think is a relative. It is the same drive leg installed on an even older Prout. Carl tries to get the owner to sell it. The owner contends he's going to get his boat fixed someday. I wager any amount this is not going to happen. It probably still hasn't. Sonic is once again officious and difficult to deal with and for some reason won't send a replacement part to A-1 Marine despite Carl's superb reputation for integrity and boatwork. I get on the phone again, allow Sonic to charge me still more money and the part finally arrives. I had not planned on the EC$ amount it takes for Carl to move the part through customs. But at least he knows where the money needs to be applied to make it happen. The Harbour has a Travelift that will take the beam on Quo Vadis. I schedule the lift for first out and last "splash" of the day. I get Carl's guys scheduled and we start.

Done in One Day, then on to France

After I get the boat chocked up at Carl's, I discover Joel has not even started priming and painting the newly ransomed steering yoke, so I do.

In what comes to be hailed as an all-time "first" at the Jolly Harbour boatyard, we manage to lift QV out of the water, repair the drive leg and put the boat back in the water in one work-day. Which means 15 minutes before the Travelift guy quits for the day at 1700. The tales of my wondrous feat circulate on the Jolly Harbour docks. So the legend grows.

During my last visit to California, Dimitri told me I should look up a sailing pal of his when I reach Antigua. Paul Eldridge is Australian-born but has been crewing on boats in the Caribbean for years. He recently married a Brazilian girl, bought a house, fathered a baby with her and became a principal in Tend-aloft, a rigging company. So he's going through some serious life passages, which most of us can relate to from experience. We met for a beer (of course) at Nelson's Dockyard, the original 18th century British base on the other side of the island. He asks how our mutual friend is doing and I observe that he hasn't showed up to crew, despite our previous discussions and my current pleas.

"Of course not," explains Paul with Aussie directness. "He's already done this on boats bigger and nicer than yours." I am thick-headed but the lightbulb finally starts to glow faintly. I'm still dealing with the boat's mechanical repairs, but engage him to check QV's rigging even though I don't think there's anything wrong with it. I mention this to one of the Jolly Harbour residents who confirms these guys are the only serious riggers on the island.

"Right," I'm informed. "Tend-aloft is Big Pete, Little Pete and Paul the Aussie." I never meet the Petes. I also learn their focus has shifted drastically from cruisers like me to the big charter boats.

Boat repair is much like medical practice. If it's your specialty, you'll find something that needs to be fixed. Paul persuades me the hardware of the jury rig staysail connection should be replaced with the "proper" gear, though it has worked fine since the Exumas. However, the specified item is not in the inventory on Antigua, so also needs to be ordered. Some days later, he and Silas arrive to go up the mast. The staysail headstay gets fixed, Paul certifies that my rig is in "fair condition"; we hear a rumble in the distance. He climbs down, muttering about lightning, and comes up with a bill for US$300 plus parts. I hand him an equivalent stack of EC$ which he proceeds to count one by one. This has been a case where each of us thinks he's doing the other guy a favor.

In mid-October, I settle my other Jolly Harbour accounts and head south to Guadeloupe, still solo.

It took 10.5 hours to cross the Antigua and Guadeloupe Channels to the anchorage off Deshaies, Guadeloupe. The passage was a bit much for me and not always pretty. Winds are tough and the currents were 1-2 kts against. But it was done and I'm not injured; just very sore. I can finally tack that big genoa single-handed with acceptable results. "Helm's a'lee!" I announce to nobody on board. I also don't see any passages down the chain of islands that will be longer. Most of them look to be 5-6 hours—or so I hope.

When I was chartering with Jean-Paul around Guadeloupe three years ago, we sailed as far north as Deshaies and took on water at L'Amer Yacht Services. (It is largely J-P's fault I'm out here. He got me hooked.) They offer a hose from shore tethered to an offshore float. The cruising guide describes it as a horseshoe. It's actually the horns of a Brahma bull that can't get its head above water—or a Creole devil sign. Something like that. L'Amer charges FF100=Euros20=US$24 just to open the tap, no matter the amount of water taken. As Jean-Paul observed back then, "That's a lot for some few liters of rainwater." I made it a point not to use it this time. My tanks are full, Monsieur FF100!

French Customs and other Strange Practices

The names of the sports teams, or gangs (Hard to tell which on most of the English-speaking islands.) are great. "Extreme Action Skull Bandits" have a logo featuring the "Death from Above" lightning skull of Vietnam days with cross bones added which give it a sort of pirate look. The "Sex Street Party Soldiers" had no evident logo on their fluorescent green T-shirts. I regret not writing down more of the other names; now forgotten.

One of the main reasons to put in to quaint, old Deshaies is that it's the first Port of Entry into this overseas department of France. I get the dink pumped up, drop it in the bay, and get the outboard on which is a real pain in the ass single-handed. I haven't figured it all out. With the dinghy tied to a fairly empty pier, I walk up the hill to a foliage-obscured sign that points to *"Bureau des Doanes"* and looks like all French national road signs. Between 1000 and 1100 on this day, *le bureau* is locked. I walk back down the hill where nobody in town admits to knowing anything about the actual hours, if any. So, I resort to one of my favorite back-up plans; one you may remember: Let's eat lunch. I'm so glad the French take food seriously. As a bonus, they served me enough of it.

That gratifying first meal ashore in France taken care of, I walk back uphill and spot this year's new model E-class Mercedes parked in front of the *Bureau des Doanes*. I figured some local fat cat must have some items to clear in and the office may be open for him. I walk in to see a nice-looking blue-eyed blonde guy in his late 20s pounding on a manual typewriter in the back room. He's dressed in a plain white T-shirt, khaki shorts, and deck shoes. I tell him why I'm here. He already knows, gives me the form, and leaves the room. He returns shortly, chastises me for giving him a copy of the vessel documentation (everybody wants the original), reads most of the visas in my passport; then makes official stamps on several things. I get the yellow copies. That has to be his Mercedes out front. I don't get it. Is he collecting enough in "unofficial" payments to buy this car? Is he the black sheep of a wealthy French family banished to this tropical outpost with a cushy government job? The mystery remains unsolved.

Reading these documents leads me to believe I'm officially cleared in with no time limit. It's a dead calm afternoon so, after getting back on board, I raise the French courtesy flag and deploy the bimini. Just as I'm about to open the bag of ice, a dark gray patrol boat approaches; then ties alongside QV without needing to ask. I am boarded by three large black guys equipped with small black pistols secured to black leather lanyards. They are wearing uncomfortable-looking combat boots (black, of course) and dark blue uniforms with "*Doanes Francaise*" patches; no nametags. The unsmiling trio inspects the boat with special attention to the medicine cabinet in the port head (but don't even look in the starboard cabinet). They are not overly impressed with my freshly stamped clearance papers and start to fill out another form asking for info in, naturally, French. I try to comply. The guy filling out the form, presumably based on my answers, makes fun of my faded, sewn-up U.S. ensign. I tell him it is old, like the Captain. He is not amused. They did not give me a copy of the forms this time.

Most of the places a cruising boat might stop along the Guadeloupe coast are still closed. They are waiting for "the season". When does that happen? One of the guys on Antigua told me disparagingly that visiting Guadeloupe or Martinique was like going to Europe. Well, that suits me just fine. I enjoy Europe. The food and wine are way better than any place else in the Caribbean. In fact, the good restaurants (if open) in these postcard coastal villages treat immigrant sailors much nicer than those up North for not that many more Euros: a currency they are still adapting to in these overseas departments. Most prices are still listed in francs. It's also striking in the French Caribbean that a town of shacks and shanties, many dilapidated into picturesque tropical squalor, will often feature an ultra-modern, shiny new public structure: perhaps a town hall, clinic or library. The architectural style is definitely 21st century European with air conditioning and, many times, working toilets. Even the postal service seems to work here. This is rare in this part of the world, plus *La Poste* has free ATMs that both dispense cash and return your card. Again, this is not something to be assumed in other Caribbean jurisdictions. If this is a result of the French "*mission civilatrice*" from colonial days, it works for me. Of course, it is Europe, but with better weather. The days have been ending in spectacular sunsets but no green flash.

Yet Another New Experience

I did something strange anchored off Anse Deshaies. I went ashore and visited the botanical gardens. The standard French tourist attraction sign advised they were only 1.5 km out of town, neglecting to include the information that it was about 20% uphill grade. Bob H. would probably know the names of these tropicals without the little bi-lingual signs (French and Latin). As one result of having a mother and a former wife who are avid gardeners, I'm surprised how many I know. Also, many of these flora are grown in Southern California. You just have throw lots more water at them on that other coast. Parrots (actually, lorikeets) and macaws are flying around under the forest canopy. The garden is on some of the acreage of an old plantation. The buildings show the local colonial/tropical architecture with carvings and cutouts of hummingbirds and butterflies worked in to the decorative trim. I can't say much for their koi ponds, though. It was a very different state of mind to get off the boat and think about land stuff for a few hours.

I'm indecisive, which is not good for a Captain, about heading down to Basse Terre the next day to get fuel and clear out. There was no wind so, I thought, a nice day to motor. I stayed inshore to observe all the scenery which meant I spent the morning avoiding fish trap floats. God, I hate them! I waited out a squall or two and was off the Riviere Sens Marina before noon. The marina entry required an S-turn through a 50 ft. rock-to-rock gap scattered with other rocks and the red marker from the breakwater, all blown into the channel by the last hurricane. This is too much like Port Zante at the other Basseterre (St. Kitts) where the steering yoke was snapped. I saw 8 ft., 7 ft., 6 ft and down to 5.5 ft by the fuel dock where both people I asked for help left or ignored me: the latter leaning on the fuel pump about 150 meters away. So, I get to try another thing I didn't know I could do. Kick out the fenders, set throttle to match speed of the wind blowing QV off the dock, step ashore from the starboard *ama* with the bow line, back to the cockpit to bring the engine to neutral, grab the pre-rigged stern and spring lines and secure everything. Thirty-seven feet of boat LOA and 16 feet of beam seem so small when you're making an open water passage and so big when you're in a tight, unfamiliar dock space.

I waited. Nothing happened. I finally walked the 150 meters up to the pump guy still puffing on his cigarette, who acted surprised to see me. I informed him in my newly-acquired West Indies French dialect (or so I thought) that I wanted everything: diesel, gasoline, water and ice. He informed me they didn't have water but did tell me which pump was which and go do it myself. Ooo-kaay. No, they didn't have any room at the marina for me to stay overnight. I pumped selected fuels, paid 40 euros for everything and walked down the dock to have lunch. This being France, it was excellent. There are clearly very different national priorities in providing services.

Lunch is followed by much maneuvering to get Quo Vadis off the dock, turned around, miss the other boats and rocks and get out to the guide-prescribed anchorage just up the beach aways. The hook goes down in 12 ft. by 1330. It is fairly rolypoly. About 1630, I notice a large diameter metal structure sticking up within a few feet of the surface. The guide said nothing about this. Caution would dictate, "Move the boat". But, to where? The anchor rode fouled and I cleared it when the wind went around to the Southwest—which it never does, I've been told.

It was fairly easy to clear out at Riviere Sens. The Customs office had actually posted office hours on the door and, even more amazing, seemed to observe them. *Sacre bleu!* You can't tell Customs you're going to stop at the Iles des Saintes so you enter your "Next Port" as some other country. In this case, that country is Dominica which is still more of a farce because there is no fuel or water service for yachts there. Everybody knows this since it is the compelling reason to put in to Riviere Sens in the first place.

Finally, the Iles des Saintes

The Iles des Saintes are a truly charming Gallic group of islands, originally settled and still largely populated by proud, if isolated, Breton fishermen. I anchored just outside the fishing fleet in 20 ft.

I heard a secondary rattle from the diesel as I was anchoring but didn't see that anything had fallen off. The ride across the channel from Guadeloupe was OK despite continued nasty "Caribbean Two-step" cross chop. You would not believe you can have two; sometimes 3, wave crests within a boatlength. With any attention lapse, one will get you. BAM! Shudder. Whoops. That gets old…fast.

But how much more of this painful narrative can you dear readers endure? Not a whole bunch, I'd guess. Quick flashback to the last passage: it was the alternator bolt falling out, wrong-sized since Pompano Beach. After more French misadventures which included walking to the other side of the island looking for the part and being offered engine mounting bolts from the beachfront motorcycle shop, I reassembled the various bits but did not really improve on the situation mechanically. After eating very well ashore and making a plane reservation, I sadly sailed away from the Iles des Saintes.

There is a Jimmy Buffet song you've probably heard with the lyrics: "Before I get to be an old man, I'm going to sail down to Martinique. Get me a sweat-stained Bogart suit and an African parakeet." When I sang it, Caroline commented, "Well, you better hurry up." How sharper than a serpent's tooth; just because I'll turn 60 on my next birthday—if I make it til then. I already had the Bogart suit on board and

I'm very skilled at sweat-staining just about anything but I don't think you can get parakeets through Customs in most places so will probably pass on the bird.

Dominica (pronounced Doh-me-neeka) is the island country between Guadeloupe and Martinique. It's recorded in the ship's log for historical and research purposes. We don't need to get into what absolute holes its two ports are during this discussion. You sailing types can coax it out of me over a ration of grog sometime. It is the only country in the world starring a parrot on its national flag.

Speaking of sailing, I did. Down to Martinique. The course to St. Pierre was 175 but I couldn't sail it cleanly with wind at 135-145. The guide informed me as how going to Martinique was no longer sailing to windward. To quote Bogart about the waters of Casablanca, "I was misinformed." Actually, it's a nice day. Sunny, 4-5 ft. seas, 15-20 kt. winds blowing in the wrong direction. So it goes. After heading in toward the Northernmost, but incorrect, village named St. Pierre for about an hour, I checked the waypoints, the chart, prevailing currents, and my sun sign and managed to turn QV toward the "real" St. Pierre which was just around the cape. See what happens to me after single-handing for this long?

Quo Vadis is on the hook off the municipal pier by 1430. St. Pierre is a quaint French colonial town, known as the Paris of the Caribbean until Mt. Pelee erupted in 1902 killing all but two of the inhabitants. One of the survivors was a drunk murderer who was locked in the underground dungeon of the town jail. That'll teach him! I call Mer on my cell phone and invite her to join me for dinner in Martinique—my treat. She declines.

Another Day in France

As mentioned, St. Pierre looks like a typical French provincial town that has been plopped down on the coast of a Caribbean island. There is a market in the town square and daily fresh baguettes. Church bells ring the hour but, with surprising sensitivity, don't start until 0500 and stop at 2000. The Gallic roosters, however, have no sense of time or even darkness and go off 24 hours a day. Maybe the moon has them fooled. One rooster really does a distinct "Cock-a-doodle-doo" in French. I'm also spotting some sea turtles in the anchorage: alive and seemingly well.

Another waterborne curiosity was the large number of French troops moving around the harbor in bright orange inflatables. One such detachment was disembarked on the municipal pier. OK, it is the tropics but these guys are wearing impossibly short shorts. The sleeves of their jungle camouflage jackets are rolled up. Some dim memory bulb tells me that the Foreign Legion are the ones who wear these short shorts in tropical zones. I know the French government likes to keep the Legion out of mainland France. But as a choice of battle dress, even for these tough troops, I sure wouldn't want to get in to a skirmish with that kind of exposure. I watch this detachment unload stuff from the inflatables on to the pier, shout back and forth at each other for a while; then sit down for what turns out to be a long wait in the sun. Some things in the military never change.

After the wait and some command I must have missed, the smaller guys shoulder enormous packs, the taller guys pick up orange and white plastic coolers just like the one you probably have, and the sole black Legionnaire shoulders an entire stalk of bananas. All of the *Legionnaires* amble down the waterfront to a small, unmarked white van. They looked like they were going on an extended picnic as they loaded the van and drove off down the coast highway. Ah, the glamour and excitement of the Foreign Legion.

The only fuel dock in Martinique accessible to "yachts" is down the coast at Le Ponton in the bay south of Fort-de-France. I head that way in very little wind, dodging fish trap floats and one entire fish farm. I wend my way into the largish bay and hit the waypoint in front of the Hotel Meridien; now dodging small, high speed ferries and looking for the fuel dock. I finally saw the pumps and realized it would be a port docking. I had rigged for starboard that morning. The dock also does not have a VHF radio. About 50 meters out, I yell for some help. The dock attendant stands up and puts down her book. The dock attendant is a good-looking French girl with a nice body. As I get closer, I see blue eyes and dark hair. I'm gaping at her a whole bunch but still manage to hand her my docklines without hitting the dock. At some point, I re-focus and kick the fenders over. I'm trying to muster my very best French so as not to embarrass myself (any more) when a French guy wearing Jockey briefs bangs the port *ama* of his small catamaran into the dock, bounces off, runs astern to grab a piece of clothesline and throws it at the cute dockhand. The short length of line falls into the water. He then tries to get his motor started. He finally does on the third try, backs out, comes around, and hits the dock again. He tosses out the clothesline again and she catches it this time while his starboard *ama* runs into my dinghy hanging in the davits. He keeps saying "Boof!" as he runs around the deck in his underwear. By now, I'm feeling pretty smug in comparison.

After fending him off; topping up with fuel and water, I clear the fuel dock with the cute dockhand offering me my lines and a charming "*A la prochein*" farewell. "Til the next time." I wonder if she was reading Camus? More likely, Danielle Steel but—I can fantasize. I head around Cap Solomon to an overnight anchorage at Anse D'Arlet.

I expect to see Anse D'Arlet empty on a Friday morning as it is somewhat remote from the city at the far South end of Martinique. It is the most packed anchorage

I've seen since the BVI. I can make out the outline of St. Lucia to the South. The next morning I clear the bay of Anse D'Arlet on course for Rodney Bay, St. Lucia. By 0830, I am passing Diamond Rock: formerly **HMS Diamond Rock**, commissioned, fortified and occupied by the British just to annoy Napoleon. Since his Empress Josephine was from Martinique, it worked. Historical anecdote has it that he was furious since Diamond Rock is barely 800 meters off Martinique's south coast." Nyah-nyah na na nyah", went the British. I don't know if **HMS Diamond Rock** ever fired a shot, or needed to.

Doanes Francais and they really mean it

After getting strongly set by current and swell for over two hours, I heard a prop aircraft approaching and turned my head just as **Quo Vadis** got buzzed at mast height by a turboprop twin. I couldn't tell what make. "What an asshole," I reflected, especially when he came around and did it again. As he rolled out, I saw written in very small block letters on the fuselage "DOANES FRANCAIS". Why were the French customs so interested in me? *Merde!* I remembered I forgot to clear out of Martinique. They have sent a twin full of agents after the fugitive *bateau Americain*. As I see the twin continue ahead and land on St. Lucia, my imagination runs to the worst possible scenarios: the welcoming committee, like a necktie party on the dock; multi-national at that. Fines, boat impoundment, more searches, confiscation of weapons, and maybe get sent back anyway by St.Lucia customs since most of the Caribbean Customs officials prefer any problem to be somebody else's problem. Only 2 hrs 15 mins from the St. Lucia waypoint, I turn back knowing I'm losing a day to middle-aged memory lapse.

Two good things result from this (I'm open to some good things): 1) I'm sailing downwind for the first time since Nassau. It is incredibly smooth, quiet and quick. 2) I see lots of very large black fins. The biggest dorsal fins I've ever seen turn out to be attached to a pod of orcas: the first killer whales I've seen. Tropical orcas. They were headed south as QV passed through the pod, largely ignored. Probably another good thing.

I was on the hook off the Fort-de-France commercial docks by 1430. I got the dink down, me cleaned up, and made it to the customs office on shore by 1500. The sign on the door read *"Ouvert tout jours* 1315-1630" and it was locked up tighter than a drum. Now, the adventure turned ugly. Nobody hanging around the docks knew where the other customs office was. I hiked a couple of miles to several official buildings including the General Ministry of Martinique and nobody knew or, alternatively, sent me to the next wrong place. And my French, at least on such a focused topic, is pretty good. I finally just walked along the commercial port until I saw a square concrete pile with "DOANES" inscribed on it. One guy in the sparsely-populated office said he did the boats. I filled out forms. He looked confused. It occurred to me he had never seen U.S. national vessel registration documents before. We talked his way through it and I finally got my copy with *"Sortie"* stamped on it by 1600 which coincidentally was closing time for this office.

I walked back to the cruise dock in the too-new deck shoes that were now wearing holes in my feet. The dock was locked with my dink and my boat on the far, far side of the gates. The security guards saw me trying to scale the wall and, after some explanation, one of them said he'd show me how to sneak in. Who would know better, right? It was much later and hundreds of miles south of Martinique before it occurred to me to wonder why the guards didn't have a key to the gate.

Well, I slashed my leg on the concertina wire, did fingertips and tiptoes on the edge of the sea wall with my body hanging out over the water, and rock-hopped back to the pier in a rising tide. I got back on board by 1630 bloody, bruised, blistered but with my clearance papers stamped, signed and dated. I violated my own cruising rule and went for the Anse L'Ane anchorage four kilometers across the bay. I barely made it by the 1730 sunset and got the hook down in 8.6 ft. I was the only cruiser in the anchorage. I put the dink down, again, for a last French dinner ashore only to discover nothing was open for dinner. I spent my last euros at the local 8-8 minimart (Like a French 7-11 but with a much better selection of good things to eat). A tired Captain dined alone, though not badly, back on board capping a 10-1/2 hour day. Tomorrow, another passage to St. Lucia in the southerly swell and 3-4 ft. chop

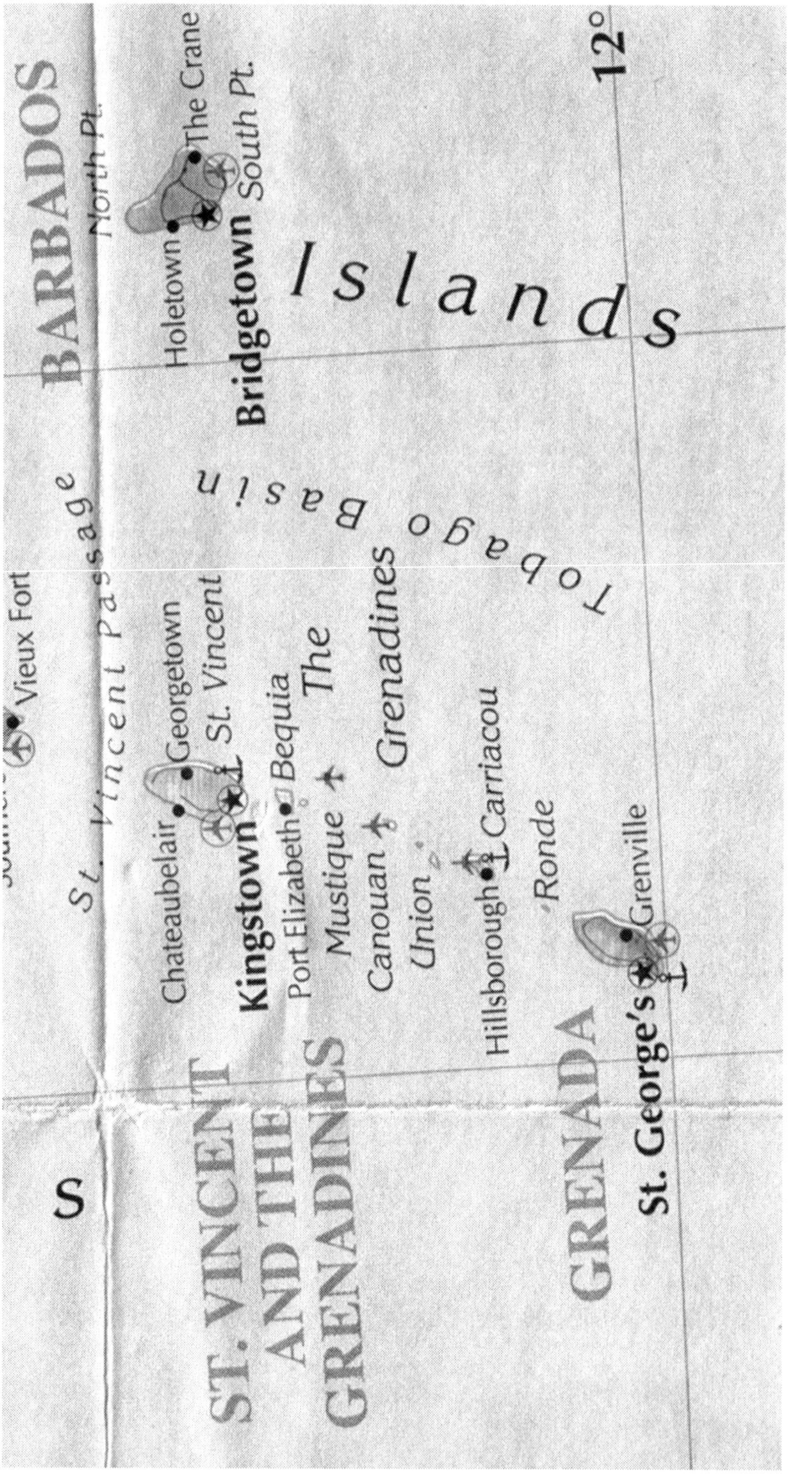
BARBADOS
North Pt.
Holetown
The Crane
Bridgetown
South Pt.
Islands
12°
St. Vincent Passage
Tobago Basin
Vieux Fort
Chateaubelair
Georgetown
St. Vincent
Kingstown
Port Elizabeth
Bequia
The Grenadines
Mustique
Canouan
Union
Hillsborough
Carriacou
Ronde
Grenville
St. George's
GRENADA
ST. VINCENT AND THE GRENADINES
S

A Year on the Caribbean Sea

On the Beach, Ft. Lauderdale, Florida

Dancing Children and Diving Ducks

This may sound like a Caribbean cliché but I really have seen children dancing in the streets and singing to themselves as they walk along. No band, no instrumental music, no Walkman or Ipod plugged into their ears. It was most definitely not for anybody else's entertainment. Just their own.

When Quo Vadis was stern-tied to the shore at Dominica—a move recommended in the cruising guide which proved unnecessary for my boat—a little boy was dancing on his back patio: a concrete slab over the stony beach. (Remember, it's the poor people who live on the beach in most of the old Caribbean.) He jumped back and forth in a bouncy style, loudly accompanying himself with the song, "This house is a happy house." Those seemed to be all the lyrics he could remember and, like children everywhere, he kept at it until he got tired. This took another half- hour of singing "This house is a happy house."

When I was walking back to Wallilabou Bay on St.Vincent (after another intrepid single-handed passage I've probably regaled you with already), a young girl in a long dress and a bright-colored head scarf tied in a front knot came strolling down the road, trilling an island song in that unforced, easy voice of an unselfconscious child. We made eye contact as she passed. We both smiled but she never hesitated in her singing.

Along with other unexpected phenomena, I hadn't associated ducks with the waters of the Caribbean. But there are quite a few and they dive for fish like the pelicans and frigate birds. Unlike those other types of diving birds, they also stick their heads underwater and look around for their piscine prey. I've been told these ducks have a nictating membrane that slides over their eyeballs like a snorkeling mask. I couldn't figure out if they consistently dove under water right away or flew back up and then dived on the fish. You'd think I'd note such behaviors as I'm getting weirdly fixated, on ducks for example, during the long weeks of single-handing. I've not really had any visions, at least none that I can remember, and the voices from the hulls no longer speak to me. While underway on these smooth reaches with Quo Vadis nicely trimmed up and steady on course, I daydream about having Mer on board and the various positions and activities we could be engaged in. (Later, during a phone conversation, she enthusiastically assures me of her cooperation to fulfill one specific sexual fantasy of mine.) How did we get to this daydream from diving ducks?

It was just about this time last December that I drove Quo Vadis out of the Hillsboro Inlet and in to the Gulf Stream. Now, I'm sitting just two miles away from that inlet, using Steve's desktop to write. I left QV on a mooring in True Blue Bay. I'm near the end of a trip away from the boat, back to San Francisco to make Thanksgiving dinner for family and the lovely Meredith who joined us. What a joy to see my children: Beth and Caroline. We celebrated Caroline's 18th birthday and noted my Aunt's 75th and my 60th, in passing. It was a wonderful long week and life seemed very good.

I had acquired an original silk Japanese kimono for Meredith. The often-abused phrase "To open the kimono" had nothing to do with the procedures of business deals and everything to do with her style in doing that very thing. She was hiding nothing.

Reflections on a Choppy Sea

The islands of the Caribbean had names long before the Europeans showed up. Today, their (mostly) Carib names are memorialized as each island's very own beer. So Antigua was Wadadli, as is their beer today. Dominica has Kubuli. St. Vincent was called Hairoun, "Home of the Blessed". Hairoun lager isn't that good, but it's drinkable. St. Lucia's beer is Piton, because they've got two big ones and are very proud of them, too. I was anchored in the shadow of Petit Piton which, of course, is the higher of the two peaks. Grenada brews Carib beer and then ships it throughout the region, sort of like the Caribs themselves who boated North to kill, eat, or enslave everybody else. They were really serious about controlling the market. When the Europeans arrived, they renamed the islands after various Catholic saints, or the day they first saw them (Dominica on Sunday), or their royal sponsors' favorite children. Since the Europeans also killed or infected or worked the remaining island-namers to death, these imported names are the ones most used these days. Except when ordering a beer.

The Europeans also spent several centuries after their arrival fighting over who held which island. They intentionally killed most of the inhabitants and, incidentally, each other's troops. One lasting result of these activities is the big, obvious British forts and fortifications. They stand out on cliff tops all over the Caribbean with an attitude like "Now we've built ourselves a proper fort!" The French forts are much harder to spot from the water, unless you're looking for them. They are still big, featuring thick stone walls with cannons sticking out of them…if you look real hard. Maybe these low profile French forts presented less target area to a British man o' war. I'm not sure how many are original Vaubans but even the knockoffs involved lots of cut rock and dead slaves.

I am continuously surprised by the contrasts. White cattle are tethered along the roadsides of the French islands, cropping the weeds between the asphalt and rolling fields of sugar cane. There's just one cow to a leash; sort of randomly spaced. I also read in the local paper that, after a long absence, the former motocross champion of Guadeloupe has made a triumphant return to the sport, winning the second moto and overall event. Yes, his name is Joel. All you old motorcycle racers reading this will appreciate the irony. I note that the competition equipment is totally up to current specs. Are the billows of white smoke rising from the lush, green hillsides the charcoal makers (*les charbonniers*) plying their ethnic and traditional trade or people burning trash which is today's air pollution? After several days' observation and one day downwind, I conclude it's probably trash.

Since Guadeloupe and Martinique are actually part of France, when the locals are not conversing in Creole, they speak French. But they change the "R" to a "W". Yes, just like Elmer Fudd when he's talking about Bugs Bunny. This usage is institutionalized: even the slogans on T-shirts use "W" which took me a while to figure out. Who started this linguistic twist? Is it like Castilian when the Spanish aristocrats adopted King Carlos' famous lisp? I still pronounce the "R", marking myself as a hopeless foreigner. Otherwise, how could they possibly tell?

Wallilabou and Carriacou, too

The Customs and entry port on the northern coast of St. Vincent & the Grenadines is Wallilabou Bay. You have already seen and will recognize this scenic indent in the island landscape if you sat through "Pirates of the Caribbean". It is one of the main settings for the port scenes. As a result, the Vincentians are quite proud of their nation's role in a Disney film. However, it is a most unlikely place for Customs and Immigration even through a new-looking sign at the Wallilabou Anchorage announces it is "Open as Usual".

The day after arriving from St. Lucia and fending off the attentions of lots of boat boys on paddleboards, I go ashore for a walk to the waterfall described in the cruising guide as about a mile up the road. I pass the washer women pounding clothes on the rocks in the stream. I pass scrawny cattle with white egrets standing on their backs. I pass nicely kept gardens with strange veggies growing in raised beds. I pass a couple of Rasta-looking guys wearing only cutoffs and dreadlocks. They pass a giant spliff back and forth and glare at me but do not offer to share. I pass another half hour walking uphill before I see water falling about 10 ft. over rocks into a small pool. The cold water pounding on my back and shoulders felt like a massage after tense weeks pulling on lines and sheets. I notice a big, old stone dam just 30 ft downstream with a hole in it. A boatload of Dutch vacationers appears. They are cheerful enough, and friendly, but the pool gets crowded.

I'm back on board by 1400 with the last of the diehard boat boys trying to sell me fruit, and anything else they think I need. Three mushroom clouds on the western horizon are set ablaze by the setting sun. After I already have the anchor light on, a 50 ft. charter boat with 10 French guys but no gals on board wanders in to the anchorage. They all start doing different things on deck, including just sitting there. Whenever I see a French boat, I always hope that one or more of these things is setting the anchor, though this particular activity does not appear to rank high in their priorities. Is this "Gay Guys Out Cruising"? Hard to tell with French guys in those skimpy swimsuits.

So now, my cruising guide warns me of the "Bequia Blast". There is some wind and some big current as I head Quo Vadis across the Bequia Channel on what turns out to be a heavy duty ride. I'm seeing 7-8 knots while the *amas* are sizzling a white wake with a rooster tail, though a small one. This is the real stuff: sailing fast and hauled tight on a reach. I only wish I could share it. A pod of larger, solid gray dolphins moved slowly across my bow as I steered over four foot waves into Admiralty Bay, Bequia. I drop anchor on a white bottom in 14 ft. and am pretty pleased with my positioning: just clear of the fishermen. When I dive on the anchor a few minutes later, I find it is upside down on about one inch of sand over rock. Lots of big breaths later, I have carried the anchor out into deeper sand at a depth of 20 ft. This is a problem singlehanding: you can't be on the foredeck and at the wheel at the same time. At least, I haven't figured it out.

Noeline Taylor runs the Shoreside Market and Porthole Café in Bequia's only town of Port Elizabeth. I go there to provision and eat. She is a well-dressed businesswoman who inquires about my circumstances. (In her world, guys don't usually shop alone.) When informed, she responds explosively.

"I been seein' that all de time. You men down cruisin' by yourselves. She back up with de grandchildren, leavin' you alone. They don' give cruisin' a chance. Tell her to get down here; try it. De divin' is good. (Meredith does like snorkeling, I think.) De water is good. (No argument: 84 degrees and clear.) Tell her to get to Bequia. She must try it." I couldn't agree more and stock up with as much as I can carry from Noeline's market.

The Knee Thing and Some Sailing

Stepping off the curb during this stroll along the Bequia waterfront, one of my few physical fears is realized. I twisted my left knee (the "bad" one). It is the first time on this voyage but is incapacitating for sailing solo. I also discover that none of the washing machines have hot water and that cold water has the effect of fixing all stains, regardless of origin. These are not worthy concerns in the great scheme of life and the universe but they are, respectively, painful and annoying; especially with no one to sympathize or laugh with. Back on board, I got the knee elevated and medicated. I also fooled the broken CD player into working with the B.B. King disc Mer compiled for me. Bonnie Rideout was stuck in there for weeks, playing "Scottish Fire" on her rousing fiddle.

The knee is much better in the morning. After ibuprofen and coffee, I decide to weigh anchor for Canouan or Mayreau, heading on down the Grenadines. The wind is stiff which should make for a nice run south. My bad decision of this morning was to try a mainsail set running dead downwind. After I got that mess cleared up, I lined QV back up for the passage and saw a consistent 7-8 knots on my course of 216 Magnetic; actually trimming sail and correcting course to compensate for the 2-3 knots westward set. It was a tighter squeeze between rocks and reef to get into Salt Whistle Bay at Mayreau than I had expected from the chart. There are a lot of immobile items like those to run into in this part of the Caribbean; not all of them well-marked.

I had allowed an extra week to get to Grenada for the plane ride home. Glad of that schedule, as I observed the lunar eclipse at Mayreau; then spent the next three days anchored in gusty, squally, limited visibility conditions. This also forced too many charter boats into Salt Whistle from The Moorings base on nearby Canouan. But, I must admit, while I'm all uptight about weather, boat condition, schedule, etc. here are a bunch of charter types playing Frisbee on the beach. Weather reality eventually conforms to weather forecasts, with clearing after noon of the fourth day. I head out to Clifton Harbor, which is the last port of entry (or exit) for St. Vincent & the Grenadines. I do remember to clear out of this country. Anchoring was fairly hairy: caught in a late afternoon squall in the 35-40 ft. depth inside the reefs. I had decided to reset the hook to get more swing clearance when the squall came roaring across the anchorage and almost blew QV into the dock.

Music and other Lessons

I had to wait until the next morning for Customs to open at a casual 0930 so dinghied ashore for dinner on Union Island. The good surprise was an excellent pan band. I am beginning to appreciate how good pan bands can be. Most of us gringos think "Thrash and Crash" when we hear about steel bands. That style of playing must be from someplace else: Trinidad or Jamaica, I'm guessing.

Before the horde of German tourists showed up for the fixed price buffet, an older gray-haired guy was stroking the pans softly and, it appeared, instructing a younger player adorned with dreadlocks and attitude. The older guy was sporting a crushed porkpie hat; wearing dark slacks and white shirt. When the band started their set, the mentor in the porkpie hat sat down on a chair at the back of the platform. They played mostly ballads, soft sweet melodies on steel and drums, and several tourist standards. Even "Yellow Bird" was not offensive as pinged from their steel.

They were good enough to record but my tape recorder was back on board since I never expected to hear these beautiful, moving sounds on my trip ashore. Then a fat, bald, red-faced German tourist spoiled it for them and for me by starting some Europop tape on his boombox and exclaiming, in English, "Jam session!" The collective look from the pan band should have killed him. I didn't wait to find out the fate of this musical Fourth Reich and left to find my dinghy.

Next morning, while I was walking out to the airport to get my passport stamped, another boat came in and anchored just where I planned to fall off to get underway. So, I needed a new plan.

The wind was up to 25-30 knots but I decided at anchor would be my best, or least risky, chance to raise the main. Another part of the new plan was to go forward over the inside reef. The charts showed it at 10-12 ft. The reef where Quo Vadis had to cross looked shallower. It was adrenaline time getting in over 200 ft. of scope with nobody at the helm, but I then managed to pass over the inside reef and turn seaward before the outside reef, which was breaking. What followed was a nice, quick ride down to Carriacou at over eight knots. This is the northernmost island and first clearing-in port of Grenada, which is not part of the Grenadines. Got all that political geography?

I had the bridle on the anchor line by 1330 after diving on the hook, well-set in sand 12 ft. down. I had purposely anchored in front of the Callaloo, reputed to be one of the best eateries on the island. I beached the dinghy fairly competently near the beachside veranda where I was greeted by an affable gentleman, comfortably seated and sipping something tall. He commented favorably on my U.S. flagged vessel, increasingly rare in these parts, and introduced himself as Roland Bullen.

The Bullen family is an old, established one in Grenada. They own several businesses, including this restaurant. Roland is a San Diego State University graduate who also just happened to be the United States Ambassador to Guyana. He had stopped by his mother's restaurant while on home leave to have a quiet drink. Well, it turned out we had both been in San Francisco for the last Fourth of July fireworks and partying, so talked about that shared experience, exchanged business cards and Stateside football stories. Unfortunately, his mother's kitchen was closed. He offered me the hospitality of his embassy should my voyages take me to that South American coast.

The End of a Chapter and, maybe, an Era

Clearing in to Grenada at Carriacou was about as complicated as polite people in a non-totalitarian state could make it. The cruising Captain gets to visit four different offices and agencies, one of which exists just to collect the fees assessed by the other three. However, I am getting good at dancing this bureaucratic waltz or, at least, inured to it. Tyrell Bay was highly touted as this really great cruiser destination on the southwest corner of Carriacou. Just before leaving for that anchorage, I bought the smallest lobster in the boat boy's live collection. It was about two pounds.

The trip around to Tyrell Bay was a little tricky. It also had three times the number of boats in it, compared to just-departed Hillsborough Bay. And the famous local pizzeria was closed! This sting was eased somewhat with the arrival of a fellow rowing a small skiff that appeared to be banged together from pieces of scrap wood. John, for that was also the name of this other itinerant entrepreneur, offered me a dozen oysters for US$10. The negotiations continued while he shucked and delivered 30 oysters for 24 Eastern Caribbean dollars. John explained his plans to expand his business and exploit the booming economy of St.Martin—by selling his wares in euros!

It used to be my job to support and encourage entrepreneurs. I saw no reason not to continue.

The mangrove oysters were delicious with the key limes also provided by John, even though the bivalves looked like snot on a rock. Close eyes and slurp from the shell. I suddenly understood why Jimmy Buffet wrote the "Just give me oysters and beer…" lyrics. Both were followed up by lobster in garlic butter and fresh-baked whole wheat bread. My only regret was a lack of Meredith to complete this "Tom Jones" dinner in proper style with a quaff, victuals and a knees-up.

The next day was one of the best sailing days of the voyage so far: a challenging but quick run from Tyrell Bay down to the main island of Grenada. I was actually sailing Quo Vadis for wind, current, distance, wave height and direction, all the things that make up the environment at sea. Sometimes I even got the sails right; often enough, I didn't.

When I inquired via VHF, I was informed curtly that St. Georges Marina and Yacht Club was full and would be all week. The harbor anchorage was also too full for my taste, besides being dirty with crummy ambiance. I departed to beat south around Pt. Saline and in to True Blue Bay. This is also the site of St. Georges Medical School, whose American students were "liberated" when the U.S. invaded this island during the Reagan administration. There are lots of local stories about that operation; some of them may even be true. One story I liked is about the Army unit leader who had to commandeer a telephone with international access to call his HQ in the States so he could ask them to send a message for the Navy ships to stop shelling them. The radios weren't compatible. Curiously, most black locals seem embarrassed to discuss the invasion and the mostly British white locals act like they are still the colonial masters. The bad guys, i.e., the ones we didn't like back then, are still in prison at Ft. George, the formerly British redoubt overlooking the main harbor.

The End of an Era

I think the age of individually, casually cruising the Caribbean in your own 30-40 ft. boat is drawing to a close. The best of that era probably lasted 30 years: 1972-2002, all within my adult lifetime. Cruising is now moving toward big charter base operations even in previously remote areas, and lots more megayachts, mostly crewed to shuttle between the Med and the Caribbean by season. I haven't been any place where it seems the conditions for cruising, as I've done, will improve or even maintain.

Exceptions might be places the megayachts don't want to go, like Salinas, Puerto Rico. The locals seem to make more money from these boats. It's not even just about the fuel and provisioning sales, though Quo Vadis typically takes 10-15 gallons of diesel while the motor yachts the fuel docks want to see take 100 times that amount. Unless the docks are out of fuel, which happens more often than I'd have thought.

Grenada Regattas and other Attractions

I'm stretched out on the aft deck sipping slowly on a sundowner; listening to the pan music wafting over the water—each note distinct but not too loud. The setting sun pinks up the fair-weather clouds framing the islets at the mouth of True Blue Bay. This is not such a bad situation except I'm still alone on board. This is a chronic condition which I have not remedied in over four months. I know, I know. It doesn't help to complain.

Another night in Grenada, I dinked around the point from True Blue to Prickly Bay to hear the most famous pan band on the island. They must have had 20 pieces which included some brass. It was worth the choppy dinghy ride in the dark. I still remember them. The good pan music reminds me of Milt Jackson on vibes with the Modern Jazz Quartet. The best is in its own class.

Wooden or Plastic?

The wooden workboats of Grenada have been the native water transportation for hundreds of years. They have no keel, are usually gaff-rigged on wooden masts, and use rounded river rocks, or crew, as ballast. These years, they aren't used for work but assemble annually on Grande Anse beach during Grenada Sail Week to race.

Racing rules are rigid at the start and finish, but looser on the course. Full body contact between crews and ramming other boats that get in the way are fairly common, if not expected. Each heat begins with designated crew from each boat, the runner, starting from a line in the sand up on the beach. At the gun, they run to their boat where other crew are holding it in the shore break. Once the runner's aboard, or at least hanging over the side, they launch. During the race, pretty much anything goes. Finishing order is established as the boats come back to the beach from the barely visible seaward mark. The runner must jump out of the boat, run up the beach back to the judges' table, and knock back a shot of rum from one of the glasses lined up there. Tactics vary. Some jump early, but then the water's deeper and the runner might have to swim. Some boats run up to the beach to give their runner a firmer footing, but it takes longer to get through the shore break upright. The regatta continues through the day with running starts, splashing finishes, and shots of rum.

The boats have inspired names. **Mosquito Bone, Lion of Judah, X-treme.** The last-named boat was the only entry with a white crew: one of them female. They actually did pretty well, winning a couple of heats, until they capsized. X-treme was eventually towed slowly back to shore, hull up, with crew hanging on. Nobody seemed concerned.

Between races, adjustments and fixes to the boats are allowed. I came across an older man sporting a fedora and hammering a big nail into the wooden mast. He was showing his grandson how to attach the rigging. I think it was the main halyard. Some boats tried to improve their performance by reducing ballast. One of the officials started complaining about people cluttering up his beach with these rounded rocks. He was completely ignored.

By mid-afternoon, the races were over, the last runner downed his shot of rum, and the judges repaired into a palm hut to evaluate the results accompanied by the remaining rum. The music has started. The Carib beer has been disappearing into race crews and spectators for some time already.

On the other side of the island in True Blue Bay, another part of Grenada Sail Week is happening. The yachts in the Caribbean Racing Assn. have gathered for their regatta. There are some serious competition boats from islands besides Grenada assembled for the event. They go out past me every morning on their way to the start line. In this fiberglass fleet, there is one black crew; the others, mostly white. A boat named Disco Inferno plays, you guessed it, disco music through on-deck speakers. I instantly dislike this boat, though it proves competitive in the regatta and places in the top three.

At dinner ashore, I find myself sitting alone near a crew from Trinidad that is short-handed for tomorrow's race. As the sometime race crew and old salt that I now imagine myself, I offer to stand in. My offer is coolly dismissed. I understand the insularity of racing crews but am genuinely surprised they don't recognize what a great offer they've just refused. I also figure if they sailed up from Trinidad, I can sail down there. The Mostly White Crew on Plastic Boats Regatta is not really as interesting to me.

Christmas is coming. I've been leaving messages on answering machines around North America. Nobody wants to talk to me. Meredith sends an embarrassing FAX to the marina (which everybody reads as it prints out) detailing reasons not to come see her including she is sick, and why this can't work out between us. The workers that agreed to come on board to help me with some boatwork requiring another set of hands don't show up. I eat another lunch alone at the outside table of Win Hop, the affordable Chinese family place within walking distance of the dock. I am depressed and still crewless.

After a couple of days sailing in and out of other bays along the South coast of Grenada, I paid for another month on the mooring in True Blue and made a plane reservation. I struck the U.S. ensign at dusk, double-checked the painter on the marina's borrowed tender to ensure it would be there to carry me ashore at dawn and watched the stars get sharper. The weather report forecast an Arctic cold front approaching California. The next day, so was I.

Doctor, Doctor

Leaving family, pals and a more friendly Meredith behind in early January, I returned to Quo Vadis on an unglamorous airplane some 30,000 ft. above the miles of ocean I'd sailed. My last few days ashore, I recruited from some internet crew lists. Two guys, two gals and a couple signed up to go sailing the Caribbean with me. When I got back to Grenada, only the two gals had confirmed their arrival dates. Neither claimed much sea experience but said they did have return plane tickets: one of my few conditions for crew.

The big yawl on the next mooring in True Blue Bay was still there. Now, someone was moving around the deck, tidying up the boat. I waved and welcomed another skipper, also apparently alone. He invited me over for sundowners. I dinghied over with some chilled beers at the appointed time. There was a ladder down the side of the white hull.

John Cocker describes himself as "an old country doctor". He had already navigated his 71 ft.-long yawl **Stitches Explorer** around the planet once and was about halfway through his second time around when he parked it here off Grenada. After some consideration, he decided he was through with this particular adventure. He cited his age, expense of operating a boat of this size and vintage and, no surprise, difficulty in keeping good crew. He enlightened me as to one way to deal with crew: have them pay for the experience. He charged his crew five pounds a week to sail with him. The underlying psychology is basic: it gives value to being on board. If it's free, people don't think sailing on a nice cruising boat is worth anything. His strategy had worked for a circumnavigation.

I also learned that Dr. Cocker had built his own plane in his barn during the course of a Canadian winter. There was a photo of him flying the tandem two-seater over Ontario. We enjoyed other evenings on each other's boats and ashore where he revealed that he was top of the class in Physics at the University of London, but was pushed toward med school by his family. Decades of doctoring led him to another business: arranging medical conferences for various specialties in interesting locales, mostly near warm seas.

I didn't think of myself as a slouch in things I'd done with my life, but it was becoming increasingly evident that there were cruising skippers that were a lot more accomplished.

I shared this observation with Bill Alvis when he flew down from California for a sea trial. **Stitches Explorer** was for sale. I found this out indirectly when Dr. John asked me to give him a hand taking it out. He scurried around the boat, doing most everything himself to get underway, as I complied with his commands and Bill watched us. The self-described old country doctor had become fairly rotund in his months ashore ("Gluttony is the only one of the seven deadly sins that leaves evidence," he had proclaimed.) but managed to take the 71 ft. boat out of the Bay with ease and competence.

Sailing in 15-20 knot trades under a full complement of sail on a yawl this size was a thrill and, to me, somewhat of a challenge. I had never before seen some of the types of rigging and basic hardware or felt the surging power of a former racing yacht this size, but it turned out that the two of us could sail **Stitches** with good results. The good doctor later confessed to me that he was greatly relieved the engine didn't overheat during our demonstration and he hoped to have an offer from Bill. He didn't have it in hand before leaving Grenada but he did leave me excellent ingredients from his medicine chest with instructions for use: how to run a course of antibiotics and other off-shore medical tips.

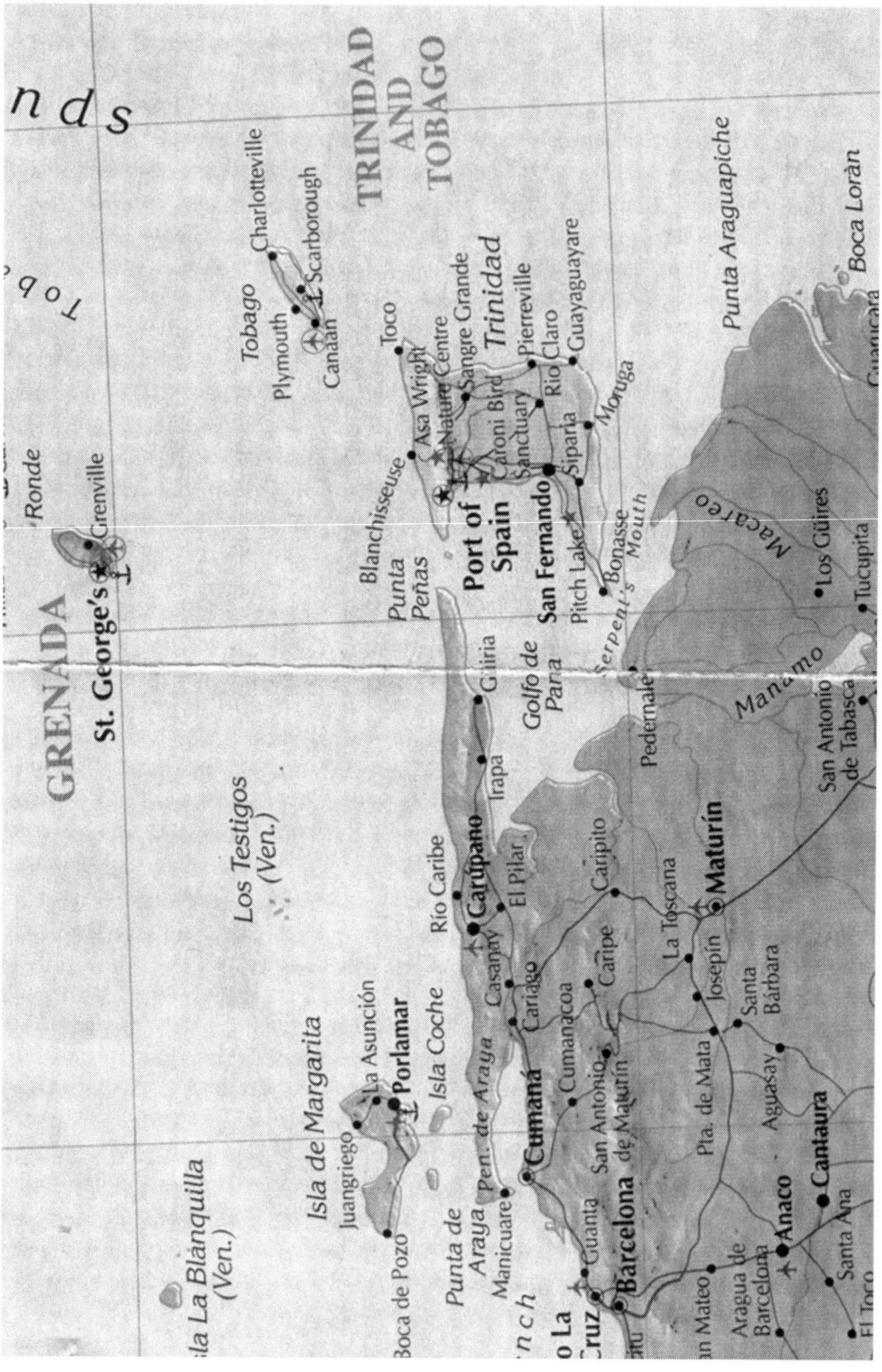
TRINIDAD AND TOBAGO
GRENADA
St. George's
Grenville
Ronde
Tobago
Charlotteville
Scarborough
Plymouth
Canaan
Toco
Trinidad
Sangre Grande
Asa Wright Nature Centre
Caroni Bird Sanctuary
Pierreville
Rio Claro
Guayaguayare
Moruga
Blanchisseuse
Punta Peñas
Port of Spain
San Fernando
Siparia
Pitch Lake
Bonasse
Serpent's Mouth
Golfo de Paria
Güiria
Irapa
Carúpano
Río Caribe
El Pilar
Casanay
Cariaco
Caripito
Caripe
Cumanacoa
Cumaná
San Antonio de Maturín
Maturín
La Toscana
Jusepín
Santa Bárbara
Pta. de Mata
Aguasay
Cantaura
Pedernales
Manamo
Macareo
Los Güires
Tucupita
San Antonio de Tabasca
Punta Araguapiche
Boca Loràn
Los Testigos (Ven.)
Isla de Margarita
La Asunción
Porlamar
Juangriego
Isla Coche
Boca de Pozo
Punta de Araya
Pen. de Araya
Manicuare
Isla La Blanquilla (Ven.)
Barcelona
Guanta
Anaco
Santa Ana
Aragua de Barcelona
El Toco

From Carnival to Margaritaville

Aboard S/V Quo Vadis, sailing Grenada to Venezuela

With the internet-recruited female crew finally on board, I am still determined to get to Trinidad in time for Carnival. The first night and day we're ready, the forecast has seas at 5-7 feet. With a green crew on their first passage, I decide to wait. On the chart, it looks easy to get to Trinidad from Grenada: just keep heading South. But it is one of the longer stretches of open water in the West Indies with consistently strong trade winds and currents setting your vessel to the West. You can get pushed over to Venezuela near the Paria Peninsula, if you miscalculate. The waters off this peninsula have been the most active pirate zone in the Caribbean in recent years. It is consistently colored Red on threat zone alert maps. The pirates are mostly shore-based, coming out in launches powered by multiple heavy horsepower outboards and, by all accounts, very well armed. One message on the Coconut Telegraph says these guys are military or ex-military renegades, which is how they got their hands on automatic weapons.

Night Passage to Trinidad

As it turns out, the key to making landfall off Trinidad rather than Venezuela is to stay to windward of the giant gas collection platform which lies about halfway along this passage. The seas had dropped down to 3-4 ft. and the trades were pretty normal at 15-20 kts. I plotted a course that would take us a little to the East of the Boca del Dragon, figuring we could fall off easier than beat up. It had taken me three days to learn this most obvious sailing strategem while single-handing down the Windward Islands. I took the wheel for my usual midnight watch. It wasn't long before the gas platform was visible, lit up like a giant Christmas tree. It is surreal to come across a structure like this out in the middle of the ocean, especially after long hours in wet darkness. It gets very real as Quo Vadis is being pushed to the West, inside the platform, by very strong currents. I keep pinching up, trying to get the boat headed Southeast. We're apparently still making pretty good speed over the surface as we come up on the platform within an hour and my trusty vessel slips by on the outside of this incongruous structure, clearing it by about 200 meters. The steel pilings and lattice supports are brilliantly lit and look unyielding.

The platform disappears over the stern and the world of the midnight watch is black again under partial cloud cover. There is a radio call from northbound cruiser S/V Pelican. We see each other's lights, confirm location and pass port to port with correct separation. I indulge about 10 minutes in thinking how nautically correct we've been when I sense, then see, a boat bearing down on Quo Vadis at about 30-degree angle to the starboard side. It is running without lights but I think I hear their engine. It looks like a sloop in the 40 ft. range with some sail up but not trimmed. I come hard to starboard, heading into it. The maneuver barely works. We are too close as the vessel I call "Bad Surprise" crashes heavily into the waves just two lengths off the port bow; never slowing, never showing any lights, and never responding to my VHF calls. I'm shaken by the suddenness and overall wrongness of this near-collision. Why no running lights? I saw nobody in the cockpit. I finally come back to course with a slight shiver as the adrenaline starts to wear off.

I'm drained and tired when I rouse Kate for her watch around 0400. I'm roused out myself about 0630 to come on deck and see Trinidad. I'm not expecting this wall of 400-500 ft. rock cliffs which nearly fills the horizon. Kate and Julie are just happy we found the place. This is their first passage with me on QV and, maybe, their first overnight passage ever. The elevation of Trinidad's north coast does not come across from the charts and I haven't picked up on it from my readings. Trinidad looks massive in the dawn light which accents the intense green of the tropical foliage growing out of the cliffs. The currents appear to have weakened in closer to shore, so our position is about 3 miles east and two north of the Boca, which is not a bad place to be. Way better than being this close to Venezuela. We just need to open up the sails and run downwind for a while. We can't check in until Customs and Immigration at Chaguaramas opens at 0830.

Chaguaramas

As the night wind died and the current surged through the Boca de Monos (Columbus supposedly named this channel Boca del Dragon since he wanted this to be China where there were dragons.), I started the engine and motored in to Chaguaramas Bay. All spaces at the customs dock were taken, so I eased the boat into an 18 ft.-wide slip with a sea sick Julie on bow lines and a not so sick Kate on stern lines. This new crew, my only crew for quite a while, came aboard to cruise back to California during the next six months. I thought this a reasonable schedule, even if it was already February. Certainly, we could get through the Panama Canal and on to southern Mexico.

Julie was a 36 year-old recent MBA graduate. Her experience on sailboats was gained from weekend sailing on San Francisco Bay and a Windjammer cruise. The SF Bay experience can provide significant knowledge of strong winds, tidal effects, boat handling and sailing in choppy waters. It can also be just going along for the ride, clenched to an immobile piece of somebody else's sailboat. That she hadn't been picked up by the Silicon Valley company where she had interned, or any other, I attributed to the demise of the dot.com economy. I also hoped her expectations on board Quo Vadis had nothing to do with her wearing that Windjammer cap. She said she knew how to tack and had a plane ticket home.

Kate was older; an organic vegetable farmer from Colorado. She had informed me she owned a Pacific Seacraft 27 which she sailed on lakes and also had offshore cruising experience: standing watches, preparing meals underway, etc. She did not get sick on this passage to Trinidad. She did, however, prove to have a consistent capacity for being correct 50% of the time. This covered the spectrum of on-board actions from "Do we have any mustard?" "No, we're out." (I found the mustard.) to "Are we clear of the reef?" "Yes," she replied from her bow position. (We weren't.) The other half of her input proved correct, which still frustrated my decision-making using that information. I never figured out which 50% category applied.

I didn't want to risk doing time in a Trinidad jail or spend it with guys who were, so I declared the Mossberg 12 gauge shotgun and the double-ought buckshot rounds. The Customs guys seemed somewhat surprised by my candor but gave me a receipt and cleared us in to Trinidad and Tobago for 30 days for US$35. I saw very few other declared weapons on their registry book, most of them 9mm pistols.

Chaguaramas, I find out, was a World War II U.S. Navy base. The harbor is now lined with boatyards, markets, cheap motels that charge big prices, marine service companies, some eating places and a Budget Marine store. It has become a major repair and overhaul port for cruising boats, originally because of its location here at the far Southeast corner of the Caribbean in sight of South America. Of course, that is why the British and, later, U.S. navies also set up shop here.

Right now, Quo Vadis needed a place to park. I had already called the Trinidad and Tobago Sailing Association and talked to Phyllis. She said she would save a mooring for QV, so we motored around the peninsula to Carenage Bay and the TTSA's mooring field. The first response to my call on CH68 was "We're closed for the weekend". Then, Wallace came on the radio in response to my reference to Phyllis and said he would meet us in a guide boat. He did; cleaned the growth off the mooring lines and ball and had QV on the buoy by 1330. Julie went ashore in their tender. Kate and I rested up for whatever was next. The days of Carnival had started without us, just barely.

An enormous bank of loudspeakers blasted this year's Carnival tunes from a giant stage on shore. The music started before midnight. The last tune ended about 0900 the next morning. The deck of Quo Vadis provided a great view of the fireworks set off with the music. Welcome to Carnival.

Sticky Wicket, Old Man

The sand beaches extend west from the Officers' Club area around Macqueripe. Between the gnarly tree trunks awash with breaking surf at high tide, families and couples arrange their territorial markers for the day, usually backing their space up to the pocked, rocky cliffs.

We walk around a wall of rocks to a longer, flatter section of wet sand where a pick-up game of cricket is underway. The closest U.S. analogy is probably a weekend touch football game. It is just as serious as testosterone, local beer, and male egos combine with whirlwind intensity in an athletic event that has no external meaning, impact or consistent scorekeeping. The attitude is fierce.

I will now oversimplify what little I know of cricket. One guy with a thick, flattened paddle about a yard long tries to keep another guy from hitting a wicket (stakes in the ground) with a hard, rapidly thrown ground ball. He does this by hitting the ball to places the other guy's team mates can't reach. These first two players are the batsman and the bowler. This contest may be the most enduring heritage England has bequeathed her former colonies from the Caribbean to Pakistan. Well, maybe cricket and the slow-acting, complicated bureaucracies distributed over the same geographic area. In all these ex-British venues, both institutions are embedded in daily life.

Clad for this outing only in my sporty red shorts, now dripping wet, I watch as a series of batsmen defend the wicket (a rusting metal folding chair stuck upright in the sand) against fiercely thrown balls sent skittering fast across the wave-wet beach. The clang of the ball hitting the chair signals the current batsman is out. I note he also loses the bat if somebody grabs a ball hit in the air.

I am the only white guy on this beach and probably the only guy over 50. In a friendly gesture, I am invited to bat. Surprisingly, since I have little skill and less experience with bats and balls, I get it. The stance is with the bat down. I rest the flat tip lightly on the hard-packed sand. If you hit the ball back successfully, you run to a post before a groundsman grabs it and throws it back. If you hit the ball in the air and it's caught, you're out—just like baseball. Cricket came first.

I whack the ball away from the wicket repeatedly with the first bowler, not disgracing myself; helped by the fact the ocean is to my right. This slows down would-be fielders as they run into the small waves to catch the ball. I can tell they did not expect this performance. Neither did I.

Another bowler, older and bigger, takes his turn. The pace picks up. He winds up, runs at me and releases. The ball is coming faster, leaving a mini-rooster tail across the beach. I hit it back, most of the time on the ground but with no control of direction. I'm just swinging, bat down, to protect the wicket. A few more hits back (The rules of this pick-up game let you hit til you're put out. Maybe that's true for "real" cricket, too.) and a third bowler takes over the position.

I smack his first bowl back. It all happens very quickly. His next run and overhead toss sends the ball hissing a little more to my left and I miss. The ball clangs into the folding chair, which falls over. The Trinidadians are gratified to strike out the old, white guy who is just as pleased to have hit in his first and, probably, only beach cricket game. It was certainly no match.

Julie took some digital images of the event. I look tan, somewhat thick through the torso, and dripping wet but also attentive: bat in correct position with a relaxed stance. My beard looks very white in these images as do I among this all-black crowd of cricketers.

V. S. Naipaul with Bake 'n' Shark

I have become addicted to the Trinidad street food, bake 'n' shark, pronounced "bacon shock". This is your traditional Caribbean johnnycake with a chunk of grilled shark stuffed in it. You then add other items, to taste. One of the items to my taste is the equally traditional hot pepper sauce. Quality of shark and the condiments on offer varies from vendor to vendor along the curbsides of Port of Spain. I determined this by sampling from as many as I could. So one sunny day I make the pilgrimage to Maracas Bay on Trinidad's North shore where, local food legend holds, bake 'n' shark originated. This tasty treat is supposedly original, and best, from Richard's shoreside stand.

About half the population of Trinidad converges on the Maracas beaches on most weekends. Richard's is just one of many snack shacks along the beach road but the line has formed at this one when we arrive. Richard does offer a tremendous variety of things to enhance your "bacon shock" including some I have never seen before. The chunk of shark is fair-sized, nicely grilled and, well, I'm beginning to think this culinary adventure could all work out. The folks working behind the counter efficiently take and fill orders. I order two, which overfills the plate but doesn't deter me from joining the crowd around the fillings table and grabbing a cold Carib beer from the ice tub.

Seating is at a premium, so tables are shared; especially those in shade. I ask to share one with a family of East Indian descent, as is about 40% of Trinidad's population. The gray-haired head of the family agrees we may sit down with them. My immediate concern is attacking the alleged original bake 'n' shark. It is as good as promised, except nobody promised me how good it would be. I took that on myself. After the first one is gone, I remember it would be good manners to introduce myself and my crew to our tablemates. So I do, adding how and why we've arrived in Trinidad.

"Very well," comes the lilting but lightly accented reply of the gentleman. "I am Vijay Naipaul, this is my wife, Risa, and our niece visiting us." I stop eating, stare and stammer. " Naipaul, as in V.S. Naipaul, winner of the Nobel Prize in literature?"

"Yes. That is correct. We are cousins. Vidi was here to visit just last year. He stayed some time with us." Wow! V.S. Naipaul (Vidi to his family, it seems.) is the only scion of Trinidad to win the Nobel Prize. He lives in London now, I've read. I express my admiration for his work and achievement. Our conversation expands. This Mr. Naipaul knows many interesting things.

"You're in Chaguaramas?" he asks. Well, close. We've also been up to the Macqueripe beaches.

"That is all technically still United States property," he informs us. This is a surprise. It seems Britain leased most of the peninsula to the United States in 1940 for a term of 999 years. Trinidad gained independence from the UK in 1975, but a 999-year lease is still legally in force. The U.S. had wound up most serious Naval activity on the island by the mid-70s and let the new government have the use of the property but the lease was never renegotiated or revoked. It had, for some reason, become a point of contention between the two main political factions.

"The U.S. has legal right to the property," Vijay continues. "Maybe you will take it back someday."

This explains the 1940 architecture of the hangars and seaplane ramps just opposite our mooring. They are like those built in the same years at Alameda Naval Air Station, my last home on shore. The headquarters building is now a seldom-used convention center. The base officers' club is a bunker converted into a disco. Macqueripe was the officers' beach. Its concrete salt water pools are now breached and crumbling. Big houses, originally built for ranking officers, are visible along the road from the former base up to the beach. There's a golf course. Is the last American facility, the tracking station, still used? I can imagine what fantastic duty this would have been in World War II: flying PBYs over the Caribbean looking for U-boats. Back to Trinidad by dusk, a trip to the O-club, a young wife; maybe a swim in the morning. No shooting. Protect that Canal!

Some Work and Some Play

Many of the Carnival nights are *"Jours ouvert"*, usually said and written *"Jouvert"*: open the day. This is celebrated with street parades and masked dancing throughout the early hours until dawn. Julie and I take a Maxi (The category of small bus called a Mini in Grenada.) to downtown Port of Spain and find space near the parade reviewing stand. Anticipating being hugged and groped by the petroleum-coated "Oilmen" (They seem to go for tourists.), we are dressed way down. In my case, in rags. Most of the crowd is pretty wasted by the time we show up except for the highly visible police. One of this year's slogans is "We Carnival Safe and Happy". And so it is.

A nattily dressed guy with a microphone comes over and asks if we'll do a TV interview. I figure we've been selected for this media moment since I am the only white guy currently sober and vertical in Port of Spain. Certainly, we're the only such couple in sight. Julie has just informed me that she unexpectedly got her period and is asking the sympathetic female producer behind the camera if any shops were open. At 0300, there probably wouldn't be even if it weren't Carnival.

She rejoins me as the interviewer freshens his make-up and we are 3-2-1 Live! on nationwide television: Trinidad and Tobago Channel 3. He told me to speak to him; not into the camera.

"Are you enjoying Carnival?" he asks. I tell him and whoever is tuned in to Channel 3 at this hour how much fun we're having at Carnival and, yes, it does feel safe while one of my crew starts her period on live TV. We miss the rest of the festivities since Julie doesn't feel safe enough to go back to the boat by herself. But not before I see the Mayor of Port of Spain directing the traffic of frolicking masqueraders past the reviewing stand turn. The irony is that several of them are costumed as unflattering effigies of His Honor. He doesn't seem to notice or take offense. Another masquerader opens a black raincoat to reveal a see-through red bra and panties labeled as "Weapons of Mas Destruction". (Most of Trinidad calls Carnival "Mas" from masquerade.) It was a crowd favorite.

Our Carnival experience is interrupted by a few hours of sleep on board. I paddled back to shore about 1100 (The outboard continues to die.) for the Parade of the Bands: music on wheels. This is one of the two Big Events. The other is the Parade of the Marching Societies.

Another big deal is the annual contest for the top Mas song. The competition was over and the winner was "De Band Coming". It took me a while to understand the lyrics with the Trinidadian inflection and, within a few days, I never wanted to hear it again. Reading the list of prior winners, I discover that the top tune for Carnival in Trinidad many years ago was "Zombie Jamboree" by Lord Invader and the 12 Penetrators. This song was a favorite of mine when I was a teenager. Lord Invader had several other #1 tunes over the years when he apparently dominated the

Carnival music scene. I missed out on these other tunes and, surprisingly, could not find a Lord Invader CD among the hundreds of bootlegs and knockoffs for sale on every other corner in Port of Spain.

The bands travel on long flatbed trucks. They are everything you think pan music is all about—amplified. I count well into the dozens of steel drums on many platforms. Some bands include brass and regular drums. A few are purists, playing only the pans. All of them are very good or they wouldn't be here. Many of the bands carry out a visual theme. Fanciful Naval costumes and American Indians seem popular. Little kids work out with vigor on their small steel pans but lack the stamina of the teenagers. I don't know if it is possible to stand still as this music pounds you like surf. Why would you?

The Marching Societies have bands, too, usually on their floats. You're welcome to join the elaborately costumed men and women, but towards the back of the group, please. I marvel at the inclusiveness of Carnival. The parading men and women are of all ages. I verify several mother-daughter dancers and at least one trio of dancers made up of three generations in a family.

We fall in behind one crew to shuffle and dance the parade route up to the Queens Park, a large expanse of green space at the North end of town. After a few blocks, one of the lavishly costumed young women in the line just ahead turns to me and asks, "Are you enjoyin' yourself?" She is not the last female on Trinidad to ask me that question as we dance, shuffle and stroll along the streets. I don't think they really mind I'm staring at their shapely, often bare asses. Especially when they're doin' some grindin' which appears to be much like a dry hump done in tune to the all-surrounding pan music. Even the grannies get into it. Especially the grannies, as the afternoon goes on.

There are stands selling snacks and drinks set up along the parade route. My strenuous if not always rhythmic efforts required regular re-hydration. There are photos of me sweating through everything I'm wearing. I started hydrating from my water bottle. When that is sucked dry, I buy some of the local beers, handed over to me as our group dances past. In some later snapshots, my shirt is off. In a few still later shots, I look somewhat drunk and still dripping wet. I don't actually remember it that way but do I recall being polite to everybody as everybody was acting very polite to me, even friendly. Variations on this experience continued for two more days.

When I went over to Mood Indigo to swap beers for charts, Joyce Davis gave me the name of her local ob-gyn. This was more useful than you might think since he practiced in the same office suite as a GP, Dr. Ahmad Rahman. My left leg had become swollen, red and painful to walk on even before the activities of Carnival. It seemed to be the least of my bloody injuries when I fell off the curb chasing a Minibus back in Grenada. Before visiting Dr. Rahman, I arranged for Quo Vadis to be hauled out at Powerboats' yard which, with Caribbean logic, works almost exclusively on sailing yachts. The fix, repair, or replace list had grown and I'm still planning to cross the Caribbean from East to West.

Dr. Rahman's office is in a modern-style medical building. I was told I'd find it near the soccer stadium. He doesn't keep me waiting long before checking me out and diagnosing an infection which started through a very small leg wound. He takes a blood sample for lab work and writes a prescription for antibiotics and pain killers. The lady at the reception desk charges me the equivalent of US$25. I find a westbound Maxi and get off at West Mall where she told me there is a good pharmacy. After collecting my pills for another US$30, I go to the book shop. In the small but distinct V.S. Naipaul section, I find a copy of "Miguel Street", his autobiographical account of growing up in that Port of Spain neighborhood, which is less than a mile away from this book shop. His use of particular words and the Trinidad rhythm of speech immediately come alive in my brain. I've been hearing them every day; now I read them. The lab work reveals, among other cautionary results, that I have cellulitis. It has not moved up my leg as far as the groin, so no hospitalization is required for treatment. This is good because Quo Vadis has yard work scheduled. The charge for this follow-up visit is even less. I wonder if I could have afforded any of this treatment and medication in the U.S.

We survived Carnival, played cricket, and ate bake 'n' shark on the beaches of the North Coast. The remaining touristy event on the list is a visit to the Caroni Swamp to see the rare scarlet ibis which is, not surprisingly, the national bird. One guidebook waxes lyrical about the sight of the bright red birds flying in to complete a color portrait with the snowy egrets and blue herons.

I splurged on a rental car and drove to the swamp parking lot. Julie wanted to get in a boat with some young guys who had nothing to do with the birds. We paid the operator of the actual tour boat. When it was nearly full, he motored down the channel out to a mangrove island and tied the skiff off to the mangroves.

Half an hour before sunset, two big flocks of scarlet ibis flew across the water into the trees on the opposite side of the lagoon. I remember a bird-watching neighbor in Topanga Canyon, where I lived many years ago, and wonder if she has seen the scarlet ibis to add to her list.

Now, I'm sure it's a good thing the tour boats don't get too close to the birds' night roosting territory but, from across the wide lagoon, all you can see of the scarlet ibis is a scattering of red dots on a green background. There also some white dots beneath them and, if you look even harder, some blue dots. The closest we get to Caroni Swamp wildlife is a couple of medium-sized pythons who are hanging from low branches over the water. They didn't move. We were back to the parking lot two hours after we'd left. While I had the rental car, we did an inland tour the next day. The crew could not agree on what they wanted to do or for how long. My attempt to keep them happy was not what management used to call "a good success".

Quo Vadis got new batteries, new rudder pindles and gudgeons (The work crew really does talk like that.), a 110V inverter so we could operate a laptop, radar repair, possible leaks plugged and, after much agonizing, a new reefer. The original one still worked but the compressor was rattling ominously when it shut off. I don't want the reefer to go terminal when we're halfway across the Caribbean, though I'm not really clear, at this point, on exactly where that is. The Stone Cold reefer is claimed to use less power and cool more efficiently than the Adler Barbour cold plate it replaces. I don't remember that it ever worked consistently and it used the same or more power. Both of my crew spent most of their time visiting other boats or on line during most of our days on the hard.

The Islands of Venezuela

My clever strategy for avoiding pirates (and the only one I could think of which included sailing from Trinidad) is to get out of sight of land before dark. The pirates in these waters are supposedly land-based with spotting towers along the coast of the Paria Peninsula and further West. This is the information on the Coconut Telegraph, anyway. A cruising boat was boarded in this same area last month. The boarders killed the captain. Some crew survived and were eventually rescued. This information was in the local press. Other details are not clear or not consistent. So we head due North from Trinidad to put distance between Quo Vadis and the mainland. The goal is to be over the horizon before turning on our running lights. The course to Los Testigos, our next landfall, is actually around 290 magnetic so this strategy, or safety precaution, or skipper's paranoia (depending how how you label the action) will add hours to our passage to these off shore islands, claimed and administered by Venezuela.

The departure from Trinidad was not encouraging. Aidan Gittens, a very knowledgeable diesel guy; maybe the best I've met so far, came back out to the boat to see why the engine cooling water wasn't flowing. He discovered air had leaked into the cooling water intake hose, breaking the vacuum. I had inadvertently knocked the valve open re-stowing Julie's bag. Lesson learned. We went in to the TTSA docks to fill our tanks only to be informed the water supply to the club was cut off for the day. NavTech finally found the correct style of light for the cockpit but it was built for interior use so didn't solve our problem. Before we cleared Carenage Bay, the wind generator clattered to a stop. That was something new. I had recovered the 12 gauge and buckshot rounds when we cleared out of Customs/immigration. Now, I propped the loaded shotgun up in the cockpit just outboard of the helm chair.

Low on water, no wind-generated power, and we're sailing in to an active pirate area. I try not to worry about another reality: this is only the second passage for this crew. I also worry we won't make our first waypoint before dark. With the tradewinds blowing 15-25 on our beam, *Quo Vadis* was making 7-9 knots, so we did. This waypoint was our reference for setting course toward Los Testigos. Just after sunset, a boat headed straight toward us. We were still near our closest point of approach to the Paria Peninsula. As the distance between the vessels closes, I chamber a round. The boat takes the shape of a Venezuelan fishing smack and continues past us on a reverse course. Apparently, the boat is manned by actual fishermen. They usually return in the morning; not at dusk.

We have 1-2 knots of Northwest current against, so I figure it will be a 16 hour passage if conditions don't change. Kate stayed up to help Julie on her watch. Julie was sea sick. I slept intermittently but comfortably as QV ran downwind in 3-5 ft. following seas.

The wind died on my midnight watch resulting in 3-4 knots speed through the water and estimated arrival at Los Testigos in mid-afternoon. I started the engine but couldn't keep good sail shape. The noise of the genoa brought Kate on deck. "Is something broken?" Her usual query. "Probably," replied the wise-ass captain, "but nothing I can see." I alter course to compensate for the current before handing off. It looks like Kate and Julie are sharing helm duties on watch.

I came back to the helm at 0730 after boiling water for coffee/tea. Fifteen minutes later, we made landfall. I identify it as Gran Testigo (This does not mean Big Testicle. *Testigo* is Spanish for witness.) Then I see Isla Iguana Grande. I ask Kate to the helm as we strike sail. Julie is still unclear on procedure and the names of things on the boat. On the lee side of Isla Cabra, I hail Coast Guard Station Testigos and receive a prompt acknowledgement of the arrival of *Quo Vadis*.

Trading Drugs for Bugs

When I dived on the anchor in 10 ft. of clear water, I observed a short drag and deep set. Kate had left the transmission in reverse after telling me "Neutral" as I dropped the hook. Back on board, I found neutral and let the engine cool down for about 15 minutes while we got cleaned up to go announce our arrival in Venezuela. It's a requirement to check in at Los Testigos and, again, on the mainland.

The Coast Guard station at Los Testigos is in a round, white-washed building that reminds me of a Dairy Queen. But instead of serving soft ice cream inside, there is a Navy Ensign who looks about 20 years old and two enlisted men who look even younger. The officer rises from his desk as I introduce Quo Vadis' captain and crew while handing over passports, boat documents, etc. They are friendly and seem entertained to have visitors to their remote outpost. They do not, however, have fresh water to sell.

As we walk along the beach toward the fishing village, a bunch of young boys throws a big net into the shallows. With much whooping and yelling, they pull the net ashore with dozens of silvery pompano flopping in it. On the way back to the dink, I buy three of them for US$1 from a nice young girl tending the freshly caught fish. Back on board, I put them in a bucket of saltwater; then covered the instruments, the mainsail, and deployed the bimini while Kate made scrambled eggs with everything for brunch. Next planned activities in Venezuela: a siesta and a swim.

After both these important events, a guy rowed over from the fishing boat anchored around the corner. He was looking for a part for some ancient boombox. When I couldn't come up with it, he asked if I had any medicine that could help his Captain's arthritis. I traded some ibuprofen for lobsters. I was liking Los Testigos. Partly, I think, out of relief we made it here without incident.

We moved the boat across the inlet to Punta Tamarindo and were back on the hook just off the beach by 1700. I boiled the lobsters and made garlic butter. Kate, a fisherperson, cleaned and sautéed the pompano. She served the fish with a papaya salsa. I opened some wine picked up at the duty-free shop when we cleared out of Chaguaramas. I was liking the Testigos even better.

One of my boat checks next morning was the water tanks. I find approx. 10 gallons in the port tank and the starboard tank nearly dry. My error is a big one— leaving Trinidad without filling everything— even with the bad luck of the broken water line at TTSA on our departure day. I transfer 4 gallons from the jerry can reserves into the 1-gallon water jugs that we stow under the sinks.

To get away from the village generator noise, we move to Playa Real. It turns out to be a popular spot with half a dozen other sailboats at anchor plus three Venezuelan fishing boats. We find a gap in the islands and anchor off the rocky point. After a fancy lunch prepared by Kate, we dink ashore where we meet Pablo and Chon Chon.

Pablo is a French charter captain based out of Cumaná on the mainland. He has a number of French ladies with him on an adventure charter: they sleep on board or in tents on the beach. As they stroll past, I smile and say *Bon Jour.* They display absolutely no interest in me. Most don't even reply which is rude in the islands, even for Frenchwomen.

Chon Chon's Place

Chon Chon is the principal guide, gracious host and major domo on Testigo Grande; maybe for all of Los Testigos. The few and isolated families in this island group protect this place and their privilege with, shall we say, great seriousness? If they don't want you here, you don't get to stay. Chon Chon is a handsome rogue of a seasoned vintage which, given where we are, could be my age. He wears his authority easily but certainly. He observes a boat crew behaving in a way he doesn't like and calls the Coast Guard guys on his VHF. That boat is gone before dark.

Chon Chon proudly shows me a letter from a fairly recent female visitor from the mainland. She assures him she can't wait to return for his *besos* (kisses). She also sends several of her literary liplocks to him. He shows me several photos of him entertaining ladies off boats visiting Testigo Grande. All of them have starlet good looks and healthy-looking, tanned boat bodies. Of course, I suppose he's not going to show off any real dogs he was photographed with. He offers Julie a conch shell gift and me a shot of Venezuelan rum. I toast to his *Salud!* He invites us to dinner at his place tomorrow night.

Chon Chon's Caribbean compound is right on the beach and appears to be assembled mostly from things that washed up there. The open front of the eating area faces the channel and the islands across the water. There is a small personal space off to one side. The most noticeable contents are a white mesh hammock, his box of letters and photos, and a bolt action rifle. The VHF radio is wired to a car battery. When we arrive, he is grilling lobster tails and the inside meat of triggerfish. He told me the day before he preferred the taste of *toro* to lobster. With their hard, shell-like exterior, I didn't even know they were an edible species. I'm very glad to report they are.

Before going ashore, I prepared Quo Vadis for a departure to Margarita tonight and a cucumber salad to take to dinner. Kate made a papaya salsa. Equipped with these contributions plus three beers, a gallon of water and a half-bottle of rum, we dinked ashore. I'm getting better at beach landings or the surf is easier. Having another body on board to jump out and stabilize the bow seems to improve things. A French crew joined us, bringing some Venezuelan Polar beer and a bottle of white wine. Chon Chon kept grilling seafood as he told everybody to put everything on his big plank table. I'm not sure why he does this for us transient sailors but I don't question him.

Ricardo, for that is the Coast Guard Ensign's name, and his two guys showed up just before the lobsters were served. They are wearing baggy shorts and T-shirts for their off-duty Saturday night dinner, looking like the South American teenagers they are. The potluck on Testigo Grande was delicious. The information gained before and after dinner was more valuable than I expected.

Ricardo informs me that everything in Margarita is closed on Sunday. We could anchor out with a Q-flag and that's about it. I decided to wait til Sunday night to sail for a Monday arrival. Chon Chon asks me, reflectively, where I'll be putting in. I know of only two places to anchor near Porlamar: in front of Hotel Concorde or Juan Marina. Chon Chon gazes out across the water; then back at me and says "Juan *Mierda* is more like it." I take it he does not care for this place. I verify the number of a boat agent, Terry Bannon. I'm skeptical of such a gringo-sounding agent but might need some help clearing in since boats are no longer allowed to anchor near customs.

An unexpected Sunday in Los Testigos provided time for Julie and me to snorkel around little Isla Calentador. Strong surge reduced the visibility to maybe 40 ft. but I could not remember ever seeing so many schooling fish, including some species I hadn't seen school before, like trumpetfish. These big schools were all very active. Is this the way the Caribbean was in the not-so-old days?

In a somewhat strange scene, Claude off the French-flagged **Wapiti** came on board and asked for a half kilo of sugar. He was on his way to Carriacou but forgot to bring any sugar. Lucky for him, we had some. He had advice on changing money in Margarita. He also had a beer and a cigarette.

All crew was up to get underway a little after midnight. By the time sails were set and we were on a course of 240 Magnetic toward Margarita, it was 0130. I took the first watch and stayed at the helm until 0530. We made fairly good speed over the surface in 10-20 knot winds, especially given a contrary tidal current and overall Northwest current effect. QV passed a fishing boat to port and a freighter to starboard. I also saw our green starboard running light was out. The port and stern lights were OK. When Julie and Kate came on watch together, I suggested a course change to 250 to get some westerly travel against the currents. The gals roused me at 0800 to get some input on a course change since we weren't making much progress according to the position checks. While having my necessary orange juice and a banana, I saw Margarita. We could steer for the land we could see, still allowing for current. I took the helm while Julie and Kate went back to bed.

Margarita-ville

The island of Margarita is a strange, engaging, and criminal place. Everything is cheap at the highly unofficial exchange rate, most anything available is for sale; all of it is tax-free. Lots of guys walk around carrying pistols: a few in uniform; most not. Some in uniform carry M-16s.

We discovered some of this after I eye ball-navigated the landmarks in to the anchorage off Porlamar. Quo Vadis was on the hook by 1130 in 9 ft. directly in front of the shell of the unfinished (and apparently abandoned) Hotel Concorde. Juan Marina has the only dinghy dock in this anchorage but, we discovered, it is seriously shallow. You ground an outboard if you drop it down at lower tides. Only the teen-age dockhand seemed to be around when we showed up shortly after noon.

We walked next door to Jak's on a partially paved, muddy path. The hostess called Terry Bannon, the boat agent. She informed me he wouldn't be back until 1700. I made an appointment, left my boat card, and made the now time-honored decision when faced with a cruising impasse: Let's eat lunch! It was a very good lunch and the beers were very cold. Jak was born and grew up in Thailand. She has managed to combine fresh Venezuelan fare with her native cooking style and Thai seasonings. The vegetables are especially tasty. I also arranged for the barge with call sign "Waterbaby" to deliver water to Quo Vadis. Diesel fuel is supposedly delivered only at 0700. QV takes on just over 100 gallons of water. I shower in some of it and go back on shore to meet Terry Bannon. He is Canadian and on time. I discover Terry is also the Honorary Consul for Canada (and, for some reason, Australia) here on Margarita. Since that is not a very lucrative position for an honest Canadian, he also handles Customs and Immigration documents. He believes he can arrange for us to clear out via Los Roques and Los Aves, offshore islands en route to Bonaire. His fee for doing everything is 96,000 bolivares. This translates to about US$32 at current street black market rates. I have been warned not to go to banks or *cambios* to change money. The official exchange rate was about 500 bolivares for one greenback dollar. Dinner at Jak's is even better than lunch.

When we dink in to the silted-up dock the next morning, Juan Baro is there. He tells me to join him and three other very gringo-acting, middle-aged skippers in his reception area. Juan looks like a caricature of a Latin American villain. His hair is slicked back into a shiny flip at his neck. He has a long, drooping handlebar mustache and holds his cigarette between his middle and ring finger as he puffs it through his mustache. He sits with shoulders hunched and knees crossed as he explains to his audience, in accented English, how things are in Margarita and what he, Juan, will do for us ignorant nautical pilgrims. The other skippers are hanging on his every word. One of them is taking notes.

Chon Chon had warned me. Juan *Mierda* does come across as very sleazy. After he assigns a time for us all to return with documents and catch his bus to the supermarket, I inform him I've made other arrangements but would like to use the marina's laundry service. He is seriously taken aback. There is a hostile flash in his deep-set black eyes before he points toward the sacks full of dirty clothes piled in the corner. Besides, his fees for clearing in are more than Terry Bannon's.

Speaking of fees, it is time to get some *bolivares* to pay them. The starboard running light lens had a hole in it like it was shot by a .22 caliber but no apparent internal damage. Maybe it just melted. I replaced the blackened bulb using a copper collar to adapt the spare (not by Lucas) to the bracket and it lights up. Now, to find a lens. The diesel fuel boat shows up just as we're ready to shove off. I ask him to come back later and, by the way, "How much?" A quick mental conversion comes out to 19 cents/gallon.

Laundry, with boat and personal ID tags inside and out, is handed over. I hope to see it again. The shopping trip to Porlamar is a mixed success: some boat parts, fresh fruits and vegetables, but no chain to secure the dinghy and outboard. Link chain was recommended rather than the more common steel cable by some cruisers, partly because you can hear chain rattle across the deck as the thieves try to take your dink. I couldn't find the jewelry shop Terry recommended for changing dollars to bolivares. One of the street touts directs me to a watch shop. The owner advises me of the going exchange rate: still around B3000 for one US dollar. I am in the process of digging a couple hundred US out of my shorts when two *policia* slinging shoulder weapons stroll in. I feel a sinking sensation in my stomach. This is, after all, a black market foreign currency deal in progress. The owner started showing me watches. I doubt the *policia* bought into his display any more than I did. They probably just stopped by for their daily take and followed this gringo into the shop.

Back at Jak's, I collected the stamped and signed "OK to be in Venezuela" documents from Terry in exchange for 96,000 of the *bolivares* I had eventually acquired. He introduces me to Don Harris. Don's official operation is called Margarita Sailing Services which specializes in rigging. I never completely figured out the extent of his actual operations except that it includes Jak's, the rigging business, the sale of inflatables and outboards (when available), and some real estate. He agrees to take a look at the wind generator while professing to know next to nothing about them.

Dinner ashore at Jak's continues to be very good. She also features half-price drinks during Happy Hour which results in the local beer costing about 25 cents. I can't remember having a beer at this price since the same event at some of the officers' clubs in the Far East many years ago. Extreme low tide was a major factor in all the crew going to the movies at the Cinex Jumbo ultra-modern, air-conditioned theater complex. The only Third World intrusions in this temple of universal pop culture were: 1) lack of popcorn, 2) the escalators weren't working. The film I saw, starring Hugh Grant, was sparsely attended. Maybe because it was in English. Maybe Hugh's boyish charm doesn't play well in Margarita. Maybe because there weren't any gunfights or car chases.

I've been tipping the dockboys, Andres and Emilio, 2000 bolivares a day. At midnight, Emilio hands me the clean laundry bundle and helps launch the dink. There still wasn't much water under the dock. I got the dink clipped in to the davits back at QV and, stone cold sober, I fell out of it. There was plenty of water under me. The boat papers and my passport were soaked. I was up for another hour, pressing, drying and cleaning stuff including my reading glasses, Swiss army knife, and Venezuela cruising guide. When I bought the new dinghy and outboard back at Solomon's Island, I was sure handling QV's tender was a skill I'd acquire with easy grace and natural ability. It hasn't worked out that way.

Heavy wakes from the local *pineros* going out at first light rocked me awake. Julie had run the inverter for five hours overnight to charge her digital camera. I had the engine running to recharge the house batteries when the fuel delivery boat showed up. The nozzle was handed up. I put it in the filter funnel and told them it was OK to begin pumping. The guy standing at the 55 gallon fuel drum started vigorously cranking the pump hand over hand. I topped up the main tank with 16 gallons for the *bolivar* equivalent of US$3.00. That is not a misprint. Three dollars American money.

As I was hanging my rinsed clothes (from last night's dunking) out to dry, "Waterbaby" came by on its rounds of the anchorage. I filled up QV's water tanks. By coincidence, they also took 16 gallons. The same amount of the clear, hopefully drinkable liquid cost US$4.60. Like most sailing cruisers who have visited Venezuela, I wish I had more fuel tankage.

After Don's crew takes the wind generator ashore, my crew moves the boat to the Southwest sector of the anchorage, nearly in line with the Juan Marina dinghy dock. We have been advised that it is safer down here and there is less *pinero* traffic with their resulting wakes. After the bridle is re-rigged on 50 ft. of anchor line, all crew go ashore for lunch and wind generator dismantling.

The rear bearing of the wind generator has seized solid. I jump in the vintage BMW 320 with a heavily-oxidized exterior to begin the parts and repairs search. As Don gets in, he adjusts the .32 caliber automatic he usually carries at the small of his back over to his right hip. I jokingly suggest he should park the BMW out of sight when we're shopping. Or maybe it won't matter. Just being a gringo will trigger the "gringo price". It also seems like a strange caliber for an automatic pistol.

As we drive around the busy streets of Porlamar, Don tells me a little more about himself. He confides he was a Navy helicopter pilot for some of the years during the U.S. involvement in Viet Nam and other nearby places. I'm thinking he was flying rescue off aircraft carriers: that sort of duty.

"No," he says. "I was mostly flying for the civilians." I hadn't heard the term used this way. Mostly, the CIA was referred to as "The Company" as in "He's a company guy." So, I joke, Air America couldn't handle all the CIA's flight requirements in Southeast Asia?

"Not where we'd go," he continued, peering through the dusty windshield. "I'd take some of the civilians into a clearing some place; sling my hammock in the cargo bay until they came back." I express surprise the CIA didn't use their own pilots.

"They had a strong preference for Navy pilots only in this operation. Not even Marines," he noted. Don also had his run-ins with his superior brass but seemed to come out better than I had.

"One Commander I didn't get along with was removed at the request of the civilians. Unsuitable for mission requirements." I knew a bunch of them that fit that description when I was in the Air Force. I didn't know the CIA would get them re-assigned if you were flying their operatives over to Laos or Cambodia or…wherever. Don also acquired a taste for good grass during his Southeast Asia excursions. He casually rolled a number as he negotiated city traffic, lit up and inhaled. He didn't pass it over.

We found a replacement bearing, and a spare, at the SKF distributor and replacement lead wires at Vemasca, the principal chandlery on Margarita. Don knew a Dutch guy who could solder the wiring back in place. At his in-home audio shop, the Dutch guy found blue/brown wires (The European version of red/black electrical leads, I am told.) that were sized right, soldered them in and verified continuity of the circuit. He wouldn't accept payment. Don offered him a meal at Jak's, anytime. Don and I are back at Jak's before 1800 where I meet Ken Hellewell. He is sitting at a table with Julie. Both are enjoying half-price Happy Hour. I ask if it's OK to join them.

Ken came in to Margarita aboard the 35 ft. sloop **Topaz**. He has sailed his vessel nearly around the world, single-handed. We find out during dinner that Ken is making the final passages of this solo circumnavigation. There are fewer than 80 sailors who have accomplished the feat including the first, Joshua Slocum, over 100 years ago. Ken will finish his one lap around the planet alone when he makes it back to Cabo San Lucas at the tip of Baja California. He rejoices in the fact that he has only 3000 miles to go. I've been bemoaning the fact that I have over 3000 miles to go. His attitude gives me a fresh perspective. This is the second time around for Topaz, he says, so he was pretty confident the boat could make it. At this point, he is confident he can, too.

Dink Removal

The wakes from the early morning *pineros* are about the same at this new anchorage. The reefer isn't keeping the meat frozen so we tossed out the old chicken and put in a case of beer to cool. After installing the repaired and re-wired wind generator, it isn't generating power in 10 knots of wind. Such a day on board fades to such a night. Sometime around three in the morning, the dinghy is stolen. The second motor (purchased in the Bahamas you may remember), gas tank, and many long-term cruising accessories were clamped on this well-equipped tender to Quo Vadis.

As I'm staring stupidly at the cut cable end, a skiff with a young guy handling the motor comes up to the stern and tells me my dinghy is gone. Oh, really? Yes. He'd seen the thieves but couldn't catch them. He asks if we should go look for the dink. My first reaction is this was a scam to get the dink back for ransom and he's in on it. This happens. Kate tells me, in a hushed voice, "He has a gun."

I get one, too. It's the Browning automatic. When I step in to his skiff, I see the boy *is* carrying a real hog leg. It looks like something made from different parts of a shotgun, a revolver, and the stock of a dueling pistol and it has a big, black hole at the end of the barrel. I don't know what we're going to do if we do find the thieves and they have any real firepower. I'm surprisingly calm and feel ready. He knows where the local bandits usually go. We head toward the village on the far side of the bay.

We make a complete tour of Bahía Mar. During the tour, he shines his light on the shoreline and makes several unplanned stops and detours to avoid the fishing nets set in the bay at night. We see nothing moving and no dinghy. I find out he is the *vigilante* paid to patrol the anchorage at night to guard against theft from the visiting cruising boats. I'm back on board QV by 0530.

Don Harris came out to collect us after I reported the dinghy and motor theft on the 0800 cruiser net. After Terry Bannon finished looking for new customers, he pronounced me an honorary Australian and drove me to the police station to file an official report. I can't honestly say, "No worries, mate."

Terry offers to stay and help with the translation and the local cops. I accept the offer but an otherwise bored plainclothes detective with little enthusiasm for preparing cruiser theft reports adamantly refuses to admit him. It turns out my Spanish is up to the task of providing answers, which the cop records with two fingers on a manual typewriter. The ribbon is so used it is nearly transparent. The office copy machine is broken. We march back out, past the excluded Honorary Consul still sitting in the waiting room, to the public lobby. I put some coins in a copy machine. This one works. I leave with Terry and a barely legible, lightly inked copy of the official police report.

At a telephone service kiosk, I call the insurance company. Leslie answers. She is the agent who sold me the policy. I take this as a good thing. She tells me what she'll need to make a claim and I agree to FAX it. She also agrees to work up some renewal rates. What next? I make a decision. Let's have lunch! El Punto Criollo is relatively expensive at $US8/each but luxuriously good.

Ken Hellewell comes on the VHF at 0830 the next morning. He informs me he will not be able to take us ashore, as he had promised yesterday, because his dinghy and motor were stolen during the night. At first, I can't decide if this joke is actually pretty funny or in really poor taste. I eventually conclude that it's not a good day to make fun of poor unfortunate me and tell him so.

 "I'm serious," he assures me. "My dink is gone. Go out on deck and look." I do. Ken has anchored just 200 meters outside QV. There is no inflatable with motor attached anywhere on or around Topaz. Bill, skipper of Interlude, gave us a ride towing Ken's other, tiny wooden dinghy to shore.

Ken and I account for two of the three dinghy/motor thefts at Porlamar this week. Yes, there is a third one. That dink was reportedly stolen off the sailboat's deck. The local establishment doesn't seem to care about the crime wave. Vemasca, or Don Harris, will sell you a new dinghy or a new outboard if they have any available, but do not seem overly concerned about robbery. Given the pace at which small motors are being re-directed into the local economy, you'd think there would be a good selection to choose from. Still, I can't find an outboard properly sized for a 9-10 foot RIB inflatable, which I now need to replace. Vemasca, the most complete chandlery, has several candidates for QV's new tender at competitive prices. Surprisingly, they have no outboards in stock. After a couple days' search, I agree to buy a used 15 horsepower Suzuki from Don. He agrees to separate the motor from the much larger inflatable he was trying to sell attached to it. Don wants list price of

US$1500 for the motor. The Suzuki has 50% more power than should be used with this size dink. It is heavy. The few features it has appear to be directed at Third World markets. I can't think of a good alternative.

Ken rows over for dinner. A fake ATM has taken his bank card: yet another Margarita scam. During the ensuing and animated conversation covering bad ports, personal values, political views, life goals, and his least-favorite ocean (Indian, it turns out.), Kate presses Ken for his age.

"I'm 39," he admits. "Me, too." I add, smiling broadly through my beard.

"You're 39, John? It's a good age," he smiles back.

"39? You're not 39! You can't be 39!" exclaims Julie, acting seriously aggrieved and stupid.

Ken is back on board the next morning with the C-MAP navigation charts. One CD covers The Americas; the other covers The Rest of the World. This is a very thoughtful gift which he loads on to Julie's laptop hard drive. Kate makes us lunch with pesto and salsa to go with the omelets; then asks me to take her ashore. Ken provided a tutorial on C-MAP usage after lunch and just before he and Julie engage in a long conversation on sexually transmitted diseases—which makes me cringe. "Over 30% of the population has genital herpes." That kind of topic. Despite this frank exchange of more information than I really wanted to hear, they decide to row back to Topaz together and remain there for a while. Kate called me on the VHF from Jak's for a ride back to QV. When I bring her back on board, she asks where Ken and Julie are. I tell her.

"Well," she responds, "It's nice Julie finally found someone her own age to talk with." It takes me a moment to process that this is girl-speak for two horny sailors having sex after weeks at sea. Kate also informs me she is feeling sick to her stomach but is not sure of the cause.

When Don discovers his soldering iron doesn't work, we go shopping for one. On the way to Radio Shack, he stops by one of his shoreside abodes and picks up Erica, previously described as the best piece of ass ever. She looks very young and too thin but has a bubbly Latina manner and a girlish sense of humor. She pretends to be a pop star, singing into one of the microphones displayed on the wall at Radio Shack. We do some other shopping, it being Don's car. Erica wonders aloud at my Spanish-speaking ability and chides Don (She calls him Papi.) for not speaking better Spanish.

Back in the car, she asks me in her Venezuelan Spanish how much a prostitute costs in America. The question is so unexpected, I don't fully comprehend it for a moment. When I absorb what she has said, I confess I don't know. It turns out Don has a pretty good idea and tells her, in dollars.

"Well," she continues dismissively, "Thirty or forty thousand will cover it in Margarita." She's talking *bolivares*, of course. Her forehead creases briefly—like she's thinking of that dollar number.

Don uses my new soldering iron on the loose wires but the mystery of the non-generating wind machine continues. I take the shunt to be repaired by Tomas, the German. He re-solders the leads correctly and charges me nothing. The wires in the generating head are re-configured by Don. I go on-line to request a wiring diagram and diode test procedure. This effort also results in no power output. During my wanderings ashore, I meet Dijk and Leanna from Isis. They own the other Prout 37 in the anchorage. I invite this friendly couple from the Netherlands aboard QV for sundowners and snacks. Dijk has lots of information on repairing Sonic drive legs and on Prouts, in general. He also offered to look at the wind generator. Julie and Ken rowed back to Topaz at sundown. I made *chorizo* and rice. Kate still had a sick stomach and sipped some soup.

Marlec Engineering in the UK provide technical support for Rutland wind generators. When I call them back, my contact Angela has gone for the day. Just as I start wailing and gnashing my teeth, Teresa takes over as tech rep. This gal seems to know her stuff and imparts it to me with charming British diction. I head back to Jak's to get Randy and his ladder. On board, I climb up the tower and configure the internals of the wind generator correctly. Or, to be precise, exactly as Teresa told me. Still no power output. Flaco came by on "Waterbaby". Sure, fill it up. I'm busy.

At 1530, I gave up in frustration and dinked over to Isis to ask Dijk to look at the wind generator. He went through a methodical check, confirming voltage generation in the rotor box as he spun the blades. We removed the generator head. I lifted it away with a mast halyard while he stood on the rail. Dijk discovered that the disconnect junction (with blades and sockets) had been pulled apart when Don's guys yanked and cut the power wire. Crawling into the aft hull, I was able to free up another two inches of wire for him to tie into. He had it fixed by 1800. I thanked him and congratulated him for his very useful abilities. This Dutchman who doesn't drink beer accepts a chilled can of Coke.

"Back at Grenada, they called me MacGiver," Dijk tells me in accented but perfect English.

I really didn't plan on spending over a week in Margarita. I called a crew conference the next morning. First, to review boat procedure and protocol and second, to inform Julie and Kate we would weigh anchor at 0600 and head for Robledal, at the West end of the island. I still needed to get a bill of sale for the Suzuki. Don still couldn't find the operating manual for the motor but agreed to adjust his labor rate since his guys had screwed up the removal of the wind generator. He never did offer to share a joint, even during the long drive we made to the North coast of Margarita to return the cement mixer. I did get to see the interior of the island and the fancy seaside mansion where the mixer was needed. Don was vague on the source of the owner's wealth.

Out to the Edge

Ken came on board for final sundowners in Margarita. QV's dink and outboard are brought up and chained to the stern cleat before he and Julie row off into the sunset. Meredith has sent me an e-mail. She will meet us in Bonaire. We can head for Panama from there. I feel like a child waiting for Christmas at the thought of being with her again. In another part of my head, I'm seriously concentrated on the passages to Los Roques and Los Aves along the route to Bonaire. The guide describes sailing there as being "out on the edge". They aren't near anyplace else. It's not likely anybody will show up to help if there is a problem.

The crew did a good job preparing to get underway so we cleared Bahia Mar at Porlamar by 0700. We raised the main and motor-sailed off the anchor toward Punta Mosquito in no morning wind. After about an hour, I saw whitecaps and rolled out the headsail. We started making 5-6 knots under sail through a fair amount of boat and ship traffic off the South coast of Margarita.

The usual fishing boats and *pineros* were motoring about. There was a *Guardacosta* patrol boat that didn't even slow down passing us. That's good. The cruise boat Sun Princess was taking a load of windsurfers and day trippers to Guamache. We sailed past the cruise ship Ocean Village in the wide channel. A few passengers waved. I was determined to go out to Latitude 65 West before turning North toward Robledal in an effort to maintain favorable wind. As we cleared Punta Arenas at the Southwest tip of the island, the wind came on our nose at 30-40 knots producing short, choppy 4 ft. waves. I took the helm and tacked inshore to the 20 ft. line which resulted in little wind change but wave size dropped to two feet. I kept this up until we got into the lee anchorage off Robledal.

QV went between the fishing boats to drop anchor in 6 ft. off the beach. More fishing boats came in after we did and anchored both in front and astern. Kate wanted to go ashore. I asked her why. " To sketch" She suggested I pay somebody to guard the dink. Considering what I'd just been through with dinghy and motor theft, I was in a highly paranoid condition and could not think through an acceptable landing scenario. No shore parties tonight, I decided. The natives were too dangerous. After dinner, we got a radio call from Topaz now en route to Tortuga. Ken plans to anchor around Punta Delgada in the bay. We agreed to rendezvous tomorrow afternoon.

It was a clear, sunny day without a breath of wind. The crew rotated at the helm, motoring over a long swell that built from 3 to 6 ft. Kate put out two fishing lines. There were no catches. I contacted Topaz about 1500 to notify Ken I expected to make the waypoint at 1540. He advised me the charts are off by 0.2 to 0.5 nautical miles around the East side of the island. This fit with my observation that the point wasn't quite on the latitude line. It also puts the rocks out just far enough to present a problem if you are approaching in the dark or strictly by waypoint navigation.

We were on the hook off Playa Caldera by 1600. Ken swam over as soon as we anchored. The bimini went up and the crew went over the side into the warm, clear water. About 1700, Quo Vadis got a call from Topaz. Ken volunteered foccacia for dinner. He brought Julie back about 1900 along with the bread and some fresh-baked brownies for dessert. I served pasta with the red sausage and onion sauce, salad, and a Chilean wine. We ate and talked til 2300—way past my bedtime. Two other cruisers and a Venezuelan fishing boat were in the anchorage by nightfall.

I see those three leave at dawn, then go back to my bunk. Later in the morning, I check fuel, oil and battery status. With the fuel remaining, QV can motor for about 24 hours which should take her 140-160nm. Oil level is down an eighth of an inch after 9 hours of motoring yesterday. I top it up with 300cc. The engine still won't start on an isolated house battery bank which is puzzling. When I enter the waypoint to the Southeast of Los Roques, the GPS tells me it is 93.7nm away. I figure that means at least 100nm under the *amas* so we could make it motoring if the wind doesn't come up.

Rotten Fish and Rocky Places

Tortuga is a study in contrasts. Three-sided stick and board structures where fishermen take shelter are scattered along the beach facing the lagoon. Behind them is a level, well-maintained airstrip. This weekend there are 10-15 private aircraft parked along the strip during the course of the day. The mostly young and affluent Caracas crowd fly over from the mainland for a swim and a picnic lunch. In a brief discussion with a couple of handsome couples, I am informed this is a routine day trip. They are tolerant but not welcoming to gringo beachcombers from transient cruising boats.

In the afternoon, all of us transient cruisers go snorkeling. Ken notes that he and I have much of the same snorkel gear including Mares fins, which are made in Italy.

"It's amazing they're not made in China," he observes. "I'd like to find some manufactured things that aren't made in China."

Later, I walked out to the point and traded packs of cigarettes to the fishermen for some of their snapper. One of the guidebooks told me cigarettes were desirable trade goods out in the islands. Another identified trading item is beer. The fishing boat **Santa Eufemia** had come in while we were snorkeling. I rowed over to see if they had any diesel fuel. The captain first said, "No. We are gasoline-powered." Then he said he had 30 liters. Since a jerry jug holds only about 20 liters, I offered beer for fuel. I paddled back to QV and returned to **Eufemia** with an empty jug and two six-packs of Polar beer. The captain took the beer and one of the crew took the jug below and filled it from a tank in the bilge. I did not get to inspect the fuel.

Ken was invited to dinner on QV to help us eat the snapper. I sautéed the fish, made saffron rice and put out chilled vegetables. When Ken came on board, we opened a bottle of sauvignon blanc. Something was wrong with the fish. It wasn't spoiled exactly. It tasted chalky and had a crumbly texture. We tossed most of it overboard. Ken said this was poetic justice for trading cigarettes for the fish. I think I was punked but can usually spot bad fish. The fishermen also said the weather would continue calm and clear. Covering some of the options for approaching or leaving Tortuga, one of the cruising guides advises to stay clear of the reefs at Tortuguilla. This does not seem like much of a problem. I plot another course to Los Roques. Kate still has a sick stomach.

After Julie comes back from **Topaz**, both boats get underway by 0930 in very light Easterly wind. Ken continues his single-handed voyage, headed for the Panama Canal. He's allowing 14 days for that passage. QV is headed for Los Roques, planning to make landfall tomorrow before noon. We take photos of each other's boats as we sail together for a while. After a few hours, **Topaz** disappeared over the horizon.

During my midnight watch, I furled the genoa to about 80% thinking that would reduce QV's tendency to round up. I thought full sail was also overworking the autohelm in following seas. Both results were moderately successful; even better after I changed the autohelm setting to aim at a waypoint off the Sepastopol Reef. At the end of my watch, I looked up to check sail condition before calling Kate. A batten was working out of its pocket on the mainsail. I was up the mast in seconds to retrieve it before it went overboard; then I got Kate up for her watch.

At 0630, the crew got me up. We had made landfall about 5nm from the Southeast entrance to Sebastopol Reef. I disconnected the autohelm after fairly successful use on this passage and took the helm. There is another way to sail to Gran Roque: continue North along the length of the island group, turn West once clear of the reef, and come in from the Northeast. That route would take another half day and there were more opportunities to anchor along this route. We entered the Boca de Sebastopol under sail at 0730, eye-balling along the east side of the central reef that divides the channel. Kate went forward to spot coral heads. She identified a school of fish as reef break, but didn't see the ripples over the shoals when I steered QV out of the channel. The channel is fairly narrow but 10-15 meters deep, if you're in it. Julie reached in front of me, took the chart book off the instrument console, and sat down on the lazarette to read the narrative description of Los Roques. I couldn't believe what she had just done. I was tense after one excursion over the reef and shouted at her to put the chart back so I could try and follow it. No profanity. I don't talk like that since I had kids. She got very piqued and yelled back at me for being rude to her. I suppress a surge of righteous indignation and concentrate on steering. I am in a new, strange place trying to avoid hitting hard, jagged things and she grabbed the chart from in front of the helm.

I considered a couple of "out" anchorages but after clearing the reef, we were close to Gran Roque. The depth drops from 90 to 10 ft. as Quo Vadis heads in towards shore. No other boats are U.S. flagged. Since Grenada, I've been impressed by the national diversity of boats cruising this part of the Caribbean. Even in Trinidad, there were fewer U.S. or UK ensigns flying from the stern. There are Danish, Swedish, South African, French, Dutch, German, and the occasional Canadian or Australian boat in the anchorages. The only U.S. boat has her anchor down in 6 ft. by 1030. The agency order for clearing in to this National Park is *Guardacosta, Guarda Nacional, Imparques, Autoridad Unica*. The last office is where you pay the fees. The *Guardacosta* guy didn't like me or was having a bad day, or both, and would only give 48 hours in transit with a *zarpe* for Bonaire. The *Guarda Nacional* didn't see us as much of a threat and stamped the papers. *Imparques* was closed but the *Guarda* guy said we didn't have to pay fees. Maybe because of our 48 hour transit? The maximum legal stay for a boat in the Park is two weeks.

I know some cruisers have sailed this roughly rectangular archipelago for all that time and longer. The winds are fairly reliable and the water is flat. In fact, the main attraction for non-cruising visitors is wind surfing. There are no paved streets or sidewalks; no vehicles except for the officials' fat-tired golf carts. Los Roques may be little-known to us Yankees but the Europeans apparently know about it. The many *pensions* are well-populated but won't serve food to anybody except their guests. The two public eating establishments that are open are surprisingly upscale considering the sand streets, and both are island resort expensive. Well, the ice cream shop isn't so pricey.

It takes about 10 minutes to walk the length of the settlement where it dwindles away at the airstrip. A Soviet-era Antonov transport fills most of the flat space off the strip, its props turning slowly when the wind blows. A daily flight schedule to/from the mainland is posted on an empty guard shack. At the internet café, an e-mail from Mer says maybe she isn't coming to Bonaire as scheduled. I sent Happy Birthday greetings to my daughter, Beth. I worried about Mer's message.

After breakfast, I check out the Francisquis anchorage by dink. It has great beaches, a reef for snorkeling and some big thatch-roofed structures on shore. I am too ignorant to figure out these were built for charter boat day-trippers, so decide to move QV to this anchorage. Before moving, it seems like a good idea to stock up with fresh water. Gran Roque has a big de-salination plant but the water hose can only be accessed by cruising boats from a beach landing. There is no charge for the water. I ask Julie to go with me to help with the dink and the jerry jugs. She responds with a non-hostile but strange "Do you really need me to go?" I tell her I think it's a prudent move or I wouldn't ask. As we hit the beach, the rigid shaft Suzuki hits the bottom and pops off the dinghy transom. I instruct Julie to get out and steady the bow while I retrieve the outboard from the beach break. A helpful fellow on the beach gets the water flowing from the hose. The Suzuki re-starts and propels us and 10 gallons of water back to QV. The afternoon is spent in total indolence at Francisquis. We swim, we snorkel, we find time for a siesta. I check out the charter cats bringing day-trippers. They look like the big ones built on St. Kitts.

Kate likes to wash down the aft deck and cockpit with seawater. I don't see the point of adding salt to the deck but she does this every day. While she does, I pad the end of the batten and re-install it in the mainsail pocket she has re-sewn. After everybody was back on board from morning swims, we pulled up the anchor and motored away from Francisquis as the day boats arrived. I called the *Guardacosta* as we cleared the Gran Roque waterfront and advised them of our departure.

I truly enjoyed sailing my boat that afternoon over to the little island of Felipe. After we got the anchor down, a weird current and light wind were blowing the boat back inshore, where the bugs lived. I decided to move further North, where it was deeper but further out from the mangroves. We passed two boats already at anchor in the cove. The last one, nearest our new spot, was the French-flagged **Phebus**. As we motored past, I waved and offered a *Bon jour* to the *Madame* sunning on the deck. I must have been in a jolly mood after today's fun, stress-free sail, so I announced *"Nous viens a la cote Français. C'est meilleur içi, non?"* Very roughly, "We're coming to the French side. It's better over here, right?" I was thinking of the bugs. She smiled and waved.

I was surprised when Pierre, skipper of Phebus and husband of the *Madame*, came over to say hello. It turns out he was just responding to a friendly overture from an American skipper on a U.S. flagged boat. He didn't want sugar, cigarettes, or anything else. Since the invasion of Iraq, there has been a general but mostly unfounded presumption in the Caribbean that U.S. and French people don't get along because our respective Presidents didn't like each other. I don't think much of either President but had no gripe with the French, as long as they didn't smoke cigarettes on my boat.

Pierre sat down on the gunwale. I sat on the coach roof and we resumed our discussion in French. He knew the anchorages of Los Roques since he and his wife cruise six months of the year in Venezuela. They return to France when the weather improves back there, around May. He's been doing this for several seasons, leaving his boat at one of the yards on the Mainland when he's back in France. Pierre throws a little Spanish toward Julie and Kate, initially thinking they are my wife and daughter. The ages could work, I guess. I explain they are not. As soon as Pierre and I say our *Au revoirs*, Julie gets in my face for not translating for her; accusing me of being rude to her. She won't quit it. I am so taken aback by her behavior, I say nothing. I purposely avoid a response so it won't be a knee-jerk reaction. Later, I think if she couldn't take part in a casual conversation in any of the languages in use, it's not my problem. Dinner is stir-fried rice with veggies and crisped chunks of ham. Wind is light overnight with few bugs and no surge. Pierre knows his anchorages.

The French are not on deck when we leave for Los Aves at 0630. These island groups are uninhabited except for occasional fishermen and lots and lots of birds *(aves)*. One group is Aves de Barlavento (toward the wind). The other is Aves de Sotavento (beneath the wind—to westward). The guidebook tells me they are made up of some delightful islands and reefs but navigation and anchoring are a little tricky. Extensive shallows, unmarked reefs, some areas not surveyed, things like that grab your attention.

We had jibed to the East end of Isla Sur by mid-afternoon. When we came back down to the waypoint, it was a little too close to the tip of the island as depth dropped to 20-30 ft. I took the helm, cleared the point and the outside shoal, then turned QV into the wind in the first bay to drop sail.

Julie was on the furling line and Kate on the genoa sheets. Depth was still OK but shallowing rapidly with the reef visible in the clear water ahead of us. Julie got the genoa about halfway furled; then started jerking on the line when it stopped. "Stalled out?" I asked and turned in the helm chair to help pull in the furling line. Julie lost the line, lost her balance and fell on the aft deck. Dropping the genoa sheets, Kate turned to her and asked if she was OK. I was still holding on to the furling line as it tipped me out of the helm chair. The sails are not down and the reef is getting closer. First, I got my hands back on the wheel. Kate and I finished furling the genoa and dropping the main. Julie was screaming in my face immediately for not helping her; accusing me of pulling the line out of her hands, on so on. After I set the anchor, I told her she was way out of line and not to behave like that again. She argued with me. I was the one being rude and didn't stop to see if she was hurt. (She wasn't.) Julie announced she was getting off the boat in Bonaire. I said OK. You know what I would have expected from most sailors who lost the headsail furling line? "Gee, sorry, skipper. I'll try to do better."

I busied myself the rest of the afternoon tightening loose screws and bolts. The new Stone Cold reefer still pulls the battery voltages down and uses too much power for useful applications while sailing. Maybe it needs a gel cell battery update.

Between midnight and first light a high frequency whine woke me three times. I could not locate the source on board. Changes in boat sounds drive most skippers crazy. You can sleep through a crashing storm but if the pitch of the normal creaking changes you're instantly awake and usually alarmed. When I got up for the last time, I made coffee and tried some alternate calculations and routes for the overnight passage to Bonaire. Wind has been coming from about 120 the last two days. The course to a waypoint just South of Bonaire is 285 Magnetic. Any course change will have to be while I'm on watch but how fast will *Quo Vadis* run over this piece of the Caribbean?

Kate and I take the dink to explore the bird lagoon. She trolls for fish while I try to figure out the exit channels from our anchorage. There are plenty of birds adorning the mangroves: mostly boobies of different varieties. Kate doesn't pull in any fish. I am convinced of the complexity of the reef and consequent opportunity to hit parts of it, as also described in the cruising guide.

After a siesta, we stowed the dinghy on the foredeck. This is good practice for a night passage in 4-6 ft. following seas but we really did it because the starboard davit line had frayed through. I took the helm to go out, putting Julie on the port bow to call out coral heads and Kate on the starboard *ama* on shoal watch. Julie never reported anything. Kate put QV over the exit shoal in 6 ft. of water when I saw it on the depth sounder. You'll remember QV's draft is just over 3 ft. It still makes my stomach sink. We needed to make an S-curve through the reef as the last exit move before heading Northwest, away from it. I had missed it in the West sun, now low on the water.

I stayed on the helm til 2000 when Julie and Kate came on together. Julie informed me she could not stand watch alone. Is this a new attitude or has this always been going on? Kate didn't like the state of the sails. QV continued West at 6-7 knots because the sail shape turned out to be good but too fast for a daylight arrival off Bonaire. After midnight, I shortened the headsail to reduce speed and sailed our actual course. When I went off watch at 0400, I gave instructions to sail on over to 63.19 West; then turn North and call me an hour out from the marina waypoint. When I woke up at 0615, the boat was at 63.20.5 West. I'll admit we are still more than an hour from the waypoint. The light was good on an overcast morning. Julie was at the helm. After six weeks aboard, she was still driving the boat all over the ocean. I input a new waypoint for the Marina, now 3nm further East. We are beating back into the 15-20 knot wind I had planned to have on our beam as we went North along the coast of Bonaire. We get a really good view of the salt works at the Southern end of the island from three different approaches.

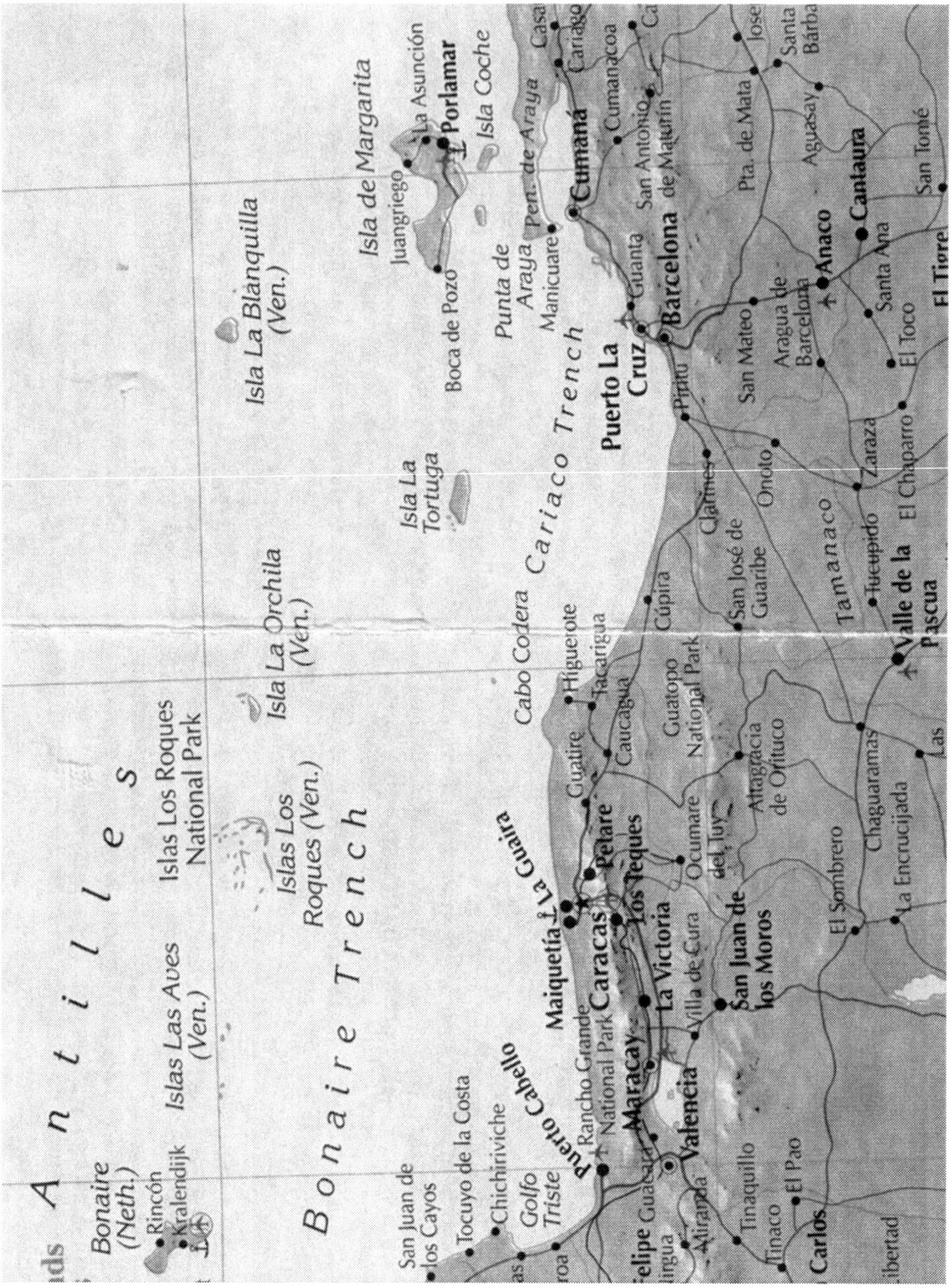
Antilles
Bonaire Trench
Cariaco Trench
Bonaire (Neth.)
Rincón
Kralendijk
Islas Las Aves (Ven.)
Islas Los Roques National Park
Islas Los Roques (Ven.)
Isla La Orchila (Ven.)
Isla La Blanquilla (Ven.)
Isla La Tortuga
Isla de Margarita
Juangriego
La Asunción
Porlamar
Boca de Pozo
Isla Coche
Punta de Araya
Pen. de Araya
Manicuare
Cabo Codera
San Juan de los Cayos
Tocuyo de la Costa
Chichiriviche
Golfo Triste
Puerto Cabello
Rancho Grande National Park
Maracay
Valencia
Maiquetía
La Guaira
Caracas
Petare
Los Teques
La Victoria
Guatire
Higuerote
Tacarigua
Caucagua
Guatopo National Park
Cúpira
Ocumare del Tuy
Villa de Cura
San Juan de los Moros
Altagracia de Orituco
San José de Guaribe
Clarines
Píritu
Puerto La Cruz
Barcelona
Guanta
Cumaná
Cumanacoa
San Antonio de Maturín
Cariaco
San Mateo
Onoto
Aragua de Barcelona
Anaco
Cantaura
Santa Ana
El Toco
Zaraza
El Chaparro
Tucupido
Tamanaco
Valle de la Pascua
Chaguaramas
El Sombrero
La Encrucijada
Tinaquillo
El Pao
Tinaco
Carlos
Pta. de Mata
Aguasay
San Tomé
Santa Bárbara
El Tigre

The ABCs of Avoiding Pirates of the Caribbean

Aboard S/V Quo Vadis, docked Bonaire and anchored off Curaçao

Bonaire, Curaçao and Aruba are the Westernmost of the Netherlands Antilles. The three islands are not too far off the coast of South America but far enough that they don't have pirate problems. This could be because the Dutch Navy flies P3 Orion long range patrol planes over their former colonies and Dutch Marines are responsible for local order and repelling any threatening brigands. These related forces are professional military, well-equipped to NATO standards and not corrupt. This overlay to the basic Dutch culture of cleanliness gives the ABCs a feel unique in the West Caribbean. They are mostly tidy, safe places where the ATMs work. Bonaire may be the cleanest of them.

Admittedly, I didn't make it to all of the Windwards Netherlands Antilles; the ABCs being the Leewards according to Dutch charts and descriptions. On British charts, the Leewards and Windwards are all in the Eastern Caribbean. But when the Dutch, who were the dominant trading power for at least one of those long-ago centuries, left their capitol on Curacao to go to Sint Marteen or possibly even to Saba or St. Eustatius, they were definitely sailing to windward. I have not been able to figure out or keep straight the whole Leewards and Windwards thing for all these years. I guess it depends on whose chart you're using—or where you start from?

The chart on QV shows we go past the Plaza Marina where I get no radio response, past Nautico Bonaire where a few exposed docks appear to have space, past the moorings which are all taken, and into the relatively new Harbor Village Marina by 0830. Juliet, off **Mistress**, greeted us and confirmed the marina office wasn't open yet. Anchoring is no longer an option at Bonaire. The entire submerged parts of the island are a National Park, strictly protected and enforced.

After the staff arrived, QV was assigned a slip for US$26/day plus power and water. Julie confirms she is leaving QV, went to the showers with Kate; then left the marina. I put the boat documents and all passports in my backpack and walked to Kralendijk to clear in. Customs and Immigration guys were downright cheerful. Not being too worried about boardings in Bonaire, I declared the Mossberg. Customs said they would send somebody to collect it from the boat at 1700. The internet café in town charged US$5/hour. It was worth it. A message from Meredith confirms her arrival in Bonaire in two days. I am ecstatic as I hitch back to the marina. The customs officer shows up only 15 minutes after the appointed hour. He writes out a receipt for the shotgun. I'm told Alfonso came by to turn on power and water but didn't. He goes home at 1700.

The next morning I gave Julie notice to be off the boat by 1800. She replied that she would get off the boat tomorrow. I informed her that it was not her call. She has announced she's leaving the boat, and she's had a day and a half to get off. She is quite miffed and reacted with personal insults. She now informs me she hurt her back and hand when she fell on the aft deck with the threat to go to a PI attorney. On Bonaire?

I spend the rest of the morning completing and FAXing insurance renewal info and premium payment. I decide to check on a hotel room near the airport for the first night of Meredith's late arrival and reserve one at the Divi Flamingo. It's on the water but away from the runways. After the water and power were turned on at the slip, I cleaned all the decks and the dinghy bottom with good results. Mer's flight was on schedule at 2100. Eladio, Master of Taxi 34, had finally agreed to a fare of US$20 and was waiting for us outside the terminal.

The marine life must be thriving in this undersea park. In the morning, we can see giant parrotfish from our window, nibbling at the algae-coated rocks on the shore. Being together with Meredith again makes me feel so good in mind, body and spirit.

When we get back to the Marina, Julie has taken most of her gear. Kate says she'll take her the items she's left. While I'm making up the queen-size bunk, Mer squares away the deck. I'm amazed how naturally she starts doing things on board after nine months away from the boat: coiling lines in a practiced manner, stowing and positioning things swiftly and correctly. The contrast to the crew that has spent the last six weeks on board is striking. I didn't expect this of her. Later in the afternoon, we go snorkeling off the entrance channel. Among all the hyper-colored reef fish, we see a baby eel. Mer thinks it is a snake. It is difficult to persuade her to snorkel after that sighting. She doesn't believe me that it's not a sea snake. I'm pretty sure they're only in the Western Pacific.

We leave the boat mid-morning to check out the beaches of Bonaire. During the transit between beaches, Mer wants to make friends with the wild donkeys that populate the interior. She has forgotten her sandals, so I offer her my three sizes larger Tevas. She straps them on and starts flopping across the sharp, rocky landscape toward the little burros.

"I look like Daisy Duck," she says to no one in particular. Well, from the ankles down, maybe. I don't remember seeing Daisy Duck in a string bikini. We encounter other local creatures during our journey through the interior. Some of them are two-legged: the pink flamingos and the humans in various colors.

Hog Country

Bonaire: Land of the Harley-Davidson. Live Free! Ride Free! It's not just printed on the T-shirts. The Hog rules, both stock and chopped. Sure, the tourist brochures tell you Bonaire is all about the diving; how the whole country is a marine park and don't hurt the reef. This is all going on beneath the water where the fishes are generally very quiet. On the two-lane asphalt roads of this Caribbean accumulation of limestone, Harleys rule. The roar of the "74 or more" machines is everywhere there is a hard surface to ride on.

The traditional native garb in this tropical clime seems to be black jeans and T-shirts. Fenders are adorned in chrome-plated skulls with red glass eyes. There is a biker couple tending to a righteous chopper as they emerge from a cheap (Well, not really that cheap in US$) roadside motel. She is not really beautiful, but blue-eyed and blonde. He has a rat tail beard and a bandana tied over his head. It could be California in the 1970s. Where else has it ever looked like this?

Bonaire is 10 miles long and 4 miles across with an outside number of 11,000 populating it. But some of the major commercial establishments are Harley-Davidson rental and sales agencies. I wonder how many of the SCUBA tourists have ever ridden before? Harleys are wicked handling, heavy machines. I think they only feel fast because the control is marginal. (Remember, I used to test bikes for a living.) But they are oh, so sonorous. Your guts rumble in synch with the big twin with each twist of the wrist. Hearing? Forget it. Helmets? What are those?

This scene really doesn't do anything for me. Nor did it 30 years ago when it could have been all mine. I really prefer the underwater realm of quiet fishies and I like 21st Century bikes that actually handle: on road or off. But, my God, Hogs are all over this small island that most bikers have never heard of. Somebody should run tours for the West Coast gray ponytail set who don't want to mess with 18-wheelers, the highway patrol, or helmets. There's none of that stuff on Bonaire, plus it hardly ever rains. It's a desert island featuring Dutch beer and decent food.

It also offers one of the top wind surfing areas in the world at Lac Bay on the windward side.

Government Affairs

While Mer and I are cleaning up after our day as tourists, a heavy set Netherlands Antilles immigration officer comes to the dock beside *Quo Vadis*. He asks, or rather tells me, about a former crew member who has come to him. I heard Julie was still on the island through one of the marina staff who had been partying with her. She had tried to keep a key to the showers until he realized she was no longer on my boat. Officer W.W. Conqet is holding a hearing at her request and he requests my presence in his office tomorrow morning. I agree to attend. Mer has been listening to all this and counsels me to take the high road and be gracious. "Don't lower yourself to her level over something like this," she advises in her balanced, mature "live in the moment" manner.

I arrive, clad in long khakis and a clean shirt. Julie's story is that I have been abusive and kicked her off the boat and she doesn't have a ticket home or the money to buy one. If this is true, she lied to me when she came aboard. One of the few preconditions made clear to all prospective and actual crew is they must have a plane ticket. If it isn't true, she has lied to Officer Conqet. She starts into personal stuff about me which he doesn't really care about. She has created a problem for him and he wants a solution. She has to leave Bonaire before Quo Vadis can leave Bonaire or else she sails away on the boat.

Most of the Caribbean island states are fiercely strict in enforcing this condition, above all others. Somebody comes into their waters on your boat, you must take them out or send them out another way. Then, you may revise your crew list and proceed to your next Port of Call. I have read horror stories of skippers who've been stuck paying for plane tickets to Europe and Australia. This is now happening to me. After listening to Julie's version for a while and my somewhat briefer story, he says, "There is a three day holiday starting at 4 o'clock tomorrow. I want this resolved before I go on holiday."

Outside, Julie tells me she only has US$400 and that's not enough for a ticket to go where she wants to go. It is enough to fly to Florida, however, where she told me her Mother spends the winter.

I go back in to ask Officer Conqet about acceptable solutions. She must leave Netherlands Antilles immigration jurisdiction or be kept on my crew list. Technically, he confides, she could be sent to Aruba (That island has a slightly different non-colonial status.) but he thinks they'll send her back. That doesn't solve our now mutual problem. Julie is holding me, my boat and the rest of the crew hostage. I trusted her when she told me she had a ticket home. I feel foolish.

At the Bon Bini Travel Agency, I am helped through the incrementally more expensive options up to a flight to Puerto Rico for US$330. Unfortunately, it doesn't leave for two days. I deliver the ticket to Officer Conqet. He inspects it carefully, reading slowly to capture all the details.

"An airplane ticket back to the U.S. Good." he decides. "I'll give it to her when she comes in. After she leaves, you can revise your crew list and I'll clear your boat out." I thank him.

Julie finds me walking back to the marina and starts complaining. "I don't want to go to San Juan. I want to go to Boston." The extent to which she still doesn't get it leaves me speechless. When I do return to the marina and Mer, I tell her what happened. Her attitude undergoes a transformation.

"Jeez, what she did is awful. How dishonest. Screw her. You shouldn't have done anything for her." So much for the high road.

The next morning, Kate informs me she is leaving. I invite her to continue as crew. It should be easier from now on. She won't have to stand Julie's watch. Mer tells Kate she can stay on board.

The day after, Kate's plane left Flamingo Airport at 0700. Coincidentally, so did Julie. At 0745, W.W. Conqet was knocking on the cabin of Quo Vadis to inform me of the dual departures. My boat could now legally leave Bonaire and he had my papers. I told him, half-joking, that Mer and I had come to like the place and asked him if we could stay for another couple of days. He said OK and signed the old crew off the entry document. He was very accommodating, actually, and apparently pleased he no longer had this particular problem. I was only a little surprised that he knew who had gone where; exactly at what time. I have learned the "authorities" of these island states usually know exactly what's going on, who is doing it, and whether it is legal. Sometimes, it doesn't matter to them. I walked Officer Conqet to the gate and wished him a Happy Holiday.

Carpe Diem on Bonaire

One reason we decided to further extend our unexpected stay on Bonaire is that any realistic hope of getting to Panama in the time Meredith had left was gone. We could sail to Curaçao; maybe on to Aruba. We no longer had the crew of four I'm told is required for the Canal.

We had been docked next to the 42 ft. catamaran Surprise since we came in to the marina. This boat had passed QV going South several months ago, with a couple on board. Now, it had that un-used look and nobody on board. When I came back from a trip to town, a woman was opening up the cabin. We introduced ourselves. DeeDee tells me the reason her boat is here but she hasn't been is that her husband died of cancer. They had sailed this far together until he was too sick to go on. This information makes a big impact on me. She has put her grief aside for now but did have some equipment maintenance and replacement questions that I was able to answer based on my recent experience chasing boat parts. I asked if she needed help moving the boat. She had friends flying down from the U.S. but thanked me. QV is staging out to a mooring but we agreed to check in on CH16 until we left for Curaçao.

I filled all the tanks with their proper fluids, paid all the marina fees and bought an out of date cruising guide to the ABCs for Nafl 10.50. (Nafl is Netherlands Antilles florin. The colonial home country may trade in Euros but in these Caribbean ex-colonies the guilder is the legal tender. Guilders are also called florins.) QV was on Mooring #10 by mid-afternoon. We spent the rest of the day looking at the abundant reef fish, the growth on the bottom of the boat, and each other in and out of the water.

It was just after the full moon. We're showered, fed and relaxing on the darkened bridge deck. Meredith can be full of surprises and uninhibited in public settings. These traits can result in embarrassing social or commercial situations but also, unexpected delights. The geometry and height of the helm chair put her directly above my legs as she pulls off my shorts and goes down on me. What is even more unexpected and erotic is the soft skin of her firm breasts brushing gently against the inside of my thighs. Later, I thank her for that added, exquisite sensation. She says she didn't really notice. She was intent on doing something else. She prefers making love under the open sky with the stars above us, the feel of weather and, I think, daring the risk of discovery.

To Church on Sunday

There is a small, stone church not far from the waterfront in Kralendijk. It is built in the austere Dutch Reformed style but, this being the Caribbean, the glass in the tall windows is all in tropical colors. I'd noticed during my last trip to town that Easter Sunday services were being held at 1000. Mer is a quite religious woman but is initially hesitant about going to this church. My long shirt and pants aren't too dirty. She, of course, wears a modest ruffled blouse and sweeping full skirt which doesn't get wet as we dink to the nearest tie-ring on the stone seawall. Everybody in the little church stares at the obvious non-natives, especially the little kids, but they make room for us in a back pew near the choir.

The Dutch minister comes out wearing the same style of vestments and hat worn by Martin Luther in his now-famous portrait. This pastor scans the varied congregation through wire-rimmed glasses and goes back into the sacristy. When he returns, the service begins. There is singing of hymns, a few of which I recognize. I kind of like that part. The minister delivers his sermon in Dutch, Papiamento and English. After the service, everybody gathers outside the door greeting each other and the minister. When we shake hands and offer "Happy Easter" to one of the well-dressed-for-church local women, she smiles conspiratorially at us.

"When he saw you had come to the services, he asked me to write out part of the sermon in English," she confides. "That was the reason for the delay at the beginning."

"Yes," confirms the beaming minister. "I rely very much on my wife. She is a school teacher."

We thank them both for their inclusive courtesy. Meredith takes photos until her subjects have all dispersed and we proceed to Sunday brunch on shore. She admits this has really turned out well. We'll wait until next morning to try for Curaçao, if the weather holds. Back on board, we stow the clothes and jump into the clear water off Bonaire. No messages from DeeDee, so I hope her friends have arrived. I feel good: happy to be alive, here with Mer and sailing in the morning.

I greet that next day early, take our passports in to Immigration to clear out, retrieve the shotgun from the amiable Customs guys, and get underway by 0700. The wind comes up by 0800. It propels us at better than 5 knots right on course to a waypoint off the Southern tip of Curaçao. The seas build and the wind increases throughout the day as Mer and I alternate at the helm. She has been a natural at the helm of Quo Vadis since the first day on the Chesapeake and continues to steer well, even after months away from the boat. She doesn't make a big deal of this 5 hour passage, noting we can still see the saltworks on Bonaire when we're almost halfway to our waypoint.

The channel into Spanish Water is very narrow but mostly deep. There is a crowded beach on one side; a cliff on the other. Inside the channel, an enormous, nearly landlocked body of water opens up in three directions. I recognize the steep bluff from the Curaçao ads. The pictures and guides don't reveal this landmark is being stripmined for the limestone. We drive around the anchorage, looking for a spot close to a dinghy dock; don't find one, so drop the hook behind the other boats. A rigid inflatable full of laughing Dutch Navy personnel of both genders motors by, ignoring us.

While I rig the bridle and we put on the sail cover, Mer comments on the dogs and kids playing on the French-flagged Lagoon 57 *Echoes*, anchored off our port side. She is attracted to both those types of animals. Something else, undiagnosed, has attacked her legs and feet. These extremities are itching and burning. I give her benadryl and apply hydrocortisone, so she can try to sleep. I suspect sea lice but I've been in the same waters and, thankfully, not affected. In the morning, I put the ladder down for a swim and give Mer another benadryl. Jeanne, who appears to be about twelve, dinks over from *Echoes* to tell us, in perfect English, about the morning bus to the supermarket from Sarifundi. Meredith wants to talk about the dogs on board their boat.

Caracasbai, Willemstad and those Fun-loving French

Sarifundi calls itself "The Sailor's Home". It is not a typical marina with boat slips or moorings. They do have a dinghy dock, toilets, phone, fresh water, and will handle mail. They also have a popular restaurant, part of which sticks out into Spanish Water, where the most notorious Happy Hour on Curaçao happens. We don't go there, having been told the bus into Willemstad leaves from the Fisherman's Harbor, on the other side of the bay. After going to a couple of locked- in piers, we finally find the rickety floating dock with an open gate and make the noon bus to town. In Willemstad, we spend the next three hours being mis-directed to every government agency in town except Immigration. Our only information is that the office is in a yellow building and closes at 1530. After 1530, I go to the Customs office which helpfully is identified by letters three feet high on the side of the building facing the main ship channel. Quo Vadis is cleared in to Curaçao for one year. The crew are still illegal immigrants.

You have probably seen pictures of Willemstad's waterfront in ads for cruise ships or Caribbean tourism: rows of brightly-colored Dutch Colonial buildings lined up behind the stone wharf. The channel between the two parts of town, Santa Anna Bay, allows for entry of commercial and naval vessels. When these ships arrive, often headed for the giant oil refinery at the head of the bay, they are admitted by opening a floating swing bridge moved by big diesel-powered outboard motors. Mer and I sit at one of the outdoor cafes in front of a brightly-colored building and take all this in.

The next morning, we are reinforced by crews from the French boats as we bravely venture forth in search of Immigration. We re-trace the sea and bus routes, walk across the swing bridge, but now press on beyond the commercial docks, through the steel gate emblazoned with "No Entry" in three languages, beyond the big yellow office building, to a regular-sized door. Inside, one Immigration clerk sits behind a glass window. She stamps our passports with a visa valid for 14 days. My boat can stay for a year but we can't. A medium-sized cruise ship of Panamanian registry is tied to the dock. A valet in white shirt and black bow tie is carrying bags down its gangway for a couple dressed very formally for the tropics. This seems a little, well, different. I am informed the ship is home to a Sea Org, that most evolved group of Scientologists, and is based here. The other ship visiting Willemstad is a French frigate. Sailors sporting those dangerously short shorts and the little white hats with red pom-poms on top are on the wharf putting rat guards the size of manhole covers on the ship's docklines.

After our foray into local government bureaucracy, our day continues like that in most mid-size European cities. We process paperwork through an officious and expensive notary, eat Italian food, go shopping, go to a movie. Well, there are some differences. Venezuelan boats hawking seafood and fresh produce are tied up along the quay to the bus station. We encounter Warren and Judith McCandless walking out of Caracasbai where they've gone diving to add to their list of tropical fish sightings.

Happy Hour at Sarifundi is conducted with Dutch precision by a no-nonsense barkeep wearing the shirt of one of his favorite soccer teams. When he rings the bell, it starts. When he rings it again, it is over. If you haven't paid for your drink by then, tough. It's full price. The place is packed with a mix of cruisers and locals. A trio of good-looking young women in tight "Sarifundi" T-shirts and jeans squeeze through this international cocktail party taking orders, including for dinner if you want to stay after Happy Hour.

Sarifundi's daily drama is presided over, from coffee to closing, by a handsome couple, Richard and Liz. He is Dutch. She is the Irish type with the raven-black hair and the blue eyes. The morning highlight at The Sailor's Home is the arrival of the van to the supermarket. The days with Meredith in Curaçao are mellow, almost conventional. It is a sweet time together. I had decided against the two of us trying to make it to Panama.

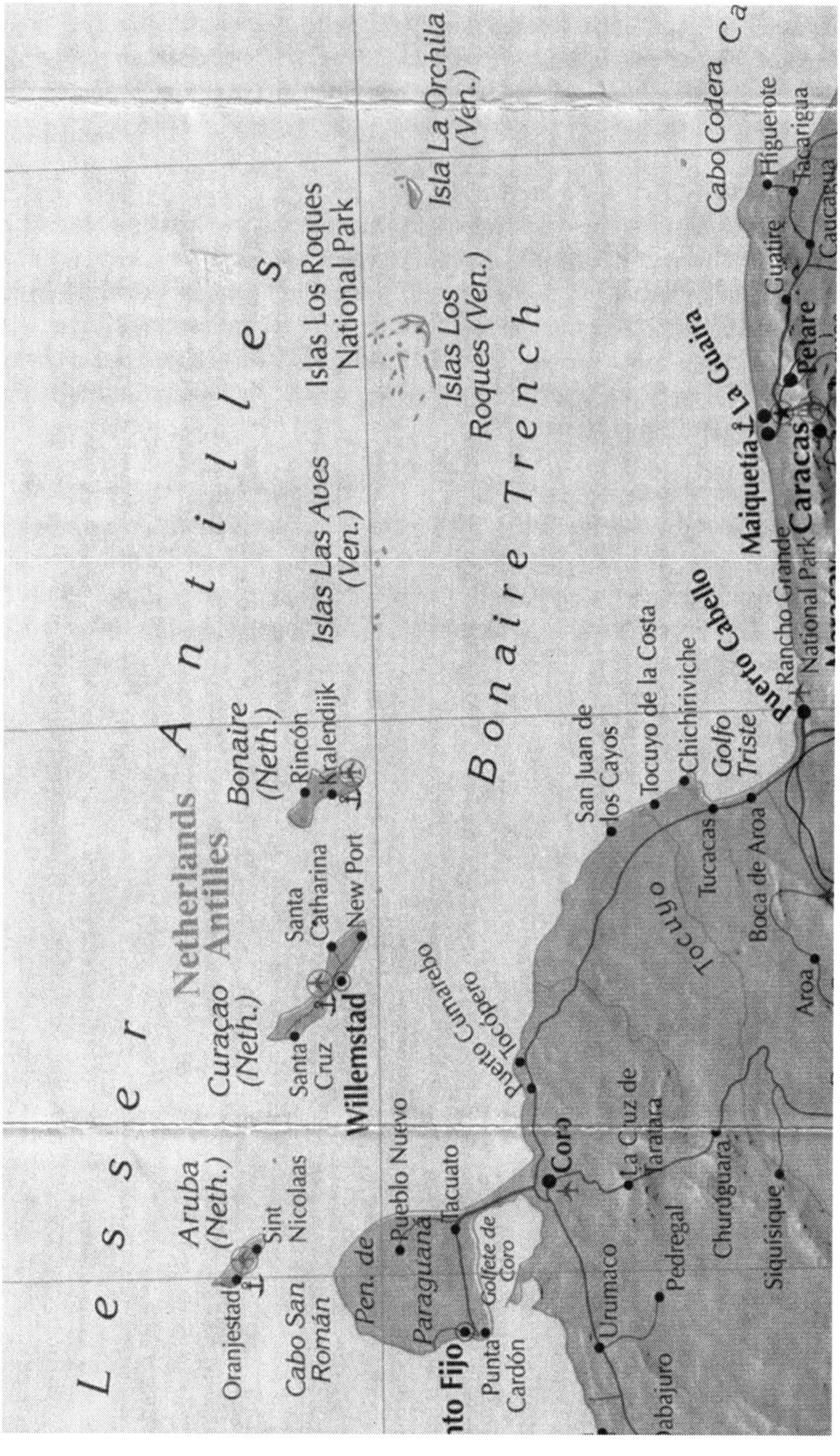
Lesser Antilles
Netherlands Antilles
Aruba (Neth.)
Oranjestad
Sint Nicolaas
Cabo San Román
Curaçao (Neth.)
Santa Cruz
Willemstad
Santa Catharina
New Port
Bonaire (Neth.)
Rincón
Kralendijk
Islas Las Aves (Ven.)
Islas Los Roques National Park
Islas Los Roques (Ven.)
Isla La Orchila (Ven.)
Bonaire Trench
Pen. de Paraguaná
Pueblo Nuevo
Tacuato
Punta Cardón
Golfete de Coro
Coro
Puerto Cumarebo
Tocópero
Urumaco
Pedregal
La Cruz de Taratara
Churuguara
Siquisique
Tocuyo
San Juan de los Cayos
Tocuyo de la Costa
Chichiriviche
Tucacas
Golfo Triste
Boca de Aroa
Aroa
Puerto Cabello
Rancho Grande National Park
Maiquetía
La Guaira
Caracas
Petare
Guatire
Higuerote
Tacarigua
Caucagua
Cabo Codera

In Curaçao

Aboard S/V Quo Vadis, in Spanish Water, Curaçao, Netherlands Antilles

I am sitting on a bench next to the *roti* hut at the end of the fishermen's dock in Spanish Water. I am eating a *roti*. A chicken *roti*, of course, because there are no fish here at the commercial fishing dock. This would not be so bad except that I am still eating alone.

I'm also wondering what they do all day inside the "*Consulat General de la Repubiqe d'Haiti*", which is on the bus route returning to Spanish Water from Willemstad. As befitting the poorest country in the Western Hemisphere, its consulate is housed in a modest one story building. Out front, a faded flag flaps on a not-so-tall flag pole inside the low, gated wall. The last news headline I saw, Haiti didn't have a government. If the local consular staff is smart, assuming there is still anybody in there, they have unplugged the phone, the FAX, and any PCs and taken night jobs at the casinos.

I wipe the dripping curry sauce from my fingers and listen to the *roti* makers (Mother and daughter, it turns out.) through the door of the hut as they chat away happily. They converse in Papiamento—the language of the Dutch Antilles. After three weeks, I'm beginning to understand it. Next, I'll probably try speaking it and make an even bigger fool of myself. So, *Kon ta bai?* How are you doing?

Since I've been cruising, I've been impressed with the originality and unexpectedness of boat names. Not the yachts but the names of the local fishing and work boats. (You've already heard my insistence that sea law mandate an international commission to vett private boat names…and reject most of them.) Now, nicely stuffed with *rotis*, I dink away from the fishermen's dock and spot an appropriate name on the transom of a local fishing boat: Thank you Lord. You may have to spend some time at sea on a small boat to really understand how good that is.

I'd like to think I'm not so easily corrupted just because of a slight ear for languages. As mentioned, I seem to be absorbing Papiamento. But I also tend to write, chameleon-like, in the style of the last writer I've been reading. While it saddens me to admit it, I'm not as funny as Dave Barry or Carl Hiaasen, those mirthmasters spawned from the Miami Herald. But why can't I write like, say, Herman Melville? Especially for these current sea sagas. On the other hand most of the world hasn't read Moby Dick and both Dave and Carl are Pulitzer Prize winners earning, as they say back on Martinique, "*Beacoup d'argent"* from their efforts. Maybe I should rethink this.

Food and Drink, again

Perhaps because I'm not sailing anywhere, I'm reverting (or whatever the correct psychological term) to cooking things. Dinner tonight was cucumber, tomato and marinated octopus salad and more. The octopus had benefited (though not in a personal way) from spending time in garlic and olive oil. What critter wouldn't? The "more" included *paella* supposedly serving 2-3 people who I figure couldn't be very hungry because this one *Capitán* ate it all, heavily seasoned with saffron from Grenada's spice market. The quantity of saffron I'm holding has a U.S. street value of several thousand dollars. I think about how to be a dealer. I admit I'm hooked on this particular, legal Caribbean herb. But my habit isn't heavy enough to sail back to Grenada for more. The sauvignon blanc employed to wash all this down is not so affordable here in the ABCs as it was on Isla Margarita but, then, what is?

Based on the four major food groups: sugar, salt, fat and alcohol, I've quite naturally maintained a balanced diet with little or no conscious effort. Fat, no problem. I frequently put together a bacon cheeseburger with avocado or, say, tagliarini with Italian sausage and grilled red peppers. Alcohol is preferably provided by a nice, spicy Zinfandel or, on especially hot days, a beer chilled to a compensating temperature. (Something German or a local brew come to mind.) But now, after however long it's been sitting alone in the Tropical zone, salt and sugar are starting to enter the gastronomic picture. I'm currently about 10 degrees above the equator. I sweat a lot.

 Hence, the necessary consumption of multiple bags of dry roasted peanuts or Dutch potato sticks. The latter are highly functional European salt substrates, apparently excluded from the U.S. market by an obviously unfair and restrictive trade embargo. This, in turn, presents the need to balance the intake of these metabolically required substances with samples from the local brewery.

The sugar baffles me. Maybe it's because I've been on Dutch islands recently. It's not a craving for chocolate although many people, mostly female, categorize chocolate as its own independent and highly important food group. Maybe the sugar craving is because I've cut out the rum—a bold if not foolhardy move here deep in the Caribbean. In arriving at that decision, I was mainly considering the question: Just how many brain cells do I have left to kill at age 60?

"Plenty!" is my right brain's immediate response "Probably more than those other bozos! And I like it like that." Now, what were we talking about? Your name again? Is your question diet-related? Food groups? What are food groups? Is there some rum? Dark, of course.

Day Tripper

Since I don't seem to be going anywhere else right now, I went back in to Willemstad as a tourist for the day. This passed mainly in a visit to the Kura Holanda museum which, I discovered, is part of the Kura Holanda urban zone restoration including the mansion, the hotel, and two restaurants good enough to be in the *Chaine des Rotisseurs* group. Mer and I had walked past this complex many times while searching for the hidden Immigration office; always too pre-occupied to stop and check it out.

The museum is incredibly eclectic, ranging from Babylonian cuneiform artifacts (original bills of lading for trade goods scratched on clay tablets) to U.S. Black Panther tracts and posters. The overall theme seemed to be black culture through the ages, broadly defined. This included the most exquisite Benin bronzes I have ever seen. This stunning art contrasted with an immense number of slave shackles and leg irons in various designs of discomfort which, bizarrely, did not look all that old and unused. Then, I found the mask gallery.

This room presented an incredible collection; including previously unseen types of African masks. I used to collect primitive masks so my juices ran to larceny. Animal masks, of course, and warrior masks but also things I'd never seen before. *Sirite*, household masks, and *sigate*, village masks featuring headpieces 3-4 ft. tall. There were ancestor masks twice that size though not quite as complex in detail and figures. Some of them featured earth mother/fertility symbols on the top with articulated arms. An arm on one of those masks held a big ladle for serving soup.

There was nobody else in the gallery and very few on the grounds at two in the afternoon. I played the wooden balaphone with its batons made of pitch. I tried all the drums. Each sounded distinctly different but all of them sounded good—with a message to send. Most of the Kura Holanda was housed in replicas of slave quarters, including a frightening below decks section in the hold of a slave ship. The rest was in the authentic, slightly restored Dutch Colonial housing from the 17th century. These structures were all around the central plaza: the site of the Curaçao slave auctions. This island was the center of that one most lucrative trade activity of the Dutch West Indies Company for about 150 years. Slave sales made that investor-owned, state-chartered company profitable which made Curaçao the commercial and political center of the Netherlands Antilles and, arguably, the most prosperous mercantile colony in the Caribbean during that era.

The black cultural experience continued, as I considered again that strange ritual of the Caribbean: A Haircut for the White Guy. You may remember some previous misadventures in this skin trade, which I do not undertake lightly.

At Lúperon, in the Dominican Republic, the young barber with the blue/white/red striped wooden pole nailed to the front of his 12 ft.-square shop proudly carved me into Capitán Juan as a Conquístador using just one single edge razor blade. In Deshaies, Guadeloupe, the one guy among many gals in the Euro-modern air-conditioned and mirrored salon thinned and trimmed my thick, wavy locks. Upon completion of that task, he decided he had given me "The Special". The tariff for "The Special", written in barely legible type at the bottom of the extensive list of services, was 16 Euros (about US$21). Now, five weeks after Mer had trimmed around my ears while bobbing on board off Bonaire, I came across Strak! Strak! while walking back to the Willemstad bus station. I cleverly interpreted this to be the name of a barbershop—in Papiamento! The hand-painted comb and scissors on the sign provided another hint. I bravely pushed open the door.

A room the size of a small gym was filled with large black guys wearing NBA jerseys. They were standing, talking, and pushing high-revving clippers over mostly black male heads. The price list for hair-related services was not cheap. I ask about a haircut with "No Masheen" as described on the list. "Man or woman?" asks the cashier by way of a comeback. I glance briefly at the clipper-wielding guys in the NBA jerseys and backward baseball caps. "Woman," I reply.

This is my strong preference for most personal activities, anyway. A gender-denominated specialist is summoned from a much smaller ante-chamber behind the big room. She looks more Latina than black. I'm still trying to explain in Papiamento about "No Masheen." and how I'd prefer to look after this encounter, when I discover she is Colombian. The Spanish starts to flow comfortably between us. After about 40 minutes of careful trimming with a very small scissors, she brings out a jar of "Hair Nutrition." She had waited until the first 20 minutes of our session elsapsed before putting on her glasses, during which she had attempted assaults on my beard and eyebrows. The label on the jar announces it is "For processed and relaxed hair." She slaps a couple of handfuls of nutrition on my relaxed hair and works it in. She then styles it into a Latino gigolo pomade helmet and resumes detail trimming with the tiny scissors. I can tell she wants me looking really good—at least by Coastal Colombian Caribbean standards.

During our conversation, I had mentioned how, being on a sailboat, I'm often out in the wind. She slicks and trims in a manner to defeat the breezes. I emerge from Strak! Strak! into the Southeast Tradewinds about 16 guilders lighter. My new coiffure is immobile. It retains its sculptured shape relentlessly, in spite of head movement or wind velocity. It lasts past the Haitian consulate on the long bus ride, bouncing across Spanish Water in the dinghy, back to the aft deck of my boat where a sun-warmed shower is hanging from the boom. Maybe I could have single-handed to Panama before the hurricanes, but then I would have missed all this.

Cruising Women and Things They Do

Leanna stopped by Quo Vadis to see if this solitary sailor was still sane. I had a pot of coffee already brewed; so we each had a cup on board. She was headed back to their Prout 37 Isis to fiberglass the interior bulkheads of the anchor chain locker. This space has very contorted access from the deck but takes on water every time you raise the anchor (like most chain lockers) and, as a result, can leak into the hulls if it's not watertight. This repair work was done on my Prout back in Annapolis two years ago and cost many hundreds of dollars. After finishing the boat work, she planned to return to Holland for 3-4 months to earn more cruising guilders for next season. Her husband, Dijk, was going to stay on their boat in Curaçao. It has a good Dutch language technical library, he told me.

Diane couldn't stay for coffee. She had to get back to their 44 ft. ketch, Lady Diane, to seal the teak deck, clean the interior of the reefer, and prepare dinner.

Back on Margarita, Don had told me about Denise. She could cook a three course meal in a Force 6 gale. "You'd look down the companionway and see her holding the pots on the stove with one foot, reading a book. If we ran short of cash, she was good-looking enough to always do some modeling…or turn a trick. A good-looking Caucasian woman in most Asian ports back in those days: $500. More in Singapore."

Sue, on Eagle Light, had successfully traced the disabling fault through the below decks wiring and repaired the boat's electrical system while they were on the hook up in the Exumas. She was a classical pianist by training.

I really didn't know, or expect, there were women like this when I started cruising. I can see how they could make life a little easier.

Meredith vs. Pirates of the Caribbean

It's been nearly a month swinging on the hook off Sarifundi Marina in Spanish Water. I have had no luck finding crew. I regularly make the trip to Xander's cyber-café in Willemstad. This journey still involves motoring the dingy to the fishermen's dock, a short hike to the bus stop, and a long bus ride to town to check on possible responses to the e-mails I've launched into cyberspace. I am excited to find one from Meredith. It begins:

"Could we make it from Curacao to a safe boat stowage on the west side of Costa Rica within 14 days? (Allowing for flight days on the 15th and 30th of June) I'm not crazy about island hopping off the coast of Columbia (sic). Not interested in forfeiting my life to a Pirate! I'd rather gut it out and sail safely out to Sea to the canal."

Many agree with her. Most cruisers and guides recommend staying way offshore of South America, even if you are eventually headed down to Cartagena. Of course, I would agree to do whatever she wants to do, as is usually the case and with few regrets. We are to the West of the most dangerous area for pirates but later, considering the other options, fighting pirates doesn't seem like such a bad way to go. Her kids and grandkids would have one hell of a story.

"Oh, yes, our dear Mamere died fighting pirates in the Caribbean. There she was, wearing her python print string bikini on the deck of a 37 ft. catamaran; sailing with her boyfriend she'd had a crush on since high school. She kept reloading the shotgun as fast as she could. He must have used the automatic between volleys from that 12 gauge. The Coast Guard said they were finally overwhelmed by the pirates only after they ran out of ammo. She was just 61."

What a fantastic story. Wouldn't you show up for her memorial service? This way of going sure beats lying in some nursing home with a tube up your nose, as long as the ending is reasonably quick. (Mer's grandchildren call her "Mamere", as Eleanor Roosevelt's grandchildren called her. Is it French?)

Well, I don't have to make that route decision right now. You probably can sail from here to Panama in 14 days but it's not likely I could transit the canal and make it North to Costa Rica and get her on a plane in that same time frame. I'd also promised my firstborn child I'd be back in June for her graduation from the University of California.

So I contract with Ben Clement to look after the boat while I look for airplane seats. This boat guardian arrangement is also required by the government of Curaçao as a condition of leaving their island country without taking your boat with you. Ben is a French Canadian guy who lives on the water near Sarifundi with his German-born wife, Serena, and then-newborn child, Cheyenne. Unless Ben is holding his baby, which is a goodly amount of the time, he is holding a beer and a cigarette because he's Canadian, eh? He has a local reputation for being reliable. We seem to get along. Ben is a pretty low key guy with a surprising amount of practical boat and fish knowledge. You run into these guys (and a few gals) in the Caribbean. They have somehow managed to immigrate (even if they're not from the former colonial country) and make a life for themselves in the local economy. Of course, I'm going to meet the ones who work on the water or on boats. It still amazes me because the residence requirements, at least the formal regulations, are very restrictive. Another example is Thompson-Neall, a British electrician who lives here. He agrees to get the burned-out parts from Rutland and install them so the wind generator can actually generate power again. I ask Ben and his buddy to work on the cabin headliner and leave both tradesmen with sums of money. Ben gives me a ride to the airport, charging $5 less than cab fare. We agree to stay in contact via e-mail but there shouldn't be a problem. Curaçao is below the hurricane belt.

Meanwhile, back at the ranch…

Diane, of Lady Diane, recommended I contact Lodie to crew from Spanish Water to Costa Rica. I'm told she owned a cat, was born in Costa Rica, and was an experienced sailor. We interviewed in San Francisco where we were both visiting family. It was agreed to meet in Curaçao the first week in November: the end of hurricane season. She suggested a family friend who wanted to crew. Jovino tells me he has lots of experience with cats and had made two offshore passages. It turned out the cats were the Hobie beach cat type and the sailing was offshore from San Francisco to Los Angeles. Admittedly, not always an easy passage but usually downwind.

Curaçao is below 12 degrees North latitude which is the limit for insurance coverage and, as the tourist brochure proclaims, no hurricane has hit the island since 1893. Until Ivan. This Category 3 storm did not head Northwest like a normal hurricane. Ivan stayed on a due West track right across the Southern Caribbean, picking up intensity after devastating Grenada: another (formerly) safe haven. I watched the weather map as the hurricane moved right up to the Curaçao symbol on the grid. An e-mail came from Ben: "Ivan due tomorrow. I'm taking my family ashore and inland." I hate the idea of chunks and pieces of my home littering some tropical shore. Miss it or sink it, I think. Ivan comes within miles of the anchorage in Spanish Water and abruptly makes a 90-degree turn North toward Hispaniola.

Family matters. I put on my Bogart suit and make it to Beth's graduation. She has a GPA of 3.84: better than either parent that took a degree from UC. Rafe has asked her to marry him. My fatherly mind is boggled. Why can't they just keep on living together? I make some time to help Caroline with her automobile handling skills until she successfully completes another rite of passage: she passes the test for her driver's license.

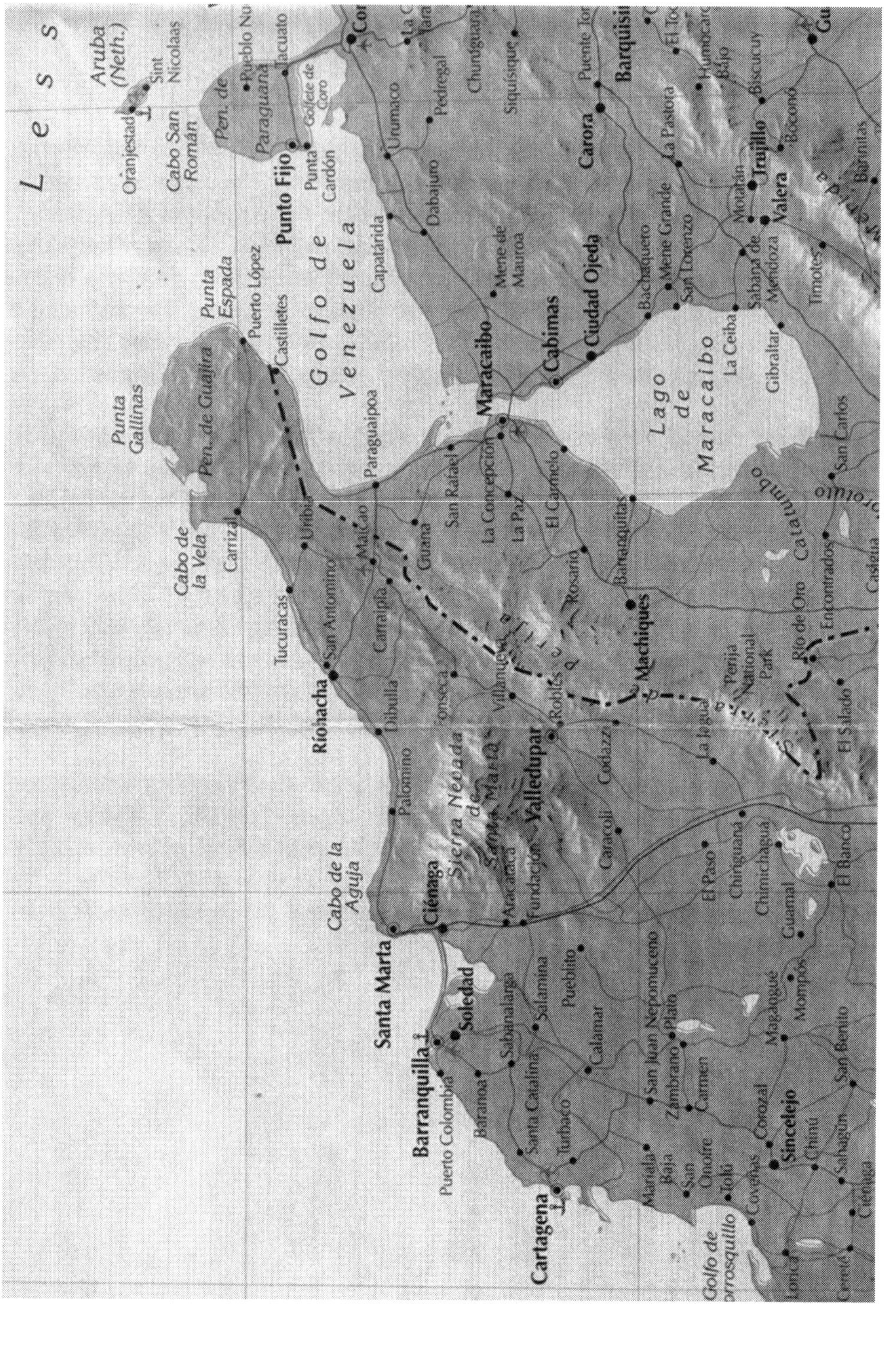

Aruba (Neth.)
Oranjestad
Sint Nicolaas
Cabo San Román
Pen. de Paraguaná
Pueblo Nuevo
Tacuato
Punto Fijo
Punta Cardón
Golfete de Coro
Punta Espada
Puerto López
Castilletes
Golfo de Venezuela
Punta Gallinas
Pen. de Guajira
Cabo de la Vela
Carrizal
Uribia
Paraguaipoa
Capatárida
Dabajuro
Urumaco
Pedregal
Churuguara
Siquisique
Puente Torres
Barquisimeto
Carora
El Tocuyo
Humocaro Bajo
Biscucuy
Boconó
Trujillo
Valera
Motatán
La Pastora
Bachaquero
Mene Grande
San Lorenzo
Sabana de Mendoza
Timotes
Mene de Mauroa
Ciudad Ojeda
Cabimas
Maracaibo
Lago de Maracaibo
La Ceiba
Gibraltar
San Carlos
San Rafael
La Concepción
La Paz
El Carmelo
Barranquitas
Maicao
Guana
Carraipía
Tucuracas
San Antonio
Riohacha
Dibulla
Fonseca
Villanueva
Robles
Rosario
Machiques
Encontrados
Catatumbo
Casigua
Río de Oro
Perijá National Park
Valledupar
Codazzi
La Jagua
El Salado
Palomino
Sierra Nevada de Santa Marta
Cabo de la Aguja
Ciénaga
Aracataca
Fundación
Caracolí
El Paso
Chiriguaná
Chimichagua
El Banco
Santa Marta
Soledad
Barranquilla
Puerto Colombia
Baranoa
Sabanalarga
Salamina
Pueblito
Calamar
Santa Catalina
Turbaco
Cartagena
San Juan Nepomuceno
Plato
Zambrano
Carmen
Guamal
Mompós
Magangué
San Benito
María la Baja
San Onofre
Corozal
Sincelejo
Tolú
Coveñas
Chinú
Sahagún
Golfo de Morrosquillo
Lorica
Ciénaga de Oro
Cereté

Colombia with Gems by the Ocean

Aboard S/V Quo Vadis, anchored off the coast and islands of Colombia

The first thing everybody and every book tells you about sailing to Colombia is "DON'T DO IT!" Sometimes, it's the last. Jimmy Cornell's <u>World Cruising Routes</u> identifies only one route: stay at least 100 miles offshore while going directly to the Panama Canal. This is intended to distance you and your boat from drug smugglers, drug smuggler-chasers (Who, uniformed or not, can be hazardous to a civilian sailboat.), regular pirates, and similar types you would not choose to invite on board.

Then there is the geographical location. The Western end of the Caribbean is where all the water in this complex Sea piles up; often into big waves. This is also where the tradewinds continue to build force after sweeping across this good-sized body of water; often continuing all night.

Whatever you do, here's what I found there: not many people along the coast, a few resort towns that cater to locals, picturesque bays, a largish wind farm (I counted 17 wind turbines spinning above the dunes of Cabo de Vela. Colombia just doesn't get much credit for its renewable energy program.), and the port of Cartagena which is the most complete original Spanish colonial city in the Americas. The word on the water is that the city of Cartagena is actually quite safe because all the big time druglords have vacation places around there and want to keep it nice for their families. So there are few shootings, safe streets, relatively little theft; basically how Miami Beach used to be for vacationing families of Sicilian descent back in the old days. Nobody wants to mess with the cartels, so Cartagena is (mostly) an island of relative tranquility.

There is also a collection of typewritten pages put together by the crew of *Pizazz*. This California couple have cruised their Beneteau 50 along the Colombian coast for several seasons. (We think she actually did the writing.) For years, it has been the only source of useful information, at least in English. People who find themselves on boats in this part of the world pass along copies of this work like it's <u>The Sorcerer's Handbook</u>. Thanks, *Pizazz*. The appeal of Cartagena to such boat people is that it's about halfway between Curaçao and the Panama Canal, providing the best provisioning and repair along that way. It also allows a favorable trajectory for a sail over to the San Blas Archipelago. The locals are mostly aware of this, especially since the big cruise ships stopped putting in to Cartagena during the last decade or so. They want visitors to believe the country is all about cheap emeralds and good coffee. Cocaine is never mentioned in Cartagena.

Getting there isn't half the fun

After delivering the homesick, seasick Jovino to the airport at Oranjestad and spending the entire day I knew (and resented) it would take to clear out of Aruba, the remaining crew of Lodie and Capitán Juan pointed Quo Vadis toward Punta Gallinas, Colombia through intermittent squalls.

After the second jibe back toward the coast, the autohelm wouldn't re-set to the new heading. We messed with it 'til dark with no solution until I realized the plug-in piece supposedly fixed by Jovino had come apart. I asked Lodie about Jovino and boats. She responded that she didn't really know him that well. Lodie then announced she couldn't steer for four hours and, in fact, she didn't seem familiar with wheel steering on a sailboat 'though she had co-owned a cat for two years. We crossed course with four commercial ships headed for the Canal before nightfall. Just before midnight, the motor tanker Mt. Alliance hailed us (in Spanish). I didn't recognize it since we were being hailed as a fishing boat. I finally figured out he had us at 2 nm off his port bow and crossing. I altered course for a port-port passing, took his stern, and both Captains wished each other a safe voyage. It is rare for a commercial ship to even acknowledge a sailboat's existence. I was grateful.

It comes to be dead downwind to the Cabo de Vela waypoint, but now I'm concerned about what other vessels are around us or hitting one of the Monjes, a group of big rocks sort of on the way to the Colombian coast. I see a beacon to the South; figured it was on Monje del Sur, so head way North to miss all of the Monjes. Lodie continued complaining about the non-responsive autohelm which was no help. I got very fatigued standing double watches so got Lodie up about dawn, furled the genoa, set the stays'l, and asked her to steer while I slept. It turned out to be a smooth ride through the continuing squalls, but slow. The rattling mainsail wakes me up every time she gets off course. I wish she'd learn to trim the sails; not least so I can sleep off watch.

After covering 170 nm in nearly 28 hours of jibing around the Caribbean, we rounded Cabo de Vela: an austere red rock and sand place. There were several false openings to the Bay, but we finally found the Pizazz-prescribed anchorage. It was obvious why the wind farm is located here: plenty of wind all day and all night. A *panguero* came up to Quo Vadis as soon as the bridle was on. He asked us for food. This was not encouraging. I had expected he had fish to sell.

Despite a weird sunset that I cannot read for weather, we awake to a serene sunrise and calm conditions. Across the anchorage, we can see the fishermen stretching from the bottoms of their pangas where they have spent the night. They don't seem to be in a hurry to go anywhere.

Cabo de Vela is about halfway along the north shore of the Guajira Peninsula. Stories are told that back in the bad old good old days of, say, 20 years ago, tons and tons of grass were shipped from Guajira; mostly to the U.S. East Coast via the Bahamas. Given the current state of industrialization and savagery in making and moving the white stuff out of this country, that period almost seems quaint. I am silently grateful to see no evidence of any boats operating in any of these modes.

I checked fuel level, oil level, alternator belt tension, and fuel line fittings: only the 14mm nut took any tightening. After setting the ship's clock ahead one hour, I got back to the serious business of course selection. It's not encouraging. The current wind direction (which we have no reason to think will change) puts us dead downwind for 130nm to Five Bays across some unsurveyed zones on the chart. We continue to troubleshoot the autohelm. Lodie correctly suggested loose wires inside the connector plug. That fixed, I cleaned all the terminals and re-assembled the unit. Both the autohelm compass and drive unit work, at least here in the anchorage.

Winds are 10-15 knots when we set sail for Bahia Cinto (one of the Five Bays), then die by 1400. We started motoring. A couple of hours later, the wind is back up to 15 so we run out the genoa and sail until it dies, again. This pattern continues throughout the night into the early hours of the next day. Shortly after the 0200 wind die, a quick calculation indicates we won't make the anchorage by the next nightfall. The engine is re-started and we motor on toward Bahia Cinto. When I rig the bridle at 1700, we are the only boat in that bay aside from a handful of dugouts pulled up on the beach. There are a few thatch-roofed houses scattered around the shore in thick jungle. The houses have two stories,big front porches and look like something from an illustrated fairy tale. You know: not really bad; just strange. We are in a very different world.

Of course the winds came up to 25 knots overnight as Quo Vadis swung on her hook; then dropped off by morning. It was a rest day which included topping up the engine oil, checking drive leg lubricant, filtering 5 gallons of diesel from a jerry can into the main tank, and cleaning the bottoms of the amas. The water was surprisingly cool. This coast is one of the few places in the Tropics where you can spot snow-capped peaks (Sierra de Santa Marta) from your boat.

The first squall blew through just as we started to weigh anchor. The winds were 15-20 after it passed so we set out. As the winds came up to 25 knots, the sea state also kept building. I put a reef in the main and furled the genoa. Running under stays'l and reefed main we were averaging over 6 knots down to Cabo Aguja. Isla Aguja sits offshore from the Cabo and I decided to save an hour by going through the channel. Neither Pizazz nor the charts tell of at least three big rocks in the middle. We saw them breaking and cleared them with Lodie at the helm and me trimming sail.

Just as we came out of the channel, another squall hit. I climbed up on the coach roof and, as I'm putting the second reef in the main, I looked forward. Dead ahead, I can see nothing but a wall of gray water as we're pointed down into the trough of the wave. I get the second reef secured pretty well and I am surprised I can do this. I didn't know until I tried. Quo Vadis does not bury its bows into the bottom of the wave but recovers with, it seems to me, a surprisingly smooth run-out as the following wave breaks around us. This wonderful boat continues to perform just like that in waves that are now running 12-15 ft. The wind stays at 35-40 knots after the squall blows off. That's when we hear sounds coming from the VHF radio over the rush of wind and water.

The Colombian Navy, based at Santa Marta, tells us "Go to 14." whereon they question our local presence, course and reason for existence. I reply in proper Spanish with boat name, registration and ports of departure and arrival. Despite my correctness, Quo Vadis is instructed to report into Bahia Santa Marta. To comply requires a 90-degree turn to port, putting the 35-40 knot winds on our beam. I don't know what the Navy will do if we don't comply with their instructions but I decide not to find out.

This, not surprisingly, turns out to be a rough point of sail with the aforementioned 12 ft. waves randomly breaking over the side. Our speed with reefed main and stays'l is 8-10 knots across said waves as wind holds steady at 40 knots. Which means that QV doesn't suffer the battering for all that long before clearing the *moros* flanking the entrance to the Bahia de Santa Marta. We end up right in front of the Naval station antenna and less than two miles out when they call to thank us for our cooperation and tell us to continue on to Cartagena. This, it seems, had been a test to see if we would try to escape as guilty lawbreakers or come in to the harbor as instructed. Lodie is furious and wants to tell them exactly how she feels. I cannot see the benefit in that. Just as we started back South, the VHF comes to life again, with a British accent directing us back to CH16.

"Quo Vadis, this is Tiger Lily. What is your size?" I inform them QV's length overall is 37 ft.

"Quo Vadis, Tiger Lily of Cornwall. We are a 33 meter schooner and have incurred severe damage and flooding in 40 knot winds and high seas just south of Santa Marta. We are making for the South end of the bay to effect repairs. Recommend you stay in." The friendly Brit went on to describe the damage they'd taken, including damage to some pieces of rigging and structure I didn't even have on QV. I did understand the part about the forward hatch being torn off by waves and the consequent flooding of the forward compartments of this 110 ft. schooner.

I switched back to the Colombian Navy channel and requested to remain in Santa Marta due to sea conditions. Denied. "Continue to Cartagena! Your visit to Santa Marta is over." I repeat my request in my most official, yet polite, Spanish citing danger to vessel and crew, harbor of refuge rule, etc. After another refusal from this same guy, a female voice from the Port Authority comes on CH14, speaking in English. I explained the situation. She confers with the Navy guys. I can hear them in the background. After a lengthy delay, she comes back and tells us to anchor to the right of the #4 buoy. She is an angel of mercy…and reason. We drop sail with winds at 25-30 kts in the bay and anchor 300 meters off this resort town. Little kids are playing on the sandy beach.

The Rio Magdalena and The Bahia de Cartagena

Bells and drums on shore in Santa Marta wake us at 0530. Is this an everyday event or a special occasion? The wind is down to 15-20 kts so the decision is: continue to Cartagena. Our course will take us across the mouth of the notorious Rio Magdalena. This freshwater feature is the source of many tales of treacherous trees and confused seas. The British guys moored next to us back in Spanish Water told of waves breaking over and into their 47 ft. sloop, leaving them with a cockpit full of sand. They were five miles offshore which, they concluded, was in too close.

The flow of the Rio Magdalena extends 10-15 miles out to sea, depending on recent rainfall and runoff, carrying all manner of flora and fauna across the course of boats crossing within that range. On this leg, that included Quo Vadis mainly because it's a left turn to Cartagena at Punta Faro, which is just past the river outlet. If we were going to get to Cartagena the following morning, we couldn't stand out too far. I was also uncertain about winds, and lack of, on the leeward side.

From deck level, you can see clumps of floating vegetation before you see the abrupt color change from dark blue to muddy brown. When you do come up to it, the dividing line between sea and river colors is cut as sharply as a paint stroke with a broad brush. I guess it hadn't been raining much in the mountains as there wasn't all that much stuff on the surface and the current didn't push us out too far. The chop was only 2-3 ft. Lodie was marveling at this extreme natural color contrast. She said she hadn't seen this before. I dodged scattered grass mats and logs. There were no dead bodies of either the two- or four-legged variety which other sailors have claimed to encounter in this stream.

Well, we didn't need to worry about any wind shadow on the west side of Colombia. As we turned South, the winds whipped right around the point and followed us at 35-45 knots. I calculated our current speed over the surface would put us off Cartagena in the middle of the night, so we furled the genoa but still moved down the coast at a sprightly clip under main and stays'l passing Punta Canoa in the dark. Then, about 0400, we spot what should be the low-lying lights of Cartagena assuming the chart is correct, our current position is accurate, and we're pointed in the right direction.

There are two entrances to the harbor at Cartagena: from the South (Boca Grande) and the West (Boca Chica). Both the cruising guide and the Coconut Telegraph advise us that in the Boca Grande, you <u>will</u> get boarded and robbed; especially at night or anchored waiting for first light. That would seem to make the Boca Chica the obvious choice. Except that those sneaky old Spaniards built an underwater wall across that narrower entrance to keep the pirates and English (often the same thing) out. I still can't figure out how they built it underwater back in the 16th century but it's still there, reportedly 6-8 ft. below the surface. The wind dies; we drop sail and crank it up.

It's still about two hours 'til daylight when the GPS tells me we're about 9 nm from the wall. There is a passage cut into this wall deep enough and wide enough for commercial vessels. This gap is supposedly marked by red and green fixed lights except when one or both of them are knocked down or burned out. If they are working tonight, they are lost to my vision against the background of the city lights on the far shore. So we go in very slowly, watching the depth decrease, until we come to a white light on a pole, keep it to starboard, and continue very slowly. I have no reason to think we can't be boarded and robbed coming in this way; it's just not a given. Past the marker, I see a dark-hulled panga off our stern. I can't tell if they are headed toward us; then it's gone. Thank God. I'm pretty sure it's the hallucinations starting.

About where the chart shows the wall might be, I spot one red light sticking up out of the water. There is no corresponding green light that I can see. We move forward. The light doesn't go away so I'm probably not hallucinating this image. The depth still looks good so we keep the red light close to our starboard side and, I think, we enter Cartagena harbor through the gap in the underwater wall. If not, since QV still draws just one meter (39 in.), at least we didn't hit the damn thing.

There is another panga dead ahead! I don't know how far I dare turn out of the channel to avoid it. If it's another hallucination, I don't want to risk it. Then, this panga is also lost in the darkness. It turns out this boat might have been real since we see lots of them fishing all around the harbor, as it starts to get light. We also see the statue of the Virgin standing in the water between the two channels leading to the inner anchorage and docks. I keep to the outside channel which shows as deeper and wider on the chart. It is very calm inside the harbor. A handful of freighters, mostly rust buckets, are anchored out. We also pass U.S. Coast Guard Cutter 911, the Lyric, swinging at anchor. It doesn't appear to have any crew on board; not even a deck watch.

After motoring down to the Cartagena Yacht Club; seeing all the berths full and nobody on the fuel dock, we loop back to the Club Nautico. It, too, appears to have full berths, so I drop the hook in front of the small, sea level Spanish fort next to the Club. A few symbolic cannons are pointed at QV. Club Nautico also has a reputation for being "less stuffy" than the Yacht Club; no jackets required. It is 0730 and time for a nap.

Club Nautico and Other Urban Delights

Folks at the Club Nautico proved very friendly. Some of them were also worried about what might have happened to the wandering pilgrims aboard Quo Vadis. After the unplanned detours to Aruba to put Jovino ashore and in to Santa Marta Bay to mollify the Colombian Navy, we were overdue to Cartagena by the standard of this passage. S/V Lady Diane made a radio call to the Club and to one of the cruising couples in port to check on our whereabouts. Lodie actively enjoyed the attention and short-lived notoriety as "the overdue boat". I was vaguely unsettled by it. It was thoughtful of Don and Diane to check on us. Later, we got word their vessel had a transmission problem and was taking on water during their passage from Curaçao to Puerto La Cruz, Venezuela. Lady Diane last reported being towed into Bonaire. I can't recall any place there to fix a 44 ft. sailboat. John, the Club Nautico manager, added his formal greeting and an orientation to Cartagena. He represented Colombia as having a more stable currency and, at the time, more stable government than Venezuela. Here, it is recommended to obtain local currency from the ATMs; not from the black market money traders like in Margarita.

In fact, there is an ATM at the Super Mercado just a block up the street. Even better, it dispenses a stack of Colombian pesos in response to my brand of plastic. So we immediately spend a big chunk of this new, blue money re-provisioning. I like Latino supermarkets. They are usually a wonderful combination of European and U.S. styles, food, service, everything, including the tiny free samples of stuff you wouldn't otherwise eat. At the sidewalk, just out front, are the pushcart vendors with the really fresh fruits and veggies at a fraction of the inside price. Lower overhead costs, I suppose. Re-stocked and re-freshed, it's time to go play *turista* in Cartagena.

First, you have to get there. We can see the skyline of The Old City from our anchorage but it's considered prudent to take a cab through some of the intermediate neighborhoods. So we do.

The old city is behind thick walls surmounted by El Reloj, a clock tower with archways in its base which give pedestrians access to the original Spanish-built *ciudad*. I don't recall if Old Cartagena is a UNESCO World Heritage site. It could be, as it is incredibly preserved yet it is still very real. It's an active, vibrant commercial city of narrow streets and courtyards under overhanging iron and wood balconies. Wall tiles on the corners of colonial buildings name the streets in 16th century Spanish script.

Lodie wants to go shopping. This is not one of my favored pursuits but I go along to the emerald shops, partly out of curiosity. All of the shops have locked street entrances; some of them have armed guards inside and out. In one of the shops, I price some emerald earrings with Meredith in mind. The counter guy asked who they're for. "*Mi nóvia*," I reply. (My girlfriend/fiancée.) "So," they ask Lodie in Spanish, "Are you the wife?" She had already warned me about this, with specific reference to her Costa Rican brother's arrangements. In this part of the world, any self-respecting man of my age and apparent class is expected to have a mistress and a wife. I don't dare tell these guys I don't have either one. I would not be respected. Lodie tells them she is not my wife without further elaboration. She buys emeralds for her granddaughter at another shop.

The Museum of the Inquisition is in the building where the real thing was conducted for about 200 years. The scales for weighing accused witches hang from a beam. (Witches were thought to be so light they would float...because they could fly. Too bad for skinny Spanish girls.) A sample question from the inquisitors might be, "How many children have you put under an evil spell since you've been a witch?" The museum's version of the Spanish Inquisition in Cartagena, as written on the wall behind the original, restored rack, explains that not all that many people were tortured to death or burned at the stake: only about 60. See, gringos? Only 60 in all that time.

I have a peculiar talent: finding good places to eat in foreign locales. Admittedly, displaying this talent in a place like Cartagena is easier than in some others QV has visited. It is far too early for any proper *Cartagenos* to have dinner (It's only about 1900.), so we have a very comfortable place with an extensive menu mostly to ourselves. Fortified with Colombian food and Chilean wine and not much poorer for the experience, we wander back into the square by the clock tower.

In this transition zone between the Old City and the New City, a dance troupe in full regalia is performing. They are very good, very athletic, and their dancing is very dirty. The musical accompaniment consists of several different types of drums; that's it. Their lighting is from the tall iron streetlamps. The dirty dozen (more or less) dancers go through three costume changes from pre-Colombian to peasant farmer to Spanish colonial. They somehow manage to do this without the music or dance ever stopping. I am impressed and delighted by the performance of these young, limber dancers framed by the 16th century architecture which defines the Plaza.

The three other tourists in the small crowd aren't as enthusiastic. The kids seem to be dancing mostly for themselves as the *chicas* whirl their petticoats (Spanish colonial outfits) and the guys start to show off with jumps and limbo moves (pre-Colombian garb mostly, but not exclusively). After almost an hour of exertion, they wind down their routines for the night and the drums stop.

San Felipe is the name of the incredibly massive fort controlling Cartagena. In the film "Romancing the Stone", it is right on the water: the parapets where Michael Douglas is pulling on the big crocodile's yellow tail drop into the harbor. The current location of the fort is inland. It is bigger than El Moro in San Juan, the previous standard for enormous Spanish colonial forts. There is a shallow, stagnant backwater behind the street shack where I just devoured a *comida corriente* (featuring fresh fish today) and a cold beer.

Did the harbor used to extend right up to the massive walls of San Felipe and, if it did, when? Have I let art dominate life? If you can call Hollywood adventure films art. There is no map or explanation in or around the fort. This isn't Disneyland or U.S. Park Service for dummies. San Felipe is in very good condition, just waiting for shot, shell, gunpowder and stores; then ready for action. As we walk down the ramps where mules used to pull up cannon, a busload of tourists arrives. Most of them head directly for the row of ice cream vendors at the base of the walls.

Goodbye, Emerald City

A cybercafé near the Super Mercado provides access to a weather site. I write down the 24, 48 and 72 hour forecasts. This is rare to find along the South and Central American coasts. The NOAA recorded forecasts out of Miami are usually too generalized for planning or don't cover this piece of ocean. If a country has a weather service (many don't), marine weather is not readily available. It is often classified as sensitive data for use only by their Navy and Coast Guard. Locals using boats (mostly fishermen) and those of us on boats who aren't locals just passing through (mostly long range cruisers) go by seasonal weather. It also helps to be able to correctly read the sky and sea conditions. Sometimes, this doesn't pan out and people on both types of boats die at sea.

Equipped with weather information, another 213,391 pesos worth of provisions from the Carulla supermarket, stamped passports and a *zarpe* obtained through Romero, our U.S. ensign nicely resewn by Simoneta from the Italian boat, and all tanks topped up with the appropriate fluids from the dock, I think we're nearly ready to go to Panama. I do pay the Club Nautico tab just to be sure. Lodie has gone to a music recital in town with the gals from Takes Me Away. I have dinner on board and read the Panama cruising guide. She hails me for a dinghy pickup about 2200.

The Colombian Navy's training ship, a beautiful white-hulled three-masted square rigger, has anchored out in the harbor. It looks like it's one of those pre-steam vessels built in Europe at the turn of the last century: the kind of ship we used to confiscate after wars. A Colombian flag the size of a sail flies from the stern. This fabric display of national pride is so big it barely clears the water when the wind dies. We pass this beautiful example of 19th century ship-building and USCG cutter 911, still anchored nearby, as we head for the Boca Grande, the South opening of the Bay. The cutter now has a chopper on the aft deck but still few other signs of on-board activity.

QV dodges small fishing boats while the big sportfishers going out after billfish steer clear of us as we clear Boca Grande about 1000. Course is set for Los Rosarios and, conditionally, on to Los Bernardos: two island groups in the Golfo de Darien lying between Cartagena and Panama.

The internet-provided weather data predicted 6-8 ft. seas offshore and winds ENE 15-20 knots. This is within the envelope of conditions to make our passage. John of Club Nautico had warned me to expect even bigger seas approaching Panama as all of the Caribbean Sea stacks up on the Continental shelf. So far, none of this is happening. There is no wind outside the Boca and seas are 3-4 ft. so we keep motoring at 5-6 knots. The autohelm holds course toward Los Bernardos.

Quo Vadis crossed over an uncharted shoal just off the Rosarios, with depths dropping to 2-3 meters; then quickly found deeper water which was also not shown at this location on the chart. My pulse returned to normal as I am, once again, reminded that it is all about eyeball navigation in this wet part of the world; especially in the San Blas Archipelago.

The small island of Tintipan provides one of the few protected anchorages in the Bernardos. I decide to press on from the Rosarios, even without any wind and the GPS calculating arrival by 1730. Getting bored motoring, I reviewed the lat/long of the waypoint provided for Tintipan and saw that it was actually the exit through the South reef, not the island. You can't check enough. This put us 4nm closer. Just South of the island, we turned West on the prescribed latitude and headed toward the spot on the chart. The water around the Bernardos provides 50-60 ft. visibility. It is as clear as anything I've seen since some select reefs in the Eastern Caribbean. Lodie observes that she hasn't seen water so clear since the Bahamas. At the indicated depths, we can see individual corals on the bottom. The diving on the Southern reef must be spectacular.

We also see three very large, very new upscale multi-story houses on the south shore of Tintipan. All had substantial docks to deep water, featuring the oversize gazebo-style party places that are part of shoreside architecture in the region. So this is where Colombian druglords come to build their beach houses. Well, three of them did, anyway. A fancy powerboat comes by as we're anchoring. One of the guys asks if I can do engine repair. I tell him I don't know much about their kind of boat, so they motor on to the furthest dock. I dive on the anchor in six feet. Towards sunset, the wind comes up to 15 knots after it being calm all day. The wind is not enough to blow away all the mosquitos and no see'ums so we light a big citronella candle in the cockpit. It seems to discourage some of the bugs. We are able to pick up the weather on the SSB. We are in a zone where the forecasts overlap: South of 10N, East of 80W. It's predicted to blow 20-25 knots with seas 9-12 ft. or 10-15 kts. with seas 5-8 ft. As you can see, there is a definite choice to be made.

A small island to the west appears to support several low-lying compounds and high-standing antennas. At night, it is all lit up including a flashing beacon. We don't know what it is. A prison? A communications/nav station for the Colombian Navy? Could it be another secret U.S. base? Or something similar set up for the owners of the big houses since it does not appear on any chart or in any cruising guide I've read.

The wind died around 0400, leaving **Quo Vadis** floating in 3-4 ft. of water. I am still not allowing for tides when anchoring. I've spent too long in the Eastern Caribbean. I stow items left out to dry which didn't, check the course to Bahia Escosés (Scotchman's Bay) at the far Eastern end of Panama, and set a waypoint to clear the reef.

Depth is back to 6 ft. by the time I push the engine start button. Nothing happens. Not a click, grind, buzz or whir. I check the battery connections. They are tight and clean. I check all the other wiring leading to the starter circuit. Everything looks connected. There are no visible shorting points, like wires touching the engine or frayed. We already know the guys with the fancy powerboat aren't going to be much help. I'm wondering about who is at the antenna compound. Then I observe, maybe for the first time, a small plug and socket connector in the white wire leading to the start button. It appears properly connected; when I pull it, it shows no corrosion. I clean both parts of the connector, spray them, wipe them and re-connect them. The engine starts right up when I push the button. It is already a good day.

We clear the reef in the channel by Isla Celeen, 3.9nm South (the previously noted waypoint) and set course. It is dead calm. In early afternoon, a few dolphins ran in front of QV to lead us to a wind patch. We set sail in 10-15 knots. The seas kept building as we crossed the open Caribbean. By dusk, waves are 6-8 ft. on top of the 3 ft. swell. Lighting flickers all around the horizon.

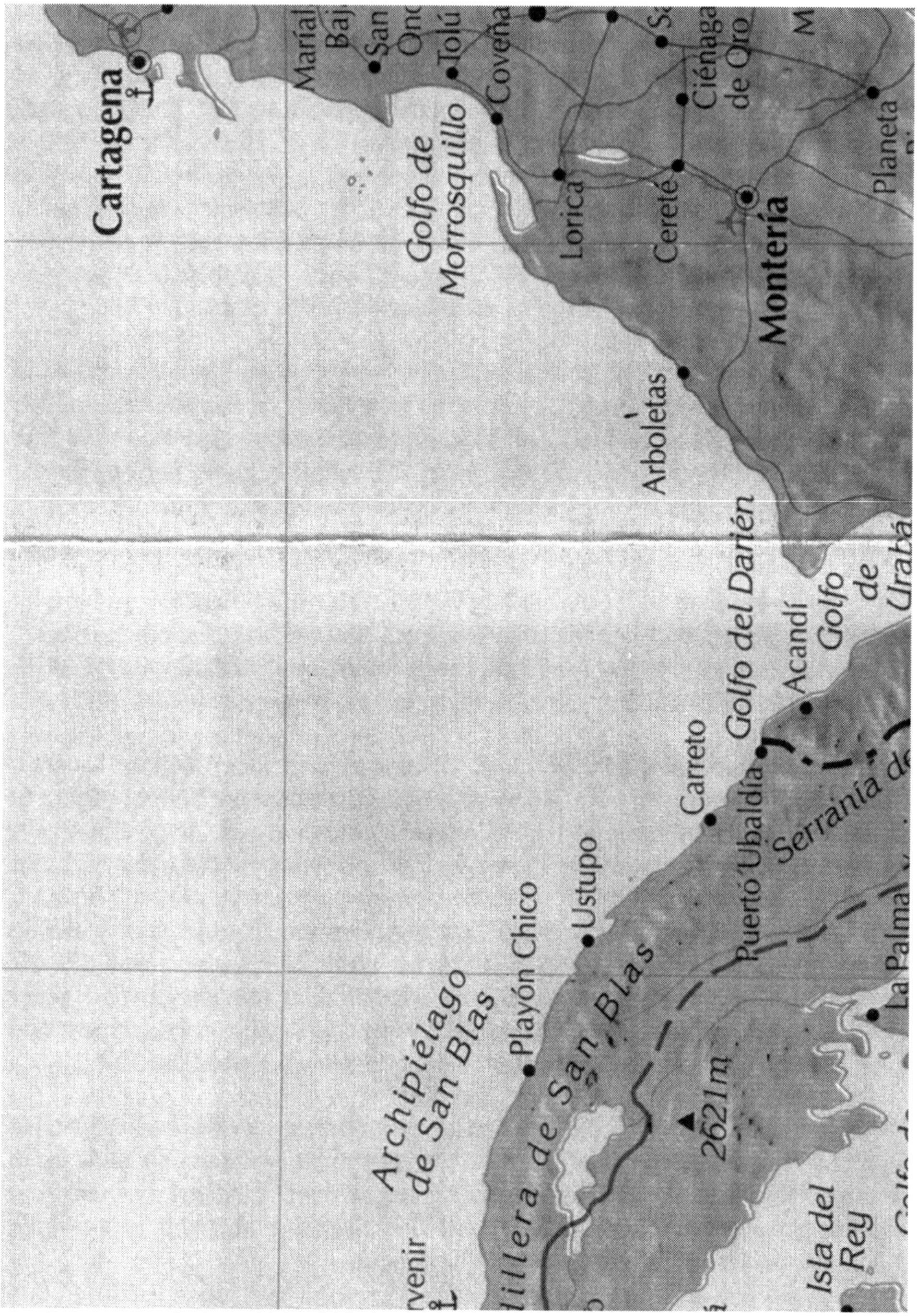
Cartagena
Tolú
Golfo de Morrosquillo
Lorica
Cereté
Ciénaga de Oro
Montería
Planeta
Arboletas
Golfo del Darién
Golfo de Urabá
Acandí
Carreto
Puerto Ubaldía
Ustupo
Playón Chico
Archipiélago de San Blas
2621m
Isla del Rey

Comarca Kuna Yala

Aboard S/V Quo Vadis, San Blas Archipelago, Panama

Quo Vadis motorsails into the night. I don't like burning the fuel but I do want to keep our speed over the surface at least 5 knots for arrival off Puerto Escosés between 1200 and 1300. I calculate it will take 11 gallons to get there. That leaves only about 10 gallons to traverse the entire length of the San Blas Archipelago and on to Colón: roughly 175 nm. This gives me something else to worry about. The seas are building though not yet to the heroic dimensions suggested by the cruising guide and John, the Club Nautico manager. Lodie is still grappling with helm control which, admittedly, is not so easy downwind on large following waves.

I'm disappointed in the boat speed but can't figure out how to get any more out of the sails. They are full and trimmed. This is when I need some serious sail-setting guys, like J-P or JB, on board. Landfall is on my watch, about 0800. Serious-looking big mountains are obscured by low haze and topped with thick cloud. Wave size continues building to consistent 12-15 ft. as QV approaches the coast. But, I am pleased to observe, the Caribbean Sea is not breaking on the Continental shelf or across the entrance to Sukunya Bay. Both conditions happen. I'm glad they're not happening this morning. We make our Puerto Escoses waypoint at 1215, according to plan but at a cost in fuel. I come back to the helm to negotiate the entrance and, hopefully, miss Scotchman's Rock which the sketch chart shows almost in the middle.

I spot the named Rock looming out of the mist. QV skirts that one; then passes the Kuna village of Sukunya. There are no people, animals, or smoke from fires. We're headed toward the anchorage beyond the village. Lodie takes the helm in 28 ft. and I go forward to get the anchor ready.

We run in to 20 ft. when I have her start calling the depth. "18, 4, 2" and "Crunch". I hear the last sound from underneath the hulls. Run aground. I go back to the helm and try to work QV off the ledge it seems hung on. When I back her down, I hit something solid astern. My first impression is that the impact was to the starboard rudder; not the drive leg. Under the circumstances, I think this is a good thing and I'm quietly thankful. I continue working the boat starboard and forward (Sounds wrong, doesn't it?), going from 2.3 ft indicated to 24 ft. under the hulls in just two boatlengths. With Lodie back at the helm, I drop anchor in 25 ft., put out 120 ft. of scope and set the bridle. By the time I finish, a Kuna guy in a dugout is along side. I gave him an orange but he wanted US$5 for anchoring. I'd heard about this charge that some of the Kuna villages have begun levying but act like I haven't. He offers to sell us some bush meat. I take this to be the small spotted animal lying quite dead in the bottom of his dugout. I counter with a request for coconuts and bananas. He takes our order and paddles off.

A light rain begins. Lodie brushes down the aft deck. I take advantage of the precip to shower and I'm in my bunk by 1500. The swell which, surprisingly, has penetrated deep into the bay wakes me up about 2100. I guess it must be pretty damn big outside. Lodie has prepared fruit and cheese. There is little breeze but no bugs. The rain started again at 0230. I got up to shut the hatches but before I could finish, it accelerated into a serious downpour. Before I could dog all the hatches and shut the companionway, the interior of Quo Vadis was soaked. Some hatches started leaking where the gaskets had dried and shrunk. These same hatches had not leaked when taking seas underway. Welcome to another of Panama's legendary features: The Rain.

Rainfall in Panama is so intense it is hard to describe, but I'll give it a try. It seems the rain drops are both bigger and come down with the density of a bucket of water dumped over your head. Visibility is canceled out by silver sheets that undulate if there's any wind or hang like a waterfall if it's still. The boat deck drums so loud you have to shout to be heard. Places that cannot leak admit water; in the exemplary case, to the interior of my boat. This is during the "dry season".

The rains in Panama have always been overwhelming to us visiting whites over the past several hundred years. One of the stories about those poor bastards trying to dig the Canal across the Isthmus is that, in some years, the rains washed more mud and rock back in to the cut than had been dug out during an entire season of excavation. The main distinction in Panama rainfall patterns that I can determine is that during the "dry season" the rain sometimes stops.

When it did, shortly after dawn, Ricardo returned in his dugout with the requested bananas and coconuts. I had doubted we would see him again. It also dawned on me that he had to go into the jungle to collect the produce. Other things I can worry about this morning include: 1) How much fuel is remaining; 2) Why the interior carpet on the port side and entryway is soaked through. The source is not evident while the worst case is that we're taking on water from the grounding.

First, having calculated 12 gallons of diesel left in the tank, I add another 5 from a jerry can. A tank measurement and the fuel gauge agree it is half full. (Notice I didn't call it "Half empty." Call me a starry-eyed optimist.) Second, I don mask and fins and go overboard to inspect the hulls and drive leg. The day is gray and misty. It looks like it should be cold but the water is tropical sea warm. There is no visible damage to the drive leg or the prop but I cruelly remember the crack at St. Kitts went unseen until half the yoke fell off. Paint is missing from the port rudder; not the starboard. The paint and barnacles have been removed from the first 3 feet of the skeg. I can't help think that was a quick, if risky, way to clean the bottom. No other hull deformation or penetration is observed. Is the water in the port side all rain? I finally discover the port water tank is overflowing. The deck filler cap appears tight so I can't figure out how the tank overfilled. The carpet in front of the navigation table is all squishy.

When I was in the water, I felt slight play in the port rudder so crawled into the aft compartment to check the coupling to the rudder. Everything looked OK with no play around the rudder post. While I'm being cheered up by this observation, Lodie calls me from on deck. Raul is visiting with another offer of *carne*. The meat consists of small, speckled dead critters in the bottom of his dugout. They don't look any more appetizing than yesterday. He seems genuinely disappointed when I decline. What are they? Agouti, maybe? He then wants to know if we want to buy a dugout: in Kuna, it's an *ulu*. A British boat had been through some months back and paid US$500 for an *ulu*, lashed it to the forward rail, and motored off. Raul thought this was pretty good business: selling dugouts to boat people who obviously had more money than sense. I can see some rich Brit bragging about his *ulu*, displayed amongst the other "native items" in his trophy room. Only partly because of this mental image, I decline Raul's offer. It's still a long way to California.

About Kuna Yala

The San Blas Archipelago is home and domain of the Kuna. Their hundreds of islands stretch along 125 miles of Darien coast, interspersed with reefs, extensive flats and deep channels. The indigenous Kuna have lived here for over a thousand years. By 1925, they got fed up with the intrusion of mainland Panamanians into their tribal homelands and rebelled. The Panamanian army was poised for bloody revenge (punitive extermination of yet another indigenous people) when the U.S. got involved (We owned the place back then, remember.) and basically said "Don't do it." Or so the story goes. Given the U.S. government and the U.S. Army's history with Native Americans, this sounds out of character.

But the Kuna weren't massacred, jailed, or carted off to reservations and today are nearly autonomous in this remote region of sea, island, jungle and cloud-shrouded mainland mountains. They maintain a traditional tribal structure. The land belongs to all Kuna but each village is governed by a first *sahila* (chief) assisted by deputy *sahilas* in a matrilineal society. A new husband moves into his wife's family compound. He may show up with nothing but his machete and his clothes. At least he doesn't have to pay a dowry.

The husband is expected to take up fishing or subsistence farming, the latter on small mainland plots. Many Kuna visit these daily by dugout. I'm not so sure how sustainable the lucrative lobster and octopus trade will be. More than once, I saw them harvesting lobster of all sizes—down to fingerlings. Most of the islands support coconut palms and most of these are individually owned. Every coconut belongs to someone. This has a couple of impacts on cruisers: 1) Don't take any coconuts, even lying on the ground. 2) Most islands have primitive shelters for the coconut guards who may spend weeks watching over the trees. The guards I saw looked very young. The men are expected to work until early afternoon. Then, the village takes care of family and tribal business on a daily basis. This is considered as much a responsibility as working. I like this idea.

Muchas molas

You have probably seen Kuna *molas* even if you didn't know where they were made. These brightly colored, intricately stitched cloth panels are actually the front and back of a Kuna woman's traditional long-sleeved blouse, so *molas* are made as a pair. A majority of the Kuna women still wear them as everyday apparel. Some of the young ones have devolved to T-shirts and jeans. Kuna women trade in *molas* as a major cash crop. The asking price in dollars seems to have doubled in the time it took to get from Curaçao to the San Blas. Still, collecting some "real deal" Kuna *molas* was one of the reasons I chose this route to Panama. I welcomed the women (always a woman) who rowed their *ulu* out to Quo Vadis with a plastic bucket full of *molas*. In one case, the vendor arrived by panga with her husband handling the outboard. I had to convince Lodie to let them come along side. She didn't want anything to do with *mola* vendors and was genuinely surprised that I did. Just so you can be a total insider, *mola* is actually a Spanish word. In Kuna, it's *morr*.

What was fascinating to me was the range of designs artfully stitched onto these pieces of cloth. There are lots of wild and domesticated animals, birds, fish and dolphins, some Catholic religious themes (the Holy Spirit as a dove seemed popular) as you might expect. But these artisanal craftswomen aren't limited to the expected. I saw rock 'n' roll guitar *molas*, a couple featuring busses (which operate only over on the mainland) and at least one Elvis *mola* design.

I favored the traditional design portraying the four distinct but related parts of the Kuna physical and metaphysical world. Each part of their world is finely stitched as multi-colored swirls within swirls. Somehow, I can really relate to that view of the way things are. I bought another *mola* of a pig with wings being led through the jungle by a friendly duck or maybe it's a seagull. I have to figure out which ancient Kuna legend that *mola* portrays…or create one to fit the flying pig and the guide bird.

Kuna women also wear gold. It is an everyday accessory for the majority who dress the traditional way. Gold is worked into intricate figures and thin leaf for necklaces. It is made into hoops which are stacked around their ankles and calves. It is formed into nose rings and earrings. It is not traded. The women are evasive about the source of the gold. It has to be from mainland rivers which are a well-kept secret. The Kuna take *ulus* to the mainland on a daily basis for hunting, tending crops, fresh water and, apparently, gathering gold.

The whole region is amazingly isolated, even from the rest of Panama. Airstrips built during WWII are used mostly by chartered aircraft from Panama City. It is an expensive way to get that vital part essential to continuing the voyage out to your boat. Sailing, which aside from collecting *molas* is what we're doing, is challenging. All the palm-dotted islands and sandy beaches cause some to say it's like the South Pacific. Many of the islands are submerged and none that I saw feature any markers. The area features channels over 100 ft. deep bordered by reefs or surrounding flats of 2-4 ft. Most boats put a lookout up the mast to find the channel and avoid the coral heads, reefs and other sharp edges under the water. After a rain, the sea is not always clear.

Kuna villages are packed on to their individual islands. Many of them are wall-to-wall huts and lodges built right to (sometimes, over) the water's edge. Some places, you have to turn sideways to squeeze between them. The experience of landing at a Kuna village is like coming across a village of Lakota on the Montana prairie today, in this century, still living traditionally in tipis, hunting the buffalo, holding tribal councils, and wearing traditional hand-made clothing. Sure, the Kuna know about television. There are some *cayucos* with outboard motors but most of the tribe still paddle *ulus* or raise a home-made sail (often patchwork) to make long passages between islands using their body as mobile ballast in the round-bottomed craft. Some of the villages have government clinics occasionally visited by government-paid medical staff but it is each village's shaman who has the real powers. The shaman can detect sorcery and does a lot more prescribing and curing with local ingredients than any Spanish-speaking intruders from the Mainland.

North to Panama! and Other Strange Directions

We find out most of this after we leave Puerto Escoses, planning to take the inside passage with the goal of making it to Akwasuit Murru and into Bahia Masargandi before dark. We head North, never seeing Puerto Obaldia (POE) with the vague understanding and strong desire that we may be legal as long as we don't actually go to the Panama mainland. The Kuna Yala is not heavily patrolled. It may be obvious already that most of the islands and other places have Kuna names. Many islands also have Spanish names. Not as many also have a third name, in English, mostly given in pre-U.S. times and frequently by pirates. Most of those guys (and a few gals) were English or Dutch. The form of name on various charts of the Archipelago is not consistent so I won't try to be, either. You experienced cruisers will understand that when we drop anchor off Kanildup, it could be Green Island or even Isla Verde in some references; maybe yours.

It is nearly 1000 and the sun high by the time we pass the deserted village, Scotsman's Rock, exit the bay and turn North. I rationalize that this is better light for the required eyeball navigation. We make good progress up the inside channel until we lose it. Quo Vadis is quickly in 2-3 ft. indicated depth but not run aground. Lodie backs out as I climb the mast. Twice she tries to get into deeper water. On the premise that it's better for me to wreck my boat, I take the helm and work QV cautiously in 3-5 ft. depth toward where I thought the channel was until, suddenly, depth shows as 40 ft.

There is lots of debris in the water from heavy runoff: another reason for staying up on the mast steps. This hurts my feet after a while so I go down to the foredeck. At Canal de Pinos, I choose to go outside Isla del Pinos into the Caribbean. The 10-15 knot North winds are still on the nose.

When we go back in to the Pinos channel and toward the entrance to Bahia Masargandi, we pass several *ulus*. Everybody waves and acts friendly, including us. One *ulu* under sail is headed South. It is crewed by three Kuna women , all in traditional clothing. Their bright red and orange headscarves are arranged to cover the lower half of their face. It is mostly for protection. Our vessels pass with less than 50 meters separation. It is a beautiful moment.

At the "Not for Navigation" waypoint, I can see big breaks to starboard. It is breaking on both sides of the entrance to the Bay. We try alternate anchorages for about 20 minutes, looking for some place shallow, but finally resort to the spot shown on the chart. I finish rigging the bridle with the boat backed down in 23 ft. I make a hot meal, we eat it and I do route planning until nearly 2100. As many of you know, this involves poring over charts that you hope are relevant and trying to figure out what the hell you're going to do next…while not sinking the boat.

At 0630, we're up and underway to Aridup. By 1600, we're anchored between the island and the South reef with the persistent North wind pushing Quo Vadis back toward the reef on a long scope. This worries me. But, when I check, the engine seems to have stopped burning oil. Or maybe it didn't run as much. I both measure and calculate we have just over 11 gallons of fuel remaining, which seems high. I thought we'd burn more. What if my calculations are wrong? The wind came to the Northeast at 15-20 knots before dawn. I reconsider destinations and decide to try for Tigre rather than the larger settlement of Narganá. I develop a waypoint at the navigational pinch point between the reef and the rocks in Playon Grande channel.

Island Hopping

We are under sail in good winds, holding 5 knots or better on a beam reach. Nothing is optimized but nothing is strained, I sincerely hope. Quo Vadis passes within 200 ft. of the waypoint. One result is our missing both the outside reef and the inside rocks. Lodie seems actively relieved about this event as we continue along miles of mostly uninhabited, savage-looking coast.

QV gets around the encircling reef and in to the deep water channel behind Tigre by noon. We drop anchor as there is a fairly large *cayuco* occupying the town dock which is a 50 ft. long concrete wall.

When the crew of the *cayuco* finish their business and leave, we move to the dock. Quo Vadis is secure by 1230 with the aid of citizens of all ages from this Kuna village. I give the kids fresh oranges but have to coax the older ones to share with the younger. Word on the water is that the Kuna are more receptive to U.S. flagged vessels than Panamanian mainly because they know we're not going to tax them, inspect them, or do similar bad things to them. Besides, gringos buy *molas*.

The Spanish-speaking schoolteacher informs me the village has diesel, fresh water and lunch. We start with lunch which consists of one leathery hot dog, rice and plantains. So much for healthy diets. Lodie fills some water jugs at the dockside tap while the schoolteacher informs me I must get permission to: 1) Be here; 2) Take any photographs. He gives me directions to the chief's house to request same. So I meet Sahila Aurelio. Few Kuna are more than 5 ft. tall and their houses are scaled accordingly. I duck my head under the doorframe, squint into the interior darkness and announce myself in Spanish. (I've memorized the Kuna greeting in the guidebook but don't want to try a conversation.) The first Sahila of Tigre returns my greeting from his hammock and invites me to sit. This is a Kuna courtesy. Chief Aurelio is formal yet cordial. He gives me permission to stay at the village for a day and to take photos of children. He says I should offer them something, like money. I'm not sure what the kids would do with it. A much younger woman emerges from the back. Aurelio introduces his wife while she shows me a large, complete two panel *mola*. I thank her and make excuses about taking care of my other business.

The owner of the diesel fuel lives at the far end of the village and wasn't home. He'd gone to Narganá; back later in the afternoon. I am escorted on my excursions by many little, snotty-nosed kids. The rest of the 12 and under population watch from in front of the family huts. Their noses are dripping, too. Lodie, a former nurse, comments on the virus that has apparently infected the village, and hopes we don't catch it. In the closely-packed, communal living style of the Kuna, any disease could be ravaging. Maybe their island isolation provides some protection.

I have never bought in entirely to the Noble Savage thing. The Kuna are used to dealing with transient outsiders. It's self-preservation. They have been known to supplement jugs of diesel with salt water, overprice or hollow-out their spiny lobsters, sell long-dead fish and similar tourist practices. I can see how they might think this all a good joke on us. Despite the escalating asking prices, the trade and barter in *molas* seems to be the most straightforward transaction. I wonder if the women know or care about their world-wide reputation? I return to the Sahila's house and buy his wife's *mola* as a wedding present for my daughter Beth.

When the owner returns, I also buy 10 gallons of diesel from a jug capped with a rag and two lobsters for Lodie's dinner. I used the regular funnel filter to transfer the fuel into my jerry jugs and the three-stage Baja filter for pouring it into the boat's fuel tank. We slipped the docklines from Tigre at 1545, intending to press on to Tuala or Kanildup. The approach to Tuala appeared difficult in low light. I plotted courses in the deep channels between the reefs shown in the Zydlers' guide. Again, it's "Not for navigation". I never did take any photos of the Kuna kids.

I do take the helm to maneuver QV out from behind Tigre and around the reef before setting all sails. Lodie's at the the helm while we hold over 6 knots on this run to make it around the North end of Kanildup at sunset. QV stays to port of four monohulls in the lagoon and runs into shallower water. I see only coral or rock bottom through 10 ft. of clear water so we back down and drop the hook on sand. I make pasta and lobster for dinner.

Winds are light across Kanildup Lagoon and light rain begins falling at 0400. I close the hatches; then crawl back in my bunk til 0700. I've spread some things on deck to dry and am just deploying the bimini when a Kuna couple come along side. Laurencio is steering while Otilda takes care of business: selling bread and *molas*. I purchase 6 loaves of bread and 5 *molas*. Otilda is dressed in the Kuna tradition, including gold and beaded anklets. Laurencio wears a faded baseball-style cap, baggy T-shirt and long pants which is what I've seen on most Kuna men, regardless of status (like Chief Aurelio) or what they're doing. Lodie changes her mind about *molas* and borrows US$20 to buy some. She had already tuned in to the Panama Net and announced the arrival of Quo Vadis. She loves cruiser nets. I'm not so sure this is a wise move since we have not officially cleared in to Panama. It is our first radio contact since Cartagena.

The lagoon is calm, the day is clear, the wind is very light so, after the Kuna couple disembarked, I started on today's "Fix it List".

Re-glue plexiglas to rim of aft deck inspection plate

Clean and sanitize port head

Check rudder steering arms and bearings

Change engine oil

Clean and oil mildewed interior wood

Check and repair headsail patch, as necessary

Tape shroud chafeguards

Fill and pump up steering hydraulic reservoir

Treat tools and cabinet door hinges with Liquid Wrench

Clean bottoms of hulls and rudders

Considering it's just a week out of Cartagena, the list is surprisingly long but, in fact, it is pretty typical. Before I start, I called Xtasy on VHF to thank them for notice of the Panama Net. The skipper invited us over for sundowners at the end of the day. Making up the list, not to mention executing the activities listed on it, makes me hungry. By now, you'll remember this Captain's solution. Lunch is chilled lobster on Kuna bread with lime mayonnaise. Some sauvignon blanc washes it down.

The appeal of scraping furry green growths and barnacles is seldom great and has completely evaporated by 1700. As it turns out, most of them are gone from the *amas* by this hour. I'm washing off the algae to get social when Paul comes on the VHF and says it's time to come over. We had already dropped the dink, so load ourselves and a bag of beer to go visit Paul and Nancy.

Paul refuses our offering of carbonated malt beverages, claiming "We've got tons of beer." It seems they've been over to the mainland recently and are headed out to The Bathtub for the weekly trash-burning and related festivities. It's quite the social event for cruisers in the San Blas Archipelago. Paul is a veteran of these parts. He reflects on the advantages of sailing a shallow draft catamaran in these waters compared to going around in a monohull with "a lead mine attached to the bottom". They are genuine, good people of considerable wit and the clever repartee goes on 'til 2000. Leaving our hosts with less beer than the tons they previously claimed, we motor home. I get the dink up and stowed. The Skipper's Special is fake burritos. Lodie says she's not hungry.

The calm continues until morning. I call Paul for any suggestions on San Blas sailing strategy. Since the wind, or lack of it, is the same for everybody, he has none. "Going to charge the batteries today." Both vessels motor out of very placid Kanildup Lagoon. Quo Vadis is headed for the deepwater channel to the Holandes Cays. Xtasy turns to starboard in our wake and we radio goodbyes. The specific cay selected for the next stop is Miriadiadup.

Before noon, we spot a mast in the Miriadiadup anchorage. The mast starts moving and then comes out attached to the rest of a vessel. We're on the hook shortly thereafter but I'm concerned about holding. When I dive on the hook, I see it laid just fine with the shank buried in white sand 25 ft. down. After a freshwater rinse, quick lunch, chart review and some course calculations, I decide staging over to the Chichime Cays will improve our passage to Portobello and on to Colón. As we start to weigh anchor, three fishermen in a motorized *cayuco* come by. The motorized part is the source of their problem. They ask in Spanish, not Kuna, to exchange lobster for gasoline. They've run their tank dry. We discuss how much they'll need to get to the mainland and I trade 2.5 gallons gasoline and 400cc of two-stroke oil for 6 bugs. They now had enough fuel to make it back to Narganá and we had a nice surprise for dinner. Their outboard starts with a little priming.

I estimate just over two hours to Chichime Cays, going around the reef rather than trying to go through with the late afternoon sun in full glare on the water. QV followed the course plots around the islands' reef and into the anchorage at 1700, never seeing less than 15 ft. However, we couldn't find any depth less than 34 ft. inside the anchorage, even up near the shore of Uchu Tippi, which had a small village. Three *ulus* full of locals came out to Quo Vadis. The folks were very nice, not banging their *ulus* against the hulls, but their *molas* weren't as nice as the ones we had.

I brought sundowners out on deck. While we're sipping quietly in the cockpit, we see three boys who look to be 9-10 years old walking a sail-equipped *ulu* over the outer shoal. They step in and push off into the gathering dusk. The nearest land is a thin gray stripe on the horizon. As concerned parents, even though all our kids are now older than these guys, we agree those little boys should not be sailing out at this late hour. But they do and are soon out of sight on the darkening sea. Just before nightfall, the girls from Uchu Tippi paddle their *ulu* out to the deep water and dump the day's garbage. For our last dinner in Kuna Yala, I prepare some of the lobsters, a salad, pita bread and open a bottle of white wine. Lodie cleans up the galley while I plot courses and punch waypoints in to the GPS for our passage to Colón via Isla Grande.

By 0530 next morning, the November Mike November weather forecast on SSB radio had already moved past the Southwest Caribbean section, so we prepared to get underway. Quo Vadis cleared the reef opening just as another boat was coming in. I can't believe they were sailing overnight in these waters. Mainly because these waters tend to be shallow and laced with reefs where they aren't profoundly deep.

I had set our course to clear Punta San Blas, the tip of the Archipelago, and come back to the inside route keeping the notorious Escribano and La Providéncia shoals to starboard.

After blowing 20 knots all night, the wind died to under six knots by 0830 with the resulting boat speed less than half that. A quick calculation confirmed that our ETA to anywhere is well after dark at this speed over the surface. The fuel remaining is calculated, measured, and gauged to be 11 gallons. It is over 40 nm to Isla Grande, so we started motoring. We went outside the shoals which extend over a mile off Punta San Blas. I can say this with certainty only because we didn't hit them. The shoals are not well-charted. The inside channel I'd chosen is mostly 60-90 ft. but does feature some surprise rocks and shallow reefs scattered about. This route was the alternative selected to avoid the prevailing two knot Southeast current in the deeper, less cluttered ocean passage. The wind continued to shift; then went calm.

I had plotted a course of 290 Magnetic which, laid out across the deep channel, missed all charted shoals, rocks and points up to Isla Grande. I had to alter course after mis-identifying which Punta we were passing. The course adjustment cleared the tall *mogotes* lining the Isla Grande entrance but I'm sweating it. The course plotted when you're rested is usually the best. Mafu Rock, right in the middle of the entrance, was barely breaking enough to be visible. How many others were not?

The preferred anchorage identified in both Panama guides was occupied by a fairly large and rotting derelict. Lodie stayed at the helm and I headed up to the foredeck to continue our search for an alternate spot to drop the anchor. I didn't get there quickly enough. Specifically, I didn't get to the bows before she put Quo Vadis up on a large patch of white coral. Our last day anchoring in the San Blas Arhcipelago was just like our first day entering this mystic realm of empty cays, cloudy mountains, coconut caretakers and, inevitably, shallow patches of dead coral. Run aground.

I worked the boat off and found a patch of sand 8 ft. under it. There still wasn't enough wind to push QV back on the anchor line, so I set it backing down, put out 55 ft. of scope, and dove on the hook. It was lying in sand with all the chain on the bottom. Since I was already wet, I checked out the amas below waterline. There was no visible structural damage, the bottoms of both skegs were stripped clean, and the drive leg looked intact. The couple cruising on Cloud 9, also home ported in an upscale Bay Area city, had observed our dramatic entrance and dinked over to say "Hi." Lodie wanted to go into town with them for dinner, so we did. Everything was closed on Monday. It's hard to believe a schedule of life goes on beyond the boat.

Cartagena Update

A few weeks after I'd transited the Canal with Steve Cherry's able assistance, he made the ocean passage going the other way, from Colón to Cartagena, on his 41 ft. ketch. He barely made it, as his boat's diesel engine surged and sputtered to a stop just outside the anchorage at the Club Nautico. You'll remember from QV's visit this is the marina considered generally more hospitable to cruisers. His update on the goings-on at the Club reminded me of another maritime commercial opportunity I'd taken a pass on: the informal transport of backpackers between Panama and Colombia. He also related the latest in local vessel acquisition methods.

Though I seriously participated in supporting the Cartagena economy, like the good gringo cruising boat, I remember events at the Club being quieter when Quo Vadis was anchored there. I seem to suffer from this chronic condition called "Just Missing the Action". Now, this is not always a bad thing as the action can include mayhem, imprisonment, shipwreck and the like. I did get the polo shirt with the "Club Nautico, Cartagena" logo printed on both front and back. You don't see those everyday.

There are a half-dozen or so boats mostly skippered by single-handers, mostly in the 30 foot range; mostly unimpressive vessels not burdened with amenities that regularly haul backpackers between Panama and Colombia. They charge US$250 per person for this marine transport service plus another $250 for a bicycle. They cram 4 to 6 of these (usually unwashed) individuals along with their packs on to the boat and give them a ride to Panama or Cartagena, usually with a stop in Portobello and the San Blas Islands. The backpackers get to visit the islands and the skipper makes a decent living. Win-win situation. Hey, it does get a little crowded on a 30 ft. boat but these are folks used to sleeping under bridges anyway, so no problem.

Well, every now and then, a fly does appear in the ointment, as was the case with one of the guys who got sentenced to 5-8 years in the Panama slammer for illegally importing aliens, of the local terrestrial variety. I later read the guy claimed his passengers claimed to have valid Venezuelan passports. These documents apparently were not so convincing to Panama Immigration officials.

Included in this elite group of passenger-carrying skippers are an Algerian, a Swede, a Frenchman (He just left on his first trip, so the jury is still out on this one.) and a

Norte Americano. Probably the most interesting tale to other *Norte Americanos* or, at least, the one with the most plot twists involves the latter.

Once upon a time (so this story begins), there was a very nice, large sailing yacht based in Cartagena. The fellow who owned this nice, large boat used to have a smaller boat. He then made a trip to Panama from Colombia and returned on the Big Boat. Go figure. His hobby was photography and his favorite subjects were teen-age girls. As a matter of fact, you could come aboard his Big Boat in the harbor at Cartagena, look at his photo albums, and actually meet one or more of his models, if you so desired. He had a local Colombiana on board who helped him manage his hobby. The two of them were an item, as well. Also involved, somehow, was this *Norte Americano* (the N.A.) whose day job, you'll remember, was the maritime transport of backpackers.

The photographer developed what proved to be a terminal illness and left the Big Boat in the custody of these two other folks. Reportedly, he wrote a will leaving the boat to them, 50:50, in the event he did not survive. He passed away a few months later. It seems as though there became a problem with the will; namely, the verification of its authenticity. The only copy to be found was in the hands of the N.A. and seemed to mostly cut out the Colombiana, even though they were also now an item, sort of. To top things off, the dead photographer's estranged daughter back in the U.S.A. initiated an action to gain custody of the Big Boat. But, this tale does not end with such wa-a-ay too predictable legal wranglings.

A couple of months later, the Big Boat was anchored back in Cartagena and the couple were doing their usual stuff in the Club Nautico Bar: wheeling, dealing, scamming. Also present in and around the open air bar were other cruisers and a contingent of locals.

A minor altercation occurs. Words are exchanged, among which the Colombiana (off the Big Boat) calls a local girl a hooker. The hooker (Um, I mean "local girl") happens to be living on board another boat anchored in the bay. She jumps in the dinghy and rows out to get the .38 her boyfriend keeps on board. It seems she had a pretty good mad going at this point. Her boyfriend says, "No problem. She won't be able to find the ammunition."

She rows back to the club with the pistol and the ammo (How wrong can a guy be?) and starts blazing away; mostly at the folks she is mad at. Everyone hits the deck. Her boyfriend approaches her to try and get her under control and, even though she is not particularly mad at him, she blows a big hole in his stomach to make her point. She goes to jail and spends the night. She is out the next morning, probably since nobody was around to press charges and, face it, she is also a local. He goes to the hospital and almost dies but eventually recovers. There is a happy ending to this part of the tale. The two of them get back together and go cruising the San Blas Islands.

As for the two folks on the Big Boat, on the last trip from Cartagena to Panama the Colombiana got upset over the attention two female backpackers were giving to the N.A., so she stabbed them both, but only just a little. The N.A. was last seen back in Cartagena, without his knife-wielding other half, but asking some of the other local legends (always reliable sources of information in a Third World tropical port) which countries did <u>not</u> have extradition treaties with the U.S. He then sailed away from Cartagena. The best guess is that he will pick her up (in the San Blas Islands?) and they will take the Big Boat on the lam. Now, what were those non-extraditing places? Let me write that down.

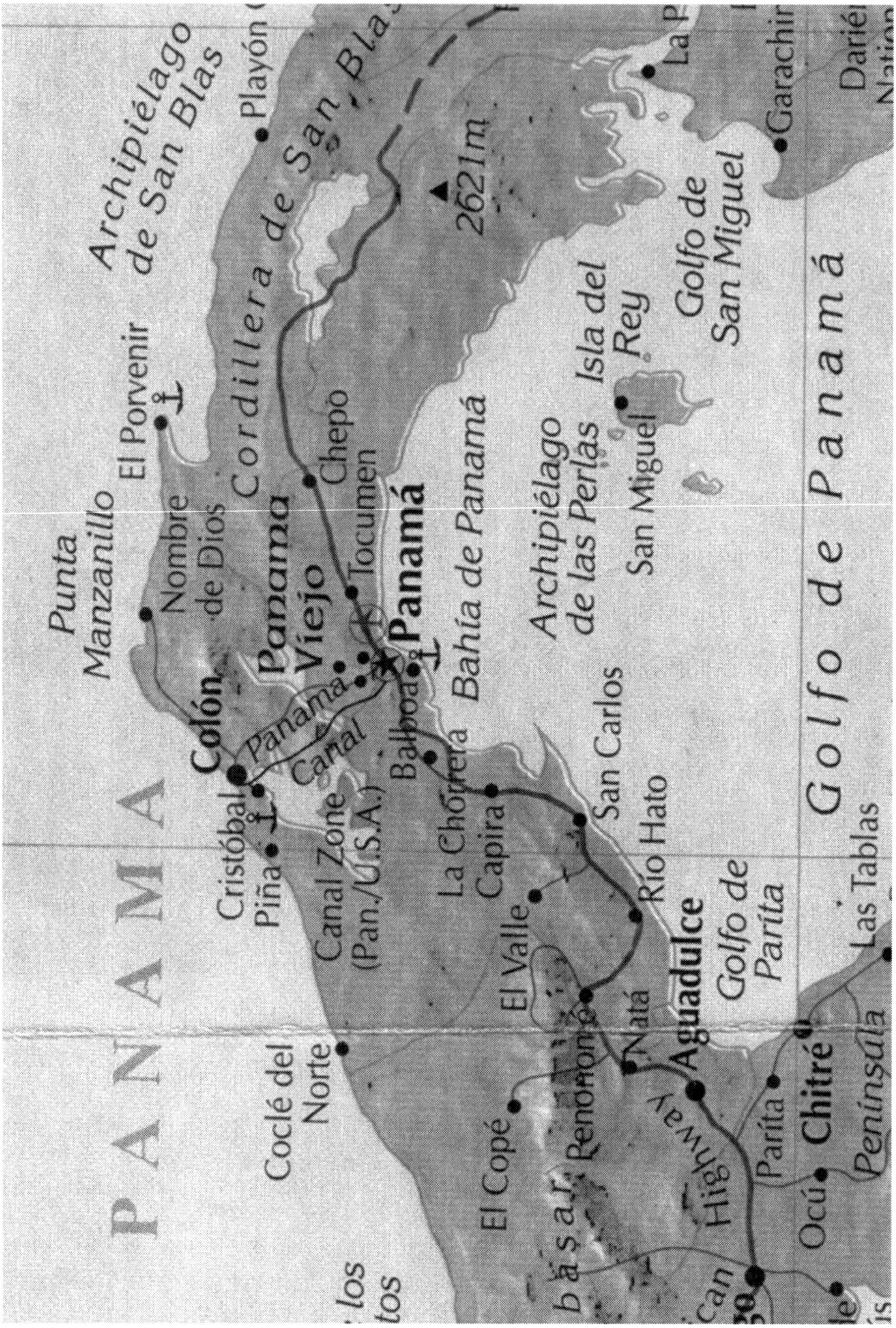

PANAMA
Archipiélago de San Blas
Playón
Punta Manzanillo
El Porvenir
Nombre de Dios
Cordillera de San Blas
Colón
Cristóbal
Piña
Coclé del Norte
Panama Canal
Canal Zone (Pan./U.S.A.)
Panama Viejo
Chepo
Tocumen
Panamá
Balboa
La Chorrera
Capira
El Valle
Bahía de Panamá
2621m
Archipiélago de las Perlas
San Miguel
Isla del Rey
Golfo de San Miguel
Garachiné
San Carlos
Río Hato
Aguadulce
Natá
Penonomé
El Copé
Golfo de Parita
Parita
Chitré
Ocú
Las Tablas
Golfo de Panamá
Highway

The Panama Canal Authority

Aboard S/V Quo Vadis, transiting the Panama Canal

The westward run after clearing Punta San Blas was spectacular. The course to the Cristobal waypoint was dead downwind with following seas 4-6 feet and an occasional set to 8 ft. I decided to jibe out past the Continental shelf and then correct course for a southerly heading back to the Colón breakwater. It was the best downwind handling and feel on Quo Vadis I can remember. We had good boat speed and sail shape. We made it to the end of the breakwater by early afternoon, started the engine and also started weaving through the fleet of commercial ships anchored on the Caribbean side waiting to transit the canal.

I couldn't raise the Panama Canal Yacht Club on any hailing channel. After we shot through the breakwater entrance at 6 knots on a breaking swell, I referred to the charts to look for the club docks. They appeared just about where the harbor chart indicated. We made one pass calling again on CH16 but still had no response, so turned in to the docks and grabbed an end tie. I managed to scrape the starboard *ama* during that procedure after Lodie's throw fell in the water and I stepped back on to the starboard bow from the dock where I had jumped off to catch the line. Then Rogelio strolled out, can of Coke in hand. He offered to take a line and said we had to move. After we re-docked, I bought 5 car tires wrapped in garbage bags for $10. Eight fenders are recommended for going through the canal. Rogelio (aka Roger) is the Dockmaster at the PCYC. This means he pretty much runs things. He offered to provide a ride and help with the entry paperwork for $25. I went for that, too. I wanted to get and keep Rogelio on my side.

The long term cruisers, sportfishing guides and other gringos inhabiting Central America usually refer to the watering hole at the Panama Canal YC as "The Star Wars Bar" since various critters from all over the galaxy gather there for liquid and solid refreshment and to conduct business. After I rigged QV for dockside, including power and water, I plunged in to the legendary Happy Hour. Aside from the distinctly different music (mostly salsa), I could see how the place gained its unofficial name and fame. I'm not sure which character I was but I was unarmed. Among the colorful characters in this scene was Steve Cherry. He had brought his ketch, Witch of Endor, through the Canal from the Pacific. Quo Vadis was docked across the fairway from his boat and next to the Swedish sloop Blusippe. Her skipper, Jon, had moored near QV back in Spanish Water.

Torture by Paperwork

Rogelio showed up at 0830 the next morning; then handed us off to JC and Roberto to go off and do everything. One of them was his nephew. *Migracion* closed at 0900 so we missed that and went over to the Port Captain and the Admeasurement Office to record our entry and request a handline transit. Both offices were in a modern, air-conditioned multi-story building out at the end of the breakwater where they can keep an eye on ship traffic. Then we went downtown to Customs. These offices were located in a turn of the last century crumbling concrete pile that looked like a set for a B movie, complete with sleazy-looking locals lounging on the steps and squinting inscrutably at us gringos. However, it wasn't nearly as crumbling as the hollowed out shell across the street that featured trailing vines and giant ferns sprouting from the glassless windows. You could read faded red letters identifying it as the (former) offices of British Steam & Freight Lines. The Customs office is where you must go to present and surrender your *zarpe* from Colombia (since we hadn't officially entered Panama til now), provide your cargo list, and get your boat papers stamped and signed so you can be in Panama, legally. As in most Latin American offices, this procedure requires several people seated behind as many desks. While I'm waiting near one of them, I hear one side of a highly emotional phone conversation in rapid, idiomatic Spanish.

"I'm all for him. It's the way to go. Viva Chavez! Viva la Revolucíon!" The speaker then slams the phone down and exclaims, to nobody in particular, "Damn. I'm going off to Venezuela!" Luckily, he doesn't leave before accepting our documents from the lady at the adjacent desk, stamping them vigorously before handing them back to me. We go back to *Migracíon*, which is now open; where our passports get stamped, quietly. Boat and crew are now officially in Panama.

The very proper lady at the Panama Canal Authority (*Autoridad de Canal de Panama*, or ACP) had informed me the admeasurer would be on board Quo Vadis at 1100 this same morning. We make it back to the dock by 1045 and he shows up at 1058. The punctuality astounds me. He is also a very congenial fellow, assuring me that he and all his ACP associates want to provide good service to all those using the Panama Canal so we will continue to patronize their facility. I am grateful and surprised at this user-friendly approach since I'm not aware we have much of a choice in trans-isthmus canals here in the Western Hemisphere.

He takes the measurements of Quo Vadis and reports 40 ft. and a few inches from the peak of the bows to the tips of the davits. He does not include the beam of the suspended dinghy. We retire to the "Star Wars Bar" of the PCYC to complete and sign several sets of forms. Some of these documents allow me to pay for the transit. By signing some others, I waive all claims against the ACP for anything they might do or anything else that might happen in their canal. We also talk about our children, have a cold drink, and he gives me a nice Spanish language brochure about the canal. The other inhabitants at this late hour of the morning include a table full of Panamanian gentlemen passing around a large bottle of rum to pour into their Cokes or Sprites. Some leave and others arrive during the time we are form-filling. All exhibit easy formality in greetings and manner of speech. This was a business meeting though I didn't catch their exact line of work.

Equipped with the completed and correct forms, I scurry off to the Colón branch of Citibank. You pay canal transit fees only at Citibank and only with a Visa card or cash. The bank, like most places in Colón, has several guards equipped with serious automatic weapons. These guards check you in through a double locking entry. I must look like a gringo guy from a sailboat as I'm admitted to the bank without being frisked. There is even a specific window reserved for those now entitled to pay to transit the canal. Today, there is no line at the window. Since QV is officially less than 50 ft. long, I pay $600 to the ACP plus an $850 contingency damage fee. I get checked back through the armed guards with my credit card receipt in my pocket. When I think about it, if I did manage to actually do some damage to the Panama Canal, $850 probably wouldn't cover it.

Even though I had braved the fearsome streets of Colón walking to Citibank, my assigned driver collects me curbside in his car and returns me to the PCYC. Lodie is having lunch with Jon, skipper of Blusippe. The yacht club restaurant features Latino-Cantonese food. There is a large Chinese population in Panama; some of whom make pretty good food. So I join them for lunch.

Jon asks me, "What happened to Gonzales… or whatever his name was?" I inform him that Jovino was put ashore on Aruba, at his insistence, after being seasick for a day.

"I'm not surprised," says Jon. "He was saying bad things about you, your boat and the whole enterprise before you even left the mooring at Curaçao. If crew is behaving that way while still at the Sarifundi Marina bar, you are going to have a problem."

"You knew this back in Curaçao?" I exclaim. "Why didn't you tell me?"

"That is not my job," Jon explains in a very precise, Swedish manner. He has a point.

It's Hard to Find Good Help

After polishing off a plate of grilled fish and fried rice, I respond to the message from Steve Cherry to come see him on the Witch. He is holding an open can and a small brush doing some wooden boat maintenance thing. Rather than asking me to pitch in with another brush, he confirms his offer to crew through the canal and extends it to go on to Golfito, Costa Rica. He says it's a good excuse to get out of the country (Panama) so he can get his visa renewed by re-entering. "And I'm not gonna charge you for it," he assures me, smiling. I interpret this to be a good thing.

I need two more line handlers to make the canal transit. The ACP requires four in addition to the skipper and the assigned pilot: one on each of the 150 ft. x 3/4 inch lines also required at port and starboard, bow and stern. Laurent, a 70ish French-Canadian off Oumiak, approached me on the dock. He and his wife would like to crew through the Canal "for the experience" since they weren't going to the Pacific but only if the transit occurred before the weekend. I also scheduled Morris, a Kuna who worked in the yacht club kitchen, to clean QV's bottom. He scrapes boat bottoms as well as pots and pans and was in considerable demand since most skippers, including me, were leery of jumping into the oily, yet crocodile-infested waters. I also contracted with Rogelio's man to provide the necessary hand lines for $50. They were light blue polypropylene.

Jon the Swede, Steve, and Bob and Zan Eisler were invited on board for sundowners. Bob and Zan had made the transit to the Pacific last week on a friend's boat, so I grilled them on "How to". Bob assured me it was "A piece of cake." while this good bunch shared a couple of bottles of good white wine. Jon had declined my invitation, saying he had to get Blusippe ready for inspection by his wife, who was arriving from Sweden the next day. I called Cristobal Signal on CH12 to get a passage time and was informed they didn't have one, yet. "Call back tomorrow."

Morris the Kuna had not arrived by 0800. I called Cristobal Signal on CH12. The operator still would not schedule a transit. I asked Roger to call on his cell phone. He did. He wouldn't confirm it but maybe we could go Friday at 1700. "Call back in an hour." Meanwhile, Morris arrived, organized his ancient surfboard as a cleaning platform and put on his equally vintage face mask. I had seen several smallish crocs under the docks so I asked him how he handled this saurian situation.

He smiles up at me and explains in fairly good Spanish (a second language to him, also), "If they come to bother me when I'm working, I hit 'em a good smack on the nose." Morris has all his limbs and most fingers, so it appears his work methods are successful to date. I mentally file this under "Best practices" in re crocs although cleaning boat bottoms amongst saltwater crocodiles may, in itself, not qualify as a

"Best Practice" at some of the more traditional business schools. Unless you are Kuna.

I tried Canal Transit on my cell phone and it worked. Quo Vadis is given a time of 1630 on 17 December to pick up our pilot on the Flats. I notify everybody and whirl into full preparation frenzy. I walk the scary streets of Colón (again) to the Texaco station for oil, filter, lubes, etc. I change engine oil, fill and pressurize the hydraulic steering reservoir, taxi to the El Rey market to provision, stow stuff on board and start the reefers, run up and get ice from Felix, the deaf bartender of the "Star Wars Bar". I forgot to mention that Felix is deaf. This can make ordering a drink, especially during the high volume Happy Hour, an interesting proposition. But, when he's not actually serving or pouring with considerable style and aplomb, he continually scans the room. He also has a couple of *señoritas* in key locations around the bar who kindly direct his attention to thirsty patrons. Felix is a local legend. The PCYC management, correctly we all agree, keeps him employed. Felix charges me US$1 for a bag of ice and I gladly tip him the same .

The Way Things Are

Most cruisers, especially of the Mom and Pop category—which includes most cruisers— make a very big deal about transiting the Panama Canal. All the more so, it seems, if they haven't done it. The cruising guides, sailing magazine articles, and the scuttlebutt around most marinas and anchorages all go on about how difficult it is to go through the canal. "Filling out all those forms" is often cited as a particularly perverse form of Panamanian torture. Price is always an object. Years ago, transit fees for all vessels were based on tonnage. Most sailboats don't displace many tons compared to, say, a fully laden container ship. Tonnage-based charges at $2/ton for, just as an example, Quo Vadis displacing 8 tons aren't going to cover an hour's wages for the obligatory transit pilot. Many, many cruisers did not seem to get this. The ACP still needs to work on its business model for handling smaller private vessels but it is somewhat more rational to apply length (LOA) rather than tonnage-based pricing. I've concluded the main reason cruisers make such a big deal out the Panama Canal passage is simply that it is something they are not used to doing every day.

One thing you soon find out is that there are three methods available to smaller vessels to transit the canal: rafted up with similar boats, center locked alone, or nested to a tug. One of the many forms presented by the genial ACP rep permits a skipper to prioritize his preference, though your first choice is not guaranteed. The conventional wisdom is that it is best to nest up to a tug. You also get a lot of unsolicited proclamations, often at the bar, that if you are so bold as to state your preference, your transit date will be purposely delayed by those vengeful Panamanian Canalists.

The morning of our transit day, we cleared out of Colón *Migracíon* with a *zarpe* for Golfito and *"puntos intermedios"*. While I was settling accounts and paying fees, a German backpacker approached me asking for a ride through the Canal. I told him QV was full. When I got back to the boat, Laurent showed up with Joceline. She was close to Laurent's age with her right wrist and hand in a cast. She gave a sort-of-Gallic shrug when she saw me staring at it. I quickly found Patrick Oswald, as was the backpacker's name, and told him to get his stuff on board.

When I moved Quo Vadis to the fuel dock to fill her up with diesel and water, most of the crew wandered off to do other stuff. Laurent and Joceline thought it was time to go have lunch at the PCYC restaurant. Lodie went to make some phone calls. Patrick was making his goodbyes with the other backpackers. I couldn't believe they were doing this kind of shit with less than an hour until our rendezvous with the pilot boat to transit the freakin' Panama Canal! I finally corralled the crew, cast off from the fuel dock at 1530, and immediately called Cristobal Signal. We were to meet the pilot boat at 1600 on Anchorage "F" and were soon circling that spot in the harbor.

"24 Daniel"

Jimmy the pilot came aboard. The first instruction he gave me was to go look at a tug that was going through, since we had requested a tug side-tie transit. He thought Smit Barbados was not a good fit for QV as it had non-standard fixed triangular fenders that were about at the level of QV's lifelines. I agreed with his assessment and we proceeded to the Gatun locks for a center lock transit, at least for now. Quo Vadis was assigned the ACP call sign: "24 Daniel", behind 24 Able, Baker, and Charlie. Jimmy was half-Chinese, reflecting the ethnic population around Colón, with 8 years experience in the ACP, reflecting how long it takes for these guys to work their way up to big ship piloting. By staying on schedule, we got ahead of SS Nordic Ice, the big rustbucket that was enabling this lockthrough and Smit Barbados, the useless tug. "24 Daniel" was last into the locks, so circled around in the approach channel until all the others went past. We were in the Gatun locks with one hour of daylight left. Jimmy didn't seem concerned.

I'm trying to hold the boat in the middle of the canal as the four ACP linehandlers toss down the monkeyfists on heaving lines, aiming at our deck from 60 ft. up on each side of the lock. They all hit someplace on the boat and three of them were secured. This is when we discovered Lodie didn't know how to tie a bowline. This knot allows the ACP guys to pull the 3/4-inch handling lines back up to the tops of the walls. Steve tied that knot and was also key in keeping QV's bows pointed straight ahead. The inrush of water into the locks makes for a quick surge but my main problem in boat handling was the wash from the tug's thrusters. The tug skipper claimed they couldn't stop running them.

QV rises up 85 ft. in the three locks and motors out on to Gatun Lake to spend the night. Jimmy started looking for our mooring buoy in the falling darkness. So did I. We spot it about the same time and Steve starts calling approach distances back to me from the bow. He picks up the buoy line and we're on the ball by 1900. Steve surprises me with a brief compliment on the successful night mooring and Jimmy soon leaves on his retrieval pilot boat. He declines my offer of a beer and tells us that he won't be our pilot the next day. It will, instead, be Cooper. "A kind of special guy," Jimmy warns us. Other cruisers have previously warned us about the infamous Cooper. "Just pray you don't get Cooper for your transit pilot." is the most common, and mildest, advisory.

Not much I can do about pilot assignment, so we put out a stern anchor in 75 ft. depth and I make pizzas for the crew: hot out of the oven. They're popular. It is very calm on Gatun Lake and a light rain starts to fall. There are few bugs and just a few sets of crocodile eyes gleaming from the dark water. You don't plan on a night swim, anyhow. The day's tension drains along with a shared bottle of red wine and I think it's pretty neat to be out on Gatun Lake on "24 Daniel".

The crew is roused and fed breakfast at 0630. I'm instructed over the VHF to call if we don't have a pilot by 0730. The pilot boat brought Cooper Ernest alongside at 0715. I introduce myself. He asks for two hangars on which to hang his "good clothes" and changes into shorts and a tank top. Joceline accommodates his request. He demands a cup of milky tea rather than the coffee offered. We can do that. He asks what fruit we have for him. I inform him that there are oranges and bananas on board which I am willing to share. "24 Daniel" was underway and into the Banana Cut by 0730. Lodie, Steve and I take turns at the helm as we motor across Gatun Lake. Cooper sits in the shade of the bimini reading a religious tract which he highlights with a purple marker. He informs me he'd like to get this transit done by 1500 so he can get on home.

We successfully dodge trash, logs and floating vegetation mats while big tankers and container ships pass us from the Pacific. We continue through the Gaillard Cut where it becomes obvious that the Panama Canal is still under construction. Enormous dredges and buckets are widening the canal to allow the Panamax ships to pass each other without stopping. However, Cooper directs me to stop QV just past the Gamboa Reach so he can make a phone call and get our transit time for the rest of the locks. I'm concerned he doesn't already have our transit time but keep my mouth shut.

I comply; hang a 180 in the canal and turn back to the dock. Cooper sternly advises that no crew are allowed to go ashore. This a security measure since 9/11. The fine for stepping on the dock is $500. Steve spots today's schedule that Cooper left on the cockpit bench and sees that Quo Vadis is scheduled to lock through at 1230 with the car carrier Queen Ace. Cooper is ashore talking into an official-looking phone when we see a 16th century Spanish galleon, one of the Black Ships, moving slowly past us. What kind of time warp is this? Wait, the Canal wasn't even finished until the early 20th century. The time-space continuum is disrupted in Panama.

Tragedy Averted in the Miraflores Lock

Cooper ambles back from making phone calls (I'm sure there was one to his girlfriend.) with instructions to follow the Spanish galleon but let the tourist day boat Pacific Queen come past. We are to side tie to the tourist boat, allowing room for the monstrous car carrier Queen Ace behind us. The ACP tries, and usually succeeds, to have a full lock every time it's operated.

QV's captain and crew follow instructions and we make it into the Pedro Miguel lock and tie on to the Pacific Queen just about on schedule. I can't help but notice the squirting leaks and mossy cracks in the walls of the lock. Most of them are at or above deck level of Quo Vadis. This is all the original civil and mechanical works, finished when Teddy Roosevelt was President. The big ships don't see this deterioration but everything still works over 100 years later. Water flows into the locks and drains back out in a rapid, timely manner. The lock gates swing open and close on command. The bow of the car carrier protrudes over our stern but is about six stories above it.

I called the Spanish ship on VHF and was informed it is La Victoria, making a goodwill cruise around some former colonies of Spain. Given the history of the Spanish conquest and subsequent overthrow by those colonies I would think local goodwill is in short supply. Maybe that's their concern. Cooper developed an interest in the international make-up of my crew and likes calling Patrick "*El Alemán*" or " The German". Patrick has no boat experience but does follow orders like a good German, including Cooper's brusque admonishments to "Pull in your line, German!"

We follow La Victoria out of Pedro Miguel lock as I call John Blake and my daughter, Caroline, to let them know our current position and expected time to the Miraflores locks. There is a web cam at the first lock which, we are told, will transmit to the on-line world images of Quo Vadis' transit of the Panama Canal. I give them the correct name of the web site while being amazed that my cell phone can connect from the depths of a Panama Canal lock to residences in California.

It takes about 30 minutes underway to reach the first Miraflores lock. QV secures to the Pacific Queen again with adept line handling by Steve. Laurent is a little sloppy. I believe he resents my demand that everybody on board, including him, wear sailing gloves. We end up looking directly into the ship's dining room where the mostly Panamanian day trippers are industriously devouring lunch. It must come with the cruise. The video cam is fixed to the railing at the top of the lock. It maybe can pick up our mast. Nonetheless, almost everybody on board "24 Daniel" goes to the foredeck and waves up at the camera. There is also a visitors' gallery at this lock which is packed. I would never guess this to be a spectator event and I would be so wrong. Again, we drop down and prepare to enter the next and last lock on the descent to the Pacific Ocean.

Cooper is urging me to speed up. I look ahead and see the Pacific Queen and the ACP line handlers are not ready to receive our lines, so I back down. This annoys him. We have 15 knots of wind and about 3 knots current pushing us forward so the stern line will be critical for this side tie. My reduced speed of approach leaves a shorter interval to secure alongside as several hundred thousand tons of Queen Ace follows right behind us. As QV comes alongside, two ACP guys finally make it over to the Pacific Queen's portside lower deck to receive our lines.

The bow line goes across and is caught by the ACP handler. The stern line is across and also caught. I look forward to check the distance to La Victoria. I look back in time to see the ACP linehandler drop the stern line into the canal. QV can't back down as the car carrier is still coming into the lock. I yell at the ACP bow line handler in English and Spanish to release the line from the tourist boat's deck cleat. By the time he complies, Quo Vadis has swung out on the bow line and gone sideways in the Miraflores lock. Cooper says to go to the opposite wall. We are stern to the opposite wall. I crank full left rudder and a throttle burst to 3000 RPM in an attempt to get the boat pointed forward. We are moving rapidly toward La Victoria as the boat straightens out. I engage reverse and go to 2000 RPM but the port side hits the wall with a sharp crack. Of course, all the fenders were on the starboard side for the planned, final side tie to Pacific Queen.

Into the Pacific

Quo Vadis comes to a stop against the wall with her forestay under La Victoria's stern line, like some sort of cartoon ending. I hold it in position in reverse at lowered RPM. My cell phone rings. It is a chipper and cheerful John Blake calling me from San Diego with congratulations for making the canal transit. My voice is steady as I am amazingly in the moment. "John, I'm a little busy right now. I'll get back to you." "OK", he says but I can tell by his tone he is puzzled.

While this little drama is unfolding, Cooper has been yelling toward the top of the wall for help. Finally, some ACP line handlers appear, looking down over the edge. They didn't expect to have a boat over here but are soon persuaded by an increasingly vocal Cooper to let down some heaving lines to seize on to our handling lines. The monkeyfists drop. Meanwhile, I order some fenders over to the port side and some of the crew squeeze them between the port hull and the wall. Eventually, we get the handling lines up to the ACP guys and down lock on the sidewall. So there is this fourth alternative for locking through the Panama Canal and, you know, it's not so bad.

Overcoming his reputation, Cooper earned his keep in those few minutes. He assigned blame completely to the ACP handler who dropped the line. Cooper knows him. "He's been working on the Canal longer than me!" he exploded, glowering. He also surprises me: he tells me the way I handled the situation was good. As we clear the last Miraflores lock, Cooper changes back into his "good clothes" and returns all his stuff, including the annotated religious tract, to his bag. The pilot boat comes alongside, matches speed and the transit pilot with the meanest reputation on the Panama Canal is off "24 Daniel". There remained a rapidly gained, strong bond of mutual respect.

Lodie and Steve, hanging over the port side, couldn't see any damage to the port hull or rudder as we motored on a low tide to the Balboa Yacht Club. We are at the fuel dock by 1600. I had remembered to chill some decent bubbly and broke it out of the reefer. I decanted it into the six real glasses on board, poured half of mine into the welcoming Pacific in the traditional ritual, and offered a toast to the crew: "Bless this ship and all who sail upon her. Especially, through the Canal." Patrick responded in English with a nautical toast concluding with the wish that my boat always have at least so much water beneath its hulls, holding his hands apart. We all drink to that and add "Amen". Patrick, Laurent and Joceline are on the bus back to Colón by 1700. Rogelio arrives to collect his four handling lines. The fuel dock guy charges $15 and offers to take our five bag-wrapped tire fenders for $1 apiece. These will be re-sold to the next transiting yacht.

While I'm showering, a guy from the Panama Maritime Authority comes on board uninvited and wants us to check in. He's talking about the full routine: go to the downtown Panama City office in the morning, go to the bank, etc. I show him our *zarpe* from Colón, just a canal-length away in the same country and same bureaucracy. He claims we need a new *zarpe* to leave from Panama City. I told him we were leaving for Costa Rica in the morning, as stated on this *zarpe*. After much back and forth, with him claiming to speak no English and me not interested in getting into a conversation in Spanish, I finally get a receipt for US$30 with the stipulation we are not getting a new *zarpe* and are leaving Balboa in the morning, which we did.

Lodie asks me, "Why didn't you speak Spanish with him?" Still wet from the shower, I reply, "He didn't ask permission to come on board." She looks puzzled. Steve grins at me. He also offers the opinion that the guy is headed to the nice restaurant just up the block to meet his wife for dinner, which $30 should cover.

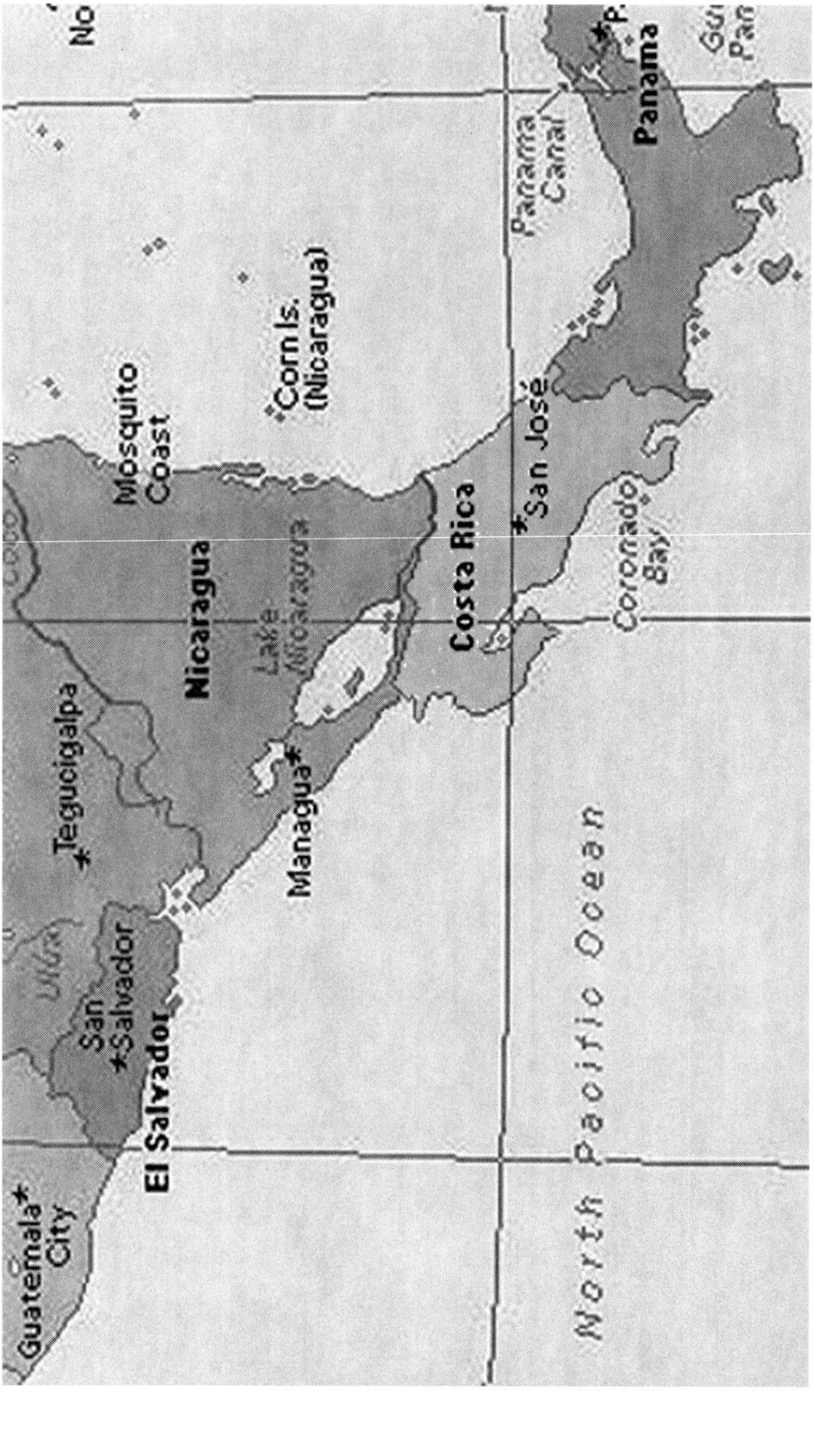
Guatemala City
El Salvador
San Salvador
Tegucigalpa
Nicaragua
Managua
Lake Nicaragua
Mosquito Coast
Corn Is. (Nicaragua)
Costa Rica
San José
Coronado Bay
Panama Canal
Panama
North Pacific Ocean

Banana Republics

Aboard S/V Quo Vadis, underway and anchored off Central America

Quo Vadis cleared the Balboa YC mooring field by 0730 and motored out the buoyed channel for the Balboa approach to the Canal. Sails were set in winds blowing NNE at 20-25 knots. These were nice conditions for our southwesterly course to round Punta Mala and on to Punta Burica; headed for Golfito, Costa Rica. We first had to sail past Taboga and the other offshore resort islands in this part of the Gulf of Panama. Golfito is a former banana shipping port, originally built and operated by United Fruit Co. to export those Chiquita bananas. It is now the Port of Entry for southern Costa Rica.

I set crew watches at four hours, working the others around my midnight watch, then chatted with Steve about cruising the Pacific. For openers, I am not impressed with the Balboa so-called Yacht Club. There is a mooring field, a fuel float and a long, narrow elevated pier from the float to a stone patio with tables. A tiny kitchen and larger bar are covered, providing rain protection, but open on three sides. And that's about it for amenities at the ol' BYC. I know, open kitchens are all the rage for chic restaurants. This place isn't one of them but it is the closest place serving food.

Steve knows some of the guys who have gravitated over to the BYC from the Flamenco anchorage, just down the peninsula. One of them sort of fades off toward the local girls hanging out on the shadowed edges of the patio. Another starts complaining about the puritanical couple complaining about him entertaining local girls on board; more specifically, bringing them back to the dinghy dock on Sunday morning. His romantic approach is to smack a $20 bill on his inevitably sweaty forehead (Hey, we are in the tropics.) and the first gal to peel it off wins a boat ride. Sometimes there's a tussle between the local girls. Other times, more than one gal gets to go in the dinghy, or so I'm told.

I have e-mailed my sweetie, Meredith, inviting her to join me for New Year's Eve in Costa Rica. In addition to being in love with the woman, I remain the hopeless romantic, still reveling in our other New Year's celebrations together: good eats and fresh sheets, enjoying local music—whatever it is, and explosive sex under the stars. She can fly direct from Miami after seeing her kids and grandkids at Christmas.

So go my thoughts and conversations both on and off watch. Steve, it turns out, is a precision helmsman. He can steer within one degree of actual course for long periods. For reference, I can hold about 3 and Lodie, 10 degrees variation. He later allows as how he was considered the best destroyer helmsman in the U.S. Navy. I get all the sails set, filled and trimmed to allow QV to keep moving well throughout the day and night. I am stoked, sailing the wind through my midnight watch; maintaining speeds above 7 knots in 5-7 ft. seas. Steve has applied the knowledge gained in his nearly 30 years at sea, plotting courses that allow safe, easy night passages; with options to save time during daylight running. It is another valuable lesson learned.

There are several points named Punta Mala (Bad Point) on charts of Central American waters. This one in Panama got its name largely due to the confluence of currents to 3 knots, strong winds like we've experienced, and the extreme yet common Pacific tides of 15-20 ft. We round this point during Steve's watch, apparently without incident since he doesn't wake me, and later clear Morro de Puercos (Rock of Pigs) on my watch. Since my former family nickname is The Pigman, sailing past this landmark amuses me. But then it doesn't take much to keep me entertained, especially on midnight watch. Some nights, it's just the moon reflecting on waves.

I haven't been much concerned about mileage during this voyage but when Steve punches the log readout just after 0800 that morning, he notes that we did over 170 nm this past day. This has been one of the best sailing days on Quo Vadis, including the distance. Things worked well.

Back to New Islands

There are so many islands promising fun times off the Pacific coast of Panama. Coiba is the largest but is a combination prison colony and wildlife preserve, so not too encouraging for casual visits. Cruising guides also advise not to pick up swimmers. This whole stretch of ocean doesn't get much notice. Steve can identify all the boats cruising this area on the fingers of one hand. Most other boats, like this one, are in a hurry to get to Costa Rica or in a hurry to get to the Canal. I intend to honor the commitment to Lodie to deliver her to Costa Rica before Christmas but also decide it's a good time to take at least one island break, so we head for the southwest cove anchorage of Cebaco. Winds have dropped from NE 15 to calm, so we start motoring. Steve now informs me that this is pretty typical of Pacific sailing: windy one day; calm the next.

What a bad surprise. There is a barge anchored in the best spot with mooring buoys scattered around it. The barge features hammocks and decorative potted palms on deck, all swaying under a canopy. One of the guys on board waves from his hammock. We're not as happy to see him. This development is new since Steve came through here earlier this Fall. It appears to be a sportfishing base which, I am discovering, is very big business. It is also another cruising anchorage spoiled. We look for another spot to drop the hook, ending up off the beach in nearly 40 ft. I can't quite dive down to the anchor but it looks buried in sand. The water is a translucent blue, even at these depths. Being back in the ocean feels so good. It is the first time since the San Blas Islands any of us have been back in the water. We all wonder out loud why we ever leave the sea. This is where I feel the best and also stay very fit, never even thinking about it. It just happens.

Another thing that happens to interrupt this tropical idyll, which includes a sweeping arc of white beach backed by jungle, is the rumbling arrival of a sportfisher. Ironically, the boats I've seen on the Pacific side are not as big as Caribbean sportfishers; mostly around 30 ft. Steve regales us with stories of guys he has met who fly down from the U.S. for a week or two, spending US$2-3000 a day to drown baitfish in the Pacific, get drunk, and have selected hookers ferried out to the barge.

It didn't make enough of an impact to warrant a log note at the time but, later when I checked the chart, it looks like Quo Vadis has gone as far South as it is going on this passage in the Pacific. QV crossed 7 degrees 10 minutes North latitude, before turning North.

Crew are up at dawn and QV is underway within the hour. Weather is holding but the wind continues NE light. I calculate we have enough fuel to motor the distance and the light winds do make for smooth seas. During the 1600 to 2000 watch, I make dinner, looking out of the galley occasionally to see the long, smooth swells getting darker. There is beef teriyaki, black beans with chopped onions, and a salad. No wine underway. Steve did two tours in Japan and relishes anything teriyaki. Lodie tells us it's the first time she has had a hot, prepared dinner underway. She says they ate cereal bars on her boat when moving. I take the helm while they sit down for dinner; then, I take a nap.

Las Islas Ladrones show up on radar just about where I expected and I keep them well to starboard. These "Thief Islands" are barely visible as blacker specks in the black sea when QV comes abreast of them. We make it around Punta Barica at the end of my watch and are in Costa Rican waters. By dawn, we are in the Golfo Dulce after passing the eerily white cliffs of Punta Blanca in the night.

Everybody's on deck as Steve takes the glasses and tries to sort out the entrance to the bay at Golfito. He suggests I slow QV's approach as we see how this develops. The water is shoal all around a fairly narrow entrance. The outside channel marker either isn't there or we can't see it.

The Days at Banana Bay

"The last time I came in here, it was from the North using a chart plotter," says Steve. Now he tells me. We slowly float North 'til we see an opening between mangrove and jungle. I spot an inside marker. The guide says to line up the buoy lights and look for a range; then go in almost to the jungle-covered shore before turning starboard to the anchorage. I never find the range (I later discover that is because the range signs are overgrown by jungle vines and barely visible even when standing right in front of them.) but I do see the high, rusty banana boat pier as a reference and keep the inside buoys to starboard.

You get pretty damn close to the shore before making the indicated turn. Steve suggested we go down to Banana Bay where he'd stayed during his trip to the canal. This suggestion seems to have merit since the first listed marina-like facility, Samoa del Sur, features one sunken sailboat leaning crookedly against the end of a pier which itself is in a slow process of sinking. There are three cruising-type boats moored out. One of them is John Cocker's yawl, the former Stitches Explorer. So, Bill Alvis did purchase it after the Grenada sea trials. It now has Trekker writ large across the transom and a freshly painted hull. The boat still looks good…and big. No one is on board.

We are docked at Banana Bay Marina by 0900. Steve knows the dockhands by name but the owner (Bruce Blevins) and office manager (Cristiano) are occupied elsewhere. He introduces me and he gets a hug from the head waitress. He also assures me the cook in the Banana Bay kitchen makes the best cheeseburgers in the whole country. And we only just got here.

Changes in latitudes; changes in attitudes

As I'm checking in, arranging for Costa Rica Port of Entry clearance, signing up for a mooring at US$10/day, and taking on fuel, Steve informs me Lodie is leaving today.

"I know!" I exclaim. "I planned to get her to Costa Rica in time for her to spend Christmas with her family up in San José. I told her we'd make it," trying not to sound too boastful.

"No," Steve continues in a sort of "You must be clueless." but still kindly tone, "She's leaving the boat for good. As in: Not coming back after Christmas."

Well, this is the first I've heard about her new plan. My first reaction is that I wish we'd spent more time out in the islands of the Golfo de Chiriquí instead of rushing to Costa Rica for her benefit. Lodie later rumbles her roller bags ashore, headed to the airport. Quo Vadis is on a mooring by noon, just down from Trekker. Lodie had complained or told me about several things she didn't like about my boat. It took me a while to figure out that these items were not the critical things to make her leave. What she really did not like is that she wasn't on her boat with her "partner" doing things the way she remembered that experience from two seasons ago.

"Well," I can't help but rationalize, "Quo Vadis has traveled over three times as far and I haven't wrecked my boat." Which is how her boat and partnership ended: on the reef at Tortuguilla, that small island near Tortuga. As it turned out, most of the stuff that she found irritating aboard QV gets fixed or replaced during the stay in Costa Rica.

Steve and I must have felt pretty chipper after a siesta since we were already ashore, under the immense conical palm thatch roof of Samoa del Sur, by sundowner time. This establishment seems to be out of the marina business and into the bar and pizza business. Is there is a lesson here? I call the airport hotel to check on Lodie and let her know we are at the pizza place. Steve tells me this is pretty damn noble of me since she jumped ship without prior notice. He's right, in that I'm no longer responsible as skipper if she's no longer crew. At least this is not the same nasty problem I had when Julie decided to leave the boat. Lodie has Costa Rican citizenship and a place to go. But, with Steve now headed back to Panama, this means I am back to single-handing.

Samoa del Sur is also the foreign battleground where crews from two visiting U.S. Navy ships got into a traditional inter-crew bar brawl during shore leave. This naval action occurred during Steve's previous stopover. It is in this environment that we find ourselves drinking and talking with Giles Liddell. He is accompanied by a young accomplice who is fixated on a televised basketball game and rarely speaks.

I expect I'm going to enjoy this experience as soon as we exchange cards. My card is typical and boring: dark blue ink printed on white cardstock with my name, boat name, e-mail address, etc. Giles' card is a transparent plastic U.S. $1,000,000 banknote with his name and phone number positioned where the Secretary of the Treasury otherwise unimaginatively prints his/her signature on U.S. currency.

Giles and Steve discover they were in the same destroyer squadron during their Navy years though not on the same ship, thankfully, or this would have become an even more intense reunion. Giles tells us he was ordered by the commander of his destroyer to become the ship's barber since, this skipper presumed, a black sailor would know how to use a razor. Giles tells the skipper he doesn't have any experience in using a razor for barbering but he still ended up with the billet for the rest of that cruise. I'm not sure how much we're being had as Giles proceeds to divulge to us the wooly mammoth re-population scheme he is currently investigating.

It seems he has information that former KGB agents (or maybe they are from its successor Russian agency, the FSB) are proceeding with their plan to grow prehistoric wooly mammoths. These modern-day mammoths will be developed from DNA recovered from fully intact mammoth specimens that have been frozen in the

Siberian ice for the last 10,000 years or so. The scarcity and novelty of these recombinant beasts will make them incredibly profitable to sell to zoos and animal parks; even to private collectors. We had by now consumed a couple of pizzas and more than a couple of beers but I do recall Giles' overarching plan was to get a piece of this DNA mammoth action. I was pretty vague by the time he outlined how he was going to go about doing this. Something about threatening to go public with the whole scheme if he weren't cut in to the deal or else he'd do it competitively with DNA from other frozen mammoths. I am wondering how this might work: either blackmailing or competing with ex-KGB wooly mammoth-growers?

We woke up on Quo Vadis about 0700 the next morning. If I had lost any DNA, I didn't miss it. Squawking birds and monkeys provided a wake-up call from the thick jungle that grows right down to the water's edge all around Golfito. Several movies have been filmed here because the jungle locations look like people imagine Africa looks, at least in the movies.

Steve thinks he might need some new pants so we walk into Old Golfito to check out the clothing store. This enterprise is a combination yard sale, Goodwill store and discount outlet. It is housed in a former United Fruit Co. building, as is almost everything else in Old Golfito. Big storage and supply warehouses have shifted roles to being diner, bar, bus station, and hardware store. Worker dormitories are now multi-family housing. There is a machine shop building set just back from the main street with dusty, rusty equipment that looks 1930s vintage and sits ignored and unused. A small locomotive that used to pull cars full of bananas sits on a short piece of track. Most of the accessible rail has been torn up and used in construction. It substitutes for re-bar and steel beams in many Golfito structures. This eroding company town and its dock are the most visible remains of capitalist colonialism. Steve doesn't find anything he likes, so goes to check bus schedules to Panama. I buy two pairs of quick-dry shorts in lime green and khaki, paying about three dollars for them. I figure they'll be good for working on the engine and cleaning the bottom. Back at the boat, I try them on. The cut, fit and color combine to make me look very gay but who, I figure, is going to see me? Steve scores a big chunk of smoked swordfish from Jay Belzinski, a local gringo fishing guide. We dine very well on board Quo Vadis that evening. I make a cold vegetable salad, and we drink sauvignon blanc with the swordfish. Jay later gives me a specialized fishing lure as a present when he discovers I have never caught a fish from QV. It's supposed to attact dorado. "It's too ratty-looking for my paying customers," he says, "but I catch fish on it."

Christmas in Costa Rica

Continuing his Christmas shopping, Steve considers the $150 sunglasses that Bruce is selling in the marina store. While he's considering, two Costa Rican ladies attired in straw hats, bikini tops and sarong wraps pop in and buy a set each, peeling crisp

U.S. dollars from their designer wallets. Steve eventually decides his $10 "Swap-meet Specials" work just fine.

On Christmas morning, I whomp up a mess of Spam and ham and eggs for a hearty breakfast on board. Steve requested the Spam. Note: Costa Rican coffee is really good. We spend most of the morning reviewing charts and identifying the anchorages from Golfito to Ensenada (Mexico) while I scribble notes based on his experiences coming down the coast. I patch sails later in the day, then we dinghy over to the open air entrance of the K&N marina, which is closed; then go down the road to the Banana Bay Marina, which is closed. I have finally figured out how to work the local phone card so I call to verify my continued existence and wish Merry Christmas to my mother, my kids, and Meredith.

Meredith informs me she has just read my invitation. She will not be joining me in Costa Rica at New Year's. But, she immediately consoles me, we will have all that time going up the coast of Mexico to be together. This response does not fill me with Christmas joy but she is right about having time together in Mexico. That Pacific coastline stretches over 3000 miles. I just hope I don't have to do it single-handed. I later mention this development and my sentiments to Steve.

"It's a long way even if you've got the entire New York Yankees with you," he confirms.

Which leaves us standing in the empty street wondering what to do next. I bet Steve the Chinese restaurant up the road will be open on Christmas. This is based on my experience with Chinese restaurants worldwide that seldom close, and least of all, on *kwai-lo* holidays. I don't know why he is so skeptical of my assessment. Hai Pin is where we have Christmas dinner. I'm still not over the novelty of the Chinese restaurant owners speaking Spanish. I know it's the only thing that makes sense; it's still strange to me. The rain starts just at dusk and continues off and on throughout the next week. I scurry back to the boat as I, once again, left some hatches open.

Steve goes through my charts and decides he might as well take all of them from the Panama Canal back to the Intracoastal Waterway. That's not what I expected but, realistically, I have no plans to visit those spots again in the near future. He has also sorted through the charts he left in the Banana Bay basket on his way South and finds some that I can use; still marked with his position checks and anchorages. I leave a like number of Caribbean charts in the swap basket.

Learning Days and Lonely Nights

The second morning moored at Golfito, I am on deck trying to take it all in and plan which fix-it items to tackle according to mood, money and availability of on-shore skills. I am only partway through my coffee when the eyes and snout of a saltwater crocodile come gliding past between Quo Vadis and the docks. Given the size of its head, the attached body is going to be 6-7 ft. long. Chama later confirms that this particular croc cruises the waterfront in the early mornings and after the fishing boats return around mid-afternoon. He further informs us there is a larger one who does not keep such a regular schedule.

First in this week's lessons is a continuing one in troubleshooting electrics. Robert, an ex-patriate German, comes on board to address the intermittent functioning of the autohelm. He goes to the interior back of the electrical cabinet and finds one side of the 12V socket has corroded away to the crumbling white powder we all dread. The problem had nothing to do with the autohelm itself. The tuition for this lesson was US$40. There is no replacement socket in Golfito or, probably, San José. This is the beginning of my education on the lack of marine supplies in Costa Rica.

Steve is off to the border town of Canoas, lugging his duffel and an equal-sized bag of my charts on to the 0800 bus. I wander around town, buying a few boat items and trying to arrange for a new companionway hatch door, until the produce truck shows up. I have not yet learned this is how groceries, including fish, beer and other carbonated beverages, are provided in most of rural Costa Rica. As a long-time Farmers' Market kind of guy, I position myself to pick out a few kilos of fresh veggies. The truck driver instead blocks my access and, bag in hand, he starts picking out produce for me. My first reaction is that I'm being scammed as a stupid gringo. Then, I realized he was selecting in decreasing stages of ripeness, so the supply of fresh stuff will last longer. It seems this is common practice, and the lesson is considerably less expensive than my last one.

The street that defines landside Golfito takes on a new look that afternoon as dozens of nubile Latinas semi-clad in tank tops with matching Spandex shorts or low cut jeans set up booths emblazoned with local and international brand names. The rampant sexist culture of Central America continues at speed as the bicycle Tour of Costa Rica rolls through town for a few intense minutes. The young ladies are flirting and, occasionally, hawking the sponsors' wares as the riders arrive. I can't tell the players without a program but there is one guy way out front of the peloton: made up of another 25-30 riders who grab water, sports drinks, and an occasional ice cream bar as they slow down briefly by the street stalls. The gals working for sponsors smile and cheer. The guys riding bikes smile and sweat. The back of the pack straggles through for another 10 minutes until that part of the event is over. Nobody is in a hurry for the girls to pack away the goodies, including them. I talk one reluctant lovely Latina out of a calendar of the coming year, now only a few days away.

The next morning the smaller, 2 meter-long caiman comes to visit Quo Vadis. It is floating on the surface just astern of the twin hulls. It knows I'm still here. Onshore, I meet and chat with Lee Newman off the Valiant 40 Jenny Wren. Her husband Merrill joins us after attending to some boat work. They are an older couple taking their time sailing South on the Pacific Coast. (I realize only as I write this, some would consider me an old guy. I don't.) We arrange to meet for dinner at Banana Bay. It turns out they were college sweethearts and now share a home in Santa Cruz. Their long term romance and care for each other seems very real and, to me, very touching. I also discover they have on board a chart of the Golfo de Nicoya including the approaches to Puntarenas. I shamelessly ask to copy this key piece of Costa Rican geography which is still missing from my navigation portfolio. Merrill agrees and insists on picking up the dinner tab. "This is our party," he explains. Both unexpected events make for a very positive day.

What do you do with a Drunken Sailor?

Between the continuing rain (Heavy at times, as the weather report confirms.), the maintenance list continues to get checked off. This includes replacing the Racor diesel fuel filter for the first time in two years. There is no water, very few particulates and all the components are in very good condition. Maybe filtering the fuel into that new stainless steel tank every single time I filled it from the Chesapeake Bay to the Panana Canal has paid off. One of my few consistent on-board virtues is reinforced. Since I have all the new parts, I put them in and thank God and the sea goddesses, again, for absolutely no fuel problems on this voyage, so far. So good.

Meredith was now in Miami, where she had again declined my invitation for New Year's Eve and the weeks after. If I were given to drowning my sorrows rather than celebrating good times and important occasions, you could argue that's what I did instead of having a sober evening ashore and great sex on board with Mer, as I'd hoped. Instead, I cleaned myself up and motored ashore about 1830 to be informed the party didn't start until 1930. I returned to find bottles of Moët Chandon chilling in hollowed out logs on the Banana Bay veranda. There is also a light buffet of *bocadillos*, the delicious "Little Mouthfuls" of Costa Rica which are yummy with or without drinks.

Through various transactions, including generous offerings from other celebrants and outright purchase, I managed to ingest lots of pretty darn good bubbly. I wasn't counting glasses, which may have been an error, as it sloshed down easily starting at dusk. I don't believe dinner was included. Around midnight, the party had migrated to the local rich guy's hacienda and my abrupt transition from multi-lingual, charming and witty skipper to catatonic drunken gringo occurred. I was even more surpised by this abrupt shift since it was not a familiar condition, personally.

Bruce got my still-conscious body back to Banana Bay; then returned to the party. (His motivation? Hard to say. Avoid property damage? I hadn't paid my marina bill?) I managed to make it through the gate, down the ramp, on to the dock, and step carefully into my tethered dinghy. My progress slowed only briefly as I managed to complete a cartwheel over the outboard pontoon and into the bay. After the initial, unsuccessful splashing and thrashing to pull myself back up over the gunwale, I had to catch my breath before trying again. I hear the distinctive slap of a flat tail on the water. My activity may have alerted at least one of the resident saltwater crocodiles. I see two yellow eyes reflecting in the dock lights, or imagine I do. I think all this with confused, misfiring synapses while my own reptile brain heavily launches my soggy body back into the dink. The synapse failures continue and the security guards get a good laugh out of my condition as they tow me back to Quo Vadis. I have avoided the toothy, subsurface grip of a croc jaw on my flailing legs but remain completely soaked, soused, and undignified beyond any Latino reason. I really do behave much better when escorted.

Latitud Ocho Re-visited

Rigging tightened and tuned, tanks topped off, wind gen blades re-aligned, reefer cleaned and re-provisioned, cluster of bananas hanging in the galley, new companionway door coated with ugly yellowish varnish installed. Oh, well, at least the newly carved out door fills the opening, locks, and doesn't look like it will fall off real soon. So it must be time for one last visit to Latitud Ocho. What? We haven't talked about this venerable Golfito institution? How could we have missed it? It's just a minute or two above Eight degrees North latitude, up on the side street overlooking the bay.

"Latitude Eight", as the Spanish translates, is one of those Central American dives that should be in an old movie. It is also the principle gringo bar of Golfito. The other cantinas are dark holes where local men get drunk and mean. Those places are screened from the street and provide frequent Friday night fights. No women frequent those places—at least not to socialize. Latitud Ocho has windows that open to the Bay and doors that open to the street. Women of all ages are found on both sides of the bar. Steve took me there my first time and explained some of the routines.

The very used-looking owner checks in on busy nights, doles out cigarettes to his preferred visiting girls, leaves the room to collect their favors, checks back in and, if things seem under control, goes home. Another time, a helpful gringo who winters out on the tidal island reminds me to beware of the fer-de-lance and other big, poisonous snakes when I'm on shore. There are at least two local names for this reptile. One name translates as "Smooth and Silent"; the other as "Three Steps" since that is how far you'll make it after it bites you. I later read that Costa Rica has only venomous snakes, including a viper with big eyebrows that hangs from tree branches. With six foot snakes and saltwater crocodiles, I wonder how they keep the tourists coming.

The ambiance of discarded boat parts, faded flags, out of date calendars and soccer on the TV attracts visiting and local gringos supplemented by a younger Costa Rican crowd who don't find the cantinas chic. "Ocho" always has nicely chilled beer and, I'm told, the barmaids pour an honest drink. These *muchachas* are good-looking but not too, and young enough but not too young, which describes most of the successful women in business in this part of the world. The crowd, ever-changing in hue and color, includes without limitation, a gang of ex-pats washed up on this shore, boat guys not yet stranded, a good number of Ticos attuned to the gringo presence if not always embracing it, and a supporting cast of colorful characters of all genders.

By mid-afternoon when I find myself through or tired with the day's boat chores, Latitud Ocho is often empty except for one of the three regular Tica barmaids; often having lunch at that time of day. The *comida típica* she is eating always looks good to this hungry sailor. She usually offers to get me a plate from the place down the street. The second time this happens, I sit down with today's hot special and the cold beer she opens for me. She goes back to consuming her lunch.

"*Grácias*," I say; then try a little joke in Spanish. "It's nice to have lunch with you."

"Well, we're on opposite corners," she correctly observes from her end of the bar, 20 ft. away diagonally. I just can't seem to get the witty banter going with these Latinas, so I shut up and eat.

When I get back to the boat, there is a very large Pacific green turtle floating along the port side. It has a deeply fluted carapace which makes it seem old, like having wrinkles. It also has a piece of black plastic wrapped around a front flipper. I can't think of a way to get the plastic off without risking some additional damage to both of us.

Once more, into the Sweet Gulf

Waypoints and route are entered in the GPS. Ah! One more thing: pay the Marina bill. Got bill, reviewed bill, adjusted bill for duplicate charges, paid bill. There was no bad weather news or, as usual, much weather information of any kind except on San José TV. Well, it must be time to go cruising. I say goodbye to Jay as he slides hooks into baitfish for tomorrow's sportfishing client. As I get into the dinghy, I hear the smack of the croc's tail off the end of the dock. He knows I'm here.

I'm up at 0520 to prepare for departure from Golfito but have left too many things to do singlehanded, so it was after seven before Quo Vadis was motoring back into the Golfo Dulce with sails raised. I went slowly the first 3 nm past the mangroves and out to the Golfito waypoint. On reflection, I'm not sure why I went slowly since I knew the route and had to make 70 nm to Bahia Drake before dark. The engine sounded funny to me. Mer has told me I always say that about the engine.

I could not find an angle of advantage to sail at the speed needed to reach Bahia Drake (They say Bahia Draw-kay in Costa Rica though, like several other places along the Pacific coast, it is named after that famed seafaring Brit, Sir Francis Drake.) before dark, so I left the engine on trying to maintain 6 knots, which I didn't until rounding Punta Llorena.

Within an hour, lots of big dolphins joined me. These guys and gals were 6-7 ft. long; colored sleek gray all over like old-style submarines. They had pronounced blowholes and a long, rounded dorsal fin. They jumped back and forth, crossing the bow, running between and under the amas. It delights me that the dolphins in the Pacific play with the boat, doing what looks to us furry mammals like daredevil stunts in and out of the water and all around the boat. But they are so in control. This pod accompanies QV for about 20 minutes which puts me in a happy mood as I change course to follow the coastline of the Osa Peninsula around Corcovado Park.

I cut some corners, hugging the coast rather than going out to all the waypoints, fully aware that if I hit an uncharted rock, anchoring before dark doesn't really matter. Penetrating my state of anxiety is the appreciation that the Corcovado coastline is beautiful. There are sea caves, little waterfalls that drop directly into the ocean from sheer cliffs, rocky islets sprouting trees of bonsai shape and perfection. Thick jungle grows right to the water's edge broken only by small, sandy beaches. It's not 'til later I find out this is the land of the very pricey eco-tourism jungle lodges.

At 1500, small, dark dolphins with sharply pointed dorsals greeted QV just as we came out of the channel inside the Rocas Corcovado. This is another good omen for this not overly superstitious sailor. They have other, probably fishy business and continue Northwest as I turn the boat Northeast, following the curve of the peninsula. A tourist panga comes blasting past after the dolphins leave, carrying the sunburned passengers back before cocktail time. I am concerned about the light, or lack of it, coming into an unknown inside anchorage on a rocky coast.

QV reaches the Drake waypoint 13 minutes before sunset. I cut around the point into the bay, staying out from the shore, and 20 minutes later drop the anchor in 14 feet. It holds, so I rig the bridle on the anchor rode. The day ends without further drama after 11-1/2 hours underway.

I'm still not that crazy about single-handing but I hear a lot fewer complaints! I critique my own decisions, though, while I set the anchor light and start dinner. Needs to be some discipline here.

I'm up at 0520, again, to make the Go/No go decision to head North to Manuel Antonio or Quepos. The wind direction is good but there is little of it (3-5 kts) so it means 55nm of motoring; another 11-12 hours. A dipstick check of the fuel level calculates out as 20 gallons remaining. That means over 12 gallons burned yesterday. I did think the gauge was dropping faster than usual. I am back in my bunk by 0630, as Quo Vadis rolls gently in a tolerable swell.

Up again at 0830, I feel good and well-rested. It's time to deploy the bimini and make coffee. I can see varnished wooden buildings peeking out of the jungle. The sand and gravel bar in front of the creek is breaking. It extends well into the bay and completely across the mouth of the creek. I'm glad I didn't try to go in there last night. Having been indulged so far today, El Capitán decides the crew shouldn't get too lazy so he makes the decision to change the engine oil. I manage to extract over two liters of old oil while putting two liters of water through my sweating body.

While installing a new oil filter and absorbent pad in the bottom of the engine compartment, I notice fuel on the exterior of the fuel pump and some drips on the pad. As instructed back in the Chesapeake after the first great fuel leak, I snug up the 17mm and 14mm fittings on the fuel line. Only the 14mm fitting would not tighten and just kept spinning. When I re-start the engine to check for possible filter leaks, a steady stream of diesel fuel squirts out of the fitting into the engine compartment. This may explain the above-normal fuel usage yesterday. While I had my head down in said compartment doing the oil change, a sloop had come in to the bay. Gale from Kattegat snorkeled by on her way to shore and asked to hang on the swim ladder to rest. Their boat had put in to find a possible fuel leak. These things can be contagious, as experienced cruisers know. Not knowing if I had the parts to fix the fuel line/pump fittings, I implemented a Capitán Juan solution to mechanical problems afloat and made lunch. It turns out to be one of the best cheeseburgers I've ever made. Well, at least this is one on-board skill where I'm improving.

The pangas servicing the resort customers don't return by mid-afternoon, as they had said. In some strange quirk of behavior, I don't want to launch the dink, put on the motor, haul out the fuel tank, etc. to go ashore. Instead, I wait for a panga ride.

The wind comes Southwest by 1700 and the two monohulls at anchor roll in the confluence of wind and swell. No pangas appear.

David of Drake's Bay

At 0530 the next morning, the radio alarm verifies that it still works. Within an hour, the resort boats are zipping around, ignoring my overhead arm waving, and little black and white birds are trying to build a nest in the boom. They will not be chased away, so I duct tape the end of the boom closed. The birds are angry and confused. I don't blame them. I am feeling the same way as it takes another hour to get the attention of anybody to take me ashore. Gilberto the fisherman agrees to take C500 and wait while I search out a mechanic at Aquila de Osa, the fancy resort.

I explain my situation to the *señorita* at the dock. She turns and yells up at a ledge in the jungle, "David! David!" The reply is the Spanish equivalent of "That's my name. Don't wear it out."

David appears through the leaves; seems to understand the problem but can't come out to the boat until after his workday at the resort is over at 1500. I persuade him to come look at it during his lunch break. This requires that I finally launch and prepare the dink for motoring. I also go through parts and spares looking for replacements for the broken bits. I have a spare fuel pump and new brass washers but, I guess, my assumption was the fitting itself could not be the thing to break. I bring David out to QV after he finishes his lunch. He peers into the compartment while I crank the engine to demonstrate the fuel leak. Diesel fuel arcs in a steady stream from the pump fitting. He then removes the 14mm fitting along with the aluminum threads and outlet from the fuel pump which are stripped on to it. He observes that it has been overtightened. There is no other culprit. This has been overzealous maintenance—by me. A red and bronze flash flies into the jungle. "*Gavilán!*" David proudly announces: a hawk.

The options for repair or replacement are limited, as they usually are when you're swinging on the hook off some tropical shore. Neither David's workbench nor mine featured a tap to make new threads so I gave him a big wad of colones and fresh tubes of JB Marineweld, as Jeff H. had recommended to have on board. David agreed to re-assemble it all with a Marineweld fix and make a new gasket. After returning him to shore and me to QV, I serviced the electric windlass and made another killer cheeseburger with yesterday's leftovers. Add to list: tap and die set.

When I returned to the Aquila dock to pick him up, David had put together a fuel line and pump arrangement using Mexican Poxy-Pol. He chose this faster-acting epoxy because JB weld would take too long to set. Thus begins my new life with

Poxy-Pol: the preferred fastener, sealant, glue, elixir, etc. of mechanics throughout Central America. It is the malleable, non-melting substitute for duct tape! David re-installed the pump, bled the lines and I cranked the engine. It worked! There was no leak and David started giggling like a schoolkid, he was so pleased with his handiwork. "Hee, hee," he smiled widely. "No fuel is coming out. Look." I do; it isn't.

While David counts another wad of colones at the conclusion of his work on board, I get a radio call from Erik on Kattegat. He has solved his fuel system problem and invites me over for dinner. First, I take David, much richer than he began the day, back to the Aquila dock. Back on board, I go for a welcome swim, clean up and go out for dinner. The dinner that Erik and Gale prepared is excellent; fairly elaborate in a solid Swedish way, topped off with a list of the Pacific weather radio nets he has used sailing South. Some days end much better than they start.

Coasting Up Costa Rica

The clanging of a ship's bell the next morning marked Kattegat's passing by Quo Vadis as they're leaving the anchorage. I have been up since 0530 but Erik beat me getting underway. Why does it take me so long? I've already used the "sailing single-handed" excuse; mainly to myself.

I eventually cleared Bahia Drake about 0700, motoring with the main up and the exhaust smoking. I smell fuel but can see no leaks from pump, hoses or filter. I set the autohelm as a pod of the small dorsal fin dolphins appears 3-400 meters off the starboard side. They did not join the boat. About 0800, the wind indicator was showing 6-10 knots on the beam so I set the genoa and cut the RPM back. The exhaust stopped smoking. Maybe the excess engine oil had burned off. It looks like about seven hours to the Manuel Antonio waypoint. There is enough flotsam in the water to pay attention and I notice the genoa luff strip is torn near the top…in two places.

By 1000, the wind had died but the exhaust didn't smoke when I cranked the RPM back up. The wind clocked around to an onshore breeze by noon so I rolled the sails out on a port tack just in time to see a pod of dolphins headed toward the boat, leaping 2-4 feet out of the water. I'm out of film! There's a green turtle floating on the surface on the starboard side and, minutes later, a leatherback on the port side. It turns its head and looks at me as Quo Vadis goes past. I pass more sea turtles. Most of them dive as the boat approaches; some don't. Are they sleeping?

The dolphin pod is now swimming and leaping on both sides of the boat. They are medium size; dappled with light gray spots. Two to four of these beautiful creatures at a time are jumping clear of the water, guiding us in to the anchorage. I dodged a shrimp boat, got the sails down and said farewell to the good-looking, athletic friends who had escorted me into Manuel Antonio. A big, green-hulled motor yacht has taken the best spot to anchor, right in the middle.

The anchorage is actually rather small but I find a spot in 18 ft. and dive on the anchor with 90 ft. of scope in the water. Hook and chain are lying in fine, silty sand and mud. Back on board, I have a shower, shampoo and a sundowner. It was really a nice day once I got over my engine anxiety. The autohelm performed, I was able to set the sails in a useful manner, and covered over 50 nm in 8 hours seeing no other boats. I sat with a drink in hand watching the same sunset as the old guy who emerged to sit by himself on the foredeck couch of his 100 ft. motor yacht.

I pushed Meredith's custom-made Bach CD into the stereo to accompany a self-indulgent dinner of smoked tuna and asparagus with mayo, followed by penne pasta in my tomato-basil-onion-garlic sauce which I washed down with a cheap Chilean red. The surf breaking on the jungle beach off the stern soothes me to an early sleep, alone in my bunk.

Up at 0610 for a planned seven hour run to Bahia Herradura. Before leaving, I checked the oil level, checked the fuel level, added five gallons to the main tank from a jerry can, raised the mainsail at anchor after an engine start, and had the anchor up by 0710. (OK, I see why it takes me an hour to get underway.) There are stunning rock formations rising straight from the sea around Manuel Antonio. They look spectacular in the early morning light with jungle sounds providing the audio background. I was off Quepos by 0800 which also served as a position check. The cruising guides identify it as a preferred anchorage but it is just a shallow road open to weather from the N-NW-W. There is no protection from swell. Glad I didn't plan to stop.

When the wind came up to 10-11 knots, I tried sailing around it on a starboard tack until QV was almost 20 degrees off course; then the wind died anyhow. I set the throttle back up to 2800 RPM and the autohelm on a course of 292. The autohelm seems to be working normally. The solution may just be reliable 12V power input but it is amazingly less hassle than when Lodie was on board. The exhaust is still smoking, but less than yesterday. By 0930, the Pacific Ocean was oily flat so I could direct all my anxieties toward the engine until the knotmeter stopped working.

It took 'til almost noon to clear Punta Judas, where it was time for a course change and the wind clocked around and came up to 6-10 knots. Running out the headsail was good for another knot of speed over the surface: showing 6.1-6.4 kts consistently on the GPS. All these Costa Rican headlands feature gnarly rocks which, of course, have surf surging and breaking over them. So I worry about the unmarked ones. I also occasionally scan the sea side to check if anything is coming from that direction. On one of these scans I see a ray fly out of the water: one, two, three times it flies 10 feet in the air. It has the coloring of a manta but is small, with approx. 2-2.5 ft. wingspan. Is it a baby? I've never heard of this or seen it before. During the afternoon, I spot some more of these flying rays. I'm in a continuing state of wonder. What are these rays doing?

Bahia Herradura, traditionally a cruising anchorage, is in the process of transforming into Marina Los Sueños and destination resort. Not my kind of place, but it has the only fuel dock between Golfito and Puntarenas. I started calling the marina on the VHF about 1400. There was no response. After about half an hour, a voice came back referring me to the fuel dock on CH12. As QV rounded Isla Herradura, I called the fuel dock and, surprisingly, was told to stand off until further notice. I didn't receive any further notice, so called back in half an hour and got clearance to come in past the breakwater. I had spent the time idling slowly around Bahia Herradura. There were only two sailboats forlornly anchored in a far corner of the Bay, away from the creeping condominiums. Nobody was aboard either of them.

A fancy new sportfisher passed me going out as I rounded the breakwater. Apparently, this previous occupant of the fuel dock had taken half an hour to fill its tanks. It was a tight squeeze to turn a cat but the dock guys were great help, using their inflatable to push the bow around. I knew they would be disappointed by my purchase of "only" 25 gallons of fuel (five of it into a jerry can) so I also bought beer, ice and water. Los Sueños is sportfisher/vacation condo expensive. If I'd had any wind, I would have gone on to Puntarenas with the existing fuel reserve. A couple of docked megayachts were changing crew as I cleared Bahia Herradura with the intent to go another 5 nm and anchor at Playa Mantas. The guide says the beach got its name from the manta rays who hatch their young there with the result being hundreds of baby rays in the shallows.

At 1630, I dropped the hook in 22 ft. not far off a highly populated beach. I stood for a while on the foredeck, which was going up and down on the surge. Somehow, this didn't seem right. I called to a boy playing in the shore break. *"Es este Playa Mantas?"* He looked at me strangely; then answered, *"No. Está al otro lado."* Well, I hadn't done this since Jost Van Dyke. I was off the wrong beach. This was Playa Blanca. I had to go around Punta Leona to get to Playa Mantas.

By 1700 I was anchored for the second time, off Playa Mantas. I put out 70 ft. of scope and had the bridle on before a sunset worthy of a postcard started backlighting the dozens of pelicans swarming in to roost in the leafless trees on the islets off Punta Leona. I didn't know pelicans did trees. It looked like a gathering of little pterodactyls. I warped the scene just a tad more, cranking up Pink Floyd on the sound system and prepared a cold dinner on board. There were no baby manta rays in the shallows. They must have all gone out to sea to practice their flying. Quo Vadis is the only boat in the bay. After dark, I called my children, Beth and Caroline, on my cell phone. Caroline confirmed she is flying down to meet me later this month. Ah, the wondrous impact of technology. Still not as wonderful as flying manta rays, though. Or my daughter coming on board.

Scrubbing, Clubbing and Reefing

I was up at 0530 as a light shower swept across the Bahia, wetting the deck. I put my mask and snorkel in a bucket, poured bleach on the black mold and went back to my bunk. The disco behind the beach hadn't shut down until after 0100 last night: a Saturday. After 0800 and a cup of coffee, I give in, again, to the lure of being able to phone people Stateside while bobbing at this remote anchorage off the Central American coast. Among those who answer is John Blake. I ask him to pick up a copy of "The Forgotten Middle" at Downwind Marine in Pt. Loma and get it to the Costa Rica YC where I optimistically hope to receive the package in the not-too-distant future. He agrees but informs me he won't be available to sail until April. I leave messages for Mer, Brian and Aynsley, and my Auntie Ro even though, at age 76, she is not a candidate to crew on QV.

I consider moving the boat in toward the beach since it is now in 25 ft. of water. The 14 ft. depth when anchoring yesterday was low tide. Since the wind was up, the surge was down, and I didn't know the inshore depths, I instead paid out more scope: over 120 ft to deal with the 10 ft-plus tidal range I'm still trying to get used to. QV slides back to 27 ft. depth and I re-rig the bridle.

It must be time to put on mask and fins and go under the starboard ama to clear the knotmeter/ impeller. Most of the really gross black mold washes off the mask. I quickly accomplish that assigned task. The impeller spins freely. As I'm having so much success, I continue, cleaning most of the weed and some of the Golfito barnacles off the hulls, the drive leg and the drive leg's lifting tackle. After this aquatic workout, it must be time for (late) lunch. On Sundays, brunch can be a salad and omelets; today, it's just for one. Some people, probably those who hadn't been scraping weed and barnacles from their boat, would consider this brunch enough for two—or three.

Late in the afternoon, I turn the anchor light on, though I haven't seen another vessel in two days, and take the dink ashore, making an uneventful surf landing on Playa Mantas. The amphibious arrival of the gringo from the *velero* is sufficient novelty for a couple of well-mannered, English-speaking kids to help me drag the dink up on the beach. I continue through the trimmed tropical landscaping to the

Punta Leona Beach Club. It is a typical weekend-at-the-club scene for the apparently sizeable segment of the local population who can afford it. Little kids are splashing in the pool, mostly on each other, or yelling "Look at me!" (In Spanish, of course.) Families are sitting at big, round tables as the young staff bring them pizzas; hot dogs for the kids. Nobody asks me for my club card as I let myself through the gate and settle at a small outside table. The cordial young waiters comply with my request for a *cerveza* and *ceviche*: two of my favorites. The experience reminds me that a whole other existence goes on for most of the world just a few hundred meters from my life on and in the water, no matter what country I'm anchored in. This doesn't get in to the cruising guides. Reading them, it's like nothing exists beyond the high water mark unless it involves provisioning. Toward dusk, as families start to pack ending their Sunday outing, one of the families helps me carry the dink back to the receding bay.

The trees on the point and islets look like black lace against the orange-pink fabric of the sunset. Fewer of them are adorned with pelicans. I plot the courses for tomorrow's run to Puntarenas to make a rising tide around noon. The surge increases overnight; possibly building on the falling tide. It isn't really that bad but wakes me up several times, including at 0530 the next day.

The winds are 15-20 knots directly on the course with a 2-3 ft. breaking chop in the bay. I'm indecisive about going this morning. I checked the oil level and filled to the top mark. I checked the engine compartment and find diesel mixed with a small amount of oil (providing added color) about a half inch deep in the bottom. The absorbent pad is soaked through. Apparently, there is still a fuel leak. So I decide it may be best to use only sail to Puntarenas, if possible, and lessen the risk of an engine fire from a fuel leak. Decision made, it proves fairly challenging to get the outboard off and the dink up in the three foot chop, drawing blood around my ankles. The whole procedure took almost an hour. After deciding to go, I further decided to go for a swim. I jumped overboard and swam around the boat. I didn't see anything new broken.

Back on board, I showered and really felt much better, especially in my left shoulder and trapezius muscle which had been sore and cramped. Weighing anchor became another long process with the wind still pushing at 15-20 knots. I finally got the mainsail up after twice clearing halyard wraps from the mast steps. This is still a tricky business for me single-handed in big wind. After all the effort, the wind died leaving the Bahia. I reluctantly started the engine and set course for Puntarenas just as the wind came back to a steady 30 knots offshore; with gusts to 40. The position checks soon reflected a big set to the West: finally almost dead to windward. I'm sailing at a 40-50 degree angle with 35 knots apparent wind and making poor progress toward Puntarenas.

By noon, waves are breaking over the coach roof. I shorten the main to its first reef (doing that singlehanded underway required all three hands) and sheet in the stays'l but still cannot point up to Puntarenas. While I was messing around with all this, my good blue oxford cloth shirt and my gray *banuela* blew overboard. I had laid them out in the cockpit to put on before checking in. It was time to start considering harbors of refuge. The Islas Tortugas showed only northside anchorages. Negritos showed none. I decided to try for Isla Cedros, about an hour away, and fell off toward a newly invented waypoint North of the island. The course should let me clear everything I see on the chart.

At speeds of 8-9 knots, it took less than an hour to make the waypoint. I worked around the North side of Isla Cedros with winds dropping to 25 knots and moved into the channel. The hook was down and bridle set very close to the *isla* by midafternoon. The set is solid but it is now only about two feet below high tide and near the shore. I washed off the salt of several breakers that had caught me in the cockpit and turned on the reefer. The ferry to Puntarenas chugged by an hour later.

Dinner on board was canned frankfurters and sauerkraut from the Netherlands Antilles. For some reason, this seemed funny to me. I was chuckling out loud to myself as I warmed up the Dutch franks, fresh out of the can. I also made a red onion and cucumber salad. Not as funny but good.

What sounded like the bellowing calls of a *caiman* woke me around 0300. The sound came from onshore, in the mangroves. I awoke the second time at 0500: it was still dark. The third time, at 0700, there was plenty of light to let me see mud banks on three sides with Quo Vadis sitting in a pool of water just seven ft. deep. A large power cat and the ketch anchored offshore are gone this morning. One guy is loading a panga on the mainland shore. Otherwise, it is very quiet. There are no daytime jungle sounds.

Maybe it wasn't such a good guess about the tide yesterday. Thirty minutes later, the depth sounder is showing 6 ft. I make preparations to get underway. It doesn't take me an hour this time. My timing and initial course are the same as the departing ferry with low-lying Puntarenas visible just 10 nm across the Golfo de Nicoya. I tried to follow the ferry but it made some course changes that may have been dictated by its draft though I saw no depth less than 25 ft. The wind built to 20 knots and the chop with it, though it was a much easier time than yesterday.

I punched in CH06 on the VHF radio and called the Costa Rica Yacht Club to request space and to check in through them. I heard an affirmative to both requests. I was further instructed to call later for a panga to come out and guide me through the channel. I passed the waypoint and got anxious trying to find the "round white" harbor buoy described in the guide. I finally decided it was the rusting 55 gallon drum floating horizontally. The depth dropped to 10-12 ft. very suddenly. I followed the docks; then turned port toward the shipwreck shown on the chart; running in 6-8 ft. The depth sounder showed 2.6 ft. before I got Quo Vadis stopped well before the wreck. It made my armpits sweat even more when I saw depths (or lack of) down to 2.3 ft. while backing the boat against the incoming tidal current and a following wind. I called the CRYC and asked for any suggestions. They said to stay put and they'd send a panga after lunch, which not so coincidentally, was also close to high tide. The anchor dropped, grabbed, and stuck hard in the mud.

I stayed busy cleaning up the galley and noted, happily, that the wind generator and solar panels were keeping the batteries topped off. That sort of thing really cheers me up. About an hour after the panga was supposed to show up; with 10 ft. of water under the hulls, I called the CRYC again. They replied they would send a panga "in just a few minutes" to guide me in. Sure. Right. I resigned myself to the long wait I have learned to expect, but not yet resent, in such tropical venues.

Carlos, Carlos, Carlos and William of the Costa Rica Yacht Club

In just a few minutes, a panga did show up with Timothy at the throttle of the outboard. He helped rig some lines both fore and aft to go on the double moorings necessary due to the extreme tides and currents in the fairly narrow estuary. This was done by 1400 with help from another panga, manned (I later learned) by ChiChi. He also took me ashore to meet Carlos Chinchilla, manager and Grand Panjundrum of the Costa Rica Yacht Club.

Don Carlos affably agreed to handle vessel and Captain check-in for Quo Vadis, making copies of all relevant boat documents. I signed the original of a new document for guest membership of the CRYC and the US$370/month mooring fee. Don Carlos also found William the Mechanic for me. I explained the three major mechanical problems and he agreed to meet me on board tomorrow at 1000 and start to work. I was to pump out whatever was in the engine compartment first. The yard could haul the boat tomorrow afternoon or the next morning. The club mooring fee will apply to the time on the hard. More to the point, Quo Vadis actually fits in their lifting well (if you don't put out fenders) and the only Travelift then operating in Central America will take this catamaran with its modest 16 ft. beam. Don Carlos also agrees to contact a sail repair guy to come by in the morning. Things are looking surprisingly up.

To celebrate, I treat myself to lunch ashore at the Club's open air restaurant, which is managed by Carlos. After three years afloat, eating lunch still remains one of my best command decisions. The whole fish hanging over the edges of my plate is well prepared; supported by fries and a salad. The genuinely friendly waiter, Carlos, brings me a cold, locally brewed Bavaria to help wash down the fish. I have another one and have now spent six dollars at the CRYC restaurant. Carlos the restaurant manager tells me it's OK if I want to run a tab. Does he know my boat is getting hauled in the yard just across the estuary? Hmm, maybe I already told him. This is a nice club, staffed with helpful people, located between the seldom-used train tracks and a shallow, muddy mangrove swamp. It is also the only yacht club in the country: a membership club for the small percentage of Ticos who can afford recreational boats. I'm thankful they accept wandering gringo sailors.

In the Yard on the Hard

Things moved at a pace not usually associated with Tico Time. William was only 20 minutes late, inspected the fuel pump, hydraulic piston, rudders, and engine. He said he could fix everything and would start tomorrow morning. I was introduced to the paint and fiberglass Supremo. He was not another Carlos. His name was Juan Carlos. He said he'd get primer, cleaner, paint, etc. and start work as soon as the boat was hauled. Juan Carlos spoke with Latin fervor and professional enthusiasm about painting the bottom of Quo Vadis in "Pedditreenidah" which he would do for US$1000. Still no answer from the sail repair guy, Francisco.

The bus into Puntarenas didn't stop for me. Twice. There was a nice-looking sand beach on the other side of the tracks and highway. It was deserted. On my way back to get a swimsuit, I was informed by Carlos that the "*Pescado Entero*" on today's lunch menu was corbina (generally considered a variety of sea trout). I was soon carefully dissecting 1-1/2 ft. of crispy-skinned dead corbina. The beach wasn't going any place.

Mario showed up in a panga at 1500 to take Quo Vadis to the yard for haulout. He said we would just tow it; no need to be under power. I started the engine and engaged the clutch, anyway. With the tide coming in, he released the slack bow line and I recovered it on board. The stern line promptly jammed in the mooring buoy with several wraps. I tried to back QV down to relieve tension on the line. It took a couple of tries as the current pushed the boat sideways whenever the line was slacked. Glad I had the engine fired up.

The slack stern line gets unwrapped from the buoy and used to straighten out QV. I scurry back to the bow and hand Mario the bow line for the short tow over to the Travelift well. With the tidal current still pushing us up the creek at 2-3 knots, we maneuvered QV into the well. Half a dozen other guys grab the rubrails and the handling lines I toss out. There are about three inches on each side: barely enough room for the slings. The forestay and furled headsail have to be released to fit into the lift. I had not been previously advised but managed the de-rigging. Both yard guys working on it hurt their fingers but they actually were clumsy and didn't use the tools I offered. Timothy bravely dived into the swirling brown gook to verify the sling strap positions and thanked me for use of my mask. Quo Vadis was out by 1545, chocked 10 minutes later and everybody immediately went home, leaving me standing on the deck 12 ft. up in the air and on the hard.

Boat Work Makes Strange Politics

During the next couple of days, Francisco the sail repair guys shows up, William and his helper Andres crawl in and out of the boat, and Juan Carlos shows me an empty can of the stuff he wants to buy. It is Pettit Anti-Fouling Paint at $150 per gallon; 4 gallons minimum needed for QV. It is in this venue that I meet Peter and Arnaud. They also have boats in the yard and have been living on them while waiting for parts, money, or maybe some combination of these factors.

Arnaud is fiercely French. He has adopted one of the three primary looks for male cruisers: a shaved head and soul patch. Tomas is from (the former) East Berlin. He is clean-shaven with longish blonde hair that falls artfully to his nose. They are both about 30 years old with non-descript sloops about 30 ft. long. They totally disregard historical national rivalry and cold war history. They are citizens of the New Europe: allied against the imperialist U.S. and, of course, these lazy Latinos. Their conversations are fascinating…at least to me. Tomas gets evasive when I bring up the Stasi. I sense that his family, like so many East Germans, were involved with the omnipresent Secret Police. He is not apologetic, but instead Germanically literal, about growing up as a young Communist and an "Esti". Arnaud offers his unsolicited opinion that it must have been terrible for Tomas because he wasn't allowed to travel anywhere, obviously an important thing for the sailing Frenchman.

"No, I could travel places," Tomas tells him.   "Where?" pressed Arnaud.

"Romania, Russia," offers Tomas without much enthusiasm.

"But what's in those places that you'd want to do?" asks Arnaud.

They are united in their disdain for the Club Manager, Don Carlos. He **doesn't** favor guys in tank tops and boat shorts sprawled in the Club lounge watching soccer matches on the TV; especially if those guys are not buying drinks or food. I rarely see the Europeans purchase anything. Arnaud, prioritizing like a true Frenchman, sometimes has dinner at the Club and complains how the prices have gone up just since he's been here. On this point, he is correct. Some menu items have doubled from about US$2 to US$4. He also doesn't like the Yacht Club's house wine. It is not French.

Impacts on the Economy of Costa Rica, and other Tales

Francisco is an Evangelical hypochondriac among other things, but a genuinely sympathetic guy. When he's not patching sails for vagabond gringos, his main line of work is furniture upholstery. The reason he gives for not showing up before was he'd been sick. He had been caring for his sick mother until she died not long ago and, he believed, he had caught something from her. He asked if I had any tablets that would help him feel better. I don't know the particulars of practicing medicine without a license in Costa Rica and don't really know what is ailing poor Francisco. I dig out some general purpose antibiotic bequeathed me by Dr. John Cocker way back at Grenada. Figuring this drug offers the least possibility of damage (Remembering the Hippocratic oath: "First, do no harm."), I give a dozen pills to Francisco with orders to take one in the morning and one at night with meals, but stop if there are any side effects. He eagerly accepts this ship Captain's prescription; apparently with unquestioning faith in my medical knowledge. What have I done?

As we itemize the sail repair jobs to be done, figure out the materials required to do them, and estimate the tens of thousands of colones necessary to accomplish all this, Francisco informs me of God's plan for us. Our names are already written in a Great Book (*Un Gran Libro*) he tells me, waiting for judgment day. For the moment, it is enough for him that I accept this, along with whatever it implies. I arch my eyebrows and articulate my facial expression, "*Interesante*."

We spend the rest of the day scavenging all over Puntarenas for items useful or necessary to the improvement of my trusty vessel, including visits to one of his pal's shop to have some pieces fabricated. Francisco maintains, with apparent accuracy, that there is no such thing as a ship's chandlery in Costa Rica. This is also the beginning of a long-running relationship with the neatly uniformed staff of the Banco Nacional: sometimes strained, sometimes cordial but always draining…my bank account. Of course, we eat lunch. Fran has a preferred sit-down stall in the Mercado Central. The entire working class of Puntarenas eats at least one meal a day in the Mercado. That includes us. I try one of the drinks made with tropical flavors, like tamarind, included in the bargain price of today's *casado*. Tamarind is a taste I still have not acquired.

Back in the yard, Fran sells me a piece of sail to cut up and patch the luff and other holes, pulls his sewing machine out of a bag, and "with God's blessing" starts to work. It is not the best work I've seen but it is getting done for 10,000 colones. Juan Carlos shows up with cans of paint featuring plain white generic labels. It has something to do with avoiding import duties. The price is just $140/gallon, a savings of $10. He also has the product sheet for Pettit Trinidad SR (this is the "Pedditreenidah" he recommended) which identifies the product as a hard epoxy paint. Whoops.

Only ablative anti-fouling paint has covered the hulls of Quo Vadis since before I owned her. Time out for a consult. Juan Carlos assures me that hard epoxy over a soft ablative paint is OK. Yards in the Chesapeake and the Virgin Islands have emphatically told me it is not, which seems logical. J.C. gets the technical representative for the paint company (so he claims) on his cell phone to assure me it is OK to use this paint. *"El Ingeñiero"* on the other end of the conversation asks me how long it's been since Quo Vadis' bottom was painted. I have to think back to the haulout at Virgin Gorda. It's been about a year and a half.

"If it's been over a year and a half," he reasons, "there's probably not much left on there after cleaning the bottom, so it isn't going to have much effect anyway." I see his point. Juan Carlos' three man crew is very efficient in getting two coats on both amas while he starts on the gelcoat.

My visits to the Banco Nacional have become almost daily events to keep up with the on-going demand for thick stacks of colones. None of the ATMs in town respond favorably to my card so, once admitted inside by the shotgun-armed guards, I take a number and wait. It's not bad, really. The bank is air conditioned, there is a water cooler, and the TV on the wall is tuned to Animal Planet or the National Geographic channel—all the time. These are the two default channels throughout Costa Rica if there is no soccer game. The waiting watchers' eyes are glued to the habits of the African lion or the stealthy stalking of the swift cheetah. The tele-transported Ticos even seem fascinated by a program on crocodiles which, if they step outside, they can see in person on the nearby riverbank. The bank staff pretends a cool indifference as they count out the piles of colones from the small metal toolbox behind their desk, but I can tell they remember me. Not many old gringos show up every day and withdraw large sums of cash. Unless they're dealing.

I have taken on the re-conditioning of the drive leg as my personal project. My, by now, intimate familiarity with this apparatus has not bred affection but I know more about it than your basic Third World boatyard guy or, possibly, anybody except Dijk Dunkers in Curaçao or Allan in the UK. Neither are currently available at the Costa Rica YC. I scrape, sand, drain, fill, lube and re-coat the drive leg between scavenger hunts and trips to the bank. This also allows me to be responsive to requests by the workers, monitor the work's progress, and is probably quite amusing to the rest of the gang.

William shows up to install the re-worked hydraulic piston and adjust the rudder bars. I add hydraulic fluid to the reservoir and pump the air pressure to over 30 psi. He turns the wheel hard both directions after bleeding the piston. The rudders are tight with no play. The installation looks good. Francisco shows up to tell me he can't make it on Monday to rig the headsail. He gives me a heavy duty snap shackle as a present. It is a Wichart: top grade marine hardware.

My compelling reason for working to make QV fully functional and seaworthy, again, is the impending visit of my daughter Caroline. I want everything to be right when she's on board. I call to confirm her arrival time and tell her I'll wait outside Customs at the San José airport.

I'm up at 0630 collecting and stowing yard work items. I also top up the drive leg lubricant after letting it settle overnight. Everything except the sails is re-rigged and the bottom paint is dry to the touch. I decide to put her back in the water so Timothy schedules it for "Right now!" since high tide at 0715 provides over 8 ft. in the lift well. A panga pulls QV to one of the floating platforms in front of the Club. This is definitely an upgrade. The small dock features a freshwater hose and accommodates just two boats. One of the perks of paying C.O.D. perhaps? By afternoon, soft black flakes are falling from the sky. This is a result of the sugarcane fields to the Northwest being on fire. Burning the cane fields is customary and seasonal in Costa Rica. The sticky black ash that falls from the skies is part of life. It makes boat decks a gummy mess.

William steps aboard, proudly displaying the rebuilt fuel pump. Francisco has brought Grebin, the young captain of the tourist day boat Loe Lani to assist with the headsail. Grebin scampers up the mast and discovers the cable is frayed. He offers to help replace it and has the swedges to re-rig the cable. His swedges turn out to be the wrong size but I visually verify he has the necessary tools. Fran and I go into Puntarenas to look for steel cable. He assures me his machine shop *amigo* can make the needed hardware. We find only plastic-coated cable in the size needed for QV. I am concerned, among other things, that maybe this steel fiber isn't so stainless but I buy the required length of it plus a few feet for insurance. As soon as I see the parts at the machine shop, I knew they wouldn't work with Grebin's swedging tool. I know to always take dimensions and make drawings but I didn't for this job. Grebin tries to make it work but, not surprisingly, just distorts the swedge. The re-rigging turns into a cobble of pressed copper tubing immersed in silicone wrapped in rigging tape. It might work.

As we install the genoa, Grebin and Francisco tell me the furling direction is wrong. They change it and Grebin attaches the tack of the headsail to the furling drum. There is barely enough cable to secure it. I furled the headsail and it worked, so we tie on the jib sheets with opposing bowlines. I am still not 100% certain on the furling wrap. It is different from Fraito's rig, done in Puerto Rico, which worked from there to here.

Caroline comes to Costa Rica

All that work was scheduled to get underway while I went to San José to meet my daughter, Caroline. I found the correct bus in town and managed to emerge curbside at Juan Santamaria Internacional 20 minutes before her flight. Forty minutes after it landed and all the passengers and crew had taken their bags elsewhere, Caroline still had not emerged. I called her mother, trying to keep any note of panic out of my voice. Our darling daughter was not on the flight. After driving four hours to Los Angeles International, she discovered a problem with her passport. It had expired.

She was working to get it re-newed at the consular offices in L.A.; then catch the flight in 48 hours, contingent on getting her passport back. I learned the bus route and schedule back by trial and error. While there are direct busses from Puntarenas to the international airport, there is no bus returning. You have to go someplace else to catch it. After wandering around Alajuela, the gritty suburb where the San Jose airport actually is located, then waiting about an hour, I jumped on the first bus with "Puntarenas" whitewashed on the windshield. It also had many other place names painted in smaller letters. This bus stopped at all of them. I was not on the "Express".

With *Quo Vadis* lacking only a working oil pressure sensor to be completely fit for sea duty, I panga'd ashore to call Caroline and see how the passport thing is progressing. I leave a message and sit down in Carlos' restaurant for juice and coffee. I'm enjoying the brief cool of a tropical morning when I get a call. It is from Kathleen, Caroline's mother and my former wife. She tells me Caroline is at the airport in San José. She dropped her cell phone in the toilet so she couldn't call me. I used the YC's office phone to call the airport and request she be paged. There was no response after 20 minutes, so I appealed to Don Carlos to arrange a ride. (The next bus from Puntarenas had already left.) She'll be OK, I tell myself. Female teenagers show up alone in Costa Rica all the time, right? You hardly ever hear about anything really bad happening to them at the airport.

Richard, who does painting and fiberglass for Juan Carlos, has a car. Soon we are speeding up the road to San José. Until we come to the long line of vehicles behind a truck wreck on the winding uphill section. Richard, however, is undaunted. He knows *La Ruta Ahuacate* (The Avocado Route). It is very scenic, the way the mule ride on Molokai or into the Grand Canyon is scenic. *La Ruta Ahuacate* presents new dimensions in Costa Rica travel: narrow and vertical.

Caroline is sitting quietly outside the passenger terminal, reading a very thick book.

"Where were you, Dad?" Good question. I am so choked up to see her my voice is cracking as I manage to introduce her to Richard. He is just the first of many Latino guys who likes the way she looks. A father notices these things.

We stop for lunch going back on The Avocado Route as Richard supposes (and I agree) the main road won't be cleared yet. Richard is concerned that we choose a place with enough variety on the menu for Caroline to select something she likes. We all ended up eating one of the *casados*. I buy Richard some gas, give him all the dollars I have left in my pocket (and decide to supplement it a little later). The family members have a shower on shore and siesta on board. William arrives to finish the last of his work, completes it and bills me US$500 for a total of US$600. I have a confused reaction. Is this reasonable or a rip-off? But, he appears to be the only game in town for Yanqui cruising boats and impresses me as a competent mechanic.

When we return from zipping through the forest canopy the following afternoon, Dawna and Chris are waiting for us outside the Costa Rica Yacht Club. Surprise! I worked with Dawna on the 2004 Presidential campaign. I later heard she was backpacking in Central America for a few months' R&R after the election. She met Chris along the way. He was acting as her male "protective coloration", an increasingly common, and useful, move for young *Americanas* traveling in Latino-land. They were both hoping to sleep on board my boat at this stage in their pilgrimage from the shores of Montezuma to the heights of Monteverde. Tom and Arnaud later offered the decks of their own boats, still chocked up on the hard, for budget tourist sleeping accommodations. Don Carlos didn't know quite what to make of it all. Frankly, neither did I. After dinner ashore, Dawna and Chris unrolled their sleeping bags on deck. They were zonked by 2100. The Captain and Caroline retired to their cabins after the nighttime shutdown routine.

Repaired, re-provisioned, with captain and crew recuperated, S/V Quo Vadis cast off her mooring lines and set out into the Golfo de Nicoya on the next day's high tide with a full crew, two of whom had never been on a sailboat before. We sailed around the Golfo in light winds with Caroline handling the helm while I walked and talked the newest members of the crew through boat functions, safety procedures, and Sailing 101.

We dropped anchor behind Isla Muertos by 1700, far enough out so the bugs might not find us. I am pleased, and a proud father, that Caroline remembers the anchoring procedure, our hand signals, and proper helm control dropping the hook. Everybody jumped over the side for a swim.

After freshwater solar showers, it was time for sundowners and my increasingly famous cheeseburgers. These food items grow in reputation and tastiness each time I make them. Cheeseburgers (Needless to say: with everything) are definitely at the top of the always popular "Skipper's Specials". What talent. The young crew stays up til 2230, chatting and pouring rum into Cokes, long after the sole senior citizen on board has headed for his bunk. The wind shifts twice overnight, swinging the boat and blowing away the bugs.

There is a nice-looking dinghy dock on the mainland shore, complete with a canopy and chaise lounges. After a casual breakfast on board, we drop the dink and paddle over. There are some elaborate structures back in the woods but only two of them look like residences. Some folks walking along the rocks respond to Dawna's grammatically correct but gringo-accented Spanish. It seems this is not Bahia Luminosa and there really isn't any "Nature Path" to explore here.

So we paddle back out, tie off the dinghy and move Quo Vadis to Bahia Luminosa. It's only around the point. This was once a yacht/crew center for Costa Rica, or so I've been told. We pass one boat half-sunken in the Bahia and one boat floating, dismasted. The dismasted boat has lots of pelicans lined up on deck. They seem pretty comfortable hanging out there. We dinked ashore, again, and went looking for Finn Johannson, identified as the manager. We found him outside a large enclosed *palapa*: the dining, dancing and reception area of Bahia Luminosa. The only visitors to the resort were two young Americanos: Keith and Erin. Besides the big *palapa*, there is a row of empty motel-style rooms, and a pet monkey. The place is not exactly thriving. One benefit of its condition is there are lots of iguanas, colorful birds, and a troop of wild monkeys crawling around in the upper branches of the ceiba trees. This is the first "getting near the animals" event for Caroline. She poses with a couple of iguanas. We run into Keith and Erin on our way back to the beach. He wants to crew on a boat. He tells me he owns a sailing cat and Erin is going home in a few days. I invite him to come over to the CRYC later that week.

Caroline and Dawna alternate at the helm as we head East between Punta Gigante and Isla Guayabo in very light air. QV enters the Estero just at slack high tide. Timothy is waiting on our floating dock to take the lines and we're secured by mid-afternoon. Dawna and Chris are good about pitching in, though not always sure exactly how to do all the tasks. They volunteered to clean the galley after meals on board and now start scrubbing the deck. They are learning fast.

Chris wants to crew as a low cost way to get back to the States but, as he put it, "You've seen all of my experience." While we're talking over the possibilities, he paused and looked away into the distance. He tells me he grew up without a father. He never even met his father until last year and Chris is now 25. He motions with his hand around the boat including Caroline, who is chatting and working with Dawna up on the foredeck, "Then to see this, how you two are…" His voice trails off. For me, the past two days had featured easy day sailing, gunkholing, and some basic "How to" instruction on the boat. For Chris, his experience of these same days and things had been seeing a father-child relationship: something he'd never experienced. How different, our takes on the exact same events. This is another life lesson I have just re-learned.

After one more watery passage through the club house showers, Chris and Dawna shoulder their enormous backpacks and go looking for a bus that will take them still closer to Monteverde.

"Thought you'd never get rid of us, huh?" Dawna smiles. Caroline had confided in me that, while she was glad to meet them and all that, she wanted to spend time together without any other crew or visitors. That's why she flew to Costa Rica. I never said anything but, as an increasingly ancient mariner and father, I am flattered by this rare declaration from my daughter.

Caroline and Captain wait for high tide and, once again, head down the Puntarenas Estero to the Golfo de Nicoya. We're going exploring with, maybe, stops at Isla San Lucas, the prison island, and the wildlife preserve by the beach at Curú. Even at the time, I realize what a wonderful feeling and great moment in life this is for me. We're provisioned, have full tanks, my kid has gained in experience and we can sail anywhere our ability, wind, and current allow. Well, perhaps with the aid of a reliable Yanmar diesel. With winds ENE 15-20, we sail into the small bay at San Lucas by late afternoon. I choose to go outside the rusting wreck in the middle, turning back into the wind and dropping the anchor a bug-deterring distance from the jungle beach. A short, deteriorating pier juts out from the shore. It was used for delivery of prisoners and provisions when this was the prison island for Puntarenas province. There are, reportedly, security guards at the abandoned prison but we see no movement on shore and no lights after dusk.

The jib sheets smacking on the coach roof woke us up at 0330. The genoa was unfurling itself in high winds. (As you sailors reading this already know, stuff like this traditionally occurs around three in the morning. Anchor dragging? Surprise flooding in a compartment? Hearing the crash of waves on the unseen reef? Thieves cutting the dinghy cables? Most, if not all, of these events happen between 2 and 4 A.M. It is a part of the lore of the sea not typically passed on to novices, unless it happens to them.) This is one reason I take the midnight watch when we're under way. Another reason is that I'm usually awake, anyhow.

The genoa would not re-furl from working on the furling line. I went forward to the drum but could not re-furl the sail by hand. Closer inspection revealed the furling line had jumped out of the roller drum and wrapped around the forestay. All I could figure out was that the pitching deck had acted on a slack furling line and yanked the slack loops below the drum. Even with that, it seemed to me *Quo Vadis* wasn't pitching as bad as Steve Cherry had described his ketch under similar conditions: jumping around the axis of its anchor rode and pitching sharply 2-3 feet. The anchor was holding; the bridle worked. Caroline brought forward a flashlight and the big screwdriver to use as a marlinspike. She quickly returned to the cockpit and pulled tight the jib sheets to control the viciously slatting jib. The big genoa ripped along the leach. My task quickly changed. Get the sail down. It tore again, nearly in half, with that stomach-churning sound you hate to hear. Somehow, I unshackled the cable and, with Caroline's help, pulled down the two pieces of former headsail. We had it in the cockpit by 0400, all balled up; not neatly folded but we did get all lines and cables secured. The anchor was still holding with winds at 35 knots, gusting to 45. I wasn't breathing that hard and the wind chill factor had precluded much sweating. There were no personal injuries that we could determine. Everything was OK.

"Well, Dad," said Caroline. "It shows we can work together in an emergency." I agreed but I had never thought, at any time, that it would be any other way. Later, it occurred to me that she might have felt uneasy in the middle of a dark and stormy night with the running rig not responding; the sails ripping in high wind, anchored all alone off an abandoned prison island in the middle of the Golfo de Nicoya in a foreign land. She didn't know these things always happen around 3 A.M.

Islands as a State of Mind

After considering the passage South to Curú and back without a genoa, we decide exploring San Lucas is a better idea. We dink ashore near the tumbledown steel pier, armed with cookies and sodas to soften up the security guards. Only there are none. No other people, either. There is just the eerie emptiness of an abandoned prison, dock, and chapel. The Administration buildings and the chapel are both larger structures than the one cell block, which is missing most of its roof. If there were many prisoners in here, they were pretty crowded.

Fishermen, or somebody else who uses two-stroke oil and nylon line, have been camping inside one of the outbuildings. There are blackened spots on the concrete floor from their fires. Large, battered pots are still in the kitchen along with several large jars of indeterminate content: mostly liquid. I stifle a gag sensation. A surprisingly intact modern style telephone booth is incongruously bolted to the porch in front of the Admin building. Caroline checks for dial tone. Wouldn't you know it? Out of service.

Several of the rooms in the main building, which is relatively grand, are home to little brown bats… and lots of them. Caroline is delighted to discover these creatures and takes some flash photos which gets them flurrying around the room for a minute or two before they return to hanging from the rafters. The only sound is the soft flutter of their small, furry wings.

A littered path as wide as a city street leads away from the cell block. It runs between rows of foundations which are what remains of the guards' and staff housing. Today, they are populated by many iguanas. Since there is nothing to harass or kill them here, many grow to 3-4 ft. long. Caroline spots a big, yellow four-footer ("*Un Amarillo*" as they're called here.) and follows him into fairly open bush, trying for a photo. Today's visual image is a young woman 5'5" tall with a buxom figure inherited from her mother chasing a mini-dragon into the jungle while smaller iguanas scuttle out of her way. Playing in the back of my brain is the sight of Caroline: a little girl about three years old running on the beach scattering seagulls to the sky while laughing that perfect laugh of little girls. But I don't feel any older; more like I'm experiencing a time lapse. Or is that the same thing?

The wide path emerges on to a long white sand beach. The only living things in sight are hundreds of bright pink crabs, standing beside their holes. As we approach, they scuttle in unison back down into their holes. If we back off, they re-emerge taking up position with claws raised defiantly. We orchestrate the dance of the miniature pink creatures, moving them in waves as we approach and retreat. Other than the crabs, we have the beach as well as the rest of Isla San Lucas to ourselves. The water is shallow and warm. The waves are small as we wade out to get wet at Playa El Coco.

Back along the path past the foundations, scaring more iguanas, we find fruit trees gone wild by the prison buildings. I swim out to the dinghy, dive under to untie the painter since the tide has risen several feet and tow it back to Caroline without slipping on the rocks. Isla San Lucas will probably be a destination resort by our next trip. Maybe it is by the time you read this. From the dreaded isolation and squalid cells of a prison island to exclusive vacation getaway in one generation. It would probably be offering overpriced rooms and panga service to the mainland already if it weren't state-owned. Hmm, is it too late to invite the Interior Minister of Costa Rica to lunch?

Winds have cranked back up to 30-35 knots, right on the nose for our return course to Puntarenas. We motor out into the chop. No finny or shell-backed friends visit us. They are apparently smart enough to stay down below the confused seas. We get soaked by the spray breaking over the bows. It feels pretty good.

Some things do go according to plan, as we make the entrance to the Puntarenas Estero on the tide. I called the CRYC about 10 minutes out and Timothy appeared in a club panga to assist **Quo Vadis** back to our floating dock on the flood tide. He and Caroline again did a nice, clean job of docking and line handling. Timothy can probably do this with most boat crews that show up at the club. I am so proud Caroline has learned to work seamlessly with him in her short time aboard.

We showered and dressed for dinner ashore. Actually, only Caroline wore a dress. I did khakis and a polo shirt. Carlos graciously seats us at our preferred table which overlooks the Estero, the mangroves on the far side and, as it gets dark, the burning cane fields glowing in the distance. I had the fish. Caroline has discovered one of the Costa Rican standards: shrimp and rice, which is made in a Creole style with intense flavors but not spicy hot. She orders it in her improving Spanish. Tonight's meal together seems especially good. I can't stop grinning ear-to-ear as I have dinner with my daughter.

In the morning, the deck is covered with black, sticky cane ash. I work at hosing it off while the black, tasty Costa Rican coffee is brewing below in the galley. Would the cane ash sweeten it? We enjoy a leisurely breakfast aboard, Caroline's last in Costa Rica. She decides I need a haircut, so trims my longish, flowing locks before we go ashore. At the airport, I manage not to cry. My boat, my home seems very empty when I eventually get back on board later that evening.

Torn Sail, Oil Leak, Green Crew and other Cruising Delights

Next day dawns cool and calm. I try to remain the same as I see the genoa is torn nearly in three, I discover the engine has leaked lots of oil and the wind generator does not appear to be generating. Francisco calls me before 0900. He is waiting for a club panga to collect him and get the sail so he can inspect the damage. We lay it out in the boatyard and match the rips. He proposes gluing and sewing it back together, sacrificing about an inch in the luff. I like the concept of both adhesive and stitches to reassemble the genoa. It turns out he doesn't have any of the materials he proposed to use for the repair. We make a shopping list for me to take to San José. He also tells me he is feeling better and attributes his overall improvement to the tablets I gave him. I am thankful for any placebo effect but prudently don't prescribe any follow-up medications. I don't want to press my luck or jeopardize his, any more.

Back on the boat, I am still trying to understand, and fix, the roller furling problem. After re-rigging the drum, I delve into the engine compartment and discover a pond of oil covering the bottom. I siphon out over two quarts of viscous black liquid. A brief engine run confirms it is still leaking but I can't find the leak point. I pump detergent into the bottom of the compartment and towel out most of the oil. I clean the galley and treat the starboard head. After this fun-filled morning, I decide it must be time for lunch. This remains one of my better command decisions, you may recall, and sometimes the only one that yields successful results.

By 1400, I am finishing up at the CRYC dining room when I am joined by Keith, the crew candidate. We talk. I learn he graduated a year ago from a college in Colorado, which sounds like a school for rich kids who ski and snowboard. I think he was trying to impress me back at Finn's by informing us that he had a dual major:

kinesiology and graphic arts. I listened but did not tell him I know what those subjects really are: physical education and cartooning. The college Phys. Ed. major was re-termed "Kinesiology" decades ago when I was still at UCLA so that most of the football team could have a more impressive-sounding major. I have engaged in a lot of physical activity (with bad knees to show for it) and cartooning (I actually drew some in a previous lifetime.) but these are not college majors I would brag about nor spend four years of tuition to indulge in. He also tells me he taught snowboarding at Crested Butte in the afternoons and started on the school's lacrosse team. Lacrosse? In Colorado? With snow on the ground until June? I admit that I didn't have any idea that Colorado had become a hotbed of lacrosse but see no point in telling him I had also played that sport.

Anyhow, Keith seems healthy if a little soft for a self-proclaimed two season athlete. He's also the only current candidate for crew to California. I propose we make a trial run from Puntarenas back into the Pacific and up to Playa del Coco, the Costa Rica exit port; see how it goes. He can get off there if things don't work out and we won't have a problem with crew lists, passports, etc. He could catch the bus back to the airport—or anyplace else. Maybe I've learned something from prior experience. Maybe not.

After another two hour bus ride to San José, I eventually find the Street of the Sewing Supplies. Francisco has directed me to this district of town to acquire the essential items for sail repair. His directions are typical for Costa Rica. "Go 200 meters from the bus station, turn right at the old church and go another 300 meters. Look for the big store; then go past that." San Jose has few street signs and the locals seldom refer to them, in any case. After being shown dozens of sewing machines of museum vintage, if not quality, I finally find the shop that carries nylon thread. One spool of about 500 meters is all that remains in their inventory. The only sales option I am given is to buy the whole thing. Another shop has urethane, the thick goop we'll use to glue the sail. The shop assistant pours it from a five gallon drum into some re-used bottles and caps them. I search hours more for sail cloth, not willing to accept its complete commercial absence, and give up only when it is time to catch the last direct bus back to Puntarenas.

William the Mechanic came aboard to search for the oil leak. He can't find it, either, so goes back to get his small mirror. He stretches down under the engine, I crank it and he says "Aha!" Oil is squirting out at the bottom of the timing gear cover. "This could be simple," he tells me. "Maybe just tightening three bolts will fix it." When he uses my socket wrench to tighten the bolts, a short length of sodden black gasket squeezes out. "Difficult to replace," he observes. *"Difícil, peró no imposible."* I actually take heart from the words: *"No imposible"*. I am even more encouraged to find the original manufacturer's replacement parts in the spares locker. Sometimes,

I surprise myself. William promises to return and attempt the *"difícil"* but advises me not to run the engine since the leak is opened up more now. Only later, do I wonder if *"difícil"* is Costa Rican mechanic's code for "This is gonna cost you, gringo."

Adíos, Costa Rica Yacht Club

During the two days waiting for the electrician to look at the wind generator, William replaces the gasket and re-assembles the engine. Francisco with help from Keith and me re-assembles the headsail. Grebin comes on board to help with its installation and will accept nothing but thanks. The others are more demanding financially which means my acquaintance with the Banco Nacional staff is renewed on a daily basis. I start carrying provisions back to the boat.

I had also volunteered to crew on Hauke Martens' sloop *Atlantis* in this weekend's CRYC regatta. His boat keeper, Gerardo, was excited about my offer and assured me how great this would be. Herr Martens arrived from San Jose, where he has a business importing German machinery. Hauke informs me he isn't racing in the regatta. Talk about your culture gaps.

So I check the tide tables, again, and we prepare *Quo Vadis* to get underway. We made a trip to the fuel dock, filled the water tanks, left tens of thousands of colones with the CRYC cashier, weaved back through the mooring field, found the channel and still caught the ebbing tide. The reefer seems to be working normally, rather than cycling in fault mode as it so often does.

Course is set for Las Tortugas which gives the option to continue to Ballena Bay if we can make it an hour before sunset. We sail through the narrow gap of Los Negritos and on to Isla Alcatraz: this rock populated only by its namesake birds. This passage on the blue Gulf between the rocky islands and the jungled mainland is postcard-perfect. I wish Caroline could have made it.

We found an anchorage on the north side of Ballena Bay inside a natural rock breakwater. I dived on the anchor which was set in fine, silty sand. Swimming in the clean, warm waters of the Bay cheers me up after a week of mostly dirty, grubby boat work. I sauteé shrimps and make a salad while all the stuff is still fresh. The reefer has actually managed to chill the bottles of Chilean sauvignon blanc, so we open one and drink it with the shrimp.

A Day in Ballena Bay

We arrange the boat for a stay and swim ashore to explore the beach. We are surprised to find a number of structures hidden back in the jungle including an accurately reproduced Plains Indian tipi. Two of the structures have an electric powerline to them, running along the trees, to power empty but working refrigerators. One of the enclosures has a long communal table with benches. It is adorned with multicolor painted signs spelling "PEACE" in more languages than I know. All of the structures except the tipi are open-sided with sections of corrugated metal or plastic overhead. There is also a wrecked trimaran on the beach: the only thing visible from the water.

There are no signs of any current inhabitants until a inflatable dinghy comes running up the bay. The sole occupant is a red-haired, freckle-faced kid who turns the dink in and runs the boat up on the beach. He takes the outboard off the transom, slings it over his shoulder and walks directly in to the jungle. He comes right back and we help him haul his boat above the tide line. It seems he lives here with his father and older brother. We also discover the trimaran was built by them and wrecked in a storm when it was anchored just about where Quo Vadis is now. The kid looks like a younger version of Huckleberry Finn but speaks only, and naturally, in idiomatic local Spanish.

"How did the boat get wrecked?" I ask in non-local Spanish.

"Just big waves," he answers. "It came loose, went on the rocks and then the beach." So now, he observes, the boat "*No sirve*."— the colloquial Costa Rican term for anything that's broken. "It doesn't serve (its purpose)". "*No sirve*," he repeats and turns back in to the jungle. I wonder how much English he speaks after however many years he's been here. Both Keith and I reflect on what kind of life this is for a 12 year old boy: living in the jungle, tipi on the beach, not going to some regular school, having a skiff with an outboard. We agree it seems like a pretty good one.

Overnight the wind had come up and clocked around, so we move to the south side of Ballena Bay, near the village of Tambor. I go overboard with a brush to clean the Estuary growth off the bottom. The new paint job is OK overall though not to my U.S. standards. There are a surprising number of new marks, stains and scrapes on the starboard side…from docking? Schools of small yellow and black fish follow around below me, eating the stuff I scrape off the hulls. I've seen this before, often with multiple fish species competing for weed and barnacles. I don't know why I'm so entertained by feeding my personal tropical saltwater aquarium. It keeps me scraping.

A good-sized motor yacht leaves to the North as I climb back on the aft deck. A crowded panga buzzes past QV and on to the beach at Tambor. I make *chorizo con huevos* and a tomato salad for lunch. The local sausages and fresh veggies are gobbled up by Cap'n and crew. Keith cleans the galley while I clean off anchor chain rust and wash down the foredeck. That seems like enough clean-up for the time being, so I sling my new hammock for a siesta on the Bay.

We clear Ballena Bay by 0645 the next morning, riding down winds of NW15 kts toward Cabo Blanco, leaving the Golfo de Nicoya and headed back to the open Pacific.

In the Pacific Ocean

Quo Vadis glides smoothly South past Montezuma where Keith, and every other 20-something visiting Costa Rica, has gone to surf, drink, and play on the beach. We round the guano-coated rocks marking Cabo Blanco; then turn Northwest, standing some distance off the Pacific Coast. The winds cooperate for a welcome change, coming East by afternoon.

The reality in Bahia Carillo has changed since the sketch chart was made. But, then, what hasn't?

The East side is wall-to-wall moorings and the West side is rolling and exposed. After making the trip back and forth, I ask the guys on the sportfisher Permit III about the nearest open mooring. They didn't think the boat would be back. It's never easy for me to snag those tandem mooring balls but we manage by dusk, just as 10 sportfishing boats come roaring in from a day of drowning bait. This small harbor is suddenly very crowded but nobody kicks us off. I am so grateful not to be ejected in the dark and have to go back over to the roly-poly West side. As a display of gratitude, I make dinner. Starting with a sardine salad; moving on to spaghetti with meatballs accompanied by a box of Chilean wine. In the morning, a 7 ft. tide reveals still more rocks we had luckily missed while motoring around the Bay looking for a parking place.

We cleared Bahia Carillo by 0630, still missing the now-visible rocks and outside reef break. We encountered some wind as soon as QV rounded the point: 30-35 knots, gusts to 40. I had reefed the main and furled the genoa to 75% anticipating some Cape effect. Then, it went calm. An hour later, the wind was back to E15-20 knots. I am still not used to the highly variable winds, including none, common in the Pacific after years of sailing the constant Caribbean tradewinds.

We pass Tamarindo a good distance off shore to clear shoal water and rocks. This is the newly "discovered" getaway, now over-populated by the would-be chic crowd. It has become Tama-gringo since the article in <u>Vanity Fair</u>. This area and Montezuma are the current hip places on the Nicoya Peninsula for the younger set who can afford it. Neither holds much attraction for me since they both have outside surf and no protected anchorages. I may even be the wrong age.

What does get me excited on this leg are multiple sightings of sperm whales. I've never seen this type of whale before. I make the first sighting: a calf. The blunt head and smooth flukes help identify it as a sperm whale. Even this baby is about 15 ft. long. There really is no such thing as a small sperm whale. We see the probable mother blow nearby. Then an adult surfaced within just a few feet of the starboard ama to check us out. It briefly looked at the boat; then sank back beneath the surface. She (or he) was the length of the boat (37 ft.) or more and displaced an incredible roiling mass of water when she sounded.

Keith and I are swimming off Playa Conchal by 1700. Tonight's Skipper's Special is the infamous 'burgers with veggies and fries. There was some more red wine in that box. For being squeezed out of a box, it's not that bad. Even day sailors will agree everything tastes better out on the water.

Few places look so forlorn to a sailor as an abandoned marina. Flamingo apparently used to be the place on this coast. It had fuel pumps, restaurant and bar, provisioning, docks inside a breakwater—all the fancy stuff. I had already changed the guidebook entry by writing "No" before "Fuel available." The boats still docked inside the sea wall looked equally abandoned. I've been told the entrance is silted up. A couple or tourist busses roll by on the beach road. We tune in the Amigo Net and hear the local gossip but no weather report.

QV enters the southern end of the Golfo de Papagayo and sails on past Playa del Coco (the town), the Islas Viadores and Playa Hermosa, on to Playa Panama. A Southbound skipper told us we'd find calmer waters there over white sand. He is right. *Quo Vadis* is the only boat anchored off the curving white sand beach. It doesn't occur to me there might be other reasons we're alone.

After sleeping in til 0730, we went ashore to place our grocery order with Marioncet at the Restaurant Guanacaste. She offers one day turnaround service with pickup here under the *palapa*. Then, we start hitchhiking into Playa del Cocos to clear out of Costa Rica. Three rides later (with Michael the German, the 7-11 truck, and the religious guy) we're dropped off by the town's soccer field and walk down to the Port Captain's office. It is staffed by a young gal and a guy in civilian clothes whose skill set includes being able to type and enter data in a desktop computer about three generations removed. This database is supposedly to monitor and verify ship movement in and out of the country. But the old computer rule of GIGO still applies. He enters whatever I tell him.

The rest of the routine involves relinquishing the boat's import document, obtained those many weeks ago in Golfito at the other end of the country. Then it's off to *Immigracion* to get our passports stamped and sign out our warm bodies, to the bank to pay the boat exit fee ($US20), back to the Port Captain with the bank receipt to get the *zarpe* verifying our exit port which, hopefully, will admit us to our next Port of Entry: San Juan del Sur, Nicaragua. As you have now probably figured out, this involves a fair amount of walking around Playa del Coco. It is an amazingly seedy beach town with the main paved street disappearing into the sand beach. There are a few truly tacky bars with regular daytime patronage, the bank, a couple of *tiendas*, a souvenir stand near the bus stop, and an ice house. Another paved road runs around the soccer field. That's about it.

The official rule in most countries where Quo Vadis has sailed is you have to leave national waters within 24 hours of the date on your exit documents and you can't stop anyplace along the way. Since it was midafternoon and we still had to pick up our grocery order, I asked the young guy to stamp our *zarpe* departure date for the next day. He agreed. This is a good idea, in general, because if you're not gone from some countries by midnight of the exit date and get caught, you have to start all over including paying a new set of fees, taxes, etc. The scuttlebutt from other, not necessarily reliable, sources was that boats that overstayed their departure from Costa Rica had to re-enter to clear out, paying both ways along the paper trail. I have to think those skippers must have done something really stupid or pissed off the Port Captain, or both.

After taking 3000 colones, the cabbie dropped us at his version of Playa Panama which was across the inlet. On the other side of the bay, Quo Vadis could be seen riding at anchor. After a long, wet, sandy slog through the mangroves we get back to the dink, still chained to the tree, and get back on board. I made cheeseburgers for dinner. The French wine purchased in Puntarenas did not, as the wine snobs say, travel well. Cane ash fell on deck throughout the night.

Papagayos and Water Balls

Our grocery order was ready. Ticas are rare in cultures between the Rio Grande and, say, Buenos Aires. They almost always follow through and often, at the predicted time. The local males are no slaves to punctuality. We re-provisioned for US$25 including a US$1 service charge. Keith called his parents to tell them he was headed for Nicaragua. I requested they, in turn, call Meredith to let her know I was, too. It was a local D.C. area call for them. The engine started, again. No faults, no alarms, and the oil level is good.

We left Bahia Culebra. (This translates as "Serpent Bay". There are many bays of this name. The Spanish must have had a thing about snakes. Maybe because snakes are rare in Spain?) We passed the Islas Viadores by 1000. The wind started building as we moved out on the Golfo de Papagayo. The Port Captain's forecast had no significant weather events predicted so I decide it's OK to head for the Murcielagos Islands which, according to the guidebook, have well-protected anchorages should we need to find safe harbor.

Halfway across the Gulf which gives its name to the wind, it started to build: 30-35 knots with gusts to 45. The sea state isn't bad, maybe 3-4 ft. but with an annoying wave frequency; more like the Caribbean. Since I had more experience steering these waves, I took the helm. Winds increased to 35-40; gusts to 50. An occasional wave breaks over the coach roof. I notice we are being set West of the Islas Murcielagos (Why are they called "Bat Islands"? And what a strange time to wonder about this.) We run out the stays'l in place of the genoa and motor to get back on course for the passage between the islands. As we come abreast of our planned anchorage at Bahia Sueño, we find it wide open to the winds. It looks like there is whitewater inside. So we continue North and drop the hook behind the tall rock cliffs of Key Point. The wind instrument is showing 20-25 knots here in the anchorage. Quo Vadis is rotating 360 degrees with the wind swirling around the cliffs into the little cove. I wonder how the anchor is doing, so dive on the hook. As far as I can tell, it's doing just fine. After more than two years, I must be getting this part right.

And so it goes for the next two days as the Papagayo, for that is what we're in, blows 30 knots with gusts to 40 here in this protected anchorage below the cliffs of Santa Rosa National Park. Quo Vadis is rolling in breaking waves from a South surge and the North wind. The boat is moving around but the anchor is holding. We try the Amigo Net again and hear lots of chatter, recipe swaps, boat locations, but nothing about weather. Quo Vadis isn't supposed to be in Costa Rica at this late date but it seems unlikely we're going to get busted by any authorities arriving by boat.

Giant balls of water 12 to 30 ft. in diameter come rolling down the channel, one after another. I've never seen such things before. I've never even heard talk about these water balls and cruisers, especially, love to regale anybody who will hold still with tales of any strange phenomenon they've experienced at sea. I read in a local newspaper that the giant water balls have prevented the fishing fleet from going out for several days and the negative impact this had on their earnings. There is no further comment on the freaky giant balls of water vapor, like they happen frequently like a well-known but annoying sort of thing, like tornados in the Midwest of the U.S.. Around 1300, the winds started to drop and fewer, smaller water balls were rolling across the surface of the channel by mid-afternoon. We may have missed a window. The wind came back up at dusk.

At 0630, the sea state looked more subdued than it had yesterday so I decide we should stick our nose out and see what's happening. The tip of Cabo Santa Elena is just over three miles West. We headed that way with winds initially at 25-30 knots. They started building to 35-40 as we approached the cape; then went to 45 kts. sustained. Quo Vadis was moving at 8-10 knots under main only. I took the helm approaching the point in confused seas of 4-5 ft. with sustained winds of 40-50 knots. I decided to come back in. We turned around OK but now were headed into the waves with winds over 40. I'm concerned about the sail blowing out. A good crew effort got the mainsail down intact but the starboard lazy jack came apart and a slide snapped out of the mast. We made only half the speed returning to anchor as going out but still had the hook set by 0845.

I tried to repair the lazy jack fitting with an electrical connector (heavy gauge), safety wire, and my new discovery: Poxy-Pol. With Keith on the winch, I went up in the bos'n's chair to re-attach and run the rigging. I crimped everything together and wrapped all the pieces in rigging tape. When I got back down out of the wind, I figured it might be good to look at some alternatives to San Juan del Sur if the Papagayo continues at the speeds and direction we've been seeing for the last couple of days. I've been told by locals that Papagayos can blow for weeks. I find two Bahías to the East, back in Costa Rica. They could work but I'm not enthusiastic about going back.

After noon, I couldn't see any whitecaps out West beyond Cabo Santa Elena. Strongly influenced by yesterday's relative calm which occurred about 1300, I decide to try to get around the Cape, again.

We were underway before that time. I took the helm just before the point. It wasn't as bad as this morning. Which meant the North wind was still 35-45 knots and when we came to a course of 40 magnetic to clear Punta Blanca, the seas were head on. It didn't seem wise to continue on that course so I fell off and headed back to the anchorage behind Key Point, which I've renamed "Keith Point". The waves were small but wind gusts to 50 knots were frequent. We tried to get back to the same spot, which was now covered in just 11 ft. of Pacific Ocean at low tide. With the hook set, I replaced a frayed line in the bridle, paid out about 80 ft. of scope, went below and made *quesadillas*. The wind died abruptly to 10 knots by 1800. I'm not going again today…or tonight. We had pasta for dinner. Carbohydrate loading for tomorrow, I hope.

Based on the relative improvement of the sea state here in Bahia Murcielagos (no water balls) and reduced winds (15-25 knots), we decided to try again for San Juan del Sur in the next country North of here. We were motoring toward the tip of Cabo Santa Elena by 0645 with just the stays'l set. This time I manage to drive Quo Vadis around the point. The course of 355 to San Juan was directly into the chop, so I fell off to a more comfortable 330. The sea conditions were still uncertain with wind shifting East, Northeast and North at 15-35 knots. We were clear of Cabo Santa Elena by 0730. I decided to give it an hour and see how things developed. By 0830, we had made 5 nm headway so I ran up the main with a second reef. It seemed everything was still under control, so about 15 minutes later we unfurled 75% of the genoa. Boat speed increased by 35%.

Conditions did not really stabilize within a tight envelope. Wind speed varied from 15 to 40 knots over a 180 degree arc. Wave heights were 2-4 ft. with very short frequency, resulting in a nasty chop with occasional cross chop on this course. There was also about 1 nm/hour of westward set to consider but the boat feels steady and manageable. I feel good we have finally made it around Cabo Santa Elena, winds are tolerable and we're underway to San Juan del Sur on a bright, blue, blustery day when Keith offers his opinion. "We've got to get out of this shit."

I had thought sailing conditions were reasonably good, especially compared to the past two days. I should have told you that all during this Papagayo, the skies have been clear and sunny. They are on this passage, too. It just blows like hell. There are lots of sea turtles on the surface near the boat, apparently unfazed by the wind and waves. They are 2.5 to 4 ft. along the shell; probably Pacific Green or Olive Ridley's turtles. I still can't reliably identify these creatures, except for the rare Leatherbacks. About 1030 and only 12 nm from the San Juan waypoint, we tack back East. I can't hold the 90 mag course I planned but QV is running pretty well, cutting across 3 ft. chop at 8-10 knots. After coming to port tack, the lazy jack "fix" parted. The failure mode was not in the eye to the line but in the epoxy. I thought that stuff was totally unbreakable. New data. This is not an immediate problem. It doesn't interfere with sailing the boat; just dropping the mainsail.

Keith looks out at the not-so-big but frequent whitecaps and says again: "We've got to get out of this shit." I nod vaguely, not feeling any real threat, and continue tacking, spotting sea turtles, and steering for a smoother ride to Nicaragua. This activity results in bringing QV within 2 nm of the waypoint by 1230. Here, the inshore winds have increased to N40-45. I point up. Keith furls the genoa, and we pull the main down against the intact lazy jack. I make out two cruise ships of Bahamas registry in port, including the four-masted Windstar. This vessel has been following me (or getting to port first) since Martinique. Quo Vadis slogs into the harbor under power with no further damage or dowsings at 1400. We find an open area in the bay 16 ft. deep where the winds are only 25 kts. I drop the anchor on a sandy bottom at San Juan del Sur. We're in Nicaragua.

Before I could rig the bridle, the *Ejercito Naval de Nicaragua* patrol boat was alongside. These *marineros* of Nicaragua are wearing purple camouflage fatigues, accessorized with shiny black semi-automatic weapons. Alexis Pozo (per nametag, rank unknown) comes aboard supported by one of his crew, Zarmosa (first name not fitting on nametag, of lower rank). Alexis checked passports, *zarpe*, boat documents, took the copies I had made of everything, and presented me with a "clean" check-in form. Zarmosa made a cursory exam of the boat but didn't seem familiar with the layout of a sailing catamaran. After they departed, Keith and I look at each other, saying together, "Purple camouflage?" We want some. I rig the bridle, put 100 ft. of scope in the water and we both get cleaned up to go ashore. There is still the requirement to take our passports and money to *Migracíon* where, we discover, young Lara Calderon is the resident *migra* official.

She assesses a grand total US$29 to bring the boat and crew of two into the country. That total includes tourist cards. There is no tip jar on her desk but she doesn't have change for US$30.

It's after 1700, so we pass on a visit to the Port Captain's office 'til morning. It must be time for dinner. I introduce us and give our boat name to the Port guards on our way to town and offer them a nominal amount to keep the gates open for our late return. They are friendly and smiling.

Welcome to Wonderful Windy Nicaragua

The usual post-voyage checks reveal that the water tanks are nearly dry, engine oil level is down and there are 11 gallons left in the fuel tank. Gasoline is available at the dock used by the local fishing boats but diesel must be requested through the Port Authority. I make the request. The response is "*Mañana.*" Let's hope so.

Mario's boat looks like something that was kicked out of Disneyland. In profile, it is a miniaturized tugboat. The hull is adorned all around with unmatched fenders, no doubt scavenged from other unfortunate vessels. A metal pipe that looks like an auto exhaust (without muffler) sticks up through the cabin to direct the combustion gases from the two cylinder engine bolted to the deck into the faces of anybody standing to leeward. The vessel's design provides the unlikely characteristic of sudden; unpredictable lurches to either side. Mario steers with a toy-size wooden wheel in a small cabin with no forward visibility. He sticks his head out the side or has his helper call out directions sitting atop the cabin. Wires run across the tiny interior space to a couple of automotive dashboard gauges screwed to the rail. Mario's boat is the harbor water taxi, crew tender, supply shuttle, and cargo carrier. He appears to have the sole franchise. Our first transaction with Mario is filling a jerry jug with fresh water. He returns with the jug for a nominal fee. OK, so far this is working.

Later, we dink ashore and make a beach landing near the Restaurant Lago Azul, soon to become Base Ops/San Juan for the S/V Quo Vadis. Yes, you are correct: the beer is reliably cold and the mostly seafood menu is reasonably priced. I can also keep an eye on the boat and anything else going on out in the harbor. Keith bought a Nicaragua phone card at the post office to call home. He can't make it work. I understand the Spanish instructions better; it still doesn't work. I bought some fresh snapper filets from one of the fish stands on the beach road. We launch the dink through a sloppy shore break and motor home for dinner. I am surprised when my cell phone works. He talks to his parents. I call Meredith. Now they know we're not in Costa Rica any more.

I make *Huachinango* (snapper) *a la Veracruzana* (an old favorite from Mexico), hearts of palm salad, and we drink sauvignon blanc. The wind continues all night at 25-30 knots.

Day 2 anchored at San Juan del Sur: wind is E-NE 35-45 knots in the harbor. Day 3: wind is down to 25 but now the LPG saga begins. More on this later. Day 4: wind is N 30-40; gusts to 50. Day 5: still blowing NE 30-45 knots. An old salt with local experience tells me, "You want better sailing weather? Wait until May." Maybe, but waiting for May then puts any Northbound vessel closer to the insurance companies' definition of hurricane season: June First. If you're not North of 32 degrees latitude by then, you're not covered in a "named storm" loss. That latitude is near the California-Mexico border. Since Quo Vadis is not just my boat but also my home, I take this pretty seriously. Dinner on board is grilled ahi tuna, cottage fries, and a salad made of sweet peppers and tomatoes purchased from the little old grandmother who was carrying them in a basket on her head. This *abuelita* was the real thing.

Getting gassed

As I was making the second batch of fries, the LPG-fueled flame on the stove goes yellow and then goes out. My first reaction is actually positive. "Good timing," I think. I saw a Tropigas outlet in town. "We can get this tank filled in the morning so we'll have full LPG tanks heading North." Full tanks last about 40 days, so this re-fill could cover the rest of the planned voyage.

Well, I was up at 0700 to change out the LPG tank. I screwed the flex hose to the second tank, which was filled in Panama, but could not twist the valve open. Just some salt in there, probably. I put the vise grips on the hand wheel but it still wouldn't move. I asked Keith to put some muscle on it and he did. He snapped the valve stem right off the inner ball valve. There was enough pressure in the "empty" tank to make coffee over the yellow flame. Since the wind was down to 25 knots, I made another excursion up the mast to try and fix the lazy jack.

After stowing the bos'n's chair, tools, glue, etc., we boarded Mario's lurching craft with two trashbags and two LPG tanks. The trimaran Sunshine came into the harbor last night. This morning we meet her British crew, Allen and Stephany, near the town's ATM. I asked them about sailing conditions. They said they were OK in 25-35 knots yesterday. "Just run a small jib downwind." So noted. But unless the wind direction shifts 180, our intended courses are to windward.

Just then, another gringo walked around the corner. He looked better groomed and was wearing cleaner clothes than any of us scruffy sailors. He was also carrying a briefcase. Allen introduces Eric Blackburn, who offered to walk with us to the Tropigas to drop off the LPG tanks still clutched in Keith's hands. (He's the muscle, remember.) I explained the need for a new valve on the full tank and a re-fill for the tank with the working valve. Aurelio responded with the Nicaraguan equivalent of "OK, come back around six." We leave the tanks on his front porch.

I spend most of the afternoon extracting information from Eric and his new book, Cruising Central America. The work is an incredible contribution to sailing and cruising this part of the planet. The only sailing information currently available is incomplete or incorrect to the point of being dangerous. He can't allow me to make a copy according to his deal with the publisher. He also has to include the Costa Rica anchorages. Quo Vadis has just sailed the length of Costa Rica, so I won't need these. Eric invites us back to his house, a modest but traditional Nicaraguan city house with high ceilings, open breezeway, and rocking chairs arranged in the coolest place. Here, we meet Rocio, Robin and Erica: his Nicaraguan wife and kids. I make copious notes and copy the waypoints for all the anchorages from here to Mexico. The kids play on the tile floor until they crawl into little hammocks stretched in the entryway for their nap time. Nobody had to tell them.

Rocio, gracious in the Nicaraguan manner, offers to make lunch. I think buying lunch for them is a better idea. It does leave more food for the house, Eric tells us over a long lunch at Lago Azul. He's been working on his cruising guide since he sailed down from British Columbia and, like the rest of us, saw the need for a complete and current guide to Central America. He worked in the coal mines up in the Kootenai Range on the Canadian side while he built his steel sloop Chickadee. He confided that mining work, being dirty and dangerous, paid pretty well. When the boat was finished, he had Chickadee trucked over the Rockies to the coast. So began his voyage to Nicaragua. In San Juan, he "bumped into Rocio" as he put it. Soon enough, Robin came along; then, Erica. The intrepid young Canadian had a family, a boat and a new home in Nicaragua.

His book looks excellent, useful and thorough. He gives names, photos, waypoints and more info for ports and anchorages along a Coast little known or well-described by others. We agree doing Mexico or Panama is not necessary for his book. Besides, he's doing this at his own expense. Current and future cruisers can sincerely hope the results of his effort have been published. Even better, maybe you're already on your vessel with Cruising Central America in your bookcase. Eric knows the area as a sailor who actually lives and sails here. I consider going back to Costa Rica with him to finish the guide.

I'd discovered yesterday the engine was still leaking. Since we're out of absorbent pads, I stop by the corner *tienda* to buy a couple of boxes of sanitary napkins to soak up the oil in the engine compartment. These have the overwhelming advantage of being widely available and cheap. This particular store also carries that Japanese superglue called "Black Werewolf" (or something like that) and the well-priced but highly rated Nicaraguan rum, *Caño Dorado*. I still have time to check the internet and pull up a weather picture. The weather forecast for the Pacific Coast of Centroamerica looks good to go. I am in full "Good to Go" good mood. I just have to pick up the re-filled propane tanks. Once I get those re-installed, we are set to weigh anchor at dawn.

The tanks were out on the sidewalk, dripping with wet, yellow, streaked paint apparently applied with a very used brush. Aurelio says that Tropigas wouldn't take blue tanks. They would only take yellow tanks; so he painted my tanks yellow. Including the valves, boat name, and safety warning labels. Meanwhile, the tanks haven't been filled nor has there been an attempt to repair or replace the broken valve so the tank could actually be used. I'm guessing he has stroked surplus house paint over the blue rust-resistant finish I had so carefully sprayed on way back in Trinidad. Aurelio said come back tomorrow at ten. Mario's vessel continues to flop from side to side as it carries us back aboard. Dinner is a cold salad. Keith tries the new rum in a mixed drink. My buoyant mood of the afternoon seems to have passed so I pass on the rum.

I spent the next morning up the mast and down in the engine compartment. Armed with the Japanese superglue, I was hauled aloft where I re-tied and re-rigged the lazy jacks. The glued pieces didn't come apart nor, so far, did anything else. This is encouraging though not necessarily permanent. It only takes six maxi-pads to sop up the oil. I can feel it still oozing around the area where William installed the new gasket. I could reach some of the bolt heads with the socket; some others with an open end wrench. I was able to take up about half a turn on the bolts I could reach. Running the engine for 40 minutes did not result in any visible leaks but I suspect that if the bolts I could access were loose, some or all of the others are, too.

Mario has never announced a fixed price for his harbor shuttle service but he makes a face at the 10 colones I give him. Only later did I think that the fare probably varies according to his mood, time of day or night, cargo involved, amount you last paid, and other highly variable factors.

The LPG tanks are gone. Aurelio informs us they may be back by six or seven tonight. His wife is making his lunch. They both clearly resent this rude interruption. Winds were gusting to 50 knots this morning when I was up the mast, so maybe we wouldn't have gone North today.

The *colectivo* to Rivas charges 15 colones/person. When the little car fills up, it rattles up the hill out of San Juan and down into the broad valley around Lago de Nicaragua. This inland body of water stretches halfway across the country. It is inhabited by the only known freshwater sharks. The long fetch across the lake results in the stiff breezes at San Juan del Sur. The lake itself is gray today; flecked with serious whitecaps. Two volcanos on islands are visible through the spray. Another passenger tells us their names and adds that one of them has been active recently.

Rivas is an old colonial city. It is also the market center for this agricultural province. It has few tourist pretensions or visitors. Horse-drawn carriages are used by the locals for in-town travel. If there is only one person, they might use a pedicab: another popular transit mode in this flat town.

The square in the old town has not been restored or cleaned up for potential tourist appeal. The positive side is there aren't any clamorous hawkers. Parts of some of the collapsing colonial townhouses are now working as restaurants. We eat lunch in one, looking through 12 ft. tall doors out to the street and in to the crumbling courtyard. The food is of Centroamerica working lunch quality and quantity. It is encouraging that several *Rivasistas* favor The Golden Chicken for their midday meal. I see the stand-up snack shop squeezed onto the other corner is also packed.

The market sprawls around three sides of the bus and *colectivo* parking area. It is a *Mercado* like those that have been the communal sites of commerce in this part of the world for thousands of years. Rivas being the commercial center for the region, some of the stalls look more permanent. Some even have doors or shutters. Everything imaginable, from freshly butchered animal parts to kerosene lanterns to children's clothing, is offered along with some things I can't identify. I have to ask what they are used for. I don't find any boat parts. This is an agricultural area.

I prepaid the water taxi to bring us back aboard on our return from Rivas, plus 50 colones to come collect us to retrieve the LPG tanks at 1800. After both light and horn signaling from the deck of QV, the unlikely boat wobbles over at 1830. Mario is not at the helm. His assistant looks up at us, grins and says Mario forgot to tell him anything. He believes me about the 50 colones, pre-paid.

We know the route to Tropigas even in the dark, by now. Aurelio says both tank valves are bad so the distributor wouldn't fill either one. (Or replace the broken valve, though this is not explained.) Both canisters are still sticky wet with the streaked yellow paint. Grandly, Aurelio announces, "There is no charge." The empty tank feels heavier, so I suspect it was charged with some amount of liquid propane though not filled before the bad valve so horrified the Tropigas employee.

Keith had offered the opinion that a lot of stuff was broken or rotted on board. In addition to the frozen LPG tank valve, the lazy jack has parted, and he found a sacrificial leather tab on the stays'l foot that had done its job. "That's rotten," he tells me but offers no fix. Now he says, "So we're going North with just one tank?" For some reason, I feel guilty not having still another spare. Something breaks on your boat every day, so why do I still feel personally responsible for this one? Well, the Captain is always responsible but I don't know that I should have expected the LPG tank valve stem to twist off or that Keith would do it by hand.

The water taxi is waiting, as requested. The gate guard with the sawed-off shotgun came on board Mario's boat with us to make a tour around the Bay. Back on Quo Vadis, I studied ports and anchorages in Mexico until I crawl into my bunk around 2100.

On the Route to Luxury

There was enough LPG in the formerly empty tank to make morning coffee. The wind had dropped to NE20-30 knots, so I decided to head for Astillero or Puesta del Sol. They're both along the same course. I bought our *zarpe*, checked the internet weather picture again, and we were underway by early afternoon. We hauled the mainsail up with two reefs as we cleared the harbor. I handed off the helm to Keith. In the lee of the next headland, the wind dropped and I unfurled 50% of the genoa. Back on course, indicated boat speed was 6-8 knots. We were running well on a reach. Even with the wind shifting around and blowing anywhere from 15 to 45, we made good progress Northwest at 7-10 knots. I did hourly position checks and course monitoring. I wanted to stay close to the coast to minimize the wave effect and gain experience running close inshore, which is one recommended strategy for the Gulf of Tehuantepec crossing.

About 1600, I decided to go into Astillero with the intent and hope to fix the tear in the stays'l so we could use it on the continuing run northward. Eric Blackburn had identified and given a name to this anchorage. As we turned into the Bay, the wind came up to 45-55 knots. I pointed up to take some pressure off and Keith furled the genoa. At the waypoint, I held QV slightly off the wind so the main would push against the intact port lazy jack. Keith pulled it down quickly and tied it off. The anchor dragged on the first three attempts to drop it in relatively shallow depths. This was very strange behavior for this boat, this skipper, and this ground tackle. I pulled the hook back up and tried again. The boat was still being pushed back in the unrelenting wind when the CQR anchor caught. I monitored position for 15 minutes, verified we were stuck, and rigged the bridle. The lights at the beach bar went on and the Saturday night party got going. I had no interest in it. Fresh fish tacos and cold white wine in the salon of QV had never tasted so good.

The wind stayed high all night: mostly 35-45 in Astillero Bay. Some cruisers have claimed the anchorage offered good protection from the howling gales "under the cliffs". There are no cliffs to the East: the direction of the wind sandblasts the few boats in the Bay, including mine. I decided to go up the mast and try the lazy jack fix, again. Back to basics: I fastened all the lines with reef knots and wrapped them with rigging tape. I went back up the mast in Meredith's going away present, this time armed with spray adhesive, sailcloth patch tape, and scissors. I managed to spray some adhesive into the rip as Keith announced the wind gauge registered 45 knots. Since the stays'l had to be largely unfurled to fix it, the resulting job was not tidy. I molded the rip together and held it in place by hand. The adhesive dried quickly in the breeze, and on my glove.

By 1100, I had winched down from my airy tasks and stowed bos'n's chair, tools and materials. There was no substantial change in wind conditions or sea state. I determined they were marginal. I also had the distinct sense that Keith wasn't comfortable with a night passage in these winds. I calculated the headings and distances for course changes to Puesta del Sol. Since it doesn't look like we are going there today, I made an alternative decision. Let's eat lunch.

That accomplished, I wiped down the photovoltaic panels and other salt-encrusted hardware with fresh water while Keith rinsed beach sand off the decks. When I woke up from a siesta, the winds were down and the seas quieter. I made steak teriyaki with veggies and rice for dinner. Keith did a thorough clean up and we both were in our bunks as the winds dropped to 20-25 knots.

Something caused me to wake up before first light. It was calm and quiet. There was no howling in the rigging. By dawn, the wind was E20-25 with no whitecaps breaking in the Bay. I roused Keith, briefed him on radio usage and protocol, and set up the autohelm. I laid in the waypoints for Machapa, Puerto Sandino, Corinto and our planned next stop: Puesta del Sol. The wind came up to 35 knots after we cleared the Bay. That same wind speed pushed QV along her Northwest course through the night.

With all sails set, including the recently repaired stays'l, Quo Vadis was making 8-10 knots with Keith at the helm. He reported minimal panga traffic and no other vessels. We furled the genoa for my midnight watch and continued running downwind at 6-8 knots. That and the following seas required lots of rudder work. I'm wondering if William really fixed the steering hydraulic piston. Quo Vadis is running under the stars in seas mostly 3-4 ft. A couple of five-footers from the starboard stern quarter splashed on me. QV passes Puerto Sandino 8 nm offshore by radar.

I correct our heading for wind and set back toward the coast as the waves permit. When Keith comes on watch at 0400, the winds are 20-22 knots. I fall into a sound sleep as soon as I shuck my gear and hit the bunk. This skipper's sleep is interrupted at 0700 when he is informed wind speeds are 5-6 knots with boat speed at one knot. I don't think that is even steerage way, so the engine goes on and the sails come down. Keith tells me he was visited by small black dolphins, leaping alongside. I congratulate him on his good fortune and crash back on my bunk.

When I come back on watch at 0800, there is the Nicaraguan coast lined with volcanos. Some are active with smoke and steam blowing out of their tops. All of them are starkly impressive in the early morning light. We motor past the deeply colored cones, hands off the wheel. The autohelm works well without bumpy following sea and winds. Against the spectacular volcano background, miles of empty sand beaches fringed with palms or jungle, and the foreground of blue Pacific, we are cruising through a postcard. Wait, there's a blue and white catamaran in the picture. We are the postcard! Somebody needs to get out there about 50 ft. to port and capture the image.

There is a variance between my two sources for the Puesta del Sol waypoint coordinates. There is no sea buoy at either of them but I see red and green channel buoys inside. I got Keith up and turned through the beach break, ranging on the volcano barely visible through the smoke from the burning cane fields. In the channel, I hailed Puesta del Sol. The response: "Come on in. We're waiting for you." A friendly greeting and channel markers. Haven't had those in a while. QV emerges from the channel into a placid, protected lagoon. Large cut stone and masonry buildings are on the North shore. I see mooring balls and people standing on a small dock area.

I request a mooring buoy but a fellow wearing a big straw hat tells me the dock is available. I inquire about the depth alongside, and the straw-hatted man tells me it is plenty deep: 4 meters. (The available information for Puesta del Sol did not identify docking as an option.) QV is guided to an outside floating finger pier. I see it has freshwater and power connections. Keith kicks out fenders and hands the dock lines. We are met by Luís and the fellow in the straw hat who introduces himself as Robert. He sees Alameda, California is our hailing port and tells us he was also from the San Francisco Bay Area. We are secure by 1030 and go ashore with passports and boat docs to register. It is the first marina I've been in since Solomon's Island (way back in the Chesapeake) that asked for evidence of insurance. Many cruisers don't carry any boat insurance, especially if they own their boat outright. Keith heads for the pool while I make us a hot lunch. We like the local *chorizo* mixed with eggs and chopped sweet peppers. I slice an avocado on top.

"Robert" on the dock is Señor Roberto Membreno, founder and owner of Marina Puesta del Sol. Later, I learn he built this well-equipped marina because he couldn't find one in Nicaragua to dock his boat after he sailed here from California. I can barely imagine the permitting process he has endured. When we arrive, it is still a work in progress. It is still the only marina in the country.

Making Music Videos

After lunch, Keith and I are the only ones hanging around the bar under the oversized *palapa*. In the early afternoon, an unmarked bus pulls up in a cloud of dust and a bunch of mostly young passengers start getting out. They're carrying satchels so I assume it's a school class trip or a group from town that's arranged to come to the beach for an outing, something like that.

I slowly realize the class consists of slim, good-looking young women. I've heard that Nicas are *muy linda*: very pretty. When I go to the clean, tiled men's room to recycle some beer, there is an older guy standing in front of the mirror fixing his hair and putting on make-up. Despite this activity, I inanely ask, "Visiting Puesta del Sol for the day?" He looks at me like "Isn't that obvious since I'm already here?" but he is polite. "Yes, it's going to be a fun day. So much to get done." Now I think <u>he</u> is being obvious. Bar, beach, pool, lagoon. OK, there's a lot to do.

By the time I amble back out toward the bar, the schoolgirls from the bus have changed into trendy dance or resort outfits, gathered on the hardwood floor under the *palapa*, and are mugging at a videocam. This is *La Nueva Companía*, a Nicaraguan pop group. They are here to shoot a video. Keith is sitting on a bar stool, leering. I try not to leer but I do begin to see just how far out of the mainstream of popular culture I really am. For me, this is usually a good thing. Cruising the coast of Central America, you don't really expect to stumble on to a music video shoot.

The sound guy starts their CD. The director acts like a director trying to direct all this bouncy young talent. The choreographer (wearing a black mesh T-shirt and tight black pants, of course) tries to get the girls to follow this dance routine he has put together to showcase the group's tunes…and *las chicas Nicas*. After a few tries, they are all movin' and shakin' in real time. The guy I met in the men's room then jumps out in front of the dancers, puts on a big smile, and starts singing their new pop hit. After a few takes, the director squints into the video eyepiece and seems satisfied with what he sees on re-run. *"A la playa!"* he commands. The young women disappear into the changing room and quickly re-appear wearing brightly-colored bikinis, mostly of the string variety. A couple of them wear hats to accent their personal style. To the beach!

Keith and I follow the cast and crew down the crushed rock path, past the boat docks, across the airstrip to the Puesta del Sol beach bar. This part of the marina is organized under an enormous *palapa*. It is visible from miles out at sea. On shore, it is next to a shallow swimming pool featuring raised concrete blocks arranged in a pattern across the pool, all of it painted blinding white. Some of the girls get up on the blocks, some stand in the water, a line of four stands on the top steps of the pool. The attending bartender unlocks the walk-in cooler and asks what we'd like to drink. *"Cervezas, por favor."* Keith and I are still the only audience but we are an appreciative, enthusiastic audience.

The music starts again, the girls repeat their dance, the director adjusts some positions and they try another take. I can't believe this is happening to us. We have been days at sea in heavy winds.

All too soon, I hear the familiar refrain of all directors on location, "Hurry up! We're losing our light." But not before they do one more take. The music starts. The girls dance in front of a golden sun as it sinks into a darkening Pacific. The director and I had already exchanged business cards. He's been very cordial about us hanging out on the set; gawking at the lovely Latinas but he does not invite us to the cast party. I wish I'd had the presence of mind to invite the young ladies on board Quo Vadis and taken some snapshots. If I ever want to sell the boat that would be a killer photo to use on the sales sheet. I haven't had a *siesta*. I have had several *cervezas*. But I'm not sleepy so I proceed to make us a hot dinner on board. It is late when we finally crash. The whole day seemed like we had slipped through a warp into another, not quite parallel, universe.

Back to Reality

The universe where we spend most of our time comes crashing back in full force. The cane fields are still burning night and day, creating a steady rain of sticky black ash on deck and dock.

Luís arranged for what must be the only mobile pumpout station in Central America to come rolling down the dock and empty the holding tanks. He also manages to fill the propane tanks with no fuss or color change. Different guys come on board at different times and bang on the stuck port turning block. They all leave without fixing it or telling me. I discover the hydraulic piston is still leaking and suspect the O-rings I found in the bottom of the compartment were not the "old ones" as William had claimed. While Keith is washing and drying the salon cushions, I trudge up the dirt road to the *pulpería*. This is what the local general stores are called. This one is open air. The proprietress provides eggs, bread, fish, veggies and beer, so we must be ready to shove off. Well, not quite. *Migracion*, *aduana* (customs) and the *Fuerza Naval* all come to visit Quo Vadis. Important pieces of paper and several Nicaraguan banknotes are exchanged. It really is nice of them to make house calls, though I suspect Robert had some influence in this matter.

By dawn's early light we are underway toward the Golfo de Fonseca. This fairly large gulf is shared, with some tolerance, by Nicaragua, Honduras and El Salvador. We're not aware of any current active border disputes although Nicaragua and Honduras sometimes go at it. I set course for Punta Consinguina, the eastern end of the Golfo, noting the presence of two reefs and two "obstructions" on the chart. Andy Spears, an Alaskan charter skipper on warm water holiday, also advised us that Speck Reef was not the size or in the location shown on the chart. Good to know. There is no wind this morning which allows us to spot turtles in a calm sea and, just after rounding the point, several very large rays floating at the surface.

The wind comes up enough to fill sails, so we set them with the breezes SW10-15 knots as we approach Isla Meanguera. Then it comes up to 25. This is a common event, well-known to most cruisers. The wind will come up when you're ready to anchor, even if it has been dead calm until that very moment. We check out the waypoint anchorage and the cove at the little village.

There's no information on holding or surrounding depths at the village, so we fall back and drop the hook. Three little boys hand-paddled a boy-sized dugout from shore to check us out. Their craft has been dug out of ceiba wood which is very light and soft, almost like cork. The ceiba is the totemic tree of Central America. It protects itself with big spikes on its trunk, sheds its leaves to save water in the dry season, and provided the kapok for all the life jackets until synthetic materials were chemically induced to float. The boys' ceiba dugout canoe is painted bright green.

Keith wants to try paddling the little dugout. Josué, Marvin and Roberto (We learn their names.) were all paddling it but Marvin claims the craft is his and cooperates. His reward is a Coke and watching Keith repeatedly capsizing the boy-sized craft. When he finally gets in, both his arms and legs stick out from the green shell, giving a fair impression of a turtle on its back. Keith wants to buy a mini-dugout. Marvin is not parting with this one. All three boys paddle back to shore.

By the time I get back on board from a swim and shower, the boys are back to entertain the crazy gringos. Two of them are now paddling plastic washtubs. Darker-skinned Josué, called *Negrito* by the others, has taken over the dugout. They paddle gleefully around QV. I made a Chinese-style cucumber salad and pasta with a red meat sauce for our early dinner. Keith cleaned up.

Morning finds Quo Vadis motoring across the Golfo de Fonseca on an oily smooth swell. I had checked the engine oil before start-up and topped it up. The absorbent pad under the engine was still all white; not much in the way of leakage. After the 0900 position check, I looked in the engine compartment for any possible leak. There was hardly any oil visible but water filled the engine space up to the drive coupling. This was new and different.

After shutting down, opening up the inspection panel, and getting Keith to restart the engine I see water spraying off the water pump drive pulley. I can't actually see a leak or feel one at any of the hose connections. I give the hand signal to shut back down and mentally debate continuing to Barillas or…something else. Since QV is floating off Punta Ampala, I decide to go in and look for a diesel mechanic. Guys in two different pangas said there was one in Tamarindo. This Tamarindo is not a fashionable resort town. It's the name of a shallow estuary at the North end of the bay and its fishing village. It has definitely not been discovered by tourists.

We motor past the breakers into the shallow Bahía at low RPM with water still spraying into the engine compartment. As soon as I had the anchor down in 5 ft. way off the beach, a panga came up to sell fish. I negotiated instead for a ride ashore and help in locating a diesel mechanic.

The first candidate was "*El Viejito*". He didn't get out of his hammock or have any tools. The second guy was in his hammock sleeping off an early Saturday drunk. He rolled groggily out of his webbed refuge but didn't have the tools or knowledge of diesels. (He was determined to make us understand his specialty was outboards.) The third *mecánico* worked at *Taller Motores Marinos* (Marine Motor Shop) which sounded promising. He wasn't there. The helpful couple who were there made several phone calls to track him down. He tells me he doesn't know about diesels, either. Maybe "Chamba" could come from Puerto Triunfo on Monday. Our guide, Douglas, guides us to the beachfront shack that sells ice and beer. I hate to think this may be the high point of our day. Back on board Quo Vadis, we put the interior cushions out to dry. I make a cold lunch. We did not get much accomplished today. Douglas agrees to return tomorrow and continue guiding our search. Though shallow, this is not a bad anchorage. I wonder why Eric Blackburn did not mention it in his guide. It's open to the South but winds are seasonal.

A 10 ft. tide puts us 15 ft. above the sandy bottom of Ampala by morning. Douglas never re-appears. Maybe because it is Sunday. My decision is to go to Barillas, the marina in El Salvador. The engine starts up and the compartment starts filling with water. I fall into a necessary routine of pumping it out by hand at hourly intervals. It's a sailboat, you might be thinking, why not sail to Barillas? First, there is no wind. Second, when it does come up, it is from the Southwest along our WSW course.

I had called Barillas on my cell about 0900 to request mooring and advise them we had a problem. They provided updated waypoint coordinates for the entry to Bahía de Jiquilisco and seemed to understand our situation. We are told to make it to the entry by 1500 to meet the guide boat. A quick calculation confirms we won't get there sailing these winds. The engine restarts without a problem except for the water flooding the compartment. I go back to pumping out the seawater as Keith steers along the 10 meter line, following the shorter inshore route.

As we close to about 2 nm from shore, a guy on a jet ski wearing only a tank top and swim trunks roars up to the boat. He yells, "Barillas is waiting. Call for the guide boat on CH16 when you're one hour out." He turns around and jets back toward shore. The Southwest wind is pushing a 3-4 ft. chop at us when we get to the southern shoal. We work around the shoal to deeper water and are just past the new waypoint when a panga appears bouncing in very rough, short seas. The *panguero* turns and motions for us to follow. There are 6 ft. breakers just to the North. I fall in behind the panga which winds through the estuary for 1 hr 45 min to the mooring field. I swing the boat 180 back into the tidal current and we're on the ball by 1700. The engine is still running.

Barillas provides, much like the Costa Rica Yacht Club, moorings in the tidal estuary of a very large mangrove swamp. A Navy guy, a National Police guy and Hediberto Pineda, manager of the marina, are alongside within minutes. Luís, for that is our guide's name, takes us ashore to sign in and get our passports stamped at the on-site immigration office, which is open just for us on Sunday. This is done promptly and appears to be a considerable source of pride for Sr. Pineda. "We promise to clear you in within one hour," he proclaims. I hope it works the same for clearing out.

When I explain our mechanical predicament, he is less helpful. "You speak Spanish well enough to find somebody to help you." From Quo Vadis' aft deck, I can see a good-sized boatyard on the other side of the high wall surrounding the manicured grounds of the marina. I hope it will be open tomorrow.

Adventures in El Salvador

Barillas is a fairly new fancy resort plonked down in an estuary miles from anyplace else. It has the requisite landscaping, tiled swimming pool, mini-mart, open air bar and restaurant, maintained airstrip—all the features of your not-so-basic Latin American place for the privileged to visit. On the other side of a small steel door in the otherwise plain concrete wall around the resort is the industrial-strength shipyard Prestomar. The yard's steady work is keeping the shrimping fleet working. This fleet is based just up the estuary. The steel door is usually locked. Most of the staff at Barillas, especially Sr. Pineda, goes to great lengths to keep these two worlds separate. Frankly, I don't get it.

Somehow, I do get through the wall. My Spanish is good enough to track down the yard foreman, Elias, and tell him about our situation. He has to check with *El Ingeñiero* but thinks he can schedule Quo Vadis into his work load. He calls the hydraulic supply store in San Salvador, the capital city, to verify they can fix the steering arm piston. They can— for US$45 with two day turnaround. So far, so good. The *ingeñiero* agrees to schedule the work and Martín is assigned to work on *el yate* Quo Vadis. First, Elias has to go find Martín. The US$ quote is exactly that. El Salvador has adopted the Yankee dollar as its national currency as part of a plan to control inflation. Besides, none of the neighboring countries would take their other money.

Martín is a cheery little fellow with a lot of Mixtec in him and a constant smile. He is polite to me, since I am Capitán Juan, without being obsequious. He is, after all, a marine mechanic. In El Salvador, that doesn't necessarily mean he costs three times the normal price. After he removes the water pump, he determines the pump bearing has seized which, in turn, shredded the seal. Seawater poured out. If the supplier has the correct replacement bearing, he can fix it. This is the "new" water pump installed at Solomon's Island. I kept the original as a spare but choose to go with Martín's solution. It's still a long way to California. I give them the bearing part number and emphasize this is the all-steel version. There is a bearing of the same size and type that is a combination of steel and phenolic material. I have no idea how I've retained this esoteric bit of data. Scary.

The market bus to Usulutan leaves at 0900. We are on shore and on it along with marina staff, crew from two other cruising boats, and our gun-toting guards. The crew from the sloop Patagonia consists of Zenco, Gloria and Tanya. They started from California; are now headed South to the Canal and on to the Caribbean. I ask them about port clearances in Mexico. Gloria explains it was tedious and very bureaucratic. "We thought we could do it ourselves since, you know, we speak good Spanish." Well, yes, they do speak that language very well since they are Argentine.

(Keith tells me later he thought they were just another Southern California couple: Gloria with natural blonde hair.) Tanya actually is a California girl, born in Berkeley. She is four years old.

The bus driver agrees to stop at a bank ATM so we can extract cash to spend at the market. The first machine he takes us to isn't working. The other ATM in Usulutan is functional. It even responds to my card, dispensing US$200 in the form of 40 very used $5 bills. This makes quite a wad of Lincolns. Gloria has the same result.

"It's better to have the small bills," she smiles.

Out here in the country, all males over the age of 12 carry machetes. When not in use this serious blade is usually slung over their shoulder, often in fringed scabbards. Guys are strolling down the street carrying big swords. The weapon of choice for guards is a semi-automatic shotgun. This is what the greeters at the door of Don Juan La Dispensa supermarket are carrying when the gringo shoppers step out into the market's parking lot. One of the greeting guards smiles; the other one doesn't.

La Dispensa has everything but I prefer the prices for fresh produce at the stalls along the street outside the gate. While I'm collecting several pounds of tomatoes for US$1, one of the older sellers comes out from behind her tidy piles of fruit and asks me in dialect,

"*Mi amor*, when are you going to take me to America?" ("Mi amor" is a fairly standard greeting in these parts, sort of like "Hon" around Baltimore.) Her query is accompanied by a big grin punctuated with random teeth. A few of them are gold.

"Whenever you're ready," I reply in my colloquial Spanish. "Let me just pay for these."

"*Ai, era una broma!*" she exclaims, letting everybody in our gathering audience in on the joke. When I tell her the trip would be on a sailboat, she acts less interested and goes back to her baskets and boxes. She allows me to take a picture, not always true with indigenous people. Keith and I eat hot dogs from a street pushcart and survive.

Now equipped with fresh provisions, I invite the family on **Patagonia** over to **Quo Vadis** for sundowners. I think Tanya is the youngest guest ever to come aboard QV. I trade my Panama courtesy flag and a Panama cruising guide for some of Zenco's Mexico charts which help to fill gaps in my chart coverage.

"Glad you can use them," says Zenco. "I don't plan to go this way by boat, again." I agree with him.

Just at dawn, a light rain coming through the open hatches wakes me. I close the hatches. I later assign myself the job of cleaning the encrusted salt and oil off the engine; then cleaning out that compartment. Keith starts de-rusting the davits. While we're so engaged, a Salvadoran Navy patrol boat motors into the anchorage. It is towing a vintage wooden ketch flying a U.S. flag. The ketch's crew of two was headed South when the boat's transmission shaft coupling broke. As is usually the case, the reason they were motoring was severe lack of wind: the same condition we'd experienced the last several days coming North. They had been adrift with slack sails for four days before they had a response to radio calls. It made our situation look pretty damn good, in comparison.

This boat was a new purchase. "Well," said Dennis the skipper. "I learned how the boat handles in light air." He was headed to St. Croix. Now, he has detoured on to the work schedule at Prestomar boatyard.

Fuel and water tanks were topped off. Bunk cushions got dried out. The hydraulic piston was delivered after only a couple of *"Mañana."* promises and installed so the steering was functional. While waiting for the part, I got majorly pissed off at the fairly new Stone-Kold reefer because it was (still) not cooling. I messed with the thermostat, on/off settings, and anything else I could glean from the 4 page operating booklet. The reason I replaced the Adler-Barbour cold plate unit in Trinidad was so I wouldn't have a problem. I ended up buying ice and putting our meats and perishables in the on-deck cooler. I had already entered the waypoint and plotted the course for Acujutla, the last anchorage identified in El Salvador. The plan is to skip Guatemala. I've heard nothing good about the port facilities or port authorities at Puerto Quetzal. The entry fee is US$100, whether you stay for a day or a month.

I provisioned again, paid the shipyard, the marina and the fee for the exit *zarpe*. I'm using my regular version of Central American Spanish with the marina staff, settling accounts and otherwise checking out. Things are proceeding along at the expected pace when Hediberto Pineda abruptly interrupts and admonishes me to speak English.

"They can't understand your Spanish!" Funny, I spoke the same language in the same way well enough when I checked in that he told me to go arrange for repair work on my own. I choose not to exchange insults with him because it is time to leave Barillas.

We wait for the ebb tide, then follow Luís' panga out to the Barillas ocean waypoint. I think I had the route down well enough to go out alone but there was no need to risk it. (I later read of another catamaran pounded to pieces on the bar and shoals at this entrance to Bahia Jiquilisco. The skipper had made a series of questionable decisions, including not using a guide boat, which resulted in the loss of the vessel.)

As soon as QV clears the strange, big break to the North of the access route, her sails go up. Based on the limited info available, the weather window looked big enough to go all the way to Mexico without stopping at Acajutla. The sea state is moderate. Winds are light and, wonderfully, from the Southwest. The fuel tank is full with 10 gallons in reserve. I set four hour watches with my usual midnight turn at the wheel. We pass by Puerto Quetzal, and the rest of Guatemala, during the night with no regret.

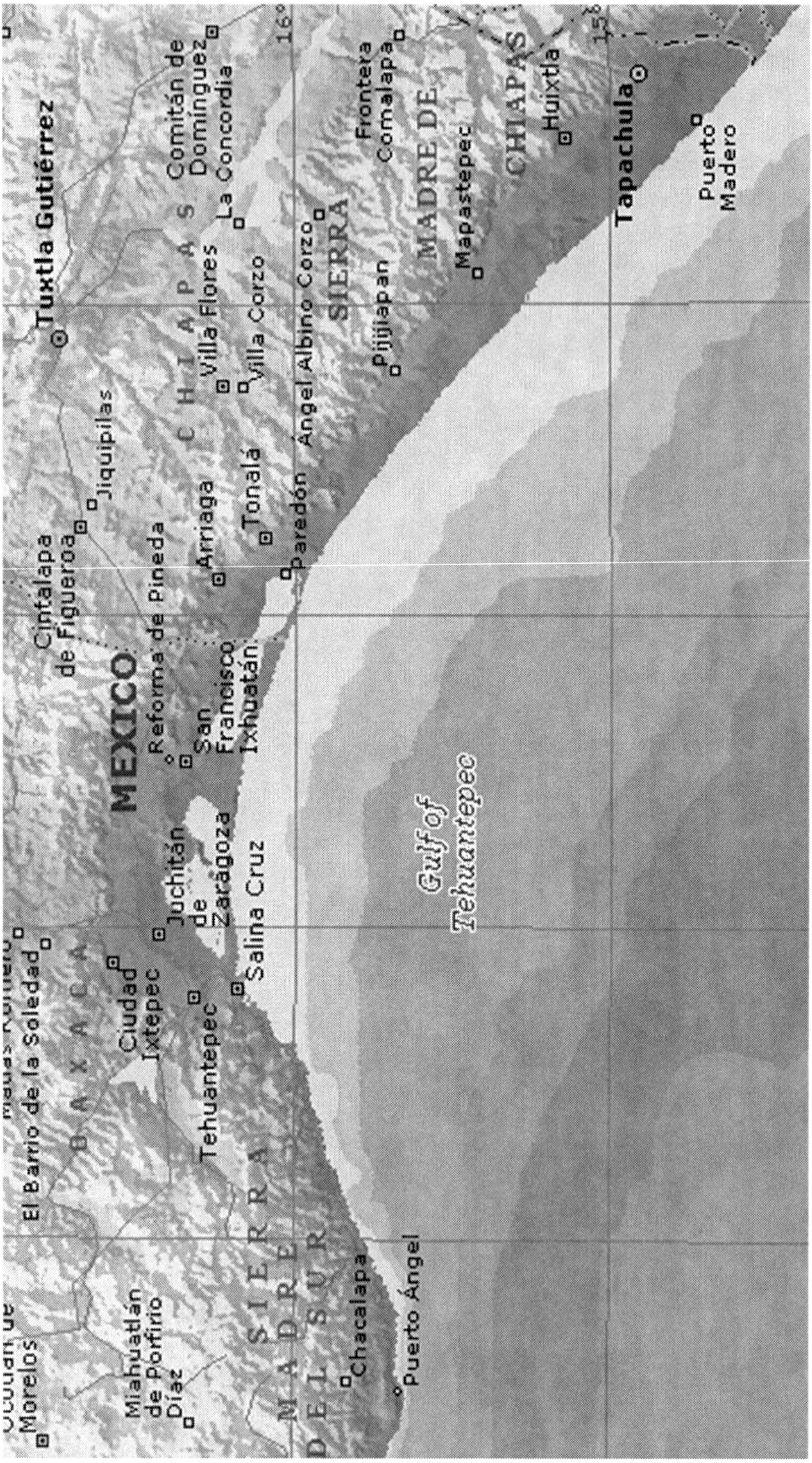
Tuxtla Gutiérrez
Comitán de Domínguez
La Concordia
Frontera Comalapa
Huixtla
Tapachula
Puerto Madero
Mapastepec
SIERRA MADRE DE CHIAPAS
Pijijiapan
Ángel Albino Corzo
Villa Corzo
Villa Flores
C H I A P A S
Jiquipilas
Cintalapa de Figueroa
Arriaga
Tonalá
Paredón
Reforma de Pineda
MEXICO
San Francisco Ixhuatán
Juchitán de Zaragoza
Salina Cruz
Gulf of Tehuantepec
Ciudad Ixtepec
Tehuantepec
El Barrio de la Soledad
O A X A C A
S I E R R A M A D R E D E L S U R
Miahuatlán de Porfirio Díaz
Chacalapa
Puerto Ángel

El Golfo de Tehuantepec

Aboard S/V Quo Vadis, docked Marina Chahue, Oaxaca, Mexico

We motorsailed from El Salvador to Puerto Madero, described as a commercial fishing port lying barely inside the Mexican border. I made the decision to clear in to Mexico at Puerto Madero, fill the fuel tank, and get the current weather forecast before crossing the Golfo de Tehuantepec. This body of water is infamous for incredibly strong North winds which come up with little or no warning and can last for days. It is about 230 nm across. For most sailors, this dictates a two day weather window to make an anchorage on the far Western side of the Gulf, preferably in the Bahías de Huatulco.

Madero turned out to be a complete hole: the worst I'd encountered on the Pacific coast. I should have taken the hint. A gringo on a sailboat leaving the dock area just as we sailed in yelled to us, "Get fuel quickly and get going."

At the same time, I was hearing radio calls in Spanish to a U.S. boat. Call me egocentric or just plain stupid but I thought the calls were directed to Quo Vadis. It turned out the Mexican navy was trying to stop the fleeing sloop and make them clear in or out, whichever they hadn't done. Trying to be correct and turning out to be naïve, I responded to the radio calls, which must have surprised the Navy guy, especially when I agreed to accept a ride to the Port Captain's office to clear in. We set the hook, launch the dink and motor in, tying off to broken and slimy concrete slabs below the rusted ladder up to the fuel dock.

The road to the Port Captain's office, which was prominently visible from both the inlet and anchorage, leads through town past the ship agent's office. There is nobody there and I stupidly still don't get what this detour has to do with us. I don't need a ship's agent to clear in to a port where they speak Spanish… or French, or English for that matter. Wrong. This Port Captain requires everybody to use this particular ship's agent, as I discover after collecting some of the entry paperwork at the *Capitanía* and being directed back to the agent. Finally, I start to get it.

The agent is "In" upon our return and wants about $50 for his services which consist of filling out a one page form and taking us to the local airport for the immigration ladies to stamp our passports. I allow as how I can handle these tasks. He informs me that this Port Captain requires an agent. Now, I understand. I negotiate a pitiful $10 reduction in fees. I didn't think until later what percentage of the Port Captain's kickback that might be and, maybe, I only succeeded in irritating him. After the airport, we move Quo Vadis to the fuel dock, rafted up outside the rustiest fishing boats I have ever seen still floating. We can't stay at the dock so move the boat back on the hook, trying not to block access to the docks. Especially after I noticed that none of the commercial boats were paying any attention to our location in daylight or in dark. There was no place we saw in Puerto Madero that looked appetizing enough to actually eat there. And you will recall, if you've stayed with me this far, that I'm not all that squeamish about Third World edibles.

Strolling out on deck at dawn revealed Quo Vadis was floating in a shallow pool surrounded by evil-smelling mud flats. The flats were coated with an oily sheen and studded with jagged trash and previously submerged wrecks. A narrow, shallow channel through the glistening mud let us dink ashore to clear out. And see if there was any provisioning at any market before heading across the infamous Golfo de Tehuantepec. The ship's agent somehow got involved in this activity and a couple of the subordinates at the *Capitanía* thought they should get some financial compensation when I tried to get a weather update. I finally ended up in the Port Captain's office. We do our introductions, smile and chat. He, finally, prints out a weather map while assuring me the three indicated Lows won't be a problem. Highs are the killers. Based on current and forecast conditions, there appears to be a two day window to get across the Gulf. Five out of six of the skippers interviewed while I was doing research for this passage had confirmed 48 hours was adequate and told of flat, smooth crossings. The other skipper (Zenco and family on Patagonia) had experienced winds to 35 kts off the lagoons at the Northern end of the Gulf but no winds higher, even in that most vulnerable stretch, and no other problem aside from motoring the final part of the crossing to Guatemala after the winds died. By now, I knew why they had all skipped Puerto Madero. Also, they were all going South with more favorable current and wind direction.

Keith and I were back on board after a pricey cab ride to the docks, got the dink and motor stowed, anchor up and were motoring out past the breakwater within an hour and a half. There was no wind. Low, oily smooth rollers passed under the *amas* at long frequency. We headed north on the 30 ft. depth line. This put us between a half-mile to a mile off the beach. The night passed quietly. There was not enough wind to sail.

The next day we were about 100nm northwest along the Gulf shore with about 130nm to go. I did the calcs after I came on watch at noon. The results showed we wouldn't make Huatulco until 2000-2100 the next night. I am never too pleased with the risk involved trying to anchor on a rocky, unknown, unmarked coast in the dark. There was still no wind as the long, oily swells slid under the hulls. I decided to cut across toward Salina Cruz which could also serve as a port of last resort, though it is not a cruiser-friendly place to put in. Based on our speed over the surface, this course change would save 4-5 hours and let us get on the hook well before dark as well as opening up the possibility to get into Marina Chahue: our planned destination in the Bahías de Huatulco.

Keith was up at 1600 for his watch. I explained the new course and plan. The seas and the engine continued to run smoothly so I went below to make some soup before crashing. I never did get to eat that soup.

Keith called down the companionway. The wind was up to 15-20 kts. Time to get some sail up. We got the main up and unfurled about 75% genoa. Within 15 minutes, it was gusting to 35 kts, so we furled the genoa, reefed the main and unfurled the stays'l. Within 30 minutes, we were seeing wind up to 45 kts. A quick position check put us about halfway across the gulf. I decided to try a course change to Salina Cruz as the seas started to build. I had never seen a sea state develop so fast. With the engine on, we could just point Quo Vadis toward Salina Cruz but were not getting any closer to that commercial port after an hour of this. It was also nearly dark by now with no moon.

I clipped in to the jack line and went forward to deploy the sea anchor. Big waves were breaking over the foredeck in a random manner as I pulled the bag out and felt for the fastening eyes. I verified which end was what by flashlight and got most of the parachute out on the deck when a bigger wave washed over the foredeck. Then, another one covered the deck before I'd made any more progress with the sea anchor. Sometime about in here, some little part of my brain told me I was at greater risk crawling around the foredeck under the intermittent breaking waves than any reward potentially to be gained from getting a sea anchor deployed. I stuffed the parachute, leads, swivel, etc. back in the bag, jammed the bag in the hatch, closed the hatch and worked my way back to the cockpit using the handrail and moving the clip along the jack line. Waves kept breaking over the decks. The psychologically unsettling part of this situation is I couldn't see them coming; then, sploosh!

The glow in the sky to the West had to be the lights of Salina Cruz' big commercial docks. I sent Keith below to make some "Pan, Pan" calls on the VHF, hailing the Mexican Navy. After three calls at 10 minute intervals in both English and Spanish, we had no response. So I asked him to make some general, "Any station" Pan Pan calls. Same format, no response. We continued radio calls for an hour. The realization came to us that we were strictly on our own. Nobody heard us or, if they did, nobody was going to respond. We were strictly on our own no matter what happened.

By 2000, the seas are 12 ft., sustained wind is 50 kts., and the engine over-temperature alarm starts going off. I hope this is just due to the cooling water inlet coming out of the water, because I don't have any clever solution to the problem otherwise.

I am back at the wheel. Keith has gone below. I glance through the helm portlight into the salon and see him lying on the starboard settee with my navy blue blanket pulled up to his nose and his eyes closed. The thing that bothered me the most about the immediate situation was that it was my blue blanket.

I can't get Quo Vadis to heave to and hold its position, so I do the only thing I can figure out to do and know how to make work. I sail the boat.

The sustained winds are at 65 kts. I am seeing frequent gusts above 80; some to 90 on the anemometer readout. These numbers scare me so I try not to look at the instruments anymore. The glow in the sky from Salina Cruz is fading over the horizon as the boat is pushed South. We are losing ground. The engine over-temp alarm starts shrilling and momentarily freaks me out. But, with just the stays'l set, I think the engine is the component that allows Quo Vadis to have some directional control and quarter into the breaking seas so I don't shut it off. I also don't want to risk a failure to re-start. Occasionally, one of these above-referenced 12 ft. waves breaks over the coach roof and into the cockpit. This is a bad surprise involving hundreds of gallons of green water. It is also mentally abusive since you can't see the waves coming. Tensing up in anticipation gets to be tiring. The wind continues throughout the night over 65 kts. (I can't help sneaking peaks at the readout; but just scare myself and wonder how the anemometer is still attached to the mast.)

I hear a dull crunch sound as the starboard davit is ripped off. I am so obsessed with helm control I don't at first see the foot square hole torn in the aft deck. The dinghy twists in the wind on the port davit, horizontal behind the boat. How much water will come in the hole? What if it pulls the stern down? What if the other davit pulls out? Pilots know that you don't want to run out of altitude, airspeed or ideas. I am running out of ideas. I'm alone at the helm, winds are 65-80 knots, the seas I can't see how big in the night, and we're being swept out into the Golfo de Tehuantepec. Well, my kids will have the life insurance and it's a good story. This is an OK way to go out, if that's what happens.

I cannot rouse Keith to come on deck so I stand at the helm until sun-up: about 0600. The morning light also reveals the sea state. Waves are 16-18 ft. with intermittent sets over 20 ft. These bigger ones seem to come in groups of three bunched closer together. Inevitably, one of them breaks on to the deck or into the cockpit. The good news is the wind has dropped to 45 kts which, by contrast to 65 during the night, feels almost manageable.

Now realizing I am hypothermic and my legs are cramping (probably due to dehydration), I again pound on the coach roof and yell down to Keith: "Hey, come on up here. I can't be the only one having all the fun!"

He is reluctant to move but I eventually get him out of the cabin to take the wheel. I show him the technique I've been using: Drive Quo Vadis up the face of a wave so that the wave breaks between the *amas* and the boat coasts down the backside into the face of the next wave. "Cowboy it," I explain, like mounting the wave crests and riding them out. The timing is important, obviously. Sometimes the sets are too close together and you still get pounded.

I am completely salt encrusted. It looks like a layer of morning frost on a statue. My hair and beard have grown crystals. I notice this in the port head mirror as I try to wash my face. I also notice my left eye is caked shut and aching. A droplet of water moving at least 65 MPH hit the eyeball just before dawn and, water being an incompressible fluid, made an impact on my left eye like a shotgun pellet. Now, I can't see from it. I collapse, dripping, on to the port settee.

For some reason, I am back at the wheel at 0900 after a deep sleep of exhaustion. Best I can calculate, we've been blown about 50nm off our intended course. I give Keith a new heading with a big compensation factor for wind and collapse for another two hours. The wind continues to abate to 35 kts, though the seas don't, so we are too far East when I wake up again. I plot a new course to get us to Huatulco but worry that we have squandered valuable daylight hours.

Capitán El Sensitivo did not realize it but Keith is physically scared. He eventually describes himself as being nauseous and feeling "weak in the knees". It hadn't occurred to me but this is now another factor to be considered in any planning. I don't recall seeing this before, except maybe when I was in Airborne training. That poor kid was eighteen, black, and recently drafted. I was three years older. Back then, that frightened soldier wasn't my responsibility. The crew of Quo Vadis is.

We are still East of Huatulco when we make landfall about 1700, so head West along the coast. It is rocky, looks unfriendly to boats and I can find no alternate anchorages on the chart or, so far, by eyeball. I also discover the depthsounder is going out. (This model sounds only to 200 ft. depth so its operation, or lack of it, isn't apparent until entering shallower waters.) The rubber-covered buttons have been pounded out of the instrument face during night. Every wave that came in the cockpit washed into the open panel. Keith also notes a slow steering response. After initial skepticism, I finally see the starboard rudder is not responding to the helm. This is because the rudder bar has snapped. At sunset, we are still 12nm from Huatulco. I enter a waypoint outside the first bay where the chart shows comfortably deep water; then plot a heading between the rocks shown, into the first protected anchorage of the five Bahías de Huatulco. The unknowns include any uncharted rocks, errors in depth charted or sounded, and, of course, my navigation.

After dark, we find out we have only a starboard running light. The masthead array is gone. It looks wet inside the red lens of the port running light. Well, at least it's the light facing the coast that works. We approach the waypoint and drop sail, turning slowly toward the rock-framed entrance. The depth sounder has quit working. A *panguero* coming out of the bay yells at us for having no masthead light. I'm now at the bow, hoping to see anything with my one working eye before we hit it. We don't hit anything, and I drop the hook in a gap between two big rocks in front of a brightly lit resort hotel on the beach of Bahía Tangolunda. As a final irony, there is no wind in this bay so we back down on the anchor lightly. It sticks. The time is 2030. This is just the scenario I'd planned to avoid 30 hours ago. Happy, touristy Mexican music comes across the water from the resort. The interior of Quo Vadis looks pretty well tossed. I can't even remember getting to my bunk but wake up there the next day with the sun already high, bright and hot.

Other boats; other crossings

Our projected 48 hour-plus weather window slammed shut in about 28 hours. We got our asses kicked by a T-pecker. We survived it with limited personal injury and a boat that could still sail, though holed in the deck and sails so tattered they looked like the shipwrecks in cartoons. What surprised me in the weeks that followed were the stories from other skippers, usually told in a lowered and cautious voice, who had also crossed the Tehuantepec, accurately described as one of the most treacherous stretches of water on the planet.

The briefest account was in an e-mail response from Ken Hellewell. He had successfully completed his solo circumnavigation on Topaz just a few months earlier, thereby becoming the newest member of the Joshua Slocum Society. "The Gulf of Tehuantepec got me, too. It was the strongest wind of my entire journey. My mainsail blew out and I was worried." This message, from Ken, after 30,000 miles singlehanding around the world. He "was worried".

Later, I was assigned a dock near the megayachts in Mexico (This is often the case due to the catamaran beam.) and struck up a conversation with one of the captains of the 100-footers parked there, waiting for their owners to show up. He had been delivering a sailboat, back in his delivery captain days, when he got caught out in the same sudden winds of the Golfo de Tehuantepec. His boat was blown 800nm out to sea in five days. They ended up sailing back to Colombia, as that was the nearest port after the T-pecker eventually blew itself out. Check the map, you'll find that landfall is south of Panama.

While I was looking for slip space in California, Bill Gribble at San Pedro told me of his friend who lost his boat crossing the Tehuantepec. That vessel was blown out to sea for two days. The boat rolled over several times. They survived that, but the boat eventually filled with water and sank. The crew was then in the liferaft for five days. The raft was spotted by a tuna boat chopper, flying a zig-zag pattern looking for fish. When they were brought ashore, the medical staff estimated they were no more than 24 hours away from dying of thirst and exposure. When we were headed North after transiting the Panama Canal, Steve Cherry told me the first of these Tehuantepec tales. His pal, another ex-Navy seaman with decades of experience at sea on destroyers and years under sail, had his ketch blown 250nm out to sea. It took him five days to tack back with a broken rig.

Why are these stories, including mine, typically related in subdued voices as if being told in confidence; in a manner that is almost embarrassed? Is it because we're afraid we screwed up? Because you know, if you've been caught out there, it's not likely you'll be saved by anybody? Is it guilt you survived, knowing other sailors didn't, or anger because it just isn't fair? I still don't know.

Hermosillo
San Carlos & Guaymas
CD Obregon
Navojoa
Los Mochis
Culiacán
Mazatlán
Tepic
Puerto Vallarta
GUADALAJARA
Morelia
MEXICO CITY
Melaque
Manzanillo
Tecoman
Ixtapa & Zihuatenejo
Acapulco
Puerto Escondido
Huatulco
Pacific Ocean

¡Viva Mexico!

Aboard S/V Quo Vadis, off the Pacific Coast of Mexico

FONATUR, the Mexican tourism development agency, was very pleased with the hard currency infusions from the ministerially planned resort at Cancún on the Yucatan peninsula. They decided to build another tourist destination from scratch on the Pacific side at Bahías de Huatulco: five small bays along the coast of Oaxaca. The town center, La Crucecita, was built only during the last 10 years. These Bahías are not far South of the older traditional villages of Puerto Angel and Puerto Escondido. These are infamous surfer and hippie hangouts and have been for decades. Huatulco is all about *turismo*.

There is now a small harbor dug into the shoreline, finished with cut rock and chock full of day boats and sportfishers. Though it's not on any charts I've yet seen and not identified in editions of the cruising guidebooks I've bought, there is said to be Marina Chahue. I try to raise the rumored marina on CH16. Enrique, the dockmaster/manager, comes back. I tell him we were caught out in the Tehuantepec; made it to Tangolunda, and would like to come in to Chahue. He gives us directions from this bay around the point to his marina, making it sound fairly straightforwad.

"Come on in, guys. It's time to relax; have a beer." His English is impeccable.

The engine starts. The drain plug pops out of the windlass when I step on the button, spilling lube oil on the foredeck. The clutch will not engage so I haul the hook up hand over hand and we go looking for the entrance to Marina Chahue. We find a narrow gap between a high natural rock wall to starboard and a piled rock breakwater so new it doesn't have any marine growth on it, yet. Broad red and white stripes are painted on the water edge of the rock wall. This is a warning to not hit the rock. It is so "Mexico". So is being unable to raise the marina. After a couple of radio calls, Barracuda comes back. He goes to CH14 to tell us Enrique has stepped out but we're not likely to have a problem with the dredge, which is in the entrance, or with the depth which is at least 6 ft.

It takes two tries to maneuver Quo Vadis into an interior slip as there is no response from the starboard rudder. After the dock lines are secure, the damage assessment begins. Everything is soaked. Lazarettes and some lockers are filled with seawater but surprisingly little is broken in the vessel's living spaces. I start pumping and cleaning out the lazarettes and tossing stuff on the dock to dry or trash. Keith is not responding to my request to help with this. He walks off along the docks.

The damage assessment continues: starboard rudder bar is snapped at the weld, the large hole in the aft deck where the davit used to be will require fiberglass work. The engine compartment is flooded, the depth sounder is out, stern light is cracked, masthead lights are gone, the stays'l is in tatters, a foot pump is cracked, the windlass... What else has happened that I'm not seeing?

Keith comes back, wedges himself into the aft rudder compartment and removes the broken pieces. David Haslam hauled his oxy-acetylene welding rig out of his boat, Nereid, assembled it and proceeded to do a very professional job of re-welding the rudder bar. Very likely because he is a professional welder, now semi-retired and cruising in Mexico. His work looks better than the original. He charged me two *cervezas* for the job. Keith declined to re-install the repaired rudder bar. I'm not sure what's going on with him but it makes me uneasy. That night Ian and Quentin, Canadians docked next to us, bring CDs over. Supported by a shared bottle of tequila, Ian does a surprisingly good soft shoe to the soundtrack from "Chicago". We provide hand-held spotlights on the aft deck. The contrast to the 80 knot winds and 20 ft. waves just two nights ago catches up to me. The emotions are not all bad. I feel resilient and happy to be alive in safe harbor. That night, I drop the Mossberg over the rail. In all the years on board, it was never fired except in practice. I'm also paranoid about jail time for having a weapon in Mexico.

The next couple of days are consumed with trips to the hardware stores, meeting workers (both real and supposed) down at the boat, and finding the good, inexpensive seafood places in town. There is also an internet café just off the tidy little plaza. The plaza was built to make this planned community look like a traditional Mexican village. When I check e-mail, I discover that my 90 year-old Aunt Peggy is not doing well. Her assisted living residence is not able to handle her as her condition declines. While I am next of kin responsible for her, I wonder what exactly I'm supposed to do about it when I'm 3000 miles from San Diego on a beat-up sailboat.

Some stuff gets fixed, like the hole in the deck, and a lot of stuff doesn't. I work on patching sails. I also clean up the engine and change the oil and filter. Bulbs are replaced to the point of having running lights but there is little marine hardware and, surprisingly, limited repair capability around Huatulco. I meet Keith for dinner in town at our favored family seafood restaurant. He is concerned that things aren't fixed (as am I) and surprises me by getting surly about my response to weather conditions.

"I blame you for the stuff in the Papagayo and the Tehuantepec ," he tells me. This surprises me, all the more because I didn't think the Papagayo crossing even was "stuff". You'll remember we waited three days for conditions to improve before continuing on to Nicaragua. He also tells me he doesn't have enough money to pay for his dinner ashore, which is one of the few boat rules. I wonder why he had the most expensive thing (100 pesos) on the otherwise modest menu.

Terry and Christine Stamper docked Reiver on the other side of us. They are senior sailors (70-something I would estimate) headed for Panama. Terry is a past Commodore of the Royal Vancouver Yacht Club but, for now, they are enjoying tropical waters.

"We haven't really cruised the Northwest that much," Terry tells me. "We're saving that for our old age." We agree to swap his vintage Mexico cruising guide for some of my still-wet Central American charts and $US20. When Christine dries out the charts, she finds them useful enough to give my $20 back.

A test run out to sea on a patched and cleaned Quo Vadis confirms the rudders work, sails unfurl and the engine isn't leaking any fluids. We taxi fuel from the Pemex station in giant plastic jugs, provision, fill the water tanks, and I get the transit *zarpe* for Acapulco from the *Capitania* at the little harbor on the other side of town. I also get a Buoy Weather printout which shows favorable sea conditions and download the predicted winds from Grib files. After dinner, we're back on board by 2130. Tomorrow, we head for Acapulco. Enrique estimates it will take no more than 30 hours under sail.

The disco woke me just after midnight and, again, at 0300. I overslept til 0700. By the time I rolled out of my cabin, Keith was gone. He left a short note on his bunk: "It's been real. It's been fun. But it hasn't been real fun!" I don't think I promised him, or anybody else, any fun.

I check with the dockhand and the clean-up guy but nobody saw Keith leave. As I'm walking back down the dock in a confused state of mind, I see Christine working on the foredeck of Reiver. She asks why we haven't left. Feeling both betrayed and sheepish to admit it, I tell her my crew has jumped ship. She replies brightly, "It's for the best, then, isn't it?"

I take her wisdom to heart, get my wallet and passport from Quo Vadis and head towards town to find a flight to go check on my Aunt. On the way, I stop at Enrique's office to cancel the *zarpe* for today. I explain the reason for the cancellation. I must have seemed upset because he assures me *"No es muy grave, Juan."* It's not very serious. Glad to hear it. There's more good news. Sight is back to normal in my left eye. The eyeball aches constantly as if it had been hit by a shotgun pellet rather than seawater moving at 65 MPH. Of the alternatives, I'll take seeing even if it hurts.

After coordinating the move of my fun-loving, good-hearted Aunt Peggy to a nursing home in San Diego, I fly back to Oaxaca. Her move to this place which is not her home is an unwelcome rite of passage for both of us. She is starting to lose it and, in her lucid hours, knows it. It is sad and confusing to see the next older generation; often people who looked after me as a child, become dependent and demented. The experience reinforces my attitude about this voyage, and life its ownself (as Pogo Possum used to say). Seize this day because you don't ever know how many good ones you still have.

I've also talked to my youngest child, Caroline. She may sail with me again, even after I confide to her the current condition of the boat. She has, unfortunately, quit college after one semester. Fortunately for me, that does make her available for other activities. She needs some time to wind up personal items.

Once again crewless (Go ahead, you can say it: And clueless!), I calculate possible single-handed strategies to Acapulco. Based on easy anchorages, boat speed and all the other factors I can remember to include, I come up with two 15 hour passages as the longest runs. This is do-able but I'm not keen on single-handing a compromised boat in unfamiliar waters. Like many things afloat, this probably reflects a mental state as much as any objective criteria. However, I've also exhausted the marine repair capabilities in the greater Bahías de Huatulco area. I'm told Acapulco offers more in this category.

Enrique, the go-to guy of Marina Chahue, arranges an introduction to Sr. Fernando Posadas Vazquez. Among other things, Fernando is the director of the junior sailing program at Huatulco, which makes him a good guy in my book. He has sailed the Acapulco route several times in his own competition days which makes him a valuable asset to any boat headed that way. He also proves to be a true gentleman: *un caballero*. He agrees to help me take Quo Vadis to Acapulco. I agree to pay expenses and to buy him a plane ticket home. First, I need to install the fish finder I bought in San Diego to use as a depth sounder. Fresh provisions would be good, too.

As I finished wiring in the new sensor and instrument (The little fish icons swimming across the screen amuse me immensely, for some reason.), Fernando arrives with his sailing gear and a bundle of charts under his arm. I knew there had to be Mexican Navy charts! Unfortunately, they are difficult for a gringo to get his hands on. The intrepid international crew clears Marina Chahue under a revised *zarpe* which includes Fernando, and QV is off Puerto Angel by noon. I am pleased to have all the ingredients on board to make *torta* sandwiches for lunch. *Tortas* have been one of my favorite Mexican street foods since the early days when Kathleen and I used to drive my old van from LA down into Baja or over to Bahia San Luis Gonzaga. We discovered *tortas* on the street carts in Hermosillo and Tijuana.

Quo Vadis passes the Puerto Escondido waypoint about 30 minutes before dark. Fernando picks out lights on shore as his navaids. I'm confirming our position with the GPS. The first reading puts QV somewhere up on the beach. Mexican charts? Navigator error? You can't check enough. Later readings confirm Quo Vadis is back in the water. All other instruments including the new fishfinder-as-depth sounder are working at dusk. So are all the navigation lights. This makes me unreasonably happy. We've seen several turtles and a pair of large, speckled rays. Fernando proves extremely competent motorsailing: hands off the wheel, just looking at the compass, stars and sails. There is some tuna boat and shrimp boat traffic across our course but I feel comfortable going to my bunk until the midnight watch. Southbound S/V Carina calls on VHF with concerns about commercial traffic. "Watch out for the big boats," I sagely advise.

At dawn, Northbound S/V Quo Vadis is off Punta Maldonado where the GPS reads 14 hours to Acapulco; 33 hrs to Ixtapa. The winds are WNW 8-12 knots which is no help at all getting to either port. Since it looks like we're going to continue motoring after 24 hours of run time, I shut down the engine to check the oil level. It would also be timely to add some fuel to the main tank from the jerry cans. That done, the engine wouldn't re-start. Fernando surmises the engine's over-temperature relay has locked out the starter motor and hot water is trapped in the engine jacket. While this is a very educated analysis, this is another first time event. I disconnect the sensor wire from the overtemp sensor, dropping the set screw into the oily bilge. The engine still doesn't turn over. I glance briefly toward shore. We are far enough off the coast to give us some time before we'd have to sail away. With the current winds, sailing would be in the general direction of the Marquesas, about 90 degrees and 2500nm off course to either Acapulco or Ixtapa.

I think, "There are other ways to do this." I give up on the hand crank, again, after smashing my knuckles in to the forward wall of the engine compartment. The 2-3 revolutions I'm able to manage are not enough to ignite the 3-cylinder Yanmar. Finally, I figured out to try to jumpstart the engine. My first efforts to do this don't start it.

Fernando is the one who suggests the successful red wire to white wire solution. We get underway under power though lacking capacity to start or stop using the controls. The poor engine hasn't been right since the Night of the Screeching Overtemp Alarm in the Tehuantepec, so I decided to go in at Acapulco and research possible diesel repair skills in that storied port.

I re-schedule us to three hour watches so Fernando will be at the helm to guide QV into the harbor, as he has done many times on racing boats. There are several sightings of terns standing on the backs of turtles floating on the surface. I see what the tern gains from this relationship but... what does the turtle get out of it? Pondering these and other questions of nature and machinery, I make hot soup and fish sandwiches for dinner. As night falls and he starts below, Fernando turns to me with a broad smile and says we go into the night as *Los Lobos del Pacifico*. The Wolves of the Pacific. I like it.

Fernando comes back to the helm at 2200. He let me sleep well into my watch. I woke up at 0130 and bustled on deck to see all five feet four of him standing tall up on the starboard cockpit bench, both arms folded across his chest, eyes focused straight ahead. The boat is trimmed and moving smoothly toward the lights of Acapulco now spread before us with no need for a hand on the wheel. We are pointed directly at the marker light on Isla Roqueta at the harbor entrance.

I take the helm as we pass The Elephant, the landmark rock at the harbor entrance, and we drop the sails. The nearest anchorage is beneath the luxurious houses perched on the south cliffs but it has a reputation for being dangerous for boat and crew. We don't go there. I hand the helm back to Fernando where he does a good job of maneuvering QV into the crowded interior anchorage on the dark, deep bay. He finds an open spot in 48 ft. depth where I drop the hook at 0300. I shut the engine down using the decompression lever on the engine block and we open up the boat to the cool early morning air. The lights of the strangely silent city sparkle on three sides.

We share a brief prayer of thanks: blessing for a safe passage, and a celebratory shot of rum. I am falling asleep on my bunk as the first cocks crow around Acapulco Bay.

Clearing the Anchor and Other Discussions

Ah, Acapulco. Pearl of the Pacific in Spain's empire, more recently reknowned for cliff divers and Hollywood scandals. The same Acapulco where, just two weeks after Quo Vadis' visit, severed heads are found rolling in the gentle shorebreak about 100 meters from our current position. The newspaper quotes the police saying it's a local problem and has nothing to do with tourists. Our immediate local problem is less dramatic but still vexing. The anchor rode is fouled on a mooring buoy tether.

Fernando maneuvers Quo Vadis around the twisted lines rather skillfully but the anchor chain has wrapped so tight the tethered mooring ball is pulled under water. He has another plan: put a line on the buoy tether and pull it up while slacking the anchor rode. I put on mask and fins to help implement the new plan. I dove down and knotted the retrieval line to the anchor rode. Fernando secured it to a forward cleat and backed the boat down. I cleared the anchor from its ensnaring loops and it swung free.

The wet and dirty skipper clambered back on board, bleeding from just a few barnacle cuts, and Fernando eased QV over to the fuel dock of the *Club de Yates de Acapulco*. The CYA is the oldest yacht club in Mexico which probably makes it the oldest club in Latin America. President Lopez Mateos was one of the founding members back in the 1940s, reportedly so he would have a place to keep his own boat. It is still that kind of place: a limited membership club, a fact which seems to be wasted on the cruisers who have described it as snooty and unwelcoming. I'm just happy the CYA has an accessible fuel dock with normal Pemex prices for diesel. I find the club manager, José Maria Marques, to be "correct" in the manner of most senior Mexican officials. Slips to handle Quo Vadis' 16 ft. beam are scarce but we can stay on the outside dock for US$1/foot/day.

The CYA features white tablecloths at lunch served by attentive waiters and a uniformed towel attendant in the marble shower room. As noted, it's that kind of club. The uniformed dockmaster introduces me to Alberto the diesel mechanic and Jorge the electrical guy. We agree on a staggered schedule for them to come on board which, inevitably, will take place *mañana*. Incredibly, they both arrive within minutes of their appointed times. To demonstrate one of our mechanical problems, I push the engine "Start" button to show it doesn't start. The Yanmar jumps to life with no hesitation.

Before that milestone event, Fernando and I enjoyed the club's pool, a hot shower and changed into clean clothes. He knows several good restaurants in town. Over two tremendous plates of seafood, we discuss the portrayal of extra-terrestrials in ancient Mayan art. We have both seen the bas-relief carvings. They show two figures in full coverage helmets and space suits hob-nobbing with the big-nosed Mayan guys wearing flowing feather headdress. It does go a long way toward explaining the Mayas' advanced astronomy. He orders and eats scallops served hot, covered in a clam paste. This is a new dish to me but apparently common in Southern Mexico. I realize that in nearly 30 years of traveling in this country, I've never been to Acapulco and Guerrero state.

Alberto and Jorge detach and take away several major mechanical pieces including the windlass. Fernando goes shopping for parts for the boats in his junior flotilla. I buy him a US$300 ticket on Mexicana. That night, we have a final dinner on shore: an elaborate Mexican version of *paella*. We're back on board by 2100. The initial attack of Montezuma's revenge hits me by 2200. I passed the night in that sorry state as I could not find the Imodium. It is no consolation that this is the first time it has happened to me in three years on board. I sleep in til 0830; then it's time to see Fernando off to the airport. I said I'd write from California. When I call Mer to sing "Happy Birthday" her machine picks up. Still, I sing into the phone, adding "Wish you were here."

Mexico no longer seems like a Third World country. The coastal cities, at least, are prosperous. People look healthy. I saw more beggars on the streets of San Francisco last summer than I've seen on this entire coast. The markets are full of food and consumer goods. The streets are full of new cars, including lots of shiny 4X4s and pick-ups. You can't find a rusty '57 Chevy with the hood held down by baling wire. Can 10 years have gone by since I've experienced Mexico?

This new century of prosperity is reflected in non-Third World pricing for boat repairs and parts at the Acapulco Yacht Club. Admittedly, "marine" is still in the description of these things so I should not be surprised the price is triple any other index of Mexican costs. It is annoying that several things supposedly fixed at Puntarenas or Barillas didn't make it even as far as Acapulco. The T-pecker has taken a severe and continuing toll. Repairs undertaken in Acapulco include windlass, starter motor, radar power cord, engine manifold, water pump (again), sails, rigging, and the wind generator tower guy wires. I should have caught that last item at Huatulco but didn't until now. Hey, at least the wind gen tower didn't topple overboard like it did off Puerto Rico.

I'm waiting for boat equipment and engine parts to return, hopefully repaired, when I'm told I'll have to move my boat during the billfish tournament hosted by the CYA. The only slip at the club which accommodates QV is shallow and inside where, strangely, the surge is exaggerated. Felix, a weathered hand who has been hanging around the docks looking for work, helps move the boat and offers to crew going North. He says he's been to Ensenada. He doesn't warn me or doesn't know about the changed conditions on the new dock. The inside surge and absence of dock cleats results in my new docklines being chafed through before morning. The impact of my boat hitting the concrete dock wakes me up. I figure out, too late, how to re-rig at the slab including setting a stern anchor to hold *Quo Vadis* off.

The insurance company puts me in touch with a marine surveyor to assess possible damage re-imbursement. Russ Dennis seems to understand my situation and *Quo Vadis*' condition. He tells me what papers and documents I'll need to prepare and send him. This conversation is, surprisingly, a real morale booster.

My morale needs some elevating as the days of coordinating Alberto, Jorge, Pastór and Febrónio go on…and on. I am also checking and, often, revising and correcting their work in between my excursions ashore in search of parts and lubricants. Meanwhile, the peso drain from the *Quo Vadis* treasury continues. Some of the work ends up being acceptable; a lot of it doesn't cut it.

It takes five days for me to reach the point of understanding I'm not going to get any further with boat repairs or parts in Acapulco. I've met another California skipper,

Gary, who named his 42 ft. sloop Landfill based on the categorical description assigned to sailboats by the San Francisco Bay Conservation and Development Commission a few years back. This is such an inside joke. I love it. He shares some steaks on board Landfill. I bring the salad and wine.

The propane store can't fill the LPG tank over the weekend. Acapulco has questionable water so I don't take on any. Felix is enlisted for his stated rate of US$75/day and a ticket home. I tell him we're going at noon. At 1230, I have to go looking for him. This is not encouraging. I get the engine (now supposedly leak-proof) started and have a weekend crowd grab the docklines. All the guys on the dock are shouting instructions at me. Many of their directions are conflicting but, incredibly, none of them are correct. I finally prevail, as Capitán Juan, and get Felix to retrieve the stern anchor from under a newly-arrived runabout while the line handlers walk QV back out of the slip. I then execute a backing turn, swinging her to port and out of the *Club de Yates de Acapulco*. We pass and hail Landfill, now bouncing at anchor outside the harbor, behind Roqueta.

As *Quo Vadis* again enters the deep Pacific, the dolphins come alongside and slice in front of the boat. It makes me smile as they leap clear of the sea and fall happily back with soft splashes. As always, I gratefully accept their guidance as an omen for a safe passage. Other wildlife sightings include several leatherback turtles (which I believe are in the area to lay eggs) and a small manta ray. Enterprising terns continue to rest on the shellbacks of other floating turtles, waiting for food. For human food, I make *telera* sandwiches at the end of my 4 to 8 watch, then do a position check. I find Felix dozing at the wheel before I crawl into my bunk at 2100. This is not encouraging but I'm too tired to do anything besides advise him to stay alert…and awake.

We make slow progress, motorsailing through the night with speeds over the surface less than five knots. The winds and countercurrent are not helpful but the engine is performing without problems, so far. I did the 0600 position check, which correlated with our arrival off Punta Papanoa and went back to sleep until 0800. I laid out hot coffee, granola bars, juice and fruit; then took the helm on a clear morning with 2-3 ft. seas and contrary winds. I soon picked up the Frailes Blancos, tall white rocks off Punta Gorda. Felix confirmed we could go inside the rocks which also put us on course for Z-town. Caroline may be able to rejoin me there. I hope so.

As we approached the bight just before Bahía Zihuatenejo, the dolphins pulled in so close to the starboard ama you could reach out and touch them. Several of these marvelous mammals started jumping clear of the water. One sporty guy jumped out and did a complete horizontal spin in the air before smacking back in to the sea. I wish I could do that. We had completed a safe overnight passage and I thanked our black and gray friends. They couldn't do anything about the heavy panga traffic or the motor yacht that barely beat us into the Bay and over to the fuel dock. We had to wait an hour to get on the dock but it was the only game in town at this anchorage.

Perhaps because they have such an exclusive, the snooty fuel dock guys added a 20% surcharge to the fuel price shown on the pump. When I protested, both of them and Felix assured me this was standard practice in Mexico. There had been no such add-ons at the CYA which I'm sure was most definitely in Mexico. Felix talked about me in the third person to the fuel dock guys, like I wouldn't understand because they were speaking Spanish. I dislike this third person treatment immensely in any language. In Spanish, I understand them perfectly, of course.

I finally hand over the demanded amount, Felix recovers the docklines, and we motor around to the marina at Ixtapa, surfing a four foot wave through the fairly narrow opening in the marina breakwater. I raised the office on CH16 and received a slip assignment. I found slip D-27 over by three motoryachts: all over 100 ft. It's this thing about catamaran beams. Shortly after we dock, a 10 ft. saltwater crocodile glides into the slip and sticks its head up to inspect us.

Expecting Caroline's imminent arrival, we had agreed Felix would return home from Ixtapa. He wants to be paid more. When I remind him that he's been paid what we agreed, he gets mad and starts complaining about no food, spittle flying from the corners of his mouth. I know this isn't about food and tell him so. He is paid 1400 pesos for just over a day's work plus 30 more for lunch. He stomps off toward the bus stop, still muttering. I continue to the marina office to sign in with the dockmaster, Elsa. She is the first female marina manager I've ever encountered in Mexico. Her manner is correct and her actions are efficient. She is good-looking with that particular Latina professional manner. Her younger, female office staff impress me as just OK.

When I return to Quo Vadis, two seven foot-long crocodiles are there to greet me. I figure the new Ixtapa marina was dredged out in their original estuarine habitat. Many of them didn't leave or have returned. It's not 'til later that I notice signs featuring a cartoon crocodile posted around the marina, mostly on the dock gates. They advise not to go in the water. If Felix hadn't complained about the lack of food and stomped off, he could have shared a dinner of smoked pork chops with sweet peppers accompanied by an avocado, cucumber and tomato salad. A hearty Zinfandel stood up to the smoked chops. I watched the smaller crocs patrolling the docks until it was too dark to see them.

It took 24 hours dock-to-dock from A-town to Z-town. The experience with Felix gives me another good reason to reconsider single-handing. Could I have done that passage alone, or with only my dolphin friends? I've gained the necessary passage-making experience and bloody well should have after almost three years sailing on saltwater. It is mostly a state of mind. Still, it would be nice to have Caroline back on board.

Between the Crocodiles and the Convalescent Home

I tuned in for the 1030 weather report but nothing came on. Despite the lack of official recognition from Mexican officials, I suspect there will be weather today. I am almost getting used to dealing with weather information as a discovery rather than a prior forecast. I'm doing personal clean-up when my phone starts playing its jaunty tune. I see an incoming number from San Diego, the town up in Alta California.

The call is from Pt. Loma Convalescent Home regarding my Aunt. She was transferred with no reading glasses and no medications. I authorize the meds and request her consulting psychologist continue with an evaluation. At first, they agree; then call me back to say their in-house shrink will do the eval. I question this approach since he doesn't have a baseline from which to evaluate her condition and I request her records transfer. I think I hear agreement in San Diego but it could be the non-committal hospital brushoff. It is frustrating.

Now as presentable as I'm going to get, I go ashore. I get conflicting information on whether the water is potable as well as where to get LPG tanks filled. I do find the DHL office to send a package of photos, receipts and damage description to Russ Dennis, the marine surveyor in Southern California. He told me in our phone conversation that he used to keep his boat at La Paz. He has been a solo skipper in a foreign land and seems to vividly remember what can happen sailing along the coast of Mexico. This makes him an immediate ally. After dispatching the package, I respond to e-mails from Caroline, my daughter, and Jeff Morehouse, my high school roommate. I ask my child to join me in Zihuatenejo and Jeff to join us wherever he can on the West Coast of Mexico.

When I return to QV with 5 kilos of ice melting in my backpack, the 10 ft. croc is lying alongside D dock, though not lurking in my slip. Before I can stow the ice, I get another call from Pt. Loma Convalescent about Aunt Peggy. They've called me to report she threw a banana at somebody. I can understand how she feels and I'm not going senile, yet. Still, I can't recall how I cut my right hand. Blood is running down my forearm as I listen to the distant, unsolveable complaints. It must be time for a sundowner and dinner.

Caroline comes to Mexico

A week passes in which I eat *ceviche* and *carnitas* ashore, observe the crocs who seem to favor my slip, gather info and read up on all Mexican anchorages, and develop an on-going relationship with Abel in the repair, re-installation and further repair of the water pump. The boat gets cleaner and more lockers get dried out. John Blake calls me from California: he's not available 'til mid-May, if then. My frustration grows until Caroline calls and says she'll be here within the week.

After catching two busses from the Ixtapa Marina to the airport south of Zihuatenejo, I jump down into the dusty parking lot. I see my younger daughter walking toward me with her bags slung over her shoulders. Her flight was early, so I'm late to meet her but I start beaming just seeing her. She sees me, and the experience of cruising in Mexico, in a different way. In her words:

Zihuatenejo, Mexico is so beautiful. The life here is so familiar, but so different. There's something that reminds me of a third world Santa Monica (where I was born). Coastal town, yes, but something more exotic. Example: there are trees with red flowers that look like hibiscus, but aren't. They have giant seed pods almost the length of my arm. The birds are distinctively patterned—like black head and wings with banana yellow bodies or white, snowy bellies with dark emerald green topsides. I saw a crocodile next to the boat. I think she/he was about 8 ft. long but Dad insists it was 10. Some people about 20-something caught sight of her/him and tied a black rope to a raw chicken and dragged it through the water. I didn't approve of the idea but I'm not self-righteous enough to say I wasn't entertained. I even approached them and took advantage of the exposed croc thrashing about with the chicken in her/his mouth for a photo opportunity. After I made sure I got a good shot, I made a comment to the young group that they ought to untie the chicken if they wanted that line back. They looked at me but made no remarks and continued to tease the large reptile. I just hope no one's dog goes missing.

I continue fixing broken stuff and puzzling over battery behavior. Caroline is signed on as crew of Quo Vadis.

Marina Ixtapa called us at 0730 to make sure we'd turned in our keys since we had our *zarpe* to leave for Manzanillo. At the internet café, I downloaded Buoyweather for Zihua, Manzanillo and Cabo Corrientes. This site is proving to be the only consistent, or available, source of weather forecasts for this part of this ocean. The key to making it useful is to accurately identify and input the buoy locations that reflect your planned route. There was no weather to indicate we shouldn't go. I was back on board by 1130 when the marina office called on VHF for me to come in, offering no further explanation.

In the air-conditioned office, Erika exlained that Mexican law had been changed a few days earlier and port clearance within the country was no longer required. She tried to refund my 257 pesos and take the *zarpe* back. I explained to her that the *zarpe* was the only signed, stamped document listing Caroline as crew. The next port might not be so understanding. After Elsa interceded, I retained one copy of the *zarpe* stamped "Cancelled". We were off the dock by 1230 and on the hook off Isla Grande by 1400. Captain and crew enjoyed a long swim in crocodile-free waters before I made a Skipper Special for lunch. Ah, the healing powers of sea, steak sandwiches and a siesta.

With all the beauty and excitement that comes with sailing, there are also its frustrations. Three, maybe four, days ago we actually began our voyage after discovering that a start battery thought to be drained was not and the cooling water was actually being pumped through the engine. All this was proven after two false starts and one escort back to Zihuatenejo from the Coast Guard and the Mexican Navy. We ventured onward with my first overnight passage. I had a strange but lingering memory of a dead parrot fish with a bloated swim bladder. The only color remaining of its once vibrant pattern was its beak washing up on; then receding from the shores of Zihua.

Moving on: lots of sleep and strange dreams, pretty much undescribable. The anchorages are almost unremarkable yet peaceful in their simple, resolute beauty. My camera stopped working and, at all times, during a visit from a pod of a dozen dolphins—the third sighting of the creatures at that. I definitely caught a few surface shots (I hope) but when three crested out of the water at once, the button stopped working. If the damned camera can't be fixed at our next shore visit, I'll be vexed to say the least. There was also a leathery-backed, olive green sea turtle coasting along in the opposite direction. I was unable to capture it on film but it will be retained in memory. I am sick, but I pray my body will soon be used to the conditions. Once again, to bed.

Mike Metteler from Warrior came by the boat off Isla Grande. He's headed to Costa Rica and we talked about passages between here and there, as well as those North. After another swim, I started dinner and noticed the start battery was at 3.34 volts and drawing down. The house bank was dropping from 13.3 to 12.9. I disconnected the B3 wire with no positive effect. The start battery appears dead. The isolator eliminator status light is out, indicating that subsystem is not working. I cannot think of a good solution. I have a spare start battery but it hasn't been used since Trinidad. Where to get it charged?

My dumb solution is to see if the engine will restart with the low voltage levels. It did but it is now 2230 and I don't want to try to go back to Zihua past the Sacramento Reef in the dark. Caroline is being very good about all this; maintaining a positive attitude. I am frustrated that another thing isn't working and just feel stupid.

At first navigable light, I get Caroline to the helm and, before weighing anchor, check the engine compartment. No oil or water is evident; the maxipads in the bottom of the compartment are still clean. It is dead calm. Neither of us slept well and Caroline starts to nod at the helm just before the Reef. We made it back into the Bay where I tried to find anchorage over at Punto Mio as suggested in the cruising guide. The area has mostly been taken up by private moorings. I spend too much time dithering over location before dropping the anchor in 14 ft. just off the beach near the few other sailboats. Caroline is tired and frustrated with my indecision. I am, too.

The start battery is reading 1.25 volts on the screen. The house battery bank reads 13.18 volts and is charging from the solar panels. Wait a minute. Didn't I have a similar condition coming down the Intracoastal Waterway a few years ago? Have I retained nothing from that lesson? How about starting the engine from the house bank with the selector in "Both" position? It works and, along with that, my brain seems to re-activate. I get out the multi-meter. A voltage check of the start battery shows 13.06 volts, which is about what you'd expect. The screen readout shows the battery voltage is 0.29 volt. The meter to the house bank shows 13.38 volts and the readout is 13.29. Close enough. It eventually occurs to me to remove the fuse and holder above the start battery positive terminal. Sandpaper, contact cleaner and reassembly result in a panel readout over 13 volts. Even if it stays calm, we have enough fuel to motor to Las Hadas.

In early afternoon, Nereida, a sloop of British registry weighed anchor and sailed out, passing very close to Quo Vadis. She is being singlehanded by Pat: a blonde, very obviously female Pat. She is headed for Alaska. I assume that means sailing mostly North and West, like we need to do. I feel like a bigger wuss than ever. Greg Morehead from Gitana dinghied by, curious as to why we've come back. I don't recall how much detail I went into. Caroline and I crashed till 1600. The plan is to eat; then sail overnight to Caleta de Campos. It should be an easy run of 14-15 hours.

We clear the Bay by 1830. Caroline is totally with it and doing a great job at the helm. I get the main up with the wind variable at 2-5 knots. The sail doesn't fill. An hour later the over-temp alarm started blasting. I check the exhaust. There is much smoke but no water discharge. I reluctantly shut down the engine. We are just off the Sacramento Reef, again. There is no wind so we have no headway. We're drifting. The closest refuge is back in the Marina. I raised the office but they could offer no response. I called the Navy. They said they'd do something. Nothing happened for an hour. I finally got a call back from the *Capitania*. (I had noticed a boat marked *Resguardo* when I was wandering around the bay looking for an anchorage.) They said they'd be out in 15 minutes. We are drifting toward Punto Carrizo but away from the Sacramento Reef. Sundown was at 2000 and I put all nav and mast lights on for ID and, I hoped, vessel avoidance. At 2030, I called again. The *Capitania* said 5 more minutes. I saw a blue, flashing light approaching QV in the darkness. It was mounted on a boat. I'd had plenty of time to rig and coil a tow line but the *Resguardo* boat motored by and tossed one. I caught it and secured it to the windlass cleat. About this time, an open launch with eight guys in dark blue uniforms and holding rifles showed up. They had no towing ability but fell in off our starboard side. *"Marina Mexicana!"* one of them proudly proclaimed. Some grinned at us; some looked serious. Caroline did a great job steering under tow while I monitored the line and prepared a back-up. The line didn't foul and we were brought to the anchorage we'd left by daylight a few hours earlier. The wind was very light from the South and stayed that way all night. I had no new or clever ideas about the engine's cooling water problem.

Anticipating another extended stay in Zihua for Abel to work on the water pump, I deployed the bimini, covered the mainsail, and put our damp bedding out under a hazy sun. I went overboard with mask, fins, gloves and screwdriver under the starboard *ama* to check the water pump inlet. It was, as always before, clear. Back on deck, I started the engine. There was no water flow in the exhaust. I advanced engine speed to 1400 RPM. Apparently normal water flow began. I backed off to 1000 RPM, basically idle, and normal cooling flow continued. With the DC reefer on, engine/alternator running, and exhaust water flow continuing, all electrical systems looked good with battery voltages over 13 volts. The Gitana crew had dinked by on their way to breakfast at Las Brasas, noting we were back again. We decided to go ashore, too, and lowered the dinghy.

The Suzuki outboard started on the first pull. It was the first time I'd used it since Huatulco. We made a nice surf landing on the municipal beach near the pangas. Caroline remembered how to jump over the gunwale with the painter and lead the bow of the dink up the beach. We had lunch, checked e-mail, told Jeff that Puerto Vallarta seemed to be a more likely rendezvous, and I bought a new insurance policy from IMIS. We're back on board by 1530. There is still no wind. We stow everything and get underway with Caroline at the helm by 1600. A half hour later, we cleared the point and the over-temperature alarm started sounding. It kept going off until the engine RPM was reduced to 2200. I'm considering going back into the Marina. Caroline informed me emphatically, "We're not going back!" I made a sandwich and took the 8-12 watch.

The over-temp alarm would stay off if we kept the engine speed between 1500-1800 RPM. Caroline came on the midnight watch she had requested. On that watch, she did not wake me, held the plotted course, and had no over-temp alarms. She roused me at 0500 reporting no traffic and no radio calls. Wind speed was N8-10 knots so I got both headsails up and the engine off. When we hit the Caleta de Campos waypoint, the wind was still up and sea conditions good. I decided to press on toward Muruata.

So, of course, the wind died shortly after 1000. On the positive side, the exhaust flow appears normal and no alarm went off up to 2300 RPM. The diurnal wind shift typical of the Pacific Coast of Mexico and California appears to have started but is very light. It feels like there is a current against us as our speed over the surface is only 5 knots motoring. There is some water in the engine compartment.

Just before noon, we passed La Niña. Yes, it is Columbus' third ship. He called her The Little Girl for size and build. There was no mistaking that lateen sail rig. I raised the skipper on CH16, who responded in an American Southern accent that she is headed South to Panama from Nuevo Vallarta— on the reverse course of Quo Vadis. I am fascinated by this famous replica in our same seaspace and impressed by its size. It is very small for carrying a crew across The Ocean Sea. La Niña is also motoring.

The afternoon passes along the rocky, scenic coastline up to Muruata. There is surf all around it with big breakers. It doesn't look like much of an anchorage to me but I pick a relatively smooth spot inside the first big rock. Caroline again did a good job at the helm and I have the bridle rigged on the anchor rode within 15 minutes of entering. It is rolly but, considering the size of the swell, acceptable. After a quick calculation, I decide to add 5 gallons of diesel from a jerry jug. When I open the engine compartment, there is oil on the water sloshing around in there. Apparently, none of Abel's fixes fixed either leak. The engine is still hot which discourages any more mopping up.

After sundowners (chocolate milk for Caroline's still-adapting stomach), I made spinach salad with blue cheese, grilled pork chops, and opened a bottle of wine. Morale improved. I crashed as my crew industriously cleaned up the galley. Two sloops came in to the anchorage just before dark.

On the way to Cabeza Negra the next morning we were joined by the little gray dolphins with the long noses until the over-temp alarm went off. We pulled the RPM back until the screech of the alarm finally stopped. I deployed the headsails even though winds were 5-8 knots which, of course, is why we're motoring. The big gray and white-speckled dolphins started jumping alongside. We can hear them breathing as they jump clear of the water and knife back in without a splash.

I sight a sea turtle in time to miss it and we round Punta San Telmo before the noon hour when the adverse winds are predicted to occur. We still encounter large swells with the cape effect. Caroline recognizes the pod of speckled dolphins, joining us again. They've also made it around the *punta*.

We could not see Cabeza Negra (Black Head) until just 10 nm out. I missed another sea turtle floating on the surface just a boat length ahead. With surge from the

Southwest and a West wind, I figured the South anchorage may not work. Though it's counterintuitive for this Coast and its prevailing winds, I go instead to the North anchorage, rousing Caroline to take the helm. We drop the hook in 30 ft. outside the shark net which protects the residents of the few, enormous, fancy mansions on shore. There is more oil and water in the engine compartment. I do not think kind thoughts about Abel. Caroline taped the instrument covers back together. It is a big improvement.

Magical Manzanillo

Las Hadas is too beautiful for words. The bougainvilleas outnumber the people. At first, from the deck of Quo Vadis all you can see are the fuschia-colored blosssoms invading every wall and planter box. Further into town, however, more varieties of colors are apparent: scarlet and sunset orange and eggshell white. They have simply taken over whatever soil has room for them to grow. Many shapes and varying pinks of hibiscus have made themselves noticed as well but they are hardly a fraction of the dominant flora.

The white spiraling and twisted architecture above the main swimming beach at Las Hadas is alluring. The actual buildings that hold the residents of the resort are stacked one on top of another like a child's building blocks, and (as Cap'n Jack has pointed out) in a way that only Mexican building codes would permit. The marina has a somewhat Mediterranean vibe around it, which I'm attributing to the white stucco walls, red tile roofs, abundant bougainvillea and sapphire waters.

Ah yes, the blue, blue water. Before our 24 hour passage which brought us to Muruata, the sea's water was teal green. Lovely but not without some murkiness. Once day turned to night, there was bioluminescence in that water. Coming in here, the water is intense shades of blue which changes from place to place.

We cleared Piedras Blancas in the morning calm on a course of 301 magnetic with 50nm to Manzanillo. Caroline stayed at the helm until nearly 1000; then hit her bunk for nearly 5 hours. I set all sails as the wind came WSW at 5-10 knots and continued on with speeds to 6 knots.

It was a day for sea creatures. I made six different turtle sightings within two hours: mostly 2-4 ft. shell size; probably Hawksbills from the heads I saw. A pod of the small, gray dolphins came by in the early afternoon but didn't spend much time with the boat. Possibly because of the weird and scary gear noises I'm hearing from the engine. I furled the sails when the wind died about 1300, then re-set the genoa when it came back up about 1500. Boat speed is OK but I get concerned that sailing the wind will take us on a more Northerly course into the coast, which proves to be exactly what happens. I got Caroline up, pointed her toward Sail Rock, which is now visible off Punta Campos, and sacked out for an hour. Caroline requested the headsails be furled as the apparent wind was now at 20 degrees. I complied.

We turned toward shore with the GPS showing 5nm to the Las Hadas anchorage. Two groups of dolphins greeted us as we entered the Bay. Caroline was first to see three sticks where the anchorage was supposed to be. We dropped the main at the breakwater and the hook in 15 ft. right in front of the swimming beach. Quo Vadis started swinging through 360 degrees, like the other three boats. The white-coated Las Hadas staff outnumbered the few gringo diners for the "Early Bird Special". Both groups are checking us out from the restaurant. I wonder what they see when they look at us.

We're anchored about 100 meters off the beach where Dudley Moore burned his feet on the hot sand in the movie "10". He had an attendant carry him back to the little pavilions which remind me of the tents at medieval jousts. The film is better-known to most of us guys of a certain age for introducing Bo Derek in a clinging white swimsuit and for introducing cornrows to white folks. This Spring in mid-week, the place is nearly empty. I see three couples under the little tents. None of them go in the water.

The next day, we go find Victor to sign in. He is at the fuel dock and in no hurry. *"Mañana OK."*

He shows us where to put the used engine oil and trash today. Getting QV on to the fuel dock looks tricky. The used oil was a result of my changing the engine and transmission oil earlier that morning. I also checked and topped up the drive leg 90W lube. It looked clean and uncomtaminated. While I was getting oily, Caroline cleaned the galley, bagged the trash, and lubed reluctant cabin hinges.

Dismissed by Victor for the time being, I went on line while Caroline did some laundry. I am able to confirm that Quo Vadis is re-insured and Jeff will be on his way to Puerto Vallarta to join the crew in a few days. I also check four positions between Manzanillo and Tenacatita on Buoyweather. They all show big seas and high, contrary winds. Based on that info, the decision for tomorrow is "No go". We provision at the supermarket, just to be safe, and get ice to pack under the meats and cheeses. This justifies taking a taxi back to Las Hadas.

I make time to advise Russ of our current status and damage repair updates. The engine over-temp alarm, indicating no or inadequate cooling water, has become a real boat-stopper. It has also supposedly been repaired three times. Some time along in here, my hair starts falling out. No kidding. I see swatches of it in the port sink. Caroline tries to be helpful.

"Well," she says, "if you're just losing your hair from stress, it will probably grow back."

The over-temp alarm, one of the prime stress inducers, went off again as we ran the engine/alternator while stowing provisions in the reefer last night. This morning, there is initially no cooling water flow. Within 30 seconds, before the engine heats up enough to start the alarm screaming, a sooty wet discharge begins. What has now become our reference point for normal cooling water flow stabilizes and even increases with RPM. The engine is rattling. When I open the hatch, I see no visible leaks in the totally clean engine compartment. I leave the engine running while I drill and screw pieces of the instrument panel in place. Putting silicone in the cracks does not make it waterproof but I convince myself it is better than nothing until we can get the factory replacement parts.

Cooling water flow is normal after an hour but so is the re-appearance of the oil and water leaks. After engine shutdown, I tape the shroud chafe guards some more; then decide to re-coil the stern anchor line into a useable condition, securing it to the lower mount of the Loran mast with a slip knot for instant access. After all this nautical stuff, I make an important announcement: "Let's eat lunch."

Today's Skipper Special included chicken *adobada*, Spanish rice, avocado with lime, and white wine. All eaters agreed on the rating: Good. I digested while plotting courses to our next anchorages. Caroline went below to read and I went under the boat to look at barnacles. The *amas* were relatively clean. I took a few barnacles off the stern sections and rudders; then removed some of the more vicious marine specimens from the encrusted nacelle. No anti-foul of any type has ever worked well on the nacelle, from the Chesapeake until right now in the balmy waters off Manzanillo.

We were off the boat again at 1700 to check on weather and crew. Weather is good enough to go. Jeff plans to be in Puerto Vallarta on May 4th. Dinner on shore was at Tacos Julio on the main street of a working class suburb outside the resort area. It was excellent—some of the most authentic food I've ever eaten in Mexico. (And I been eatin' hyar in May-hee-ko nigh on to thirty y'ar, pardner. Hard to believe I'm that old.) I bought some sponges for air filters, we caught the bus and were back on board by 2115.

In the town we went into from Las Hadas, there was a boy standing on the corner of one of those concrete, curb-like street dividers. He was holding an accordion between his hands, another accordion (probably in a different key) was dangling off the back of his left hand and he had a guitar strapped to his back. And I want to learn just one musical instrument while this kid alone was carrying <u>three</u>. Well, two were admittedly the same kind but, none the less, damn.

Another surprise was the incoming phone call after 2200 from my former wife, Kathleen. She wanted to speak with Caroline, no surprise, which she did for about half an hour. I left my cell phone re-charging with the battery selector switch set to house bank only.

Don't Believe Everything You Read…and other Life Lessons

Cap'n and crew of Quo Vadis were up, weighed anchor and moved to the cramped fuel dock by 0830 where we had to wait for a crewed motor yacht to fill, and fill and fill. Why do I always get there just after the only empty motor boat in port? We're slower? Victor says the water is potable so I filled, but still treated, the water tanks while waiting for fuel. He charged us 120 pesos for use of the dinghy dock which I thought was excessive and 560 for fuel, which I didn't think was so bad.

When we cleared Bahia Santiago, the wind came to SSW15-18. Caroline was not feeling so great and crashed in the cockpit on some cushions. I am sailing the boat downwind in 4-6 ft. swell, generally doing 6-7 knots until I finally realize it would be good to change course since we're being set in to the beach. QV clears Punta Graham by 1430 and we change course for Tenacatita.

Approaching Cabeza de Navidad, I could not figure out the approach from either Charlie's or the Rains' cruising guides. I sent sick Caroline to the foredeck to watch for rocks under the surface. The rock configurations above sea level did not match the books and the waypoints, which are inside the Bay, route you through the peninsula. They are not so useful when Northbound. The chartlets and charts don't look correct. Between Piedra Blanca, which is shown on the approach, and a submerged rock are two more good-sized rocks: one is three-pointed; one is flat and jagged. All extend out past Piedra Blanca ending in the submerged rock which, contrary to the information, isn't so submerged. It was breaking when we got there. I doubt whether you can safely pass on either side of Piedra Blanca coming in to Tenacatita.

I elected to go around everything before turning North into the bay. Caroline stepped to the helm to handle anchoring. She is feeling better after barfing. The anchor is dropped and the bridle is rigged by 1630 at some distance from the half dozen sailboats in the Northwest anchorage. A big blue motor yacht comes in an hour after our hook is set and anchors way too close. I really don't like that. This behavior seems to go along with larger motor yachts or, in the Caribbean, Canadians.

We motored out of Tenacatita mid-morning. Most of the Southbound cruising crews we have met said they liked this anchorage best. The bay is good sized and the water clear but we need to meet Jeff at Puerto Vallarta. Caroline felt the boat was sliding sideways instead of responding to the helm. I couldn't detect much difference in handling but I would like to tighten the rudders. The apparent wind is no better than 40 degrees when we come to our course, but the headsail set improves our speed through the water by a knot and a half. We continued motoring at 2200-2500 RPM with no over-temp alarm for the rest of the passage.

There are many strange-looking buildings located at long intervals along this coast. Some have towers and walls. Are these drug lord redoubts? I thought I had the references for going in to Bahía Chamela memorized from the guidebook but I didn't identify the islands correctly, so kept going all the way up to the beach in the far Northwest corner of the bay. Whoops. We turned back south to the Isla Passavera anchorage and set the hook in the lee of the island about six boatlengths from Kokua III, a sloop out of Los Angeles. Caroline was miffed by my error.

I made a meal of *chorizo con huevos*, served with avocado and limes. Caroline went for a swim until that was ready. I re-read the guidebook; then swam over to introduce myself to Eb and Pamela. About dusk, Eb yelled over that we were too close. Even without my heightened sensibility about crowding in anchorages, I agreed, but it was largely because Kokua is not swinging on the hook and Quo Vadis is; so we ended up stern to stern. I roused Caroline up to the helm and moved 100 meters East to an apparent calm spot. When we dropped in 12 ft., conflicting tidal current and wind did not allow a natural, hard set. I signaled the helm to back down, one of the few times it has been necessary. She executed the re-anchoring flawlessly but didn't see the need for it.

The small gray dolphins joined us as Caroline guided QV out of Chamela in the morning. I set the sails while she slept during the second watch to make sure I could still do that part of the job single-handed. That feat demonstrated, the over-temp alarm went off. I throttled back. The alarm still woke up the crew, making her a little grumpy.

Another dolphin pod visited us in the afternoon. This time it was the big, white-spotted guys and gals. The winds came Northwest as we approached Punta Ipala, having followed Kokua III most of the route. They grabbed a good spot and the rest of the reasonable anchorages at Ipala were blocked by a net on floats. The place was very surge-y with rocks all around. It's also fairly deep. I don't see why this is such a good anchorage, as described by the guidebooks. I had to shorten scope so we wouldn't swing in to the rocks if the wind changed. This isn't the first or, as it turned out, the last Northern Mexico anchorage that would be, at best, marginal on other cruising grounds I've experienced. I made *fajitas* for dinner on board. We still had fresh chiles, avocados and tomatoes to wrap into them. Ipala is a bumpy place which interrupted sleep for all on board. QV did not hit the rock wall when the wind shifted South during the night.

When we started the engine to weigh anchor, the over-temp alarm sounded. Perhaps, by now, this should not have come as a surprise. I ran the RPM up and down until water flow started from the exhaust. This was increasingly strange. This also delayed our departure but we started closing on Kokua III and a large motorsailer out ahead of us as we approached Cabo Corrientes—site of the fearsome "washing machine effect" caused by the meeting of currents and winds at the South end of Bahía Banderas. We stood out a little over 3nm to avoid inshore currents in wind only 0-5 knots. Our GPS positions did not match with the chart. It often located us up on the beach…or on the rocks. I believe the reference datum are not compatible. Caroline went to her bunk after her early watch. I saw two turtles basking on the surface and a very large black fish with a small dorsal fin. This critter was at least 15 ft. long. I decided this must be a basking shark and nobody was there to correct me.

It's over 30nm from the Cabo over to Puerto Vallarta. I enjoyed cruising along the scenic South coast of Bahía Banderas until the high rise skyline of P.V. came into view. I started trying to raise Marina Vallarta with no response. A couple of hours later, we're entering the channel as two tourist ferries are motoring out. Finally, a response from the marina. After I give them the boat's dimensions, QV is assigned to slip A9. Into the big marina, make a 180 around the dock to slips A9 through A11 all of which are blocked off, in repair, or under construction. I work into A12 with difficulty. It has no hook-ups. A brief examination reveals A9 will take only a short, narrow-beamed boat. There's been a screw-up by the marina staff. At the end of a tiring passage, it is a major annoyance.

Cecilia, from the Paperman agency, overheard our arrival and comes down to the dock. She informs me the Port Captain in Puerto Vallarta still wants to process clearances for his port. Our boat documents were, you may remember, rescinded at Ixtapa. She wants US$20 to develop Puerto Vallarta papers and process them. I don't want to aggravate any Mexican Port Captains, so agree to the deal. Oh, and she'll need our passports. Everything will be back to us by 1300 tomorrow.

I walk a longish distance, asking directions to the marina office. There, the staff of three are totally clueless about slip conditions as they sit in a sleek, air-conditioned office wearing crisp white blouses. After much discussion, they finally decided QV could move to M12-13. The distance from A to M, as you may have figured out, is essentially the other end of the marina.

The wind has come up for the first time today, making it more difficult to maneuver QV back out of the cramped end slip, turned around in the fairway, and back on to M dock in a side wind. The line handlers have all gone to the wrong side of the dock space. Quo Vadis is finally secured, again, at Marina Vallarta by 1800. Caroline takes a key and heads for the shower. I look for an internet kiosk to inform Dr.

Morehouse of our location. The marina wants US$65 for two days. I'm not in a good mood.

Mood improves when we go ashore to have a local pizza. My Daddy Defenses go up without prior warning when the pizza place guy starts hitting on Caroline. She is freshly tanned, noticeably better toned after a few weeks sailing, and has inherited her long brown hair and looks from her mother. The young Mexican guy wants to steal her. "She is a jewel," he informs me. "Guard her well." It sounds better in Spanish and I take his advice to heart. We're back on board by 2130 where the tired, warned father records the battery levels in the ship's log and crashes in his bunk.

Doctor Morehouse, I presume. Well, actually, I know it's you, Mad Dog.

Today is Cinco de Mayo. Yesterday Cap'n Jack's high school friend Dr. Jeff Morehouse joined us on board Quo Vadis. I am familiar with him as my sister Beth dubbed him "H". But for the sake of formality, Jeff will do. (H is his middle initial.)

Thinking a weather update would be timely as well as contribute to self-preservation, I'm up early to listen to the Puerto Vallarta Net on CH22. Nothing comes in on the primary VHF. I cannot get consistent copy from the Net on the hand-held VHF and they are supposedly just across the Bay. I put fresh batteries in the portable SSB radio and ran up the antenna for Amigo Net. I sat through the usual gossip for 15 minutes waiting for the weather. I cannot understand Don. This has been true since Bahías de Huatulco. I get no substantial weather info except there is/was/will be a big Pacific high.

I hook up the hose and shore power. Caroline industriously starts cleaning the boat after I decline such offers from Horácio, Hector and Chaca. My contribution is to search for an LPG refill. I leave the canister at the appointed collection place and return to find Caroline still working on the exterior. She finished up while I made cheeseburgers: a perennial favorite Skipper Special, you'll recall. I cleaned up the port head and made up the port bunk. I am optimistically expecting Jeff M. to join the crew of *Quo Vadis*. He does. We review weather and possible sail plans to Cabo San Lucas.

Jeff is a technically excellent sailor with offshore experience. His navigation skills were originally developed during his years as a Navy officer. His ability at calculations has been honed in more recent times as a Professor of Mechanical Engineering. I am lacking both qualifications, but we share a sense of humor and a long history. I rowed first starboard oar to his stroke for three years on our school crew. We came second in the Nationals. He was a serious, studious type in high school, so his nickname was Mad Dog, of course. After siesta, Jeff offers to sponsor dinner. We get fancy. I start with oysters. Caroline finishes with a dessert crepe. I believe Jeff also had something to eat. I feel a somewhat surprising sense of relief to have him on board for the next passage.

On to Cabo San Lucas! With just a few items to take care of before shoving off

The Captain was up at dawn, which cracks surprisingly late in these latitudes and season, to make the crew list and coffee. Cecilia came by to pick up the revised crew list and passports and arrange check out for tomorrow morning. As this is still required by the Puerto Vallarta Port Captain, it is another US$20 for her. I know it is legally not correct. Later, I find out that a couple of renegade Port Captains are trying to keep the pesos flowing in their personal fiefs and, indirectly, into their pockets.

I tune in to the PV cruiser net and inquire where to refill LPG tanks. I'm told to take a bus toward Ixtapa and get off at the *Gasera*. There is no sailing weather offered on this net so I bring up the Amigo net to hear yet another combination of garbled talk and static. While I'm reeling in the antenna, Gerardo Beltrán came by and offered to work on the over-temperature problem. I hope I didn't sound desperate or over-eager but I agreed to have the engine compartment open for business early next morning.

I took the LPG tank on the bus as Caroline and Jeff left for the Super Mexicana market to provision for the crossing to Cabo San Lucas. The bus was well out into the countryside when I figured out it had probably passed the *Gasera*. The driver confirmed it was back down the road so I hopped off and caught the next bus back. Everybody was back on board Quo Vadis by 1330. The LPG fill had cost 18 pesos, taken about 30 seconds and was no problem. This makes me even more moody about the run-around I experienced in Nicaragua. The bus rides cost about the same as the LPG. The tab was 920 pesos for provisions and Caroline's "must have" item: new board shorts.

After siesta, all the crew got cleaned up and went in to Puerto Vallarta for Cinco de Mayo. Either we had missed them or the festivities were very subdued. We watched the sun set into Bahía Banderas while trying a selection of six different types of tacos and listening to street musicians.

Jeff and I were up before 0700 the next morning. It was still cold and dark. We both went back to our bunks until 0800 when I turned out to tune in the cruiser net. The only weather was the local daily forecast. They probably saw it on TV. No useful info. I prepared the engine compartment for Gerardo's arrival and, staying optimistic, set up the SSB receiver for Amigo net. All static. No weather. Also, no Gerardo. No answer on Gerardo's phone.

To while away the idle hours, I started through the engine manual troubleshooting tree for overheating. A defective thermostat was one cause. I had a spare thermostat. That was about the only part of the cooling subsystem that had not been replaced or re-built. I started in to replace it. See what happens when you get fanatic about a boat problem?

Two hours later, I had the new gasket and thermostat back in and the cover on. Gerardo appeared a little after noon so I let him bust his knuckles re-tightening the hose clamps. I started the engine. There was still no immediate cooling water but slightly more flowed out when it did start. Gerardo took the discharge hose off. He thought the flow was still below normal and wanted to check the water pump on the premise that the impeller, though new, may not be properly seated. When he opens up the water pump, we discover one lobe of the impeller is missing and another is cracked all the way through. I had one more spare impeller. The re-assembled water pump appeared to move cooling water around the engine jacket and out the exhaust at all engine speeds, including idle. With the extra set of mechanic hands, we tightened the decompression kill cable and the alternator belt. Gerardo wanted 500 pesos for his contribution. I made another trip to the marina ATM.

Leaving that machine and Gerardo with the pesos it produced, I stopped by the internet café. I could not get the Buoyweather pages to open. The Intellicast weather page opened but only showed high altitude winds over the Baja peninsula; nothing for the Mexican mainland coast or Sea of Cortez, where we are now and plan to sail soon. The crew went to the showers while El Capitán pumped the gook out the engine compartment, re-stowed fuel and lubricants, and closed up.

Cecilia came to the dock with our *despachos* and *pasaportes* about 1230. The fee was 220 pesos but she didn't have change for 250. I am no longer surprised. I took the crew ashore for a late lunch, first checking out of the marina office. They wanted 1500 pesos including a four day power and water surcharge. We finally made it to "La Colequita", a marina restaurant where all three of us filled up on killer seafood washed down with *cervezas*. This was the best 300 pesos I'd spent all day.

We left just after dawn, raised the fuel dock on CH68 and moved in to the dock space without waiting for a motor yacht, sportfisher or panga. I left another 318 pesos in Puerto Vallarta and called the *Capitania* on CH13 to clear out S/V Quo Vadis with crew of three aboard for Cabo San Lucas. There was no additional charge.

Clatter, Clatter, Bang!

We are motor-sailing the Pacific in winds W6-8 knots when I go below to make lunch about 1230. Jeff and Caroline both heard something that sounded funny in the engine compartment and called down to the galley. The over-temp alarm went off by the time I got back to the cockpit. I stuck my head over the stern to see no cooling water exhaust flow. Engine cool-down wasn't possible since we had no cooling water, so I killed it with the de-compression cable. I thought I had heard the water pump clatter and break. The only question in my mind was the metallic noise, since the impeller is rubber but, in any case, it was the water pump just "fixed" by Gerardo for 500 *pesos*.

Jeff's calm input was that we should continue on like we're sailing to Cabo. If I haven't mentioned it before, the good Dr. Morehouse has to leave us in four days. Something about teaching his classes back at the University. I wanted to go back to Puerto Vallarta, and track down Gerardo. We started sailing long tacks in light winds. Everybody finished lunch while I paced and fumed. I did manage to set the watch schedule: Caroline 12-4, as requested; me: 4-8 and Jeff: 8-12, since he's a morning person. I remembered to turn off the reefer. I also dug in the parts locker for the spare water pump. It had no impeller and the exit piping was askew. I found a third spare impeller (I can't believe I had that many spares.) and started re-building the pump to the specs in the O&M manual.

Of the choices available at dusk, I chose to sail West away from the mainland's rocky shore, even though it was dead slow at 3 knots. If we managed to fix the engine, we'd be 36-40nm closer to Cabo. If not, it would be only that distance to sail back downwind.

Everybody made their own sandwich or snack for the evening meal. We were still full from the lunch I finally got around to preparing: roast chicken and spinach salad *vinaigrette*. The sunset is a brilliant red that darkens into a beautiful, clear night. It's too bad we're sailing very slowly on the wrong course. Las Tres Marias, the 3 prohibited prison islands, are still visible off our starboard at dark.

The navigation lights are working. The instruments are lit up and functioning. All the crew does a good job standing watch and saving power as Quo Vadis moves slowly through the night under sail.

Jeff relieved me an hour early so I could get some sleep before starting on water pump replacement. A short nap, supplemented by fresh coffee, appears to be enough to get me started. The way the single Yanmar is installed in this Prout, the front engine access panel has to be removed to get to the water pump. This panel is at the rear of the fuel tank compartment where I also store lubricants, reserve jerry jugs of diesel, and other things oily. Getting all this stuff out, and re-stowed securely for conditions at sea, is a time-consuming part of most engine work. It is no different this morning, though I'm getting better at this job and don't drop the wing nuts as much.

The pulley has fallen off the water pump drive shaft, which explains the clattering noise. I find the nut and washer in the bottom of the engine compartment. I feel really stupid and I admit it.

"That was bad Captain-ing. I should've figured out the actual problem right away."

"That was bad engineering analyis," responds Jeff, trying to absorb some of the blame. "You should always trace down and verify the fault before trying to come up with possible solutions."

Caroline is totally blameless in the company of two experienced systems engineers, one of whom is still practicing and teaching the science. I know I can make, and have made, better decisions.

I finally figure out how to re-install the pulley. I add a lock washer under the nut and facing washer. The drive belt is in good condition: no nicks or chafing. Exhaust water flow appears normal at idle, 1500, 1800 and 2000 RPM. I add 300cc to the engine oil, up to the top mark on the dipstick. *Quo Vadis* is underway under power by 1030 while I clean, stow and close up.

The wind is rising but coming around NNW, closing out the angle on our starboard tack. Swells are 4-6 ft. at 12-15 second intervals. Caroline was sick before lunch and took some Bonine. I made soft tacos which worked to make Jeff sick after lunch. He said he felt OK after throwing up. My only personal affliction is continuing to hear strange noises from the engine compartment.

Across the Sea of Cortez

During her midnight watch, Caroline was able to hold a course around 270 magnetic, pushing up to 290. I was able to hold our calculated 290 course to Cabo, right into a nasty chop which gave a bumpy ride and no sleep for those off watch below. I tried 270 as a possible point of sail; also allowing engine shut-down. It was worse. I tried 330 for motoring. Every heading was worse than our course but all headings were bumpy with breakers over the bows and spray into the cockpit. When Jeff came on watch, we shut down and added the last 10 gallons of reserve to the main fuel tank. This provided 21 gallons (measurement and calculation agree) which should allow another 30 hours motoring, if needed. I calculate we can be there in 25 hours or less. The GPS agrees.

Last night, the bioluminescent algae were appearing in the wake of the boat. It looked like the boat was leaving a trail of green stars that appeared as soon as the water was disturbed but would dissipate within a few seconds. Magic. Today, the Cap'n and Jeff woke me to see what looked like orca whales: a small pod of four or maybe more. I saw the nose of one: a Mexican orca.

We left Puerto Vallarta 2-3 days ago. We are headed for Cabo San Lucas, where everything is expensive. I have had the 12-4 watch both day and night and tonight will be my third night. I thought last night was the last time. How wrong I was. I'm exhausted. The plan is we drop Jeff off in Cabo, re-fuel and then move on for another overnight, two-day passage. Oh, goody.

Jeff stays at the helm, with a queasy stomach, into the wind and chop. After Caroline takes the wheel at noon, I make a lunch of spinach salad with *lardons*, followed by a cheese and sweet red pepper omelette. It doesn't occur to the insensitive skipper until later that I might be the only one with any appetite for all this food. The seas are short, sharp and 3-6 ft. throughout the day, making an uncomfortable ride all around the quadrant to our course. The winds never allowed setting the genoa to any advantage.

Supper is soup and a sandwich. Caroline feels better, and is holding down that amount of food when she comes on watch at 2400. Jeff is still not feeling so good. I'm concerned that he's become dehydrated. He agrees and takes in some more fluids. The seas build to 6-9 ft. during Caroline's watch. I can feel the change and go up to the cockpit at 0300. She's doing fine at the helm, charging across the growing waves. I'm the one who is worried.

Landfall comes after first light. I had already spotted the Cabo Falso light 26nm out. The lights of Cabo San Lucas and San José del Cabo make a glow in the sky. I've been turning the bows of QV slightly sideways to the short 3-4 foot chop in an attempt to give the crew down below a more comfortable ride. Jeff thinks this is a new technique, or maybe just a strange one, and tries it when he comes on deck. He takes Quo Vadis in to the fuel dock at 0930. The passage was exactly three days from Puerto Vallarta. The boat's knotmeter log shows it has traveled 334nm since leaving those sunny shores.

In Baja California

I pay for the fuel and Jeff, now feeling better or maybe just relieved we made it to Cabo, announces he'll pay for a slip in the marina. We are both shocked into momentary silence when the girl behind the desk in the marina office informs him that such payment will amount to more than US$100/day for my 37 ft. vessel.

Jeff looks at me; then back at her. "Where do you think we are?" he asks. "At Hilton Head, back in South Carolina?"

She smiles but I doubt she really knows where, or how much, Hilton Head is. Jeff bravely puts his credit card on the counter and informs me, "You're buying dinner."

I also make a real breakfast on board the next morning before seeing Jeff off to his flights home. Before leaving Quo Vadis, he helps with the tools so I can tighten the nuts on the starboard rudder bar. The starboard rudder snugs right up and exhibits no play.

The transit bus to the airport leaves from the Hotel Fiesta Marina. This is one of the wa-ay too many Cabo hotels populated by over-decorated, spoiled young *gringas* who snap orders at the Mexican staff— in English, of course. OK, this is Cabo but it is still Mexico so some of the orders aren't understood. At least, not right away. In the hotel lobby, Caroline and I embrace Jeff, wishing each other safe travel and confusing both the *gringas* and the Mexican staff. The presence on board of my pal of 40 years has boosted my morale and provided relief and amusement to Caroline. It's been a surprising comfort to have this former Navy officer, Professional Engineer, and my schoolboy crew stroke on Quo Vadis as the *de facto* engineering officer while also double-checking my navigation. Jeff hoists his bag into the back of the bus for the next perilous leg of this journey: in a Mexican-driven mini-van on Baja roads.

I had been warned that Cabo San Lucas was one of the most expensive ports in Mexico. It is. However, this Port's *Capitanía* shows no interest in payments or documents for vessel clearance. It is the only benefit evident in an otherwise charmless place.

Along a long Coast

The next morning I changed the engine oil and filter, bought ice and fresh-baked bread, and took off the trash. When Caroline came back from her shower, we made ready to get underway. The timing to Bahía Magdalena (referred to by many gringos as Mag Bay) has become marginal, now requiring we make it in 30 hours for a safe passage and a timely arrival rather than 32.

For the first time I can remember, the Buoyweather info (Winds NW3-4 knots off Cabo Falso) was wrong. We were in seas 3-5 feet at 3-5 second intervals with winds in excess of 30 knots. QV took a couple of breakers over the coach roof. Sure, we were experiencing a big cape effect late in the morning but the West shore conditions also remain uncertain. The final decider was I couldn't see the point in starting a long passage soaking wet. An hour out from Los Arcos, the Cap'n aborted today's passage to go back to the San Lucas anchorage. We'll try again tomorrow at 0630.

Quo Vadis was on the hook off a noisy hotel beach by 1300. I dove on the anchor in 20 feet. It was not a great set but one fluke was buried and all the chain was curved on the bottom. Caroline was asleep by the time I got back on board. When I came on deck after my siesta, the boat was under the looming bow of one of those big "party hearty" cruise ships. There was another of the same type anchored behind it. I still hate having big motor vessels come in and hog anchorages. After the jet skis, banana boats and pink-skinned tourists were packed away for another day, the crew of QV went for a relaxing swim and took a hot shower. Dinner on board was based on the infamous cheeseburgers, with a small salad and red wine. We agreed they couldn't be eating any better on the floating rental apartments looming off our stern.

Yesterday, we made our 30+ hour passage to Magdalena Bay. (Insert sigh of relief here.) On my watch the night before I sighted some mysterious streaks of wake-like froth being made alongside but independent of the boat. Watching the patterns and movements of these streaks through the water, and the size, I came to the almost certain conclusion that these frothy streaks in the water were caused by the night time visit of dolphins. I stick by this as a true story.

The streaks of light through the water would dodge this way and that, zig-zagging along playfully; matching the speed of the boat. Sometimes appearing as an individual line, then joining up with another to swim together for a time; then going out of my range of sight completely. I think the reason I was able to make out their trails was the bioluminescent algae in the surrounding ocean. How cool ☺.

The next morning, when I awoke there was a thick, gray fog completely surrounding us. This burned off by 1100 or so. Just a little before that, more or perhaps the same dolphins accompanied us until we were just three hours away from Magdalena. What splendid creatures they are. It seemed almost as if they were escorting us to our proper destination.

After clearing Cabo Falso the second time and getting headed NNW, I decided to try Mrs. Charlie's inshore sailing strategy for avoiding big seas on the way to Bahía Magdalena. By 1600, we were still 121nm from Mag Bay. There was no way we could make it with daylight if we continued on the inshore route. Quo Vadis came to the Mag Bay course of 295 Magnetic just before Punta Lobos. Wind and swells are on the nose but it is a possible 20 hour passage.

I had forgotten about fog. It surprised me on my watch, cutting visibility to less than a quarter mile. I hadn't been in fog since the Chesapeake, nearly three years ago. Visibility improved to about a mile by 1100. It was clear enough to see a dolphin couple jumping in synch; starting about 500 meters to starboard and coming right over to the boat. They accompanied us for nearly two hours.

The seas never lay down during the night with wind chop on top of a 4 ft. swell. Sometime during the night the second reef line (blue) parted where it loops to the boom. A quick check revealed the first reef line (red) was also frayed. I can't figure out the immediate cause: the main is not reefed and—why now? After the dolphin couple left, I laid the boat into the trough of the waves, added fuel to the main tank from the deck jerry jug and topped up the engine oil.

The wind is building to 25-30 knots. Predicted 4 ft. seas at 4 seconds are also happening. We're taking a bashing this afternoon. We pass Tosca, a supposed anchorage which looks highly unlikely to this skipper, and are anchored in Man o' War cove off Puerto Magdalena by 1815.

Caroline was at the helm, doing a great job. Within 15 minutes, I have the bridle rigged and the boat secured. My stalwart crew makes a smooth transition from Helm to DJ, selecting tonight's tunes. I makeshift repair the salon table and start dinner as the sky darkens. I fell on the table in the chop coming North. We dig in to a *caprese* salad, *linguine* with clams, a *baguette* and white wine.

After dinner, I calculate the fuel requirements for local purchase and Caroline discovers the starboard head sink door is torn loose. It's the same one Lodie broke off; maybe the same hinge. The starboard head won't drain. It is cold overnight. All the crew took another blanket to their bunks.

In the morning, I tune in SSB 8122 for weather. There is nothing. Thinking my timing is wrong in this different time zone, I try 8224 an hour later. Nothing. I also discover the port head is not working. It feels like the pin holding the pump diaphragm has come out, again. The starboard head is filling but not draining. I bucketed out both heads and added disinfectant prior to plunging in to disassemble and, hopefully, repair them. I checked the engine oil level. It takes 500cc after two days' running. A water leak, probably from the pump, is leaving crystallized salt all over the interior of the engine compartment. None of the multiple Mexican mechanics, all the way back to Acapulco, have fixed these problems despite the many days and many pesos spent.

We're still in Magdalena Bay. Dad's trying to get the heads fixed so we can crap on board. I've taken it somewhat for granted up until now. I woke up with Billie Holiday playing over the boat's speakers. What a nice way to wake up. It enabled me to walk arm-in-arm, knee-to-knee with her down a forest path in my dream before waking. Lucky me. ☺

As I continued cleaning out the heads, I dropped the bucket overboard. I got the swim ladder down and my swim suit on as it slowly drifted away. Bucket recovery becomes a major challenge. The water temperature is chilling and, let's face it, this has not been a fun morning. I need to focus. I say out loud, "I can do this." The water is not numbing enough to mask the piercing cold. I can barely take breaths as I stroke and kick but slowly make it back to the boat with the bucket. Caroline grabs it and hands me a towel. When I'm dry, I glue and screw the salon table and the head sink door. I am not pleased but not surprised if it is caused by stress, that I am still losing big quantities of my hair.

Lunch is beef tacos with everything. In the afternoon, I enter all the waypoints from here to San Diego. The GPS says it's 548 nm. That box of chips and the hand-held VHF both get new batteries. A cold fog starts rolling in at 1930 as I make a late supper.

On shore in Puerto Magdalena, there were three sisters aged 10, 9 and 5 that were so cute and so helpful. I thought they were, anyway. I bet Dad could argue. They were an inspiration to learn Spanish. So far, the children have been the only people I've wanted to have a conversation with but have been incapable of it. The sisters lead us to the little store that had a few things we wanted as the oldest kept laughing at me. I don't know if it was positive or negative but I laughed, too. I couldn't help it. I tried to make conversation. How old are each of you? Are you all sisters? Is the guy running the store your Grandpa? That's about all I could manage.

When Dad and I found out there was no diesel fuel in Magdalena but only in Puerto San Carlos, we went back to the boat to get the fuel and water jugs ready to take aboard the abuelito's panga. (When we later found out the representing Capitan at Magdalena would have delivered the fuel to the boat, we were pissed, but that's later.)

We made the panga trip to San Carlos and as soon as I jumped off the panga, I slipped on the slimey rocks and fell—BOOM—right on my ass. It didn't hurt much but, man, was I embarrassed. The girl about my age who was riding with us (the only other passenger) made her disappearance fast. So my ass was wet the rest of the day but no green stains, so I'm happy.

We cruised all over town in this guy's red pick-up truck. I also made a lame attempt at making conversation with him. Is this your house? You like music? Music is important. I listen to a little. (Lame=Me.) Anyway, we drive all over; get diesel which forces me to sit inside the truck. I had volunteered to sit in the truck bed because of my dampened backside. We pick up a few other things: water, tortillas and beer. "Yee-haw!" she exclaimed in sarcastic excitement.

The water is mesmerizingly clear, by the way. It looks wonderfully inviting but it is 52 degrees F. Ha! No. Not going swimming. But lovely to look at. On the way to and from San Carlos are beautiful white sand dunes. The wind is whipping the sand around in little cyclones. We make it back to Quo Vadis; Dad refuels.

Fuel Tales, Head Travails and Small Whales

Nica's cousin met us at the landing and drove us to the Pemex station. They were out of diesel fuel. He drove us to the API which is the official government office for permitting and dispensing commercial quantities of diesel fuel. Who knew? I was interrogated as to why I hadn't brought my boat to Puerto San Carlos for re-fueling. Engine problems, my poor daughter could be stuck on board, scary passage to Magdalena, etc. Well, Señora Lorena Ochoa C. was very sympathetic. She made out a receipt for 115 liters of diesel and offered to let Caroline stay with her if the boat couldn't be fixed or she didn't want to continue. I thanked her politely and went to have the fuel pumped. I didn't tell her that Caroline was still game and I was the one who was getting tired of this voyage.

As I finished double filtering the diesel and cleaning up, Gregorio the Magdalena Port Captain came out in a panga full of fuel jugs. He was very upset we'd already bought fuel from API. It was his deal to provide boat fuel. He also had some scathing comments about Nica (I can't tell if the old guy flat out ripped us off or he really didn't know fuel was the Port Captain's privilege.) Gregório still cleared us in with a copy of Quo Vadis' documentation and the Puerto Vallarta *zarpe*; then stayed to have a beer. I guess he didn't look very closely at the *zarpe*. It still has Jeff on the crew list since the *Capitanía* at Cabo San Lucas wasn't doing anything about *zarpes* or clearances.

After he leaves QV, I open a beer and make fish tacos with fair results. After finishing the beer and the fish tacos, I reviewed our anchorage and sail plan options, again. There is nothing I like; only long passages and/or marginal anchorages. The anchor light goes on at dusk. I tell Caroline about the housing offer from Sra. Ochoa; she says she'd rather stay on board with me. She remains cooperative and optimistic. Possibly because she doesn't need to pump three inches of water from the lazarettes (Where did that come from?) and fix the heads.

Once I figured out what was broken, I found all the necessary parts in my third (and last) Groco marine toilet fix-it kit. I seated old and new valves and gaskets with Teflon marine lube, got all the pins and screws lined up, and things generally went back together well, until the foot pedal spring snapped making it impossible to open the toilet discharge. Undaunted, I cobbled together a repair with a rigging ring, opened the newly serviced inlet seacock and…the port head seemed to be working. I cleaned up both heads and disinfected the deck areas and seacock wells; then disinfected myself. Caroline had made a hot lunch of shrimp noodles and cleaned up the galley.

The winds do not permit some of the preferred routes North, including direct to San Juanico. Caroline started doing a T-chart analysis of possible options for us, ranging from "Cross the Bay to Puerto San Carlos, park the boat, and take the bus to California" to "Keep going North to Abreojos". "Abreojos" emerged from the T-chart listing (+/-) as our best alternative. At least, based on the information we had.

At dawn, I got the SSB antenna up and actually heard weather information. Tropical cyclone Adrian is off El Salvador, making it miserable down there, and winds NW35-45 forecast for the outside of the Baja peninsula on Friday, becoming calm by Sunday. OK, we need to be tucked in safely somewhere on Friday and be prepared to motor after that.

Port Captain Gregório came out to Quo Vadis, raising the question of my having three or two crew on *zarpes* from different ports. He and I both recognize it is a problem we can't solve here at Puerto Magdalena. While in this apparent state of accord, I quickly get the anchor up and head South under sail.

I'm exhausted, so this will be comparatively brief. We left Magdalena Bay at 11:30 this morning; got to Santa Maria right before eight and sunset. So many dolphins today! It was unbelievable. There were massed schools of fish on the way out. You could tell from the swarms of birds overhead and pods of dolphins below. Feeding frenzy. No joke. In one pod, I could distinctly make out one brown body sans dorsal fin. It was a sea lion swimming along with the dolphins. I couldn't get a picture so I was pissed but I got over it.

Dad and I also spotted what Dad thought was a pilot whale. I have no idea except it was big, gray and had a small dolphin-sized dorsal fin, so who am I to disagree? I was stoked about that. A bad part of today was I cried.

The guidebook anchorage in Bahía Santa Maria, beneath the cut in the mountains, proves windy and exposed. Caroline picked her own spot and went in after nearly 8 hours underway, beating to windward. She is getting good, both at selecting the better anchorage and the boat handling to set the hook. She started seafood pasta for dinner while I rigged the anchor light and pumped some liquid from the engine compartment. I put together some salads and we opened a Chilean white.

Again, we are alone in the anchorage. Some pangas are beached by a fishing settlement to the North.

Are we really in Mexico?

Did I mention it was cold? In Vallarta, Cabo and South of all that, I'm sweating. In Magdalena and Northward, BRRRRR! Wind and temps make me bundle up like it's winter in Central Coast. Fuck it's cold! Now that we're in Abri...blah, blah (I want to say "Abierto". That's not it, something like "Abri-ho-hos"...don't care.) it's not so bad. Big winds, but we were expecting that. Still some bioluminescent algae in the night but less intense. Still plenty of dolphins. Yayy! Though I was so cold last night I did not care. All I cared about was defrosting after my watch. Surrounded by fog during my second 12-4 watch; so thick I could hardly make out the bow of the boat.

When day came, it warmed up. I got awakened in the middle of a REM cycle, though. No bueno. No me gusta. I survived. We got here to Abri-ho-hos and I peeled off my layers, got some food, took a hot shower, took a long nap (Surprise.) and all is well. How did El Capitan put it? 157 miles closer to San Diego. Big whoop. I would be more excited, but this sailing shit is work. It tires me out. We've actually "sailed"— without the motor— only a few hours (12? Dunno.) the entire time I've been on board. It doesn't really matter to me because we're getting there. Woo-hoo! Really, this time.

I was up before light to get underway on a course to Abreojos that also preserved the option of going in to Juanico if conditions deteriorated. I roused Caroline at 0700 and she was at the helm, ready to weigh anchor, 20 minutes later. When she started the engine, I stuck my head over the stern to check the exhaust flow. There was none. No cooling water; some smoke. She ran the RPM from 1000 to 1800 in 200 RPM increments, trying to start flow. Nothing happened until the over-temp alarm went off. God, how that sound makes me crazy...or crazier. She shut down the engine. I re-evaluate our options, including sailing back to Puerto San Carlos. Hoping the engine had cooled enough not to cause more damage, I decided to try to start, again. Exhaust flow began at idle and continued up the RPM range at normal volume.

Caroline got me up when a thick fog set in during her watch. I did a radar check. Frankly, I had not anticipated fog as a navigation problem and hadn't warned her. It is very much a concern along this coast and I just forgot. She did the right thing to get me up. Nothing was visible on radar at a 16nm range scan. This is not surprising since we have spotted no vessel traffic for the last two days and there are no obstacles on the chart crossing the mouth of Bahia Vizcaino.

The passage last night wasn't so bad except for the fog. But it is still too frickin' cold to be Mexico! I have the suspicion that during one of Dad's watches, he made a sudden turn and went to southern Chile because it's all desert landscapes and Antarctic winds. No me gusta. I didn't pack for this blustery cold crap. I packed for hot and sticky with sweat climates. I hope I can fix my legs. Eww.

The anchor is down in 14 ft. about 500 meters off the beach, the bridle is rigged and the engine shut down by noon. A hot lunch of *chorizo con huevos* accompanied by avocado, sweet peppers and onions is on the salon table by 1300. The wind is confusing, clocking all around and building.

There is little protection in this anchorage off the low sand spit at the village of Abreojos. This doesn't stop us from taking long naps this afternoon in what, for Quo Vadis, are rolly conditions. We are usually flat and stable at anchor.

Today we went ashore to Abreojos (Ha! Got it right this time.) and got fuel and some food. No bell peppers? How do they live? Joke. But lots of salty stuff. When we were coming in with the dinghy and trying to beach ourselves, a wave came up behind the dink and tossed Dad out. We were half expecting that. We were soaked, but OK. Nothing got destroyed. The tow truck that hauls fishing pangas hauled us up on the beach.

We found someone to take us around town in their pick-up much like we did in Magdalena. His name was Juan de Dios; translates as John of God. We stopped for lunch when we were done with everything and made fun of the female pop singer "Princesa" (gag) on Mexican TV. She sounded like I would imagine Brittany Spears sounding if she sang in Spanish. Right when we were leaving, Princesa started singing "My Heart Will Go On". (Double gag) The trip out in the dinghy wasn't much drier. We needed the tow truck again to pull us out to the water. All the food we bought stayed dry, even the bread, thankfully. Joy ☺.

Somehow, much of both Dad's and my clothing is getting wet while on board, inside. Inside closets, drawers, on the shelf by my bunk…I don't get it. And it's very aggravating since today it was overcast and windy all day. It's not much better than Magdalena; at least there it was windy and cold and sunny. The fog makes the evenings very damp and uncomfortable. Our clothes (including the only long sleeve shirt I brought: me=dumb) are never dry.

Caroline and I were the only customers for lunch at Amelia's place. We had good, basic *pescado* and *carne asada*. I still get voracious for both dishes, even after years of traveling and eating in Baja. I knew the delay for lunch would mean rougher surf conditions as the tide came in but still decided the restaurant meal on shore was worth it, for both of us. I had just enough pesos left to pay Amelia.

Surf was breaking 2-3 ft. on the beach by the time the dinghy was towed back to the water. The dink was packed with 10 gallons of fuel, 5 gallons of water, 2 six packs of beer, 2 bottles of wine and four boxes of groceries. I still couldn't get the pin out of the motor lock-down, so it was carving a deep furrow in the wet sand. Caroline held the bow until she was knee-deep. I yell at her, "Jump in." and push the dink out between the breaks until I'm waist deep; then throw my soggy body over the gunwale. The Suzuki starts on the first pull. I push it into gear just as another wave breaks over the bow. I managed to stay in the dink and we made it back to QV with everything. I'm happy.

I started the engine and reefer as we stowed provisions, cleaned up and rinsed the salt off our bodies. We bagged and stowed our soggy clothes. The engine started making a transient rattling noise just before the planned shut down time. I don't know what to look for unless the water pump is broken, again. There is a big swell with the incoming tide, making the boat rock. We go to bunks early but sleep uneasily. At 0630, I went on deck where I could see nothing but thick fog. It was below limits for safe navigation. Is this what Steve Cherry was talking about when he warned me to keep my "eyes open" around Abreojos? I went back to my bunk and shut them.

At 0730, I started breakfast and opened up the engine compartment. The alternator belt was lying in the bottom and the water pump belt was hanging loose from its pulley. The interior of the engine compartment was seriously salt-encrusted from the leaking water pump. The pump seal was shredded. This was the new one installed at Ixtapa. I conclude Gerardo screwed up all these items by not installing the new (and my last spare) impeller according to the manual and my direction at Cabo San Lucas. I dug out the "old" water pump, re-built while drifting along with Jeff and Caroline en route to Cabo, and installed it. I put the belt back on, got the alternator belt on and adjusted it with help from Caroline. Gerardo had not done this correctly, either, and I hadn't caught it. Everything looked good, so we started the engine. There was no exhaust water flow.

I had forgotten to re-open the inlet seacock. Caroline shut down the engine and I opened the seacock. Either we got lucky or we got it correct. When she re-started the engine, the cooling water flow looked stronger than it had prior to installing the replacement pump.

However, so did the flow leaking out of the water pump inlet. I recalled this piece would not tighten up when I tried to re-build the pump. It was a half-thread off from aligning in the proper position so I'd wrapped it with Teflon tape. The Teflon tape proved useless with the brass fitting. The fitting needed another half turn or pipe joint compound, neither of which were attainable. Considering the poor alternatives, I re-assembled the pump with hematite instant gasket on the threads. While I was hoping the stuff was curing to a hard seal, I turned to my traditional remedy for problems on board: We ate lunch. I made cheeseburgers with everything, my excellent home fries and put out some cold brews for Captain and crew. This may be my true, or only, talent on a sailing vessel.

The water pump fix does not look encouraging as the inlet pipe still moves. I re-installed it anyway and clamped on the newly trimmed and dressed hoses. This time, I remembered to open the cooling water seacock before starting the engine. The inlet side of the pump did not leak and the exhaust flowed normally. Nothing changed after five minutes, so I shut down still hoping the gasket material would continue to cure. While indulging in this wishful thinking, I checked the engine air filter. It was solid oily gunk on the inlet side. This is one of several possible causes of white smoke, as cited in the operating manual. The old sponge was replaced with new, clean sponge we'd bought at the neighborhood market in Manzanillo after the original air filter disintegrated.

The starboard storage bin leak continues, so I pumped it out. The port sump was filled, too. That usually happens only when we're underway. I pumped it out. I closed up the engine compartment and bagged my tools by 1900. Caroline was a good help and very patient. She brought in some semi-dry items as the incoming tide again pushed a big, rolling swell through the anchorage.

I re-entered the Abreojos waypoint as an exit that, at least according to the charts, is clear of the reefs and rocks on the outside and the sand bars on the inside. I ate a salad and sardines for dinner. The propane for the stove ran out while Caroline was making herself a turkey melt. The tank ran empty after 17 days. I had figured it could go 20. It must have been all those Skipper Specials for lunch.

There was enough LPG to boil water for coffee the next morning. More good stuff: no leaks from the inlet side of the water pump or through the seal at the bottom. Cooling water flow is good. I added fuel to the tank through the Baja filter and oil to the top mark of the dipstick. We were underway for an overnight passage to Turtle Bay; on course for the exit waypoint when I spotted a local fishing boat on a route between the reefs and shore. I told Caroline to follow the boat and try to stay on the 5 fathom line. It was relatively calm, which made the reef break harder to see.

The plan worked. We emerged into deep water, got all the sails set, and had a very large whale come very close across our bows: maybe two boatlengths off. It was so big it had to be a gray whale but it is late in the season for migration. We saw another large whale a few hours later. It was not quite as big as the first one. She was headed away from shore. Do some gray whales stay in these waters year 'round?

It was cold on the night watches with wind on the nose at 10-15 knots and choppy seas. The wind died after I came on watch at 0400 just as the fog brought visibility down to about 500 meters. I passed Isla Asuncion and Isla San Roque a little too close for a night passage. Sizing the islands for distance is difficult in the dark, especially with their short light towers. The fog lightened just enough for me to pick up the navigation lights outside the bay and, a few minutes later, the town lights behind Bahia San Bartolomé.

This morning we arrived in Turtle Bay. Apparently, the natives have a different name for it and only gringos call it Turtle Bay, but I forget what it's "supposed" to be named. Right now, I am listening to Pink Floyd's "Dark Side of the Moon". Good choice by me. I have been reading Dave Barry's "Bad Habits" and it has so far (halfway through) been consistently funny. Another good choice. I have asked Dad for his library in his will. This is not a morbid request, since he often refers to his will in miscellaneous conversations. I didn't think it would be too macabre or selfish.

A very gringo-looking Miguel paddled out in his kayak offering laundry services for US$5/load. When I asked him about fuel, he said his *amigo* Jorge Salinas would bring water and diesel he purchased from the Pemex station out to the boat. (I've read that it's traditional at Turtle Bay to buy fuel from the pier which is 10-20 ft. above deck level, depending on tides, and currently collapsing. The fuel is also expensive but, until now, it was the only game in town. I support Jorge the novice entrepreneur, having been one myself.) About an hour later, Jorge panga'd out to QV and announced his pricing structure: diesel for US$2.50/gallon and water for 10 cents/liter. I ordered 124 liters of diesel and 200 of water. He returned with 120 liters of fuel, even more liters of potable water, and one of his sons. With all tanks filled and the morning fog burning off, I put up the solar shower and started hanging out wet stuff. Caroline got up just after noon, so I started making one of my favorite brunches: *chorizo con huevos* with fresh veggies. The crew from the M/V Linda Faye motored by in their tender and asked to borrow SAE Allen wrenches. It so happens I have the most complete collection of these hex head tools (both SAE and metric) on the Pacific Coast of Mexico. (Don't ask why. It's a long story and not that interesting.) I was happy to share tools and asked them to return the wrenches by tomorrow, in case the weather allows us to continue slogging Northward.

Alternatives Afloat

Today we met the crew of a luxury motor yacht, the Linda Faye. Their names were William, Will, Bill and Richard. William went by Skip, since he was the skipper of the boat. Skip, Will, Bill and Richard were all very nice and friendly, and well-seasoned sailors. They have done, and do this, a lot. They gave us food and showed us around the boat, since I had never been on a yacht like theirs before.

Everything was electric and, it turns out, they do all this cruising on some rich person's (like owner of the vessel) dollar. Lucky guys. Not only did they feed us yummy yellowtail tuna and beer, but, before we were taken back to our boat, loaded us up with produce, eggs, ground beef and the fish we didn't devour on board. How generous! Sincerely, that caught me off guard.

One of the guys, Will, was a photographer and lived all over Asia for a while. On a separate occasion, he got to meet Hilary Swank and her husband who were both apparently pretty chill. Richard was a Canadian and at one point bought a VW bug with a buddy of his and drove from the middle of Canada to Brazil. How fucking cool is that? Bill is an all 'round mechanic/repair guy and had his head in the compartment with the stabilizer they were trying to fix so I didn't get to learn too much about him except he was from Arizona and very nice.

Skip was obviously the man in charge and knew everything there was to know about boats and he could speak French and Spanish. Good guy. All of them were between 40 and 60, I'd say, but that's just a guess. All of them were really, truly very nice, funny and generous, and good people. I can't say that about everyone I meet.

We were delivered back to QV with gifts of food and all Allen wrenches carefully accounted for by Skip before the Linda Faye headed out for San Diego. Caroline wanted more fish tacos, so I made some with the yellowtail and fresh coriander.

I was up just after dawn. It is overcast, cold and I can't get any weather on the SSB, so I go back to my bunk. By the time Caroline comes up, I have discovered a leak from the bottom of the water pump and conclude the seal is gone on this pump, too. This is not so surprising since it had been sitting dry for over two years but…I have no more pump seals. I adjusted the pump drive belt to a better tension and washed some of the crystallized salt off the encrusted engine.

We take the LPG tank ashore to meet Miguel. He can't find the LPG tank fill guy, but showed us where the town market was and went home for lunch. There is an internet connection operating in the computer store. I use it to verify insurance coverage for Quo Vadis is bound and send a message to Russ, the actually quite helpful adjustor, advising him of our location and status. By the time this is accomplished, the Chinese restaurant has opened. It seems they had been closed for lunch.

Things continue in this strange, Baja sort of way. I find the LPG guy but he didn't have any LPG. He sent us to Ramales who, it turns out, doesn't really fill LPG tanks. A guy hanging out on the street sent us to the boat repair shop, way out of town and up the hill. We walk, we hitchhike, we ride in the back of a pick-up, we walk some more. We find Agarmex in a junk-filled courtyard behind a concrete wall. OK, maybe it wasn't junk. It was boats and machinery and batteries and motors and parts of motors.

Yes, they could fill LPG tanks but they couldn't do it without the permission of *El Jefe* who, unfortunately. was not there. At least they didn't try to paint the tank a different color. "The chief" of Agarmex eventually does return. He approves the tank fill and also tries to fix the first water pump. His repair effort is impeded by the fact he doesn't have the correct size bearing or seal for this pump. Ysidro Cholo is a proud man. He informs us that since he is *El Jefe*, he decides the work and the charges. He confirms the impeller is in good shape and charges nothing. The LPG tank fill is some nominal amount. Back on board, I re-connect the tank and close up the engine compartment without further repairs. The wind has come around to WNW and 48 hour storm clouds are building.

Caroline keeps control; El Capitán keeps getting crazier

A Northeast wind fills the sails as we clear Turtle Bay. We are making 6-7 knots toward Punta Eugénia. When we get there, the wind is still Northeast. I need to decide whether to go on the East side of Isla Cedros which offers no protected anchorages from Northeast wind or to the southern bay, Bahía Sur, which the guide says provides shelter from Northeast to Northwest. I discover the course to East Cedros is into the swell and wind, reducing our speed over the surface to about 3 knots. This makes the predicted time to anchorage 7 hours. It looks like 4 hours to Bahía Sur. Either way, we are in a nasty, confused sea state with sharp-edged waves 3-4 ft. I'm glad they're not any bigger.

The GPS and compass readings do not agree. I was warned by a skipper I met in Barillas of a 20 degree magnetic anomaly off the Baja coast. Now, I can't remember if it was near Isla Cedros. North of Isla Natividad, the wind came to Northwest 25-30 knots. We continued toward Bahía Sur in the sharp, short seas. It's a bad ride. Quo Vadis is running under stays'l and main only as winds build to 35 with gusts to 40. My stays'l repairs are tearing out on the starboard side. I'm pumping water out of the engine compartment every two hours. Caroline is sick and has gone below. When QV finally reaches the bay, the entry waypoint seems to be off and the cove is choked with kelp. My misery doesn't need company but I still rouse the sick Caroline to take the helm.

She does a great job steering a 180 turn through the kelp and into the wind. I drop the hook in the Northeast corner of Bahía Sur. It doesn't hold. The boat is blowing back into the rocks just 150 ft behind us. I go forward to get the hook back up in 35-40 knots. I am starting to think this anchorage isn't tenable. Caroline remains very controlled at the helm and effective at maneuvering the boat. I get the anchor back up; she moves the boat toward the Big Black Rock. Avoiding catching my fingers in the cleat, windlass or other such painful experiences, I drop the hook again in 22 ft. QV blows back immediately but it held. I paid out 130 ft. of scope and discovered the anchor rode had come unraveled just beyond 120 ft. Caroline nudged the boat forward while I adjusted the scope to less than 120 ft. The anchor still held with only 5 times scope. The wind is mostly from the North and Northwest to 40 knots; making two ft. whitecaps inside the anchorage.

I made comfort food (cheeseburgers and fries) for dinner. Caroline prepared some little cakes with lit matches stuck in them to celebrate her Happy Half-birthday. She is 19-1/2. I am very touched and proud. This anchorage is bouncy, rolly, with a big swell that continues even when the winds drop after sunset. So far, anchorages identified in the Mexico cruising guides have mostly been awful. Or is this as good as it gets? I am concerned. Caroline seems calm.

She works Quo Vadis through and around the kelp beds and out of Bahía Sur. She sails Northeast winds with the genoa and the main set until the wind shifts through North to Northwest by mid-day. I reset the sails and unfurl the stays'l. The boat is moving along at 6-7 knots. When Caroline comes back on watch, she uses 25-30 kt winds to good advantage. She maintains 8-9 knots with regular long 10 knot runs, even with the genoa furled to less than 100%. It is overcast and cold with that same short 3-4 ft. chop. We're able to keep it on the port quarter for most of the crossing back to the Baja peninsula.

There are some anchoring options on the Baja mainland. We opted for Bahía Playa Maria and had the anchor down, well-set, and the bridle on by 1945. Later, we actually watched a sunset and enjoyed sundowners. Caroline made a plate of *crudités* and a *paella* for dinner, served with white wine on a fairly calm night. The knot log reads 84nm for today's run of 12 hours. I spend some time trying to figure out alternatives to the 60nm passage to Escarpada but come up with no good solutions. I checked distances, headings and calculated transit times from here to all our likely anchorages up to San Diego. After all these days and nights underway, we are barely halfway up the Baja peninsula from Cabo San Lucas. Caroline has been mostly up beat but has her opinions.

Last night's anchorage was one of the strangest we've used. It looked kind of Martian. On top of that, the winds were 30+ knots and no matter what direction they were coming from, we weren't protected. The waves would slowly build; then one would rock us really hard. Then, they would die and the cycle repeated. There has been lightning the past two nights which I've been enjoying. There were two sea lions frolicking about the anchorage. I may or may not have gotten a picture.

On my watches, when I'm not worrying about parts of the boat breaking or enjoying visits from marine mammals, I think about Meredith. Not just the super-charged sex, though just thinking about us is a turn-on. The boat will be in the yard for a few weeks after we make it to California. I'll go back to D.C. and spend that time with her. It's been over six months since we've been together.

I am going to propose marriage to her again. She turned me down before I left Northern Virginia to come back to Quo Vadis but I'm confident she'll accept this time. We can start planning for a Fall wedding. It will be four years since we hooked up at the high school reunion. I'm thinking this should be a Major Event. She never had a wedding; just something in front of a judge, so I want this to be a real celebration. We can have the ceremony in Christ Church in old Alexandria. She's been a long time member of this colonial-era congregation. I love it that the naves of this church feature statues of its two most revered members: George Washington and Robert E. Lee, both native sons.

I can see the wedding as an evening ceremony with candles, big white bows tied at the ends of the pews, and banks of Fall flowers all over the place. What color are Fall flowers? Orange and yellow, maybe? She will choose a piece of music for the recessional that has some brass in it. She told me she likes sacred trumpets. First, I think it would be fun to have the reception at the Cameron Club, where the high school fraternities used to hold semi-legitimate, unchaperoned dances—sometimes serving beer. Then I figure not many people would appreciate the irony and, anyhow, I heard it burned down. So we will have the reception at Mount Vernon, where Mer used to play as a little girl. Her house is walking distance from George and Martha's former property. I know this because we've walked it. There must be some part of it we can use for our marital purposes if I make an adequate donation to the Mt. Vernon Ladies Society, which actually runs the historic place. I'll have enough money from the sale of Quo Vadis. The boat should sell quickly because there aren't many cruising catamarans on the California market. Meredith will wear white flowers in her hair and be dressed beautifully, of course. She always is except when she's naked; then she looks even better.

Hmm, I know she has been going to Quaker meetings lately, too. From what I've read, at a Quaker wedding everybody just sits there until there's a "sense of the meeting" that you're now married. That's not exactly what I was going for but I suppose if she wants to…we could. Do we get to jump over a broom? Or is that something else?

On other watches, I have vivid mental images of us walking together through tall, yellow grasses from our house down to the river. During our last trip inland from Tidewater Virginia, I was surprised how affordable some of those places still are. It is a clear, cool day. We are both wearing sweaters and short jackets. The river is not specific but there is nothing on it; no boat in the picture. It is a Golden Age.

Reefs, Shoals, Seaweed and other Nautical Events

The Punta Canoas anchorage is marginal but pressing on to Escarpada is pushing into darkness. The surge sweeping around the point is acceptable with QV pointed into it bouncing in 9 ft.of water about 200 meters from the surf line. I didn't realize until after 2000 that the tide was going out and the surf line was moving toward us. Conditions still looked OK as of 2230. Caroline decided I needed a haircut while it was still light. Maybe my hair is not falling out as much.

The next day's passage is past the Sacramento Reef and Isla Gerónimo, a route requiring some planning and watchfulness, but that is not our immediate worry because no cooling water flows through the engine when we start it up before weighing anchor. This is not amusing as it is dead calm.

When the over-temp alarm goes off, I cringe and I start considering what alternatives we have if this water pump never flows cooling water again. I already know the seal is shredded. The engine compartment is seriously salt-encrusted, so I do a few housekeeping tasks like cleaning the throttle cable and spraying WD40 on any pivot points I can reach. Before opening up the water pump, I ask Caroline to punch the engine start button. This time, cooling water flow starts and continues.

Caroline took to her bunk with diarrhea and that overall yucky feeling. I messed around with different sail configurations until the West wind clocked around on our nose. A key waypoint is at the channel between the Sacramento Reef and Punta António. We have been warned to expect heavy kelp, uncharted rocks and strong currents here. It doesn't seem that bad except the proper bearing to clear the visible parts of the reef is not a good match to the published waypoint. It seems like this has been happening more lately. Dolphins pay leisurely visits every two hours.

The first big patch of kelp and the sucking swirl of water over a submerged rock got my attention. I roused Caroline and sent her forward on kelp and rock watch. She saw no more kelp or rocks until after we cleared the reef and headed toward Isla Jerónimo. Quo Vadis started running into extensive, thick kelp beds on our 330 course, so I asked Caroline to steer West to avoid them. She skirted the beds while I worried about getting QV stuck in one of them or tangling kelp in the prop. After about an hour and half, I relieved her at the helm and turned back North toward the anchorage. As we're getting ready to anchor, the wind comes up to 25 knots after being absolutely no help in getting us here.

Caroline picked a spot that looked calm, away from the village; brought the boat into the wind and cleanly dropped the main. She took some Imodium and ate some hot soup and warm tortillas.

We were dodging seaweed (kelp beds, actually) like it was land mines. It made me feel kind of like a weenie. "Oh, no! KELP! Hurry, miss it or it will destroy us all!" Ri-i-ight.

Caroline discovered an apparent leak in the port head about three days ago. There is about half an inch of water covering that deck in the morning. The leak occurs at anchor and underway; not all the time and, so far, always to that same level. I sponge it up before getting Caroline to the helm for our trip to San Quintín. It is a bash on our direct course, so we fall off to smooth out the ride. I end up working the boat around the apparent wind but not getting to the waypoint very quickly.

As expected, it got choppy with 25-30 knot winds in the afternoon. I had planned to be at anchor before it got too bad. Once again, the guidebook sketch and chart did not fit with the waypoint position. I got confused; headed toward a cluster of volcanic peaks but my perspective was wrong. As I motored West along the North side of Bahía Santa Maria, I got the sick child up to look for stuff I couldn't find but not before I went past the entrance to the Bay at Punta Entrada.

Some gringos fishing from a really small boat gave vague directions: go back but don't try to enter the estuary. While not trying to enter Bahía San Quintín, I drove Quo Vadis into 6, 5, 3 ft. of water and onto the sand. I backed her off; found the channel (18-24 ft.) and then ran her into 7, 6, 5 ft. again. Frustrated, I dropped the hook in 6 ft. off Punta Entrada. Thirty knots of wind were blowing across a whitecapping bay. There is no apparent shelter. Just as we got our foul weather gear off, a panga came by. I asked to follow him in. He was initially reluctant but said OK, and took off. I twisted my right knee in my rush to weigh anchor; then followed the panga in a deep (30 ft.) channel inside Punta Azufre. We dropped again in 10 ft., immediately swung over a 2 ft. depth, so relocated East about 500 meters. Again, the hook went down. Caroline did a good job of moving the boat so I could set the anchor in winds now consistently at 35 knots.

We arrived in a bay that was supposedly connected to a lagoon that was supposedly connected to San Quintin, the town. We never made it to San Quintin. We spent hours motoring around looking for the mouth of the lagoon. We thought we saw it but were not confident enough to go in since we all but bottomed out. No bueno. We anchored just outside the mouth of the lagoon when a panga came close enough for El Capitan to flag it down. They (being the two fishermen aboard la panga) agreed to escort us into the valley of the lagoon. There was literally a 30, sometimes 40, foot valley down the channel. On either side was a steep shelf that was very easy to bottom out on—being the shelf was less than 4 ft. deep.

Once we saw where other boats were anchored, Dad asked how much our escorts would want in payment if they were to lead us the rest of the way to San Quintin. The panga guy asked for 100 dollars, American. Ha! I'll say it again. Ha! Yeah, right. So we found a semi-decent spot to anchor and spent the night.

Even his companion in the panga looked at the guy like he was crazy. I was thinking 100 pesos. A woman aboard the nearest boat (which appeared to be anchored here on a long term basis) came on deck, smiled and waved. Later, one of her male companions rowed over from their tire-girdled hulk and asked for cigarettes. I still had some packs from my failed attempts at barter with the fishermen in Venezuela. As I made *linguine* with clam sauce, I could not imagine what brought the three of them to live on that boat in this miserable anchorage. Could this be an improvement over their life on shore? The allure of San Quintín escapes me completely. I also wrapped my right knee in elastic bandage.

At this very moment, it is 2 minutes away from 11 o'clock at night at Ensenada. We have made it this far! Yayy! I've never really recalled a time I believed in God, but I've been thanking Him and praying for His blessings since 5 this morning. Let's re-cap, shall we? Yesterday morning, between 8:00 and 8:30, Dad decides we should leave San Quintin.

I was up at 0630 and… Surprise!..actually heard weather on the Amigo Net. Armed with this unusual information, I got Caroline up after sponging up the port head leak and pumping out the sump. We had some discussion about timing; then made ready to get underway for an overnight passage to Ensenada, the last port we'll visit in Mexico. After all these weeks, it seems strange.

I had prepared exit waypoints to supplement range bearings for the channel and the back range sketches I had cleverly made coming in to San Quintin. Somehow, all of them were messed up and I put Quo Vadis on a sand shoal in 2 ft. of water. I backed off the shoal into 4-6 ft. of water and Caroline came to the helm. She found the deep channel and, expertly reading shoal depth, currents and wave action, took QV out to the 5 fathom line and beyond. It was a fairly long run to clear the rocks off Cabo San Quintín. Sea lions cavorted around the boat before we turned North.

There is no wind that day or all through that night to help our boat sail Northward. One result is that we are motoring over big, smooth swells. Another is that, for the first time I have owned this boat, I can see the bottom of the fuel tank. This is not good. I added the final 5 gallons in reserve at San Quintín, for over 18 gallons total. I get Caroline to the helm at 0430 and tell her to call me by 0500 so we can anchor at Puerto Santo Tomás and go in for diesel, then prepare to go below to my bunk. As we're passing the Punta China limestone quarry docks, I spot a tug. I can't tell if it's anchored or moored but assume that facility has diesel fuel and, hopefully, will sell us some of it.

Determining the tug did not have a tow attached to it, I began a very slow approach. I could not find the quarry docks to tie up, but Caroline saw some one on the tug with two fishing lines out. We approach the tug and request permission to come along side and buy fuel. The guy fishing went below to check with his Captain as I rigged lines on the port side for Caroline to handle. The Captain of the Cemex tugboat Polaris appeared on deck and approved our request. He asked for our jerry jugs.

They filled two 5-gallon jugs, handed them back between the pitching vessels in the proper two-handed way of professional mariners, thank God, and refused anything but our thanks. I had started filling the main tank through the Baja filter (how appropriate) when Quo Vadis surged into the steel hull of the tug with a loud crack. I proposed we cast off. The Mexican Captain agreed and his crewman handed our lines back to my crew. I will never forget the sight of my daughter Caroline, looking splendid in yellow foul weather gear, as she skillfully tended our lines to keep us positioned while we took on fuel to complete this passage. She then recovered the lines with "*Grácias*" to the Mexican crew.

I filtered nine gallons of the still warm, fairly dirty fuel into our main tank: more than enough to motor to Ensenada. The wind still wasn't up when I came to the helm at 0830, feeling well-rested, and started calling Baja Naval on the VHF for a slip. Both heads seem to have become a problem, again.

Arturo caught our docklines by 1030 and brought 120 liters of (somewhat cleaner) diesel down to the boat. We put our stuff out to dry, rigged fenders and docklines for the harbor surge, ate a big Mexican-style brunch on board, and Caroline called her mother. I called John Blake to get information on current transient slips in San Diego. He informs me there were some available at the Customs dock earlier in the day but they can't be reserved. It's first come, first docked.

We ate fish tacos on shore served by a genuinely nice owner, drank some chilled beers, and watched the off-road racing vehicles come into town on their trailers or in the backs of trucks. (Was it the season for the Baja 500? It has been so many years since I've done that.) We cleared Mexican immigration, presented a copy of the paid marina bill to release our international exit *zarpe* and arranged for Arturo to shove us off from our fairly tight slip in Baja Naval at 1615. I found the one-stop government shop for gringo sailors (CIS) to be a welcome, fairly efficient change from the prior method of clearing in or out of Mexico. I also wanted to tell the loudly complaining gringos, who apparently had not bothered to learn any Spanish or read up on the requirements, to shut up and go home. I kept my mouth shut. Who knew that I could? The gringos continued making fools of themselves which should not have surprised me but continued to annoy me.

Arturo showed up at 1620 with another guy. I gave them cold Cokes and requested they hold the stern lines to the cleats to pivot Quo Vadis off the dock. Then, when she is pointed out toward the harbor, toss the stern lines to my crew (Caroline) at my command. Arturo understood, and complied. The other guy looked completely baffled. Despite his bafflement, we cleared the docks and were underway toward the US of A by 1630.

Just before passing the Ensenada harbor breakwater, we heard a horrible sound from the engine compartment. I called Caroline to the wheel, brought the engine to idle, and opened the access hatch. A half-inch bolt had come loose, letting the alternator fall down and the belt go slack. I checked exhaust flow. The water pump was still working. Do we continue or go back? A quick check of their condition showed all batteries over 13 volts and total of 1.3 amp-hours (out of about 350 available) used from the house bank. My quick calculation of power consumption by the running lights, instruments and radio came to 26 amp-hours. This is how much energy we'd use if we just sailed overnight to San Diego. There was more screeching from the engine. I pulled the belt off the pulley and the screeching stopped.

Caroline looks at me wistfully from her position in the helm chair. "We're going to San Diego," I tell her, "without the alternator." She grins in approval and points Quo Vadis away from the harbor, toward Islas Todos Santos.

San Diego
Tijuana
Tecate
Mexicali
Rosarito
Algodones
UNITED STATES
Ensenada
La Bufadora
Tucson
San Felipe
Nogales
Puertecitos
BAJA CALIFORNIA
Gulf of California
MEXICO
Isla Ángel de la Guarda
Punta Prieta
Hermosillo
Isla Cedros
Guerrero Negro
Bahia Tortugas
Guaymas
Díaz Ordaz
Santa Rosalía
BAJA CALIFORNIA SUR
Pacific Ocean
Mulegé
Loreto
Isla Carmen
Villa Insurgents
Ciudad Constitución
Isla San José
San Carlos
San Juan de la Costa
Isla del Espirito Santo
Isla Santa Margarita
Pichilingue
La Paz
San Pedro
Todos Santos
San Lucas
San José del Cabo
Cabo San Lucas
N

American Customs and Other Behaviors

Aboard S/V Quo Vadis, docked San Diego, California

Two of those "4 days/3 nights/5 meals a day" type of cruise ships pass us before sunset. I don't think of Ensenada as an exotic port of call. Or Cabo San Lucas, for that matter. I interpret their apparent course to be in the shipping lanes. I planned to avoid that stretch of Pacific Ocean. Sailors headed North from Ensenada are also advised, however, not to hug the coast. Given these two parameters, I lay in just two courses to San Diego. The waypoint defining the end of the last course is just outside the San Diego sea buoy…or such is my intent.

Caroline comes to the helm 15 minutes before midnight. There is a big swell from the WNW. It is smooth since we've had only light winds. The sky is cloudy and shedding a light sprinkle. When I relieve her at 0300, I see she has made a good distance and I see the glow of city lights. Tijuana, I think?

The next navigation aid (hard to miss it) is the white/green aero beacon at North Island Naval Air Station. That sucker is visible a long way out which, of course, is why it's there. I think briefly of Admiral Morrison's stories when he was running the base ("One guy worries about special weapons; another guy worries about enlisted personnel retention.") The guys he's referring to are Navy Captains or Admirals like himself. Special weapons are nukes. Enlisted personnel are swabbies. After he retired, Adm. Morrison was a director on my corporation's Board. His oldest son, Jim, was a high school friend and classmate. I make a mental note to call the Morrisons after we get squared away in San Diego. Mad Dog gave me their current phone number when he was on board.

I make out the lights on the Coronado Bridge, strings of bright dots arching in the black night. I tell Caroline I'm pretty sure that we're seeing the bridge to San Diego before she goes below to her bunk.

"Dad, you're not messin' with my mind, are you?" After thousands of miles, she can't believe we are this close to her final destination aboard *Quo Vadis*. She wants to go home after we clear in to the U.S.

The wind comes to our port beam as a light rain begins falling. The main is full and driving but this is one time we don't need the extra speed. I want to enter San Diego Bay by daylight. At 0400, we make the waypoint, coming way too close to the sea buoy. I didn't pick up the buoy visually until it's about 50 meters away. Am I more than a little dingy at this point? I hope not. Within 20 minutes, I hear a new noise and feel vibration, including significant hull vibration. The engine must be the source but I can't pinpoint the cause. While I'm chasing around the boat investigating this event, I stray out of the main channel into 21-22 ft. of water beneath Point Loma. Who knew it was that shallow? My Uncle Barney is buried up on top of the Point in Ft. Rosecrans. I rouse Caroline out to put her keen eyes to work. I found our way back into the ship channel, missing some more buoys as we cut through them. This is more excitement than I'd planned. Finally, I got Quo Vadis lined up on the red/green buoys for the entrance to San Diego Bay.

Caroline took the helm as I tried to figure out the approach to the Police/Customs Dock. During the days I had sailed on San Diego Bay, I'd never had to go there. Caroline advised me it was shoaling and saw 6-5-4 ft. when I took over the helm and stopped the boat. I backed down very slowly from the shallows, thereupon being in a position to read the triangular sign that says "DANGER SHOAL". San Diego sailors know the one. Neither Caroline nor I did, obviously. Now, we do.

I finally figured out to go around the other side of the markers and confirmed the dock location on the VHF with an incoming Pilot boat. We rigged for starboard docking; fenders in place. Caroline jumped to the dock with the bow line about 0520. I put out a stern line. Battery voltage was good and the scary vibration had dissipated, so we let the engine cool down for 15 minutes before I went ashore to call U.S. Customs. I had been informed you have to pay for their overtime before 0800.

Breakfast had just been served to my intrepid crew, when Customs Officers Gomez and Zykos stepped on to Quo Vadis. Caroline finished eating while chatting amiably with the Border Protection guys. I surrendered QV's exit *zarpe*.

It was a strange sensation dealing with my own country's Customs agents on board Quo Vadis. I filled out forms, provided copies of boat documents, and tried to be as polite with these officials as I had at every other Port of Entry during the past several years. Initially gruff, maybe because of our early time of arrival, the agents eventually decided we weren't much of a threat and, since I was the third owner of Quo Vadis, the import duties on this British-built vessel probably had been paid. I got a waiver on the US$25 sticker for the boat. They told me to apply on line. I wasn't charged for any overtime.

I waited until 0730 to call John Blake. He said he would be down to the docks in an hour, and he was. It seemed strange to order in English when John sponsored an American-style breakfast at the Red Sails restaurant on Shelter Island. He also offered me his BMW 733 and a key to their house. I'm not too tired to be grateful and should be able to handle the car. It has the same instruments, engine, and the 5-speed transmission just like my 633 stored in one of Meredith's garages.

I picked up a bottle of bubbly on the way back to the Customs Dock. Back on board QV, we all celebrated life its ownself, to quote Pogo again. We had completed a long passage. Tired, but mostly intact and in good spirits, we especially celebrated the 1172nm Caroline and her Dad put under Quo Vadis' twin hulls double-handing her from Cabo. We were back in the USA.

It's just past midnight on Saturday. I'M ALIVE! Thank all that is holy and good in this world. I called Mom as soon as I thought she would be awake. We got to San Diego in the dark of night—around 4 a.m.—and putted around until we could see what almost had to be the customs dock (which we confirmed with a pilot boat.) Dad made breakfast but, before I could finish, customs showed up and had Dad fill out a form while I ate. Anyway, I called American Airlines and right in the middle of making my reservation (with Mom's divine permission), my phone ran out of batteries. Of course. So I called back on Dad's phone but before I could speak to anyone, Dad had to move the boat. Of course. So we moved to a more permanent docking where I tried, one more time, to book a flight from San Diego to San Luis Obispo. This time I reached Ethel and she was one of the nicest people I have ever dealt with from American. We booked me a flight with only a one hour layover in LA. I met John Blake for the first time and we went out for another breakfast.

I met with Wayne Morrison at Shelter Island Boatyard in the afternoon. I gave him my initial fix-it list and he identified a 21' wide slip suitable for Quo Vadis. We agreed to move her into the boatyard Monday morning. I called Russ Dennis, the marine surveyor for the insurance company, to let him know.

Caroline dressed up beautifully in a kind of summertime layered look. I found a clean shirt and some khakis that fit and were reasonably dry. We were both off the boat to pick up the Blakes by 1800. Caroline treated us all to excellent Thai food accompanied by appropriate wines. She paid for dinner with her remaining US dollars. Dixie Blake told me, when Caroline went to the ladies' room, that she'd never had that happen before. It is a rare event when your children buy dinner. Next morning, I called family and friends to advise them of our status (alive and docked) and location. I left Mer a short message.

Tonight is the last night aboard Quo Vadis for me. I leave in about 8 hours to board my flight on American Eagle for LA; then only an hour from LA to SLO. Me=lucky dog. The Blakes were great.

Well, first I got a lovely massage from Antonia; then Dad and I got a pizza from Gus's as a late lunch and rented "Apocalypse Now" while we were waiting for the pizza. We each ate most of our halves of the pizza. As soon as we were done, we went to John and Dixie's for dinner. It took a couple of hours, so it worked out all right. Chris Blake, their son, hung out for a while. Dad toasted him and me, as the next generation. The guys talked "Air Force". (Chris was a newly-minted USAF lieutenant; just assigned to pilot training.)

After 7 P.M., John and Dixie left to go see a Padres game. Dinner conversation was fun. I learned that Dixie won a beer-tasting contest held by "Bobbo" against mostly males. Go, Girl! Anyway, when the Blakes left for the game, Dad and I did the dishes; then Dad went to check his e-mail while I made popcorn. When he took another half-hour, I made him promise to stop. When he did, we watched "Apocalypse Now". I cried a couple of times. This is why I'm not in the military. Anyway, good Coppola film.

Thank yous to the Blakes, then Dad and I went home. Me, with clean laundry. We got back on board, I packed and all seems OK. Dad is gonna let me borrow "The Amazing Adventures of Kavalier and Klay". I'll send it back to him. I hope the flight goes well. I'll probably write again. I'm disappointed I didn't write more poetry. Oh, well. What is, is. A low key day: good way to end the adventure. Well, almost end it, anyway.

During one of the many cold, night watches bashing Northwest off the coast of Mexico, Caroline confided that one thing she really wanted to do when we got to California was watch a movie and eat popcorn. I was happy to accommodate her and the Blakes made their big screen TV available. I was a little surprised at her choice of films, especially after six weeks underway.

Putting her on the flight the next morning was a very emotional time. I was losing my best single crewmember since Mer was on board. Caroline had more presence and cool than I did on the final legs of this Mexico passage. She came through every time. I was stressed about the boat, the future and, ironically, putting my daughter at risk. It seems I forgot things I had learned from painful prior experience. Now, my job is to get Quo Vadis repaired, made seaworthy, and figure out how to continue to San Francisco Bay. Some cruisers have told me that was the most difficult part of the passage North.

I came back from the airport with the Sunday paper and some current boat magazines. As soon as I'm on board QV, the friendly gal working at the Customs dock office walks down to my slip and hands me an envelope. "This came for you this morning," she smiles. On the outside it says: John Hutter Slip 25. On the inside is a FAX. It's from Meredith.

Dear John,

These are the most difficult, gut wrenching words I've ever had to say. I've fallen out of love with you. I'll always feel a deep sense of kindredness, caring and concern for you but I'm not in love with you anymore.

I've lost the desire to be physically intimate.

I've slowly and steadily been pulling back and detaching from our relationship over a long period of time. I've come to realize that I want to withdraw from our pairing and be a free agent again-on my own. Now I know that I value solitude and autonomy over attachment.

The FAX goes on. As my eyes well up with tears and my throat gets tight, it gets harder to read. It ends: *With profound regret and heart felt compassion, Meredith*

This voyage is over.

Final Transmission from S/V Quo Vadis, lying San Diego, California, USA

Subject: Voyage of the Quo Vadis

S/V Quo Vadis arrived California 0500 3 June 2005, entering San Diego Harbor at the end of a 3000nm leg North off Mexico's Pacific Coast.

Crew on board, according to the zarpe from Zihuatenejo: John Huetter, Captain, 61, USA. Caroline Huetter, Commodore, 19, USA.

Boat battered; sails tattered from Golfo de Tehuantepec crossing. Crew weary but intact.

Dr. J.H. Morehouse (aka "Maddog") crewed the 3-day crossing of the Sea of Cortez, after flying from US East Coast to come on board.

Unless the voyage continues to San Francisco Bay, this completes a 3-1/2 year journey from Chesapeake Bay via the US East Coast, Bahamas, Caribbean, South America, Panama Canal and Central America.

Thanks to all my friends on shore for your support. John Huetter

Printed in the United States
130780LV00001BA/5/P